Mycophilia

Mycophilia

Revelations *from the* Weird World *of* Mushrooms

EUGENIA BONE

RODALE.

Mycophilia

From the Greek,
myco = *fungus,* philos = *loving*

Disclaimer

This is not a guidebook and should not be used to identify mushrooms. Nor should the reader think that because the author ate a wide variety of wild mushroom they would have the same results. Meaning, while I lived to tell the tale, you might not.

Mention of specific companies, organizations, or authorities in this book does not imply endorsement by the author or publisher, nor does mention of specific companies, organizations, or authorities imply that they endorse this book, its author, or the publisher.

Internet addresses and telephone numbers given in this book were accurate at the time it went to press.

Rodale books may be purchased for business or promotional use or for special sales. For information, please write to:
Special Markets Department, Rodale, Inc., 733 Third Avenue, New York, NY 10017

Printed in the United States of America
Rodale Inc. makes every effort to use acid-free ∞, recycled paper ⊙.

Photograph and artwork credits appear on page 337.
Book design by Christopher Rhoads

Library of Congress Cataloging-in-Publication Data

Bone, Eugenia.
    Mycophilia : revelations from the weird world of mushrooms / Eugenia Bone.
        p.   cm.
    Includes bibliographical references and index.
    ISBN 978–1–60529–407–0   hardcover
    1. Mushrooms—United States.   2. Fungi—United States.   I. Title.   II. Title: Revelations from the weird world of mushrooms.
QK605.B65   2011
579.60973—dc23   2011030328

Distributed to the trade by Macmillan

    4   6   8   10   9   7   5   3   hardcover

We inspire and enable people to improve their lives and the world around them.

www.rodalebooks.com

To the members of the New York Mycological Society:
my companions in the woods

Contents

INTRODUCTION

I have always loved to eat mushrooms. Even as a child, I found mushrooms to be satisfying in some mysterious way that other foods simply were not. That flavor has a name now, umami, a word borrowed from the Japanese. The noun *umami* means "good taste" in Japanese, but in English it is generally understood as meaty savoriness, the flavor of the non-essential amino acid glutamate, as found in steak and cheese and MSG.

My appreciation for mushrooms, especially wild mushrooms, might be in the blood. We have a family story about how my mother went into labor with me in a restaurant in Florence while eating tagliatelle with truffles, and the waiters had to clear off a couple of tables so she could lie down. My grandmother used to can honey mushrooms (using a technique I now know could have taken out the lot of us with botulism poisoning), tender rubbery discs seasoned with parsley and garlic that she added to braised rabbit dishes during the winter. And my parents were foragers, too.

Our family didn't really participate in any sports. Unlike the middle-class kids I grew up with in suburban New York, we didn't ski or sail. We foraged. When we were on the beach, we gathered mussels and sea snails, seined for whitebait, and collected blueberries. At our home in Westchester County, we collected watercress and dandelion greens, and I was still in elementary school when my parents taught me how to identify a morel.

Likewise, they made sure I could identify the death cap, *Amanita phalloides*, and the destroying angels, *A. bisporigera* and *A. virosa*. Within 6 to 24 hours of consumption *Amanita* induces severe vomiting, abdominal pain, and diarrhea, then jaundice, kidney failure, liver deterioration, and convulsions. Finally, in a matter of days, death.

"Just don't touch it!" my mother would say. "Don't even look at it!" my father would rejoin.

As a child, it seemed magical to me the way mushrooms suddenly appeared where they were not the day before. And indeed, in hunting them with my family, I felt like finding mushrooms was a kind of conjuring: If I concentrated hard enough, if I longed to find one deeply enough, the mushroom would reveal itself to me.

But then I grew up and moved to New York City and, except for preferring dishes on menus that included mushrooms, I didn't really think about them for 20 years. That is, until my husband, Kevin, and I bought a cabin in Colorado and I met a gal named Peggy Lindsey. Peggy was, at the time, the masseuse at the Ouray hot springs. She was also a regional arm wrestling champ. We conversed during the pummeling she gave me: she, energetic and friendly, and me, responding between grunts through the face hole in the massage table. She told me about the mushrooms she found on the nearby Uncompahgre Plateau, the chanterelles and porcini that, when circumstances were right, came up in abundance. I didn't have many friends in Colorado at the time, and when she invited me to join her on a mushroom hunt, I was motivated not only by my love of eating mushrooms but also by my need for company.

We drove along rutted roads, past miles of aspen trees quaking and quivering in the sun, until we reached a deep pine forest, cool and quiet as a graveyard. There were not a lot of mushrooms up that day, but Peggy showed me a small patch of bright orange chanterelles littered among the pine needles, and pointed out one porcini, a *Boletus edulis*, growing on the periphery of an open grassy clearing in the woods. If I had seen those chanterelles in a market basket, I would never have felt confident identifying them in the wild. But observing them growing in their habitat was a different story. All their minute variations—some were stumpy, others open like a flower—which can never be fully conveyed in a single or even a few illustrations, revealed a sort of cohesiveness in form and color. It was more like recognizing family resemblances. We found about 2 pounds of chanterelles that day, and once home we sautéed them with butter. We rolled up the slick, fleshy nubbins of mushroom in delicate crepes with *queso anejo* cheese, sweet and sour as the milk burp of a baby.

My husband is one of those hiking people. His first Christmas gift to me was a sleeping bag. ("But it zips up to mine," he said when I looked at him for an explanation.) The truth is, I couldn't understand the attraction of clambering over scree only to reach the top. I recognize that other people find this immensely rewarding, but true to my upbringing, when I connected to nature at all, it was via food.

A few weeks after the mushroom hunt with Peggy, I reluctantly agreed to a hike up Bald Mountain, near our cabin. We had company, and company expects to climb mountains when they're visiting Colorado. We had walked maybe 5 minutes when Kevin called for me to come and look. He'd found a mushroom with a cap as big as a salad plate and a stem so fat I couldn't get all my fingers around it. Right away I recognized it as a porcini. It didn't look at all like the small sample Peggy had shown me, yet I knew it the way you know when you have met someone before. One minute we were walking through a forest, and then, as if by magic, we witnessed the conversion of the forest floor. Everywhere, *boletus*: big spongy mature specimens and hard young ones that looked

Hunting mushrooms on Bald Mountain

like beige softballs growing in tidy rows along the side of fallen timber. I took off my jacket and filled it with mushrooms. I took off Kevin's jacket and our guests' jackets and the kids' jackets, too, and tied the sleeves to sticks so I could carry my haul like a hobo's pack. Kevin and our guests continued up the hill, but not me.

After gathering as much as I could carry, I returned to the car and pored over each individual in the hoard, until the rest of our party had reached the summit and walked back down the trail. Once home, I totally ignored our company. I divvied up the mushrooms into meals. Some of the big caps we grilled on the fire with a few slabs of eggplant, and I ground the two together with garlic and salt and lemon juice. We dipped big tortilla chips into this lewdly earthy dip, washed down with cold beer. We sliced up the rest of the caps and cooked them with farfalle and chicken broth and lemon zest, and then threw all the stems into an oxtail and posole soup. And so my husband's desire for a hiking partner has come true. I now accompany him enthusiastically, but while he forges ahead, his long strides covering the miles, head high, breathing in the view, I walk in circles, head down, checking the foot of every tree.

But mushroom hunting in Colorado can be lousy, and because of drought, it was lousy for years. So I decided to step up my game. At first, I joined the New York Mycological Society (NYMS) in the hopes of finding new, more bountiful hunting grounds. The composer John Cage, an avid mushroomer, founded the current incarnation of the NYMS, and many of the older members remember hunting with him. This was the first time I'd joined a club, any club, and I liked the fact that it was so easy to socialize. After all, everybody was interested in the same subject, and the other members were charming and weird and erudite. Nonetheless, I stayed mainly on the periphery of the club, taking note of information pertaining to organized mushroom hunts where I might hit mushroom pay dirt.

Before long I started to attend forays—first those organized by the

NYMS, then farther afield. I traveled all over the country in the ensuing years, once in the spring to look for morels, again in the fall to find
chanterelles or porcini or matsutake, and in the summers in Colorado.
These organized outings, put together by mycological societies or professional mushroom hunters, are kind of like Trekkie conventions for
mushroom enthusiasts. There are classes on dyeing fabric with mushrooms and on mushroom cultivation, lots of mushroom eating (called
mycophagy), lectures by academics, and guided walks in the woods
with knowledgeable leaders.

"Mushroom hunting is not simply a matter of traipsing through the
woods after it rains. It is an art, a skill, a meditation, and a process,"
writes David Arora, a persnickety genius whom I like to think of as the
high priest of mycology and author of the classic guide *Mushrooms
Demystified: A Comprehensive Guide to the Fleshy Fungi.* Of course, he's
right. Mushroom hunting, or "the quiet hunt," as it is also known,
requires knowledge both of the organism and of its habits and habitats.
Ultimately, I recognized that learning the biology of mushrooms was
how I was going to increase my effectiveness as a mushroom hunter.

Like many people, I had always assumed mushrooms were a plant.
They're not. Mushrooms are the fruiting body of fungi, just as apples
are the fruiting body of apple trees. When you kick up the duff in the
woods, that white fluffy-looking stuff under the leaves and rotting
wood is a fungus, a network of branching tubelike structures one cell
thick that traces a vast pattern underground, like a living spiderweb.
Fungi are organisms that comprise their own kingdom of life, equal in
complexity to animals and plants. There are an estimated 1.5 million
species, second only to insects in number and diversity, and only 5 percent of them have been identified. Fungi outnumber plants by a ratio of
6 to 1 and make up 25 percent of the Earth's biomass. The biggest single
living organism on Earth is a fungus. It is 2,200 acres in size, weighs

6,286 tons, and lives in the Malheur National Forest in the Blue Mountains of eastern Oregon. Some fungi are so tiny they live between the cells of other organisms. The first terrestrial creatures may have been fungi, and they are more closely related to us, evolutionarily speaking, than they are to plants.

It slowly became evident to me that fungi were everywhere: We inhale 1 to 10 spores with every breath, as many as 300,000 spores a day. They live on every surface, in every organism to some degree or another, and some can theoretically live forever. They function as a shadow immune system for all plants, a shadow digestive system for trees, and are the source of some of the worst plagues of man and animals and crops, and the best medicine we have. Fungi can decompose all sorts of organic compounds, even petroleum and sarin gas; and given enough time, they will likely evolve to recycle all the rest of our chemical inventions. Indeed, as the mycologist C. J. Alexopoulos put it, "scarcely a day passes when we aren't helped or harmed by fungi."

I also came to know of the existence of a small but intense—and intensely quirky—group of people who knew all this: brilliant people like the guiding light of the NYMS Gary Lincoff, author of *The National Audubon Society Field Guide to North American Mushrooms*, whose knowledge is huge and whose delivery is borscht belt; the great mycologist Tom Volk, with his earplugs and blue hair and sleeve tattoos; Britt Bunyard, the punster mycologist who edits *Fungi* magazine; Mark Miller, the bantamweight, quick-witted spawn maker at Lambert Spawn; Daniel Winkler, the German-born Grateful Deadhead turned world expert on *Cordyceps sinensis,* which grow from the heads of caterpillars and have been treasured in the Chinese pharmacopoeia for centuries; John Getz, who was there when the business of wild mushroom harvesting in America blew open and got married in his favorite matsutake patch; Elio Schaechter, the eminent microbiologist and notorious flirt;

and the entrepreneurial Paul Stamets, the "Steve Jobs of fungus." The list goes on and on. These were folks who live every day with an intimate knowledge of a huge segment of the natural world that I didn't even know existed. It was on par with finding out there were people who knew what caused the Big Bang, but the language available to communicate that revelation was incomprehensible to normal people like me, and so they could only marvel among themselves.

I became someone who, when a friend mentioned LSD, would say, "You know that it's synthesized from a fungus." Or if someone mentioned that the potted trees on their patio weren't doing well, I'd say, "They are probably missing their symbiotic fungal partner"; or if they complained of dandruff, I'd observe they might have an overgrowth of fungus on their scalp; or if the discussion turned to the Gulf of Mexico oil spill, I'd point out that if it weren't for an evolutionary gap between fungi that can decompose some parts of wood and fungi that can decompose all wood, there wouldn't be any oil in the first place; or God forbid, if someone mentioned truffle oil, I went into a spiel about how truffle oil is flavored artificially, and the bottle costs more to produce than its contents. My husband said I was getting a bit tedious. But I couldn't help it. I was seeing fungi everywhere.

At a screening of *Know Your Mushrooms*, a documentary by Ron Mann, Gary Lincoff, who stars in the film, told the audience, "People who are into mushrooms see them everywhere and they think mushrooms are responsible for everything." Which is true. Mushroom fanatics do see the solution to just about every problem on Earth in mushroom biology. It's a bit crazy. On the other hand, they *are* everywhere. And I was finally seeing them, too. It was like on a hunt: At first you see nothing and think there are no mushrooms up, and then you see one, and then the pattern recognition sets in and suddenly you see them all over the forest floor.

Then came a breakthrough that for me was the greatest of all. Slowly but surely, as I learned more about the huge role fungi play in nature, I started to understand that everything on Earth functions as an ecosystem; in fact, an ecosystem within an ecosystem within an ecosystem. Since 1979, there has been what the mycologist Bryce Kendrick calls an "explosion of knowledge" about the microscopic world. Scientists now know that within a spoonful of soil there is an incredible complexity of microscopic, interdependent life; that every complex creature—every plant and animal and fungus—is an ecosystem of coordinated organisms. I came to realize that no thing on Earth can properly be considered a single entity, but I am and you are composed of multiple life-forms, from different kingdoms of life, all working in concert to be me or you. And every bird (and the tree it lives in) is an ecosystem that participates in an ecosystem that eventually scales up to the planet. This notion has totally upended my idea of what an individual is, be it plant or animal or fungus, or person or place. In light of the new science, the singular noun "I" is obsolete because in reality, "I" is a community.

One spring weekend in Long Island I was walking with my friend Gia. I noticed that there were lots of dead ants on the sidewalk, but some were still alive and in a big hurry, and I saw a queen traveling, too. I pointed out that the colony looked like it was on the move; maybe the original nest had been poisoned. Gia said she was surprised how observant I was, that she hadn't noticed the ants at all. Silly as it sounds, I was kind of proud of myself at that moment. And then, immediately after, humbled. I realized that it was only because I had been paying attention to fungi for the past 10 years that I had developed the habit of looking beyond the end of my own shoe.

This book chronicles my learning curve. It touches on all aspects of mycology in the United States today: the festivals, forays, and camps; the biology of fungi; commercial wild crafters; the cultivation of exotic mushrooms, including truffles; the history of the ubiquitous white button mushroom; mushroom nutrition (they are considered a superfood now); the traditional and new science in medical and medicinal mushrooms and nutraceuticals; psychedelic mushrooms and ethnomycology (the study of psychedelic mushrooms in culture); new technologies utilizing fungi; and fungi's role in the symbiotic planet. I have had the help of many smart, passionate, and inordinately tolerant people in sorting through what was for me often very difficult literature.

But I was never a disinterested journalist, observing from the sidelines, gleaning just the information I needed to get to the next chapter. I found the subject utterly engrossing. There were many nights when I couldn't resist reading one more article with the word *ectomycorrhizal* in the title, even though I could hear my husband click off his reading light and pull up the bedcovers. At first I may have been, as a friend suggested, the Lucille Ball of mycology, blundering my way through the science and foisting myself upon a tight-knit community, but I've come a long way since then. I mean, I would never have guessed that I would become one of the presidents of the New York Mycological Society, and that like them, I would become a full-fledged mycophiliac. But here I am.

Chapter 1

FORAYS AND FESTIVALS

My journey into the realm of fungi started with basic venality. I love to eat wild mushrooms, but I don't love paying for them. They're hellaciously expensive in Manhattan where I live. The problem was: How to find them? And then I learned about the New York Mycological Society (NYMS) and their promises of guided mushroom hunts. It sounded good. Plus, the price of membership was right: $20 a year.

The NYMS offers lectures on fungal biology, slideshows of mushroom photography (Taylor Lockwood's show packed the room), a banquet featuring mushrooms during the winter (a Roman Feast, a Cantonese Banquet), many small guided walks, and a few big forays every year, the most popular being the Morel Breakfast.

When I first joined the club, I tried to mask my true motivation. At the winter lectures, I pretended to be interested in all mushrooms, nodding with phony delight at the slides of inedible molds or polypores or *whatever*. The truth is, I was embarrassed to admit I was participating in a scientific club mainly in anticipation of spring, when the morels came up and the hunting would begin. But shortly after the announcements for the Morel Breakfast went out, I realized I was not alone in my greed. Everyone in the club was horny for morels. Free, fresh, fat morels.

Morels are probably the most fetishized of all wild edible mushrooms. There are numerous Web sites devoted to hunting morels, replete with near pornographic close-ups of the wrinkly capped fungus, or shots of copious morel blooms or children happily posing with gargantuan specimens. Morel Web sites boast breathless postings of morel flushes throughout the country. (I am particularly fond of the online morel sighting maps, which are updated daily during the season, like tornados on a midwestern weather map.) There are around 10 regional festivals throughout the midwestern states, at least one anthropological study on rural community morel hunts, and morel paraphernalia of all sorts for sale. Theories abound as to why morels are so culty, but Tom Nauman of www.morelmania .com says it's because morels are well-known in the general population. I think Nauman is right. The morel is *the* American wild mushroom.

The Morel Breakfast—held the first weekend in May, when the morels are generally, hopefully up—is always prefaced by a flurry of e-mails, first the very hush-hush directions to our spot, an abandoned apple orchard in New York west of the Hudson River, then the admonitions not to hunt the orchard and pick all the mushrooms prior to the breakfast, and finally people looking for rides to the hunting grounds. I have a car and so drove a handful of ladies and their baskets and walking sticks, their tick spray and suntan lotion and water bottles, to the home of an amiable couple who live on the way to the orchard and who put out a bagel and lox spread for the club at their own expense. At the breakfast, our foray leader, Dennis Aita, explained that morels are the fruiting bodies of a fungus. The fungus is the organism and the mushroom is the organ of sexual reproduction, like a fruit or a flower.

There are many types of fungi (which can be pronounced as either fun-ghee, fun-gee, or fun-jai, though most mycophiles say fun-jai), and not all produce mushrooms, but the fungus *Morchella* does. There are quite a few species of morels—no one is sure how many—but we were hunting *Morchella esculenta* (*esculenta* is Latin for succulent and delicious). Dennis told us to look for *M. esculenta*, aka the gray or yellow morel, under dying apple trees. The fungus that produces morels lives in association with the roots of the apple tree. When the tree fails, the fungus fruits in order to spread its spore—and subsequently find a new host. In essence, to find the morel, you have to find the tree.

Which is not such an easy thing. The club hunts an abandoned apple orchard surrounded by residential developments, and the place is overgrown with pricker bushes, but we hunt there for two reasons: The morels have been fruiting there for 25 years, and it is in nearby Rockland County, an undemanding commute for New Yorkers who tend to be infrequent drivers.

Eighty people showed up that year, about a third of our membership. They were mostly older, retired people, but also young parents herding children, holding their wiggly kids' arms while they smeared on the tick repellent, plus a few French people. I'd only hunted in Colorado prior to this, and where we go, in the West Elk Mountains, there are about 10 billion acres of wilderness per person. It is rare to see anyone else in the woods. It is common to get lost. Not so at the NYMS morel hunt. As soon as we were parked and assembled, Dennis gave the word, and in an arthritic charge, dozens of people crashed into the woods, most following those who seemed to know where they were going. It felt a little like the stampede that occurs when they first open the doors of a Black Friday warehouse sale. I struck out in the opposite direction.

The NYMS, whose logo is inspired by *The New Yorker* magazine's mascot Eustace Tilley (the dandy in the top hat) looking through his monocle at a mushroom, had a couple of starts and stops during its 100-plus-year history, but the avant-garde composer John Cage (1912–1992) and a few friends resuscitated it in the late '50s. Cage's belief that music is meant "to sober and quiet the mind, thus rendering it susceptible to divine influences" also describes the mushroom hunt—or at least, a mushroom hunt without a crowd—the quiet but intense contemplation of nature that reveals a hidden mushroom. Cage turned many folks on to mushrooming. I've met a number of people with no particular interest in fungi who claim to have hunted with him. (In New York, that's kind of like running into people who've said they've gotten drunk with Norman Mailer.) But he created many true converts. One is Paul Sadowski, who prepared Cage's music for publication and is now secretary of the club.

Back to the hunt. It took me some time just to identify a dying apple tree. To be honest, the whole orchard looked like one gigantic bramble patch, filled with buzzing insects and senior New Yorkers in khakis, but after a sweaty hour I got the hang of it and started to crawl under the thickets and through the poison ivy, the shiny red leaves tiny as squirrel ears, to check the base of the decaying trees.

As I crawled under one tree, eyes narrowed to avoid scratching my corneas with twigs, I spotted one large brown morel. And then I saw *her*. Apple cheeked and undaunted by the thorns, her gray bun pulled askew by snapping branches, crawled an elderly lady from the opposite direction toward the very morel—the *only* morel—I'd spotted.

I deferred to her, of course, as if the fat morel between us were a seat on the bus.

꩜

The history of amateur mycology in America (from the Greek, *myco* = fungus, *ology* = study of) is not that long. While immigrant groups and Native Americans gathered the mushrooms they knew were edible or medicinal, as a hobby mycology didn't gain momentum until the 1880s. Botany—which included fungi in those days—was one of the most popular of the sciences for hobbyists. During the Victorian era, the sciences achieved their cultural authority: Natural history and natural philosophy became science, and science became a profession. For decades, though, fieldwork conducted by amateur mycologists contributed to the body of knowledge, and amateurs collected many of the samples that fill botanical garden archives in the United States today.*

The instigating factor that may have led to the advance of mycological societies in America was the death, in 1897, of Count Achilles de Vecchj, an Italian diplomat residing in Washington, DC. The count died from eating *Amanita muscaria*—the fly agaric. This is the most iconic of all mushrooms—the one with the red cap with white spots on it—and, except in the count's case, not fatal, although it can make you very sick or get you high, depending on what part of the world the specimen comes from, how you prepare it, and how much you eat. The death of the count, which was a widely publicized sensation, led the United States Department of Agriculture to issue public advisories about toxic mushrooms. Although the Washington mycological club had been organized 3 years before the count's last meal, his death, and the subsequent publication of Charles McIlvaine's 2½-pound tome, *One Thousand American Fungi*, describing hundreds of edible (although not always tasty) mushrooms, ushered in an increased interest in fungi, and regional mushroom clubs began to, well, mushroom. Today there are at least 95 mycological societies in North America, three regional clubs, and one national club. There is also a professional club, the Mycological Society of America, which organizes conferences and publishes the scientific journal *Mycologia*. For the amateur or hobbyist, learning about mushrooms in order to eat them but avoid poisoning is definitely one of the reasons why people join mycological associations.

*In recent years, the advent of new, exclusive tools like electron microscopy and genetic analysis—and their growing importance in mycology—has widened the gap between most amateurs and pros.

Amanita muscaria

Most mycological societies have a scientific advisor affiliated with the club who instructs the members on regional identification. This is important, because the toxicity of mushrooms can vary according to their habitat, their age, and their method of preparation, and because mushroom identification books can be deceiving. What does "edible with caution" mean? The New York Mycological Society has a number of expert amateurs, but our guru is Gary Lincoff, the author of *The National Audubon Society Field Guide to North American Mushrooms*, a menschy, approachable fellow whose knowledge is as encyclopedic as his collection of mushroom-themed T-shirts, which he wears over long-sleeve shirts—a look not every man can pull off. Experts like Gary are keen to disabuse members of wives' tales like poisonous mushrooms tarnish a silver spoon, mushrooms that grow on wood are safe, mushrooms that animals eat are safe, and mushrooms that can be peeled are safe. (All untrue.) Their portfolio of sayings usually includes witticisms like "No mushroom is poisonous until you eat it" and "Leave one mushroom for the mycologist and one for the doctor."

In 1973, the North American Mycological Association established a toxicology committee, and in 1982, they created the Mushroom Poisoning Case Registry based on voluntary information from the regional societies and the American Association of Poison Control Centers. Only ½ to 1 percent of poisonings that are reported to poison control centers each year are attributed to mushrooms, and of that, according to a

30-plus-year summary of poisonings, about 1 percent end in death. Indeed, more people die of shark attacks than mushroom poisoning. The majority of reports describe gastrointestinal disturbances like vomiting and diarrhea stemming from eating a wide variety of species.

Mushroom poisonings are not necessarily simple to define. When a combination of species is eaten, the culprit may be unclear. The health or circumstances of the eater may be a factor in poisoning, as well as allergic reactions to the proteins in a given mushroom. Additionally, mushrooms may be contaminated by bacteria and molds, or by environmental poisons like pesticides or radiation, and the symptoms from these pollutants can be mistaken for mushroom poisoning.

Of the 1.5 million species of fungi projected to be out there, perhaps 5 percent have been identified. Of that 5 percent, maybe 10,000 species produce fleshy mushrooms, and about 400 of them are poisonous. In a field that is constantly evolving, these numbers are speculative, but in general, of the 400 species that are poisonous, 20 are commonly found, 6 of which are lethal. (And of the 2,000 or so species that are probably edible, 100 are widely picked and 15 to 30 are commonly eaten.) The challenge, then, is to know your mushrooms.

There are many types of mycetismus (poisonings caused by eating mushrooms), but only three types of poisoning dependably kill.* Amatoxin poisoning is the worst. It is responsible for 90 percent of all mushroom fatalities in this country, and probably in Europe, too. Amatoxin poisoning is caused by eating either the destroying angel (*Amanita bisporigera*) or the death cap (*Amanita phalloides*), the mushroom that famously killed Sam Sebastiani Jr., a member of the Sebastiani Californian wine family in 1997, and possibly Emperor Claudius (AD 4–54),

---

*That doesn't mean new toxins aren't being discovered. One syndrome, called rhabdomyolysis, which causes a breakdown of skeletal muscle tissue, has recently been described in a Japanese *Russula* species.

among other species. One cap of an *A. phalloides* will make you very sick,
even do you in, especially if you exhibit symptoms within 6 hours of eating. Symptoms start with gastrointestinal pain, vomiting, and diarrhea
that subside after a day, leading, unfortunately, to a false sense of security,
because without prompt treatment, 40 percent of patients die within a
week of the onset of symptoms. A few days after the first symptoms, the
patient suffers hepatic dysfunction, sometimes renal failure, and even
liver necrosis. With prompt intervention, 80 to 90 percent of patients live.
In Europe, injections of the compounds silibinin and silymarin, extracts
of the milk thistle, are used to treat amatoxin poisoning. In the United
States, treatment consists of IV fluids and penicillin—although there is
no evidence that penicillin, an antibacterial medicine, does any good.
Nor are there data to suggest which protocol is more successful.

The second serious type of mushroom poisoning is orellanine (or
cortinarin) poisoning. It is rare in the USA. Three species of *Cortinarius* mushrooms will cause delayed-onset renal failure within 2 days to
2 weeks after eating the mushroom. The symptoms start with nausea,
vomiting, and anorexia, followed in hours or days by kidney problems.
Three to 10 caps will produce irreversible kidney failure, more so in
men than women. The novelist Nicholas Evans, author of *The Horse
Whisperer*, had a kidney transplant in 2011, having mistaken *Cortinarius speciosissimus*—also known as the deadly webcap—for porcini. At
the time of this writing, his wife and brother-in-law, who ate the mushrooms as well, were on the kidney transplant waiting list.

The third killer is gyromitrain poisoning. *Gyromitra esculenta*, the
false morel, contains a particularly toxic hydrazine called monomethylhydrazine, the same stuff from which missile and rocket propellant is
made. Two to 5 cups of this mushroom will cause a gastrointestinal
phase (nausea, vomiting, diarrhea), followed by fever and fatigue. Severe
poisoning leads to liver toxicity or renal failure, coma, and death.

A poisonous morel (left) and edible morel (right)

There are lesser poisonings, too, usually nonfatal but still unpleasant. One is Antabuse syndrome—named for the drug prescribed to manage alcoholism. Eating certain mushrooms with alcohol can make you sick, hence the name of the poisoning. The most famous example is the inky cap mushroom (*Coprinopsis atramentaria*), also known as the tippler's bane. Pantherine syndrome is a sort of inebriation—it's like being drunk, sometimes dead drunk, as in a virtual coma—caused by eating *Amanita muscaria*. The psychoactive effects of "magic mushrooms" are known as tryptamine poisoning (psilocybin, the active ingredient in the magic mushroom, is a tryptamine). It is most often administered intentionally and is characterized by euphoria, distress, uncontrollable laughter, hallucinations, and agitation, often followed, for a number of days, by a feeling of well-being. About 4 grams of dried psilocybin mushrooms will cause intense hallucinations. "Talking down" the patient is the usual treatment. Some species in the *Clitocybe* and *Inocybe* genera cause muscarine poisoning, which presents as sweating, drooling, and gastrointestinal disorders, and in very severe cases, coma—although the relationship between the degree of poisoning and the dosage is unknown.

Mushrooms, like all living things, are chemically very complex. Not only do they vary chemically from strain to strain—within a single species—but anyone can have idiosyncratic reactions to a mushroom. When I eat the bright orange chicken mushrooms (*Laetiporus sulphureus* and *L. cincinnatus*), my lips and tongue tingle in a freakily unpleasant way, a reaction some people have to an amino acid present in the mushroom. Slippery jacks (*Suillus luteus*) give some people the runs. Laughing jims or gyms (*Gymonpilus spectabilis*) may have you tripping and vomiting at the same time. Toxic compounds that can irritate digestion exist in some mushrooms that become perfectly edible when the toxin is degraded by heat. The morel is an example of a mushroom that should never be eaten raw. But cooked, it is one of the most delectable of all.

That's why the NYMS morel hunt is so well attended. We all wanted morels. So I was definitely bummed out to be driving home empty-handed. And adding insult to injury, that very woman who had picked my only morel was taking a little open-mouthed snooze in the backseat of my car, her basket of morels hugged tight in her arms, while I coped with the traffic over the George Washington Bridge. Later, in my frustration, I spent $40 for a half pound of tired-looking morels at an overpriced grocery store in SoHo.

It was clear that I needed to hunt an environment that offered a bigger payload.

I'd learned that the real morel action was in the Midwest, so the following year I signed up for the Illinois Morel Mushroom Hunting Championship, held the first Saturday in May.

Finding reasonably priced round-trip tickets from New York to Peoria on the first weekend in May was a lot easier than finding a

mushrooming companion. I was rather surprised none of my mycological society friends were game, as there could be lots of morels to be
had: morels to find, morels to bid on at auction, dried morels to buy at
tables loaded with morel-themed doodads and gizmos—everything for
the morel hunter and her codependents. Maybe it was the Peoria thing.
Anyway, I ended up going alone.

The Illinois State Morel Mushroom Hunting Championship was
founded in 1996 by Tom and Vicky Nauman, proprietors of Morel Mania,
Inc. (www.morelmania.com), a Web site that was created to market Tom's
hand-carved morel Shroom Sticks™ (he carves 800 to 900 walking sticks a
year) and is devoted to morel-related education, activities, and products.
There were almost eight million hits on the site in 2009. In 2007, the year
I went, the championships were held in the windy city of Henry, a small
central Illinois town on the Illinois River composed of tidy houses, cut
lawns, and flowering lilacs. Hunters from all over Illinois and several other
states inundate the scant hotel accommodations or set up tent communities on the fairgrounds where the festivities are held.

By the time I got into town, it was early evening. I checked into my
hotel, the Henry Harbor Inn, on a dirt road next to the river. The brochure
that came with my room key read, "Welcome to Henry. Best Town by a
Dam Site." The hotel was bustling, the parking lot full, and every car had
a big cooler in its trunk.

I arrived for the hunt early the next morning. Very early, like, the
third person to register. So I had plenty of time to eat pancakes in the
dining hall. That's where I met Dave Mallery, as a result of pronouncing
the s in Illinois, and his asking where I was from.

Dave is a longtime resident of rural Illinois, and he represents a certain kind of picker that I saw milling around the breakfast buffet: the
camouflaged outdoorsman. They were almost all men, with short hair
and families and, based upon small talk, conservative values. Not all

were enthusiastic morel eaters, and few ate them in any way other than sautéed over steaks or battered and fried. I'd met similar hunters before in Colorado. Mushroomers seem to have regional characteristics that reflect their local politics and lifestyles. Hunters from communities that are politically liberal and collegiate like Eugene, Oregon, were often hippies hunting for their culinary and medicinal pantries. Hunters from New York exhibit a kind of ambition in the forest—Gathering 2.0—and my Californian colleagues seem just as happy to find fiddlehead ferns as they are to find morels. Dave explained the morels were late this year, and I guess he felt sorry that I'd come so far for a sparse hunt, because he offered to take me out after the competition for some hunting on our own. I ate my pancakes in a state of euphoria. Not even 12 hours on the ground and I'd found someone who would share his spots with me.

After breakfast, I went outside to wait for one of the four idling yellow school buses that would take us to the hunting grounds for the competition. I stood against a building to escape the wind—it was a chilly 55 degrees—next to a couple who were doing the same. We started talking. Al Nighsonger is a biker with all the trimmings: leather jacket, jackboots, a long gray ponytail, a smoker's cough. He represents another type of mushroom hunter—one I've met in the commercial morel forests in Montana: hard living, off the grid, a live-free-or-die outlaw type of man. His wife, Dee, is a steady, self-confident woman with a lovely melodic voice, a former Iraq War air force gunner in a soldier's cap.

"You come with us, and you'll find mushrooms," Al promised. "We'll look for you on the golf course."

We did indeed go to a golf course—which troubled me: The thought of searching for morels on a trimmed green seemed unsporting, like an Easter egg hunt on a lawn. We all bundled out of the buses, negotiating walking sticks and wicker baskets, and Tom Nauman, a stocky, bearded fellow, clambered atop an ambulance parked near the clubhouse to explain the rules: At the end of 90 minutes, a siren will sound, giving

Hunters take off across the golf course at the Illinois State Morel Mushroom Hunting Championship.

notice there are 30 minutes left in the hunt. After 119 minutes, a siren will sound twice, notifying hunters they have 60 seconds in which to turn in their mushrooms to officials. (At this point, the assembled group started looking at one another in confusion.) Sixty-one seconds after the final siren has been sounded, hunters will be penalized 10 mushrooms for lateness. Anyone more than 10 minutes late forfeits his or her mushrooms. No pooling mushrooms, no getting unauthorized help. No damaging the fungus that lives belowground.

Then, after a few words about how big the hunt had become in its 12 years of operation and, to my relief, some general directions regarding the elm woods beyond the range, Tom pulled the trigger of his starter gun and off we all ran, a rather undignified crowd of 300 flapping across the grass in our rubber boots. Al and Dee headed west into the woods, and I followed.

Dee disappeared right away, but Al led me along, a 16-ounce can of Busch beer in one hand, smoking cigarettes the whole time, pointing with his lit butt at one tree or another. In the Midwest, given the right temperature and rainfall, morels may be found in abundance under dying elm trees. And due to Dutch elm disease, a fungal blight, there are a lot of dying elms.

"You'll find morels under that there elm," he said, pointing at a dense thicket. While Al sat on a stump, I crawled under, my clothes and hair tugged and ripped as I pushed through. But sure enough, I found morels. I knew they were growing under a dying elm, but the undergrowth was so thick I couldn't see the tree. I could only look over my shoulder at Al, who gestured for me to keep going, keep going, with a wave of his hand, and I obeyed, crawling like an infantryman through the nettles and briers. Using this technique, Al and I found about 35 hard-won morels, and then the siren blew and we had to head out of the woods. Because we shared a bag, I couldn't submit our morels for competition. Actually, everyone was grousing that there weren't many mushrooms, although most people seemed to have collected a few pounds in the 2 hours we hunted.

An auction followed the hunt, and somewhere in the middle of it, the hunt winners were announced. I didn't care about the $200 prize money for the most morels collected, but I did covet a trophy once I saw it on display: a tacky plaque shaped like the state of Illinois with a little resin morel attached. (And indeed, as the young man who won the trophy took his check, there were some intentionally easy-to-overhear comments suggesting he had colluded with other mushroomers and they were set to blow their earnings collectively at the bar.) Biggest mushroom (6 inches tall) and smallest mushroom (½ inch tall) also won prizes, although I knew an even smaller mushroom had been found. On the bumpy bus ride back to the fairgrounds, a young lady held up an absolutely miniscule specimen for me to inspect, but when we suddenly hit a rut, she dropped it.

Hunters from around the state brought mushrooms to sell at the auction, and they were expensive: Prices varied from $50 to $90 a pound—about what high-end gourmet shops in New York were charging that year. The auctioneer, a fellow in an emergency orange coat and motorcycle boots with spurs, held up half-pound bags of morels for everyone to look at. One fellow, a trotter jockey from Florida with a blond crew cut, filled a cooler with 16 pounds of these pricey mushrooms, peeling off

50-dollar bills from a wad of cash as thick as a steak. Dave sat next to me at the auction, and he explained that some hunters soaked the mushrooms to make the bag heavier. At one point, a shaggy pale-eyed dude from Los Angeles shuffled over and asked if I was the New York reporter who was just there to have fun, and then proceeded to tell me he always finds morels after he's done a good deed, and that he didn't want to come out and say it, but he thought it was due to divine intervention.

I'd heard stuff like this before. Hunters who stumble upon a great patch of mushrooms have been known to wear the same clothes again, thinking they bring them luck. Some hunters carry a small basket so as not to alert the mushrooms, or pretend they are not really hunting at all, just walking in the woods, acting casual, so as not to jinx their chances. "Never say the *M* word in the woods," they'll warn, and never pick the first morel you see, because they send a signal underground to the other morels and then they'll all go into hiding. There is certainly a feeling of inevitability when you do find them—almost like it is your destiny to find that mushroom. After all, many fungi live underground. They are by their very nature mysterious. But on the other hand, one of the trophy winners was a PhD in mycology, so obviously he enjoyed an edge based not on superstition, luck, outwitting the mushroom spirits, or by agreement with God, but because he'd taken a lot of biology courses.

After a pork chop sandwich—a delicious though architecturally challenging meal as the bone was still in—Dave took me to a spot he'd scoped out beside the river earlier in the day. We hunted a sandy bank of dying elms across the road from river wetlands. It was strewn with the kind of garbage that people chuck out of their cars—I kept expecting to stumble over a corpse, and was jittery enough to jump at the sight of a naked, discarded baby doll haphazardly buried under a sprinkling of damp pine needles. But mushrooms don't care about the aesthetics of their place, sometimes they even seem to prefer beat up and run-down areas, and true to form, this one was blanketed with blond morels. I picked about 3 pounds with Dave, and we talked about mortgages and colleges and all the stuff that preoccupies middle-aged people regardless of how cool their sunglasses are.

That night at the Harbor Inn, I did an inventory: a hefty 4 pounds of nice-looking morels that I distributed among four pie boxes I'd brought along. There was a steak house within walking distance, and after convincing the waitress to restock a salad bar that looked like it had just returned from a transatlantic flight, I ate. I was ravenous. It was $4.99.

The next morning, I had a tentative plan to hunt with Al and Dee at their spot "where no one else ever goes," but as I couldn't get hold of them early, I signed on for the morel hunting tour with Tom Nauman. I balked at the $75 price tag, but Tom said it was way worth it, plus I'd get some swag. While I waited for our group to convene in the arts hall, I perused the morel merchandise. There were morel-themed refrigerator magnets, salt and pepper shakers, napkin holders, statuettes of all sorts, T-shirts, hats, aprons . . . I almost bought a pair of resin morel wire earrings, but when I tried them on they looked like misshapen beige warts hanging from my earlobes.

About 20 of us took a bus, driven by a bottle-blond driver who told me repeatedly how she could never stand to live in the rat race that is New York City, to a lovely farm. We scrabbled under bramble, through woods, in and out of fields, Tom pointing out dead elms with no mushrooms under them, all the while talking about how many hits the Morel Mania site had gotten that spring. Tom had told us to look for morels at the base of elms whose bark was shearing off, and I saw one tree that looked promising. Indeed, I circled it, and found a few morels at its base. As I checked the leaf litter for more—mushrooms will often come up at the drip line of a tree, a circumference determined by the tree canopy—a young couple approached with vexed expressions. "We saw this tree from 50 yards away," he said, his eye on my small cache of mushrooms, and she nodded. I shrugged and left—I think I had all the mushrooms anyway—but I felt a little like I'd been accused of stealing someone's cab.

Luckily, Al and Dee were hanging out in the fairgrounds parking lot drinking coffee when we returned. I couldn't get my freebies fast enough— a bottle of water and a thin volume called *Find the Tree, Find the Morel*, written by a teenage wunderkind on the Illinois hunting scene—before I hopped in my car to follow them to their mysterious grounds.

We passed the airport in Peoria and pulled into a military installation. Dee showed her pass and, after yucking it up for a few minutes with the baby-faced boys holding automatic rifles, drove us to a beautiful moist forest deep within the base. What they'd said was true—we had the woods to ourselves. However, the forest was at the end of a firing range, and practice was going on. Guns popped and crackled and bullets whizzed overhead periodically, buzzing through the high branches, nipping off twigs. I hunted with my shoulders bunched around my ears, trying to make my head a smaller target. "Oh, that's just the police practicing," said Dee, utterly unperturbed. "Now if it were machine gunners, I'd say walk low."

We found many pounds of big morels, and Dee told me that she and Al had gone hunting on their wedding day, which was in May. Sitting in the plane, my bag stuffed with pie boxes brimming with morels, I thought about my flight over, how I'd felt the lone mushroomer then, and how different my experience in Illinois actually was. Were the people so nice because of a kind of morel brotherhood? I don't know.

Maybe it's just Peoria.

So began my period of attending mushroom forays with specific targets in mind. A mushroom I especially coveted was the candy cap, one of several closely related *Lactarius* mushrooms, which refers to the pearl of milky juice (mycologists call it latex) that seeps out of the stem and cap when you pick it.

Years earlier, I had tasted a candy cap at a public relations event hosted by the chef and author Jack Czarnecki. He made a sweet compote with the mushroom and served it over cheesecake. The candy cap was a revelation to me: redolent with the smell of maple, marvelously silky and spongy in texture, earthy and meaty and sweet. When you eat a candy cap, your skin smells like maple sugar. When you exercise after eating a candy cap, your sweat smells like maple sugar. When you make love after eating a candy cap . . . well, I leave that to the imagination, but . . . *yes.* Candy caps are native to northern California, and although you can purchase them dried from wild crafters and distributors through the Internet, I was hungry to find them for myself.

That's why I signed up for the SOMA Wild Mushroom Camp in Occidental, California. SOMA camp usually takes place over a weekend in mid-January. I'd paid $300 and checked off my packing list, which included a sleeping bag, compass, and "favorite whistle," among many other items not usually owned by people who live in New York apartments, then flown across the country to spend 3 days with 160 fungal-minded people. The SOMA camp (SOMA is an acronym—and a double entendre—for Sonoma Mycological Association and the holy drink of the Indian sacred text, the Rig Veda) had occupied a Christian summer camp that squatted amid young redwoods and rocky outcroppings; the cabins, shower houses, and dining/meeting hall all transformed from one obsession to another. Everything at SOMA camp was mushroomy: the names of the cabins (my travel companion and fellow New York Mycological Association member Arlene Jacobs and I were, coincidentally, assigned to the *Lactarius* cabin), the mushroom-shaped nametags, the mushroom paraphernalia for sale in the public space. It was like a Trekkie convention for mushroomers.

On the walls were sign-up lists for classes like "Introduction to Mush-room Dyes," "Toadstools, Mushrooms, and Beyond," and for the forays, and a map of the United States stuck with pins representing our home-towns. Arlene, a former chef de cuisine at Jean Georges in New York, is a petite woman with short hair and tidy, efficient hands. She's good at all sorts of crafts, and she put her name down for Mushroom Paper Making and Botanical Drawing. I signed up for the longest forays, ready for the deepest woods, hoping for the most bountiful hunt. And as we were eagerly writing our names down, ensuring our spots like college students jostling for a seat in a celebrity professor's course, we eyed the other participants: about 50 middle-aged people in jeans and camo and khaki carrying straw baskets, as well as a smattering of bearded mountain men in suspenders and plaid. Arlene and I were the only people wearing black.

A small foray was organized for that afternoon, and while I waited in the parking lot beside the vans, a man in huge hiking boots with red laces and a moustache that lay on his upper lip like a sleeping baby hedgehog struck up conversation. He told me he was a leading expert on Arctic polypores and that he was reporting on the camp for a food mag-azine. Naturally I asked him which one, but when he told me and I blinked vacantly, he didn't say another word, just got in the front seat of the van and closed the door.

We drove about 10 minutes north to Westminster Woods, a forest with wide, hard trails that must have been tromped all summer long by young Christians. And though we looked, and I looked until the final whistle to return to the vans, it was too dry and cold for mushrooms.

It was a rather dreary start to the weekend, but we were cheered after a few glasses of wine in the afternoon and a first-rate class on mushroom salads with the chef and gleaner Elissa Rubin-Mahon (Dungeness crab and roasted chanterelles, Thai-style grilled oyster mushrooms with mint). By the time we had ambled around to the ID tables, we saw that others had had more luck foraging. There were easily 40 different species on display, each coded with either a place-setting symbol (which indicated it was edible) or a skull and crossbones, and as we lingered, listening in on the open and easy sharing of mushroomy information, I realized that there were two castes of people at the camp: those who were interested in fungi primarily from a biological standpoint and those who were interested primarily from a culinary standpoint. In the first group were men who rather aggressively corrected each other's identifications, as well as nerdy scientific types who inspected the samples with magnifying glasses and rolled the Latin names of the mushrooms over their tongues like sour balls. I am of the lower caste: a belly feeder, interested in hunting for the pot.

Setting aside the obvious problems with poisonous mushrooms, there are a few guidelines to eating wild edible mushrooms safely. First, know your mushrooms. As Gary Lincoff likes to say, "Any mushroom is edible once." Eat only one species at a time the first time you eat them (combining species will make it harder to determine which one you are having a bad reaction to). Eat only young, very fresh specimens. Mushrooms should not be eaten raw. Mushroom cell walls are made of chitin (pronounced ky-tin), the same stuff that crab shells are made of, and it's hard to digest. It is actually a 1-4 linkage of glucose—kind of like a very thin, crispy candy. But it is supertough stuff: Chitin's strength, along with turgor pressure

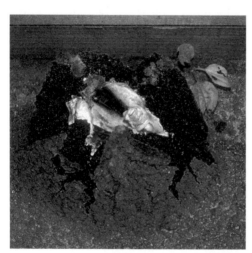

Mushrooms breaking through asphalt

(that's when the contents of a cell push against the cell wall—sort of like your flexed muscle pushing against your skin), gives mushrooms the ability to push through the earth, even through solids like asphalt. It's a wonderful adaptation, but we don't have the stomach enzymes to digest it. Chitin, however, is broken down when you cook the mushroom. Cooking also releases nutrients that are trapped in the cells. Plus, eating raw wild mushrooms could give you worms.

The next morning, our first full day, Arlene and I attended the foray we had come so far to join. The camp population had swelled overnight, the weather had warmed up, and the forest we visited, Point Reyes, was spectacular. Candy caps are symbiotic partners with a variety of plants: The fungus grows on the roots of huckleberry, tan and live oak, and conifers, all of which share this forest with redwood trees. I'd never seen redwoods before, and walking in that deep, grand forest, coming upon a grove of huge trees with dozens of mushrooms growing in the middle, was as magical as anything I'd ever experienced as a child, when such encounters were full of mystery and meaning. A young biology student with enough facial hardware to set off an airplane security alarm pointed out my first candy cap, the fungus *Lactarius fragilis*. They are small, cinnamon colored, and smell like maple syrup, and I promptly became hyperfocused on collecting them—as many as I could. At the same time, my greed and gluttony, those vices that propelled me from one patch of mushrooms to the next, were somehow smothered under the greatness of the trees, the somber quietness of the woods, the diffused green light that made the forest feel like a dream.

I returned to camp with about 5 pounds of pristine candy caps. Already, the whole trip had been worth it: the expense, the hassle of arranging to have the kids picked up from school, everything. I tried to be as low key about my haul as I could because I was afraid someone would ask me to share, though I did want one of the top identification dogs to check them out in case I had included an LBM (little brown mushroom) of bad repute. My mushrooms garnered more attention than I would have liked—despite the fact that the ID tables, by day 2, were laden with mushrooms—but no one asked for any. It was an indication of my inexperience and naiveté that I was even worried: Mushroom hunters never ask to share.

In the afternoon, Arlene and I attended Lawrence Millman's lecture "Making Fire with Fomes—Cree Indian Divination" and discovered the moustached Arctic polypore expert was the fellow I had inadvertently insulted when I didn't recognize the magazine he was writing for. His accomplishments, which he shared during his introduction, were impressive. A member of the Explorer's Club, Millman has written 11 books, including *A Kayak Full of Ghosts*, and has adventured in many places, writing articles and such. The lecture, scheduled for 1 hour, quickly threatened to run overtime, what with digressions into the trials and tribulations of camping by oneself in the tundra, so we went to peruse the sample tables where Dr. Else Vellinga explained that mushrooms are identified three ways: by their morphology (what they look like), by examining their spores with a microscope, and by analyzing their DNA.

Historically, fungi had been organized into two groups: edible and poisonous. It was the Swedish mycologist Elias Magnus Fries (1794–1878) who organized mushrooms based on morphology—their size, shape, color, surface features, odor, gills or pores, stem, veil (a membrane connecting the cap to the stem), spore color, habitat, and so on. His system was modified over time, and in the 1950s mycologists like Rolf Singer reworked his classifications. Nevertheless, most of Fries's genera are holding up quite well under the scrutiny of molecular biology (DNA analyses and the ability to identify the relationships between different fungi by their genes).

Mycologists use the same scientific classification system as all the other biological disciplines: life, kingdom, phylum, class, order, family, genus, and species. Within the kingdom of fungi there are seven phyla or subkingdoms, classifications based on their reproductive structures (which can lead to some very disparate fungi, like white button mushrooms and the rusts that attack wheat, being classed together). The higher fungi—those with the most obvious and complex fruiting bodies, including most of the mushrooms we find in the woods—belong to two phyla. The Ascomycota, which include morels and truffles, produce spores in sacks and are called cup fungi, and the Basidiomycota, like button mushrooms and porcini, produce spores on tiny structures that look like little baseball bats. Actually, the Basidiomycota are the true mushroom fungi. Technically, mycologists don't call the fruiting bodies of Ascomycota mushrooms (in fact, they don't use the term *mushroom* at all, not when talking science), but everyone does in common usage. Ascomycota tend to be smaller, and there are more species, but most are molds and yeasts. Some molds are known as Fungi Imperfecti—and are classified as Deuteromycetes, a kind of dumping ground for fungi whose sexual cycle is not yet known.

Fungi are named by genus first, like *Boletus*, then the species, *satanas*, always in Latin or Latinized, and italicized in print. Often the names are descriptive, as in *Trametes versicolor* (*trametes* = one who is thin; *versicolor* = variously colored), and in print, the name or initials of the mycologist who first described the mushrooms (and published that description)* may follow: Fr for Fries, L for Linnaeus, AHS for Smith, and Fuck for Fuckel. Many mushrooms have common names as well, like hen of the woods, but these are problematic, as people from different regions will use different common names: Hen of the woods, for

---

*Sometimes there is a race to describe and name a mushroom. The mycologist Dr. Roger Heim named *Psilocybe wassonii* for his collaborator, R. Gordon Wasson, the father of ethnomycology—the study of mushrooms in religious practice—and the modern discoverer of psychedelic mushrooms. But another mycologist, Dr. Rolf Singer, published a description of the hallucinogenic mushroom first, so he got to name it: *Psilocybe muliercula* (*muliercula* means "little women").

example, is also known as ram's head or sheep's head. It's generally best to use the scientific names because they are the same wherever in the world you find the mushroom.

Determining the phyla and genus of a fungus based on morphological characteristics has its limitations when it comes to describing the microscopic majority of fungi. Genetic taxonomy has helped mycologists identify many more fungi than just those that produce large fruiting bodies. And it turns out some mushrooms that don't look at all alike are actually closely related, like a morel and a truffle. "It's like finding out a whale is more closely related to a cow than a fish," said the mycologist David Hibbet. (On the other hand, the theoretical biologist Lynn Margulis argues that leaning too heavily on genetics to identify organisms is a slippery slope. "Even if there were identical gene sequences in the bark of a banana tree and the skin of a dog, we would still classify a dog not with a banana but with wolves and jackals.") Mycologists are currently shifting species into different genera like crazy, and all current taxonomy utilizes DNA analyses.

"It's like early-onset Alzheimer's," said Gary Lincoff. "By the time I'm 80, I'm not going to know any mushroom names at all."

Mycological festivals and forays tend to focus on more technical presentations during the day, like taxonomy, and jazzier stuff at night. SOMA camp was no different. During the evening, I attended a lecture by Gary Lincoff, a top biller on the foray circuit. I'd overheard him at dinner telling a companion, "I was at the movies the other day and I realized there was nothing about mushrooms in the film. It was as if the actors didn't even know mushrooms exist!" Lincoff, who is known in mushroom circles as the Woody Allen of mycology, is probably most famous for having written *The National Audubon Society Field Guide to North American Mushrooms*, in which his editors insisted he invent loads of common names for mushrooms that didn't have them. At his lecture, he told us that when he was writing his field guide, he sat around at night with his friends, looking at slides and coming up with common names. One picture was of a mushroom that was orange on the outside and white on the inside. It looked like a boiled lobster, and so he called it the lobster mushroom. I'd always assumed the lobster mushroom tasted like fish.

I also attended a presentation by Elio Schaechter, gentleman microbiologist, who showed rather disgusting slides of fungal infestations of the body (tongue, toenails, scalp) and then flattered me immensely by holding my hand gently during another mycologist's lecture on mold.

Throughout the weekend, we met enthusiasts of all sorts; earth mothers and hot young chefs and men of the wood-chopping, outdoorsy variety who thought Arlene and I were troopers for traveling so far. We ate mixed wild mushroom tacos that night and drank some of the great wines of Sonoma and traded business cards with other mycophiles, fully intending to keep in touch.

Back in New York, I dried the candy caps (they are used fresh in savory dishes, dried in sweet dishes) and froze them in glass Ball jars. Over the course of the following year, I prepared them many ways, but the dish that best evoked the place where I found them was baked apples, a few of the mushrooms pressed into the flesh of each apple before it was topped with butter and cinnamon. The apples were mapley and mushroomy at the same time, as woodsy and sweet and delightful as anything I've ever eaten, and not just because of their fine, unusual flavor but also because they came from a grove of redwoods on the edge of a forest through which I could see the great blue.

When I told my husband, Kevin, I was planning a camping trip with Wild About Mushrooms, a late spring morel and porcini mushroom hunting foray in the Sierra Nevada Mountains, he got a little glum. He'd been trying to get me to camp with him for 20 years, and except for one time when we camped at the Great Sand Dunes in Colorado and I spent the night slowly sliding down the dune in my sleeping bag, I'd always declined. But here I was, after maxing out my credit card at EMS, heading west to hunt mushrooms with David Campbell, a well-known California-based mushroom hunter who collects for personal and commercial purposes, and his crew.

The Mushroom Man story is a perennial in regional newspapers: A local mycologically savvy fellow or gal with a silly moniker like Fungus Bob or Wolf the Mushroom Man, or Wildman Steve Brill (who works the parks in New York City), is leading a group on a foray, where he/she will explain the joys and hazards of mushrooming.* David doesn't have a tag, but he is definitely well known on the northern California mushroom scene. He certainly looks the part of a mountain man: Tall and bearded, he has that aloof, hooded-eye quality of someone who might just leave you in the woods if you piss him off. For decades he has been an obsessed wild mushroom enthusiast and sometime commercial picker, wandering the mountains to collect morels, porcini, chanterelles, and matsutake, among others, which he has sold to chefs and mushroom distributors. A former president of the Mycological Society of San Francisco, David has volunteered at the local poison control center for the past 15 years and led forays for paying clients like myself, affably sharing both his prime picking spots and his favorite wines. "At this point I'm in it to educate people," he told me.

David is used to people like me nagging him to identify every anonymous-looking brown mushroom in the woods, which I've come

---

*While most professional mushroom hunters seem to be men, a Mexican study found that women are actually more adept at mushroom hunting. The men in the study "climbed higher, traveled further, and used 70 percent more energy than the women, who made more stops but seemed to know where they were going."

to learn is rather bad manners. (It's a bit like leaning too heavily on your Spanish-speaking companion while traveling in Mexico. One should at least try to learn a few words.) The identity of many mushrooms is absolutely obvious to someone like David, who said that after a while differentiating between two mushrooms is like telling the difference between an artichoke and an asparagus. The most commonly reported mushroom "poisonings" are not poisonings at all but the result of panic reactions when someone eats a mushroom they've picked, then, on second thought, questions their identification, setting off a series of dramatic symptoms.

To wit: I usually hunt porcini during the summer in Colorado where I have a cabin, but one year I got skunked. Fearing I'd have no fungi to haul back to New York, I turned in desperation to Yvon Gros, a French chef who owns the Leroux Creek Winery in Hotchkiss, Colorado, and always finds mushrooms. I'd been begging him for years to show me his spots—even got him drunk a couple of times and then hit him up for his locations, but Yvon can hold his tongue and his liquor. That year, however, he owed me quite a few dinners, and I could sense the weakening that only guilt can bring. He promised to take me to the Grand Mesa a few days before we were to return to the city.

The Grand Mesa, in western Colorado, is the largest flat-topped mountain in the continental United States. At about 10,000 feet, it is covered with lakes, streams, and pine forests. National park access roads crisscross the summit, giving remote access to recreationists of all sorts. We piled up in Yvon's truck: his wife, Joanna, and my husband, Kevin, and we headed up, up, up. We were at the very top of the mountain when Yvon hit the brakes.

"Ah, beautiful," he said in his French accent. All over the mossy bank, pocketed between gray rocks, were a hundred clusters of young white mushrooms. I didn't recognize them but Yvon was ecstatic. "Oooh, these are wonderful in the ohm-let!" But what were they called?

"Spa . . . Spo . . . something. It is related to the oyster. Ah! What does it matter? They are delicious. But only when very young, like these."

The mushrooms smelled appetizing: clean and earthy. We collected at least 6 glorious pounds, fantasizing about all the ways we were going to cook our haul. But that evening, Kevin and I had a dinner engagement and had to leave the mushrooms for processing later.

The next morning was our packing day, with a million things to do. Before committing a couple of hours to cleaning and cooking and freezing the mushrooms, Kevin decided a positive identification was in order and got out the books: the National Audubon Society's field guide and *Mushrooms of Colorado and the Southern Rocky Mountains*. He put his finger right on it: *Clitocybe dilatata*. Edibility: poisonous. We called Yvon.

"But I ate a pound of them last night and I feel excellent," he said. Kevin told him to go to page 746 of Lincoff's book. There was a long pause.

"I'll have to get back to you," he said.

Yvon called poison control, and was put on hold (not what you'd hope to have happen), during which time he started to sweat profusely and freak out over every little grumble in his tummy. He finally talked to a mycologist who explained that if he had muscarine poisoning, he would have known it within half an hour, and somehow he'd dodged the bullet. He promised not to eat any more.

I was very confident about my ability to identify a morel by the time I signed up for the WAM trip in California. I was less confident about the foray's housing arrangements. I'd traded numerous e-mails with David expressing my qualms about the whole camping thing, and he told me I could stay at the Ice House, a hillbilly joint 8 miles down a curvy road from the campsite. "But then you'll miss the campfire cocktail hours," he said, so I asked him to lend me a tent and hoped for the best.

I drove from Sacramento to the Crystal Basin, stopping in Pollack Pines, as per my instruction sheet, to "top off" my gas tank. The town seemed carved out of the towering forest and smelled like melted snow. I drove up into the mountains, and as I drove I saw first patches, then banks of snow, and watched the thermometer on my dashboard roll steadily backward: 65, 60, 55, 50, 45 degrees. I passed the Ice House, which had lots of big-wheel vehicles in the lot, as well as a lone police car, its cherry light rotating soundlessly. I was shivering in my travel clothes when I arrived at the campsite: a damp, snowy peninsula jutting into a reservoir, covered with giant pine trees thrusting into the sky like missiles, dwarfing the picnic tables and fire pits beneath them. It was late afternoon, and I was the first customer to arrive. David was there, his van disgorging gear, as was Julie Schreiber, a winemaker who was helping with the foray.

Julie helped me pitch my borrowed tent and then turned to other duties, pointing out the good news that it was too cold for mosquitoes. I crawled inside my tent and crawled out again and then started looking for morels.

It's probably safe to say that for most of the history of drinking wine and eating bread, intimate knowledge of yeasts—the fungi behind fermentation—was anecdotal at best. Mushrooms, on the other hand, are much easier to see and speculation about their biology exists in recorded history as far back as the recipes for their consumption. Mentions of mycophagy (from the Greek, *myco* = fungus, *phagy* = eating) in ancient texts are multitudinous—it's like trying to track references to eating fruit—but it is fair to assume they've always been eaten.

In Western culture, the oldest mushroom recipes (versus cooking methods, such as the parchment-baked truffles eaten by the Egyptians) can be found in *The Art of Cooking* by a Roman gastronome named Apicius, of which there have been more than one, including Marcus

Gavius Apicius (about 80 BC to AD 40).* *The Art of Cooking* might have originated in a Greek culinary monograph, and recipes have likely been added over the centuries. There are recipes for Truffles or Mushrooms in Coriander Wine Sauce, Truffles or Mushrooms in Savory-Thyme Sauce, Rosemary Mint Sauce for Truffles, and so on.

The Romans were undoubtedly mushroom lovers. They even used special amber knives and silver bowls called *boletaria* to cook and serve them. But not all cultures appreciate fungi. The English have tradition-ally characterized mushrooms as being unhealthy, bad tasting, and spir-itually degrading, a phobia that many Americans have inherited: "Fungophobia," fear of fungi, is how one 19th-century British naturalist described it. Mycophobia is another such term. But some of that is changing now, as more people become culinarily savvy and confident about eating wild-crafted products.

I found morels coming up through the grainy spring snow, a little melted puddle around them as if they were secreting antifreeze, near the outhouses that were strategically placed every 50 yards or so along the campground road. Throughout the trip I would find morels in the most debased places: next to fire pits and under picnic tables, and though David explained to me that morels like "disturbed earth," they seemed to me sociable, as if they preferred to be around people.

I snacked on provisions I had brought for dinner, and that night I lay in my icy tent, falling into periodic chilly unconsciousness, then awakening again to listen to the comings and goings of people as they arrived throughout the evening and gathered by the campfire, but I was too cold to go outside and socialize. By 6:00 a.m., however, the birds were ferocious and I could smell coffee, and so I got up to meet

---

*The Greek author Athenaeus, who wrote *The Deipnosophistae* in AD 200, described Apicius as "very rich and luxurious," a man who spent "myriads of drachms on his belly" and, according to the Roman authors Seneca and Martial, devoured his whole fortune. When his money got low, he killed himself with poison at a fabulous last-meal banquet rather than curb his appetites.

my fellow campers. Unfortunately, during the night my sleeping bag had sprung a leak, and I emerged covered with tiny feathers. Additionally, somehow I'd managed to get my fashionable black camping outfit into a patch of tree sap, and the feathers that adhered to those spots (mainly, to my dismay, on my behind) remained stuck there throughout the trip. I looked like a pigeon chick whose feathers were still growing in. I also found a morel behind my tent.

Sven Revel of Fairfax, California, was our chef. That morning he whipped up a batch of scrambled eggs with morels that tasted all the better because we were eating outside and the air was chewy with smoke fire and the morels had been picked moments before. There were about 12 of us, people from all walks of life: a sex columnist, a psychiatrist, a winemaker. Even as we introduced ourselves, everyone kept glancing at the ground, eyes trawling for morels like searchlights. "It's a disease," apologized the psychiatrist. David explained where we were going to hunt and how we were going to foray using the buddy system, and then everyone promptly took off on their own.

Mushroom hunting is a solo sport, made up of people who thrive on the rush of revelation, however modest, and people who like to be alone. They will head deep into the woods, off the trails, under the scrub, looking for virgin territory. And they often get lost. Every fall there are newspaper articles about a mushroom hunter who finally emerges from the woods, exhausted and dehydrated after spending the night lost in the forest.

They also tend to find bodies. "Mushroom hunter finds head," is a typical headline. One pair of hunters I heard of found a suicide hanging from a tree but decided to keep hunting for a few more hours before heading out of the woods to call the police. And mushroom hunters dream about mushrooms, too. I have a recurring dream where I ecstatically gather obese, soggy morels in an abandoned formal garden.

I was looking for morels with all my heart, but I couldn't help staring at the trees. Many were clearly old growth, with giant girths and trunks that shot up in the air as high as my apartment building, speckled with Day-Glo green lichens. Scientists today recognize that every tree is an ecosystem of animals, plants, fungi, and bacteria. Those glorious giant pines and all the life they supported demanded a kind of veneration, and I was distracted by their presence. So once I had checked all the out-houses, I wasn't actually finding many mushrooms anymore. David, who I think pitied me because I had come a very long distance to par-ticipate (this was becoming my MO), gave me a few pointers: Forget con-centrating on specific trees, instead stand still and just look around.

David commented on what he called the "greed factor" when it came to mushroomers. "The possession overcomes people," he said. "I like to shake it up by pooling mushrooms." He must have noticed my panicky look because some people in our group were even less effective than me. "But we won't," he continued. "People become attached to a particular mushroom." And indeed, in looking over my finds at the end of the day, I was amazed that I recognized almost every one. I remembered where I'd picked it and the exhilaration I'd felt when I first saw it.

That night, Sven made a smoked pork loin stuffed with sausage and morels and a sauce of morels and caramelized onion, all on a small pro-pane stove. It was like a miracle. Everyone was rather grubby, with earth under their fingernails and pine needles in their hair, and so relaxed that no one jumped at the occasional gunfire of campers elsewhere in the woods shooting, I guess, at the full, full moon. I asked the psychiatrist about our mushrooming obsession, and if it was somehow wired deep within us, like a lizard brain thing, and she said yes, she thought it was evolutionary: Just as having an orgasm inspired people to have sex, the rush of finding a mushroom inspired people to gather.

Before heading back to the airport in Sacramento, I drove to a nearby campground. The Memorial Day weekend was over, and the campgrounds were deserted and exhausted. I came upon an ugly, unused campsite, a puddle of stagnant water beneath the picnic table. Behind the site was a low sloping hill covered with morels. I picked them in a frenzy, as if fearful they would disappear before I'd gathered them all. Among them I noticed a brown convoluted mass, rubbery and asymmetrical. I got up close. It was a false morel, a *Gyromitra esculenta*, which David had pointed out was not edible, or at least, not edible for me. *Gyromitra* are heat labile: Boiling the mushroom in water can reduce its toxic gyromitrin, which converts to monomethylhydrazine when heated, but the boiling water must not be drunk nor the fumes from the boiling water inhaled. However, the toxicity can vary from specimen to specimen, depending on things like altitude, so eating it is a risky business. The false morel is, according to Denis Benjamin, a doctor and mushroom expert, "an edible mushroom that sometimes kills."

"It's delicious, if you want to go there," said David.

Some people do. When I was a child, we used to buy our live Christmas trees from the nursery of an old Italian named Nick Mastropietro in Somers, New York. He was sweet and wrinkled as a dried apple. Nick once pointed out a mushroom growing beneath the Christmas trees in his nursery, and told my father he ate them. My father flipped out: He recognized it right away as an *Amanita muscaria*, the mushroom that killed the count, and that is generally described as poisonous. But Nick said, no, they're delicious.

"But it's strange," he continued. "After eating them, I always fall asleep."

"I told him, 'You're lucky you wake up,'" said my dad.

I tried it once: Two mushroom experts, Larry Evans and Daniel Winkler, stopped by our cabin in Colorado en route to the Telluride Mushroom Festival one August, armed with a big basket of *A. muscaria*. They sliced and boiled a few of the younger specimens, then sautéed them. There was no gamesmanship: I could try them if I liked. I'm glad I did, because they were scrumptious, buttery and mild. My tongue and lips tingled a bit, but so slightly I was quite sure my reaction was psychosomatic. Shortly after eating them, however, I fell into a heavy narcotic-like sleep. It was, to be honest, just like the sleep the doctor puts you into before a colonoscopy—the Michael Jackson drug. When I woke up about 2 hours later, I was wearing one shoe.

There is a saying that there are old mushroom eaters and bold mushroom eaters, but no old, bold mushroom eaters. But actually, there are. There is a subset of wild mushroom hunters who are what Campbell calls expert mycophagists: people who eat or at least have tasted a wide array of mushrooms. A *really* wide array. "I stopped counting at 100 species," he said.

In 2000, Ken Litchfield, a Californian who has been studying and hunting mushrooms for more than 50 years and teaches mushroom cultivation at Merritt College in Oakland, conducted a casual survey of mycophagists' 20 favorite mushrooms, and the results were published in the Internet newsletter *The Fungizette* the following year.* Some of the entries were startling: Michael Wood, editor of www.MykoWeb.com and a burly, enthusiastic man prone to pronouncements like "THIS is the best wine in Colorado," then trying another and saying, "No, THIS is the best wine in Colorado!" pointed out that his #20 favorite mushroom, the false morel (*Gyromitra esculenta*), "CAN BE VERY DANGEROUS." (Indeed, 2 to 4 percent of all mushroom fatalities are associated with false morels. Eaten raw they can be lethal.) "Eat it with great caution, if at all. I try to have one meal of it a year . . . it's just TOO GOOD to ignore." The lists ranked mushrooms that I was unfamiliar with, and many eaters selected mushrooms other than the heavy hitters

---

*Litchfield is a kind of Johnny Appleseed of the fungal world. In his native northern California, he likes to spread spores by chewing mature mushrooms and spitting the mash into cracks in wood or over rotting forest duff. Ken has been struck by lightning twice. The only other person I know who has been struck by lightning twice is Moses Pendleton, one of the founders of the dance troupe Pilobolus—named for the fungus.

(morels, porcini, chanterelles, truffles) among their top three: mushrooms like man on horseback (*Tricholoma flavovirens*), lion's mane (*Hericium americanum*), and the shaggy parasol (*Chlorophyllum rhacodes*).

Throughout my years of attending forays, over and over again I encountered confident outdoorsy men with beards and shaggy hair who dabbled in a kind of mycophagic adventurism that struck me at first as being as much about chest thumping as it was about gastronomic pleasure. "For those who embrace the risky nature [of mycophagy] the danger confirms the ultimate triumph over a world they understand and respect," wrote Gary Alan Fine in *Morel Tales: The Culture of Mushrooming*. But I came to understand that in the process of trying any mushroom that they can satisfactorily determine won't kill them, these expert amateur mycologists gain knowledge about fungi that the microscope cannot reveal: They study the interaction between fungi and people, particularly our digestive tract. However, mycophagy is as much an art as a science, and the variability of people's tolerances is such that one guidebook will tell you slippery jack is edible, and another will tell you it is not. Ultimately, the edibility of certain mushrooms depends on the collector.

The father of American mycophagy is Charles McIlvaine, author of *One Thousand American Fungi* (published in 1900). He discussed in detail the edibility of many species, most of which he tasted himself. There are many entries like this one, for *Amanitopsis nivalis*: "A strong, unpleasant bitter [*sic*], which appears to develop while cooking, renders it unpalatable. It is harmless, but its use is not advised." (The book also includes recipes like "Toadstools with Cheese," which is particularly odd since the word *toadstool* has traditionally implied poisonous mushrooms.) As McIlvaine advised, "There are other species which contain minor poisons producing very undesirable effects. These are soon remedied by taking an emetic, then one or two doses of whisky and sweet oil. . . . "

While there may be some machismo or old-fashioned showing off going on, expert mycophagy is also about education, to help people better understand the diversity of fungi and appreciate the complexities of their biology. When I attended a lecture by Ken Litchfield, who is given to saying ballsy things like "the best mushrooms have worms in them," Ken put a piece of an *Amanita phalloides*—the death cap—in his mouth and chewed. It is impossible to absorb enough amatoxin through your skin to cause death, but chewing them? The audience, as I am sure Ken expected, was awash in "Oh my Gods!" and "Holy shits!" But after chewing quite audibly, he spit it out: The death cap has to be metabolized in order to decimate your liver. "It's a stunt," said Ken, "but it makes a point."

I asked Michael Wood about this practice. "I know people who eat *Boletus satanas*," he said. (This hellishly red, wicked-looking mushroom is generally listed as poisonous.) "It grows on their property so they eat it. People all over the world eat foods that need special treatment, like cassava." Wood is right (I later learned that he has tasted over 150 species), but the key word here is *treatment,* and what distinguishes mycophagists is that in order to eat all these different mushrooms safely, they must know them well, and it is the knowing that is, ultimately, the sport. Charles McIlvaine wrote, "There is but one way to distinguish the edible from the non-edible fungi; that is by mastering the characteristic of each species one by one." It's like Ken Litchfield said while he munched away on that bit of death cap: "Knowledge is power."

Back at my B&B in Sacramento, I went over my mushrooms. David Campbell had also pointed out *Agaricus subrufescens*, sometimes called the almond mushroom, a baby-pink gilled, almond-scented treasure in the same genera as the white button mushroom. They were too delicate to bring back to New York, and I wondered if I would have the confidence to eat them if I found them in the Catskills or Central Park. It dawned on me that I would never have the nerve to eat more than the few mushrooms I recognized from restaurant menus unless I got serious and learned the Latin binomial and the taxonomy and, bummer, the complex biology.

And so I started to attend conferences, and there I learned not only that the science was not tedious at all, but completely alarming and bizarre and beautiful, and that the mycologists, the people who are hyperfocused on fungi all the time, were the most delightful collection of oddballs with a mission that I'd ever met.

Chapter 2

CONFERENCES AND COLLECTORS

I eased myself into the study of the biology of fungi by attending events that trended more toward education than tromping around in the woods. The first science-oriented congress I went to was the 33rd annual Northeast Mycological Federation (NEMF) foray on Cape Cod one rainy October weekend. I'd picked up my fellow New York Mycological Society members Paul Sadowski and Alice Barner on the Upper East Side at 5:00 that morning: Even a crummy driver like me feels competent on the streets of New York at 5:00 a.m., but after 5 hours of being hemmed in by 14-wheeled Wonder Bread trucks going 70 miles per hour, we were all pretty jittery. Luckily, the bar was open when we arrived at the Eastham Four Points Sheraton, where the foray was headquartered.

NEMF is a federation of 18 mycological clubs stretching from Canada to Virginia, and each year, one or more of the clubs hosts the foray. The year I attended, 2009, the foray was hosted by the Boston Mycological Club and was attended by 240 or so people: the usual crowd of middle-aged to ancient hobbyists wearing whistles and pulling wheelie luggage (but who would turn out to be bankers, filmmakers, literary agents, and pediatric surgeons), a scattering of hippies and outdoor enthusiasts, and quite a few professional mycologists who lent a little celebrity sheen to the festivities.

I was aware that this was not going to be an acquisitional trip: I didn't even know what kind of mushrooms grew on sand dunes, and the rules of the foray called for avoiding excessive picking anyway. Instead, we were to pick only the best specimens for species identification. Nor was the trip about snazzy accommodations and sexy restaurants, though that would have been nice. The Sheraton is like a hotel version of a fast-food restaurant. My room, which I shared with Alice, faced an indoor pool where a lone lady in a swim cap breaststroked at about 1 mile an hour up and down the length of the pool for what seemed like the entire weekend. The place smelled like chlorine.

The NEMF foray followed the format of some other forays I'd been on, but with more programming. There were walks in the day during which specimens were collected, identification sessions and technical lectures in the afternoon, and entertaining lectures in the evening. In addition there were socials, games like the Polypore Pitch, where contestants chuck the tough, leathery mushrooms into various-size baskets, and an awards ceremony (honoring heaviest fungus found, best specimen, etc.). The indoor ID tables were set up in the Marconi Room (Marconi, a Nobel Prize winner for inventing the telegraph, also has a beach named after him in nearby Wellfleet), as was a kind of bullpen for the professionals and a select few amateur mycologists and their microscopes. The Marconi Room also housed the secretary of the foray and the database coordinator, whose jobs were to maintain the master list of species found. This year, the coordinator was a former NYMS member who had forsaken the club because it had been trending toward belly hunting. My friend Paul was on a microscope near Rod Tulloss, a tall, shy fellow and well-known *Amanita* expert whose proximity had made Paul blush, as if he were sitting next to Beyoncé. Bart

Buyck, the curator of the mycological herbarium at the National Museum of Natural History in Paris, had the *Russula* group station (*Russula* and *Amanita* are genera of fungi, like panthers and horses are genera of animals). Other mycologists came and went, like our own Gary Lincoff, who has probably seen and held more species of mushrooms in his hands than anyone alive today, and the DNA boys.

Mycologists study fungi (not just mushrooms), and fungi are still mostly mysterious. That's because they are very small—often only noticeable when they fruit as mushrooms or molds, which only some do, and they live in inconspicuous places: underground, in dead matter, or as symbionts of plants, animals, or other fungi. In fact, anyone whose heart's desire is to name a species would do well to enter mycology, since only 5 percent of an estimated 1.5 million species have been described, although most are microscopic plant pathogens, or tiny soil or aquatic fungi. Traditionally, botanists lumped fungi together with plants. But in fact, fungi outnumber plants 6 to 1. Fungi constitute a huge, unique kingdom, the Kingdom Fungi, which represents a wide range of lifestyles and morphologies. This group of organisms is as complex as the kingdoms of plants and animals. Indeed, animals, plants, and fungi are nature's most complex life-forms.

The 17th-century Swedish botanist Carolus Linnaeus, known as the father of taxonomy, determined there were two kingdoms of life: animals and plants, and then he divided these two kingdoms into different classes (mammals, reptiles, cactuses, etc.). He based his classifications on morphology—does it have thorns or horns? In 1866, after the invention of the microscope, the German biologist Ernst Haeckel proposed three kingdoms: animals, plants, and protista, a kind of grab bag of simple microorganisms. In the 1930s, the American biologist Herbert Copeland proposed four kingdoms, adding monera, which consisted of prokaryotes, organisms whose cells lacked a nucleus. In the 1960s, the American plant ecologist Robert Whittaker proposed a five-kingdom system. This system was mainly based on differences in what an organism ate and how it got its food, and it led to the inclusion of fungi, the fifth kingdom.

In the 1970s, molecular comparisons led to yet another redefining of the kingdoms, which split the prokaryotes (Kingdom Monera) into two kingdoms. In 1977, Carl Woese, an American microbiologist, took the long view: He established the three-domain system, composed of bacteria, archaea, and eukarya, in which the different kingdoms fall, and this has proven a durable and widely accepted scheme, though there have been other classification ideas since then, each responding to new knowledge about the relationships between microscopic life forms.

"You have to remember," said Gary Lincoff when I asked him about this shuffling about of kingdoms, "it's all just opinion. If you want to call a mushroom a plant, who's going to stop you?" (Lincoff teaches botany at the New York Botanical Garden. "One of the first questions I bring up is: What is a plant? Is a mushroom a plant? It depends on how you define plants and mushrooms. It all depends on what the meaning of 'is' is.")

Many scientists use cladistics (from the Greek *clade*, meaning "branch") to classify species of organisms. Cladograms, which look like genealogical trees, are diagrams that show the ancestral relationship between species, starting with an ancestor organism. Based on a variety of criteria, a cladogram can reveal the evolutionary relationship between plants, animals, and fungi.*

In universities, the study of fungi is typically taught in the botany department, though one could argue it should be in the department of zoology, because based on biochemical and ultrastructural criteria (ultrastructural refers to cells and their parts that can be seen with an electron microscope), fungi are actually more closely related to animals

---

Systematics, a word often confused with *cladistics*, is the study of the diversity of life. Cladistics is one of the ways of looking at systematics. Taxonomy is the science of classifying organisms.

than plants. The most compelling argument for this strange familiarity is their lineage: Both fungi and animals spent more time together on the same branch of the tree of life than either had with plants.

Additionally, fungi and animals share more morphological and structural cellular features than fungi and plants do. For example, the cell walls of fungi are made of chitin—the same substance as crab shells and squid beaks—which doesn't exist in plants. Plants make their own food by converting sunlight into chemical energy. Fungi, like animals, can't make their own food; they produce enzymes to digest the food they find. Fungi retain their carbon reserve—the nutrients they can call on for energy—the same way animals do: as glycogen. Plants store their energy in the form of starch. Animals and many fungi are aerobic respirators: They respire atmospheric oxygen in (to produce energy) and release carbon dioxide out. (Other fungi are anaerobic fermenters—like yeasts. They are able to oxidize molecules in the absence of oxygen.) Plants do the opposite (carbon dioxide in, oxygen out).

There are other indicators of animal and fungi similarity, like the fact that we share 80 to 85 percent of the same ribosomomal RNA (where proteins are manufactured inside the cell). This is why it is so hard for animals to fight off fungal infections—what kills the fungus can also be harmful to humans. Indeed, it's hard to believe that fungi are genetically closer to us than they are to plants because they seem more plantlike, but to put it in perspective, we are more closely related to plants than we are to the *Escherichia coli* (*E. coli*) bacteria that live in our guts.

Most of the mycologists at the NEMF foray were kept busy identifying the mushrooms brought in by us, the paying guests. Indeed, within hours of arriving, people were trolling the landscaped edges of the parking lot, looking for mushrooms. In the rain. By 5:00 p.m. the sign-up sheets for the classes and seminars and forays were posted, and there was quite a bit of competition for spots, made even more frantic by the fact that there were about 25 people to every pencil. I didn't know what to sign up for: Beech Forest? Great Island? Punkhorn Parklands? Someone pinned up a picture of a baby *boletus* mushroom and a couple of elderly ladies swooned over it, carrying on about the mushroom's cuteness in high-pitched voices, like it was a grandchild. I signed up for the Beech Forest walk.

The next morning at breakfast, the president of NEMF warned me that if I drank coffee before the foray my "back will get wet," which I didn't quite understand until someone on the bus explained that there was rain in the forecast and no outhouses in the forest. Our guide was Keith from Truro who looked like a fit Colonel Sanders. He said we might find *Clitocybe nuda*, the blewit, which grows under beech trees, and lots of colored lichens (lichens are included in mycological studies because even though they are a combination of a fungus and a single-celled alga or bacterium, the fungus part is really dominant, having enslaved its partner to photosynthesize food for it). "I'm lichen that!" yelled Keith, who laughed uproariously then held his nose, acknowledging his stinky pun.

In the park parking lot, Keith had us coordinate our watches, warned us about ticks, and pointed to the woods. We hiked in, at first as a group, but soon individuals peeled off like prospectors in search of their own claims. Beeches are beautiful trees. Even under bouts of rain, the beech forest emitted a pale green light, like the light from a firefly, and each of us staked out our particular grove to explore. I looked under my trees, kicking aside the wet leaf litter, finding nothing, and kept glancing at the groves taken by other hunters that I was sure were more fruitful. But then I remembered what David Campbell said about just standing still. And of course, that's what it took to see them: a dozen lavender mushrooms scattered beneath the glowing trees, gently rebuking my covetousness.

After lunch I sat in on the mycologist Renee Lebeuf's "Mushrooms and Smells" lecture, where she explained that some people are anosmiacs—people who cannot perceive odors (commonly caused by brain jostling in car accidents)—and others are hyperosmiacs, people with an abnormally increased sense of smell,* and that one's smelling ability can be developed. Renee, a low-voiced Canadian who clearly hated her microphone, pointed out that quick-rotting mushrooms rarely have smells, and that mushrooms smell less intense in cold weather. Some mushrooms have two smells, one for the stem and one for the cap, and dehydration can either increase or eliminate the odor of mushrooms. Then she covered the range of mushroom smells, sort of like a wine wheel: bitter (onion or garlic), bitter almonds, sweet almonds, anise, maple syrup, chicken bouillon, curry, rotten cabbage, bleach, mealy (like flour), cucumber, a smell like when you iron clothes, flowers of various sorts, bubblegum, tar, ether, honey, coconut, tangerine, raw potatoes, celery, pear, fish, rotting meat, burnt sugar, and sperm.

One of the most popular presenters on the foray circuit is Tom Volk, a mycology professor at the University of Wisconsin–La Crosse. Lots of people in the mushroom scene call Volk the rock star of mycology, and for two reasons: He is adept at speaking to popular audiences, and he is heavily tattooed, with earplugs (not the kind that muffle sound) and blue bangs. Volk had the 8:00 p.m. slot on Saturday: the prime time of the

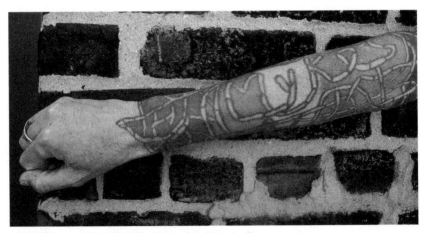

Tom Volk's tatoos depict fungal hyphae and spell "mykos."

*Hyperosmia, which, unless you are a wine connoisseur, is considered a medical condition, is also a side effect of psilocybin, the hallucinogenic chemical in *Psilocybe* mushrooms.

foray. His lecture—part lecture, part stand-up act—called "Spores Illus-trated" helped me understand some of the biology despite myself.

When a mushroom is up in the woods, or anywhere else for that matter, it is up in order to disperse its spores, and most fungi use wind to do the job. A significant difference between spores and seeds is that spores don't have a lot of food stored in them. As a result, spores are incredibly light, so light that mycologists surmise airborne fungal spores from Africa and Europe ride winds across the Atlantic and over the Pacific from China. But there are lots of different fungi, and some have evolved very strange yet effective methods of spore dispersal to ensure their survival.

Spores are tiny. They are individually microscopic, ranging in length from 3 thousandths to 25 thousandths of a millimeter (the naked eye can't see anything smaller than about $\frac{1}{10}$ of a millimeter). They come in nearly every color imaginable, from white to black, and in a variety of shapes, and this probably has some bearing on how spores are dispersed. For example, some spores that are forcibly ejected are aerodynamic, like footballs; the asexual spores of some water-dwelling fungi are shaped like tripods that land on submerged leaves and grip them like little burrs. Looking at spores through a microscope is one of the ways mycologists identify mushrooms. (Another is checking the spore colors, and that is done by making spore prints—laying a mushroom cap gill side down on paper for a few hours—and observing the patterned dusting of colored spores.)

Some spores hitch a ride on the aerial parts of plants. Some fungi eject spores in synchronized ejections that creates a mini air stream that increases the spores' travel distance by 30 times. Others shoot their spores from catapult-like devices, the most impressive being the tiny *Pilobolus*, a mold that grows on herbivore dung. The 1-centimeter-tall fruiting structure (it's not exactly a mushroom) grows above the excre-ment, orients its stalk toward the light, and shoots the spore glob on its tip 35 feet per second, summoning a thrust *10,000 times* the acceleration experienced by space shuttle astronauts at takeoff. It shoots spores 6 feet up and 8 feet out, to land in a patch of grass where the spore is consumed by an herbivore, passes through its stomach where the animal's internal heat activates the fungus's spores, and then germinates on its dung, bringing the cycle full circle. (One hundred years ago, scientists used to have contests to see whose *Pilobolus* culture could shoot the farthest.) Another fungus, the sphere thrower, suddenly turns itself inside out in order to expel its spores.

Fungi use animals to disperse their spore, too. Truffles emit the odor of certain mammalian pheromones that stimulates animals to dig up the fungus. (It's an odor that turns on the human diner, too.) The netted stinkhorn, a truly repulsive-looking mushroom, smells like rotting meat (actually, it's the spores that stink). It attracts flies, which pick up the sticky spores on their legs and transport them to another stinkhorn or a new habitat.* A rust fungus infects certain plants and induces them to grow dense leaves that look like flower petals at the tips of their stems.

These pseudoflowers are brightly colored and smell sweet, and on them are sticky spores, which insects encounter and transport to other plants.

Bioluminescent mushrooms may glow in the dark to attract spore-dispersing insects at night—mushroom expert Larry Evans likes to call them insect discos. In

Netted stinkhorn

*The stinkhorn is distinctly phallus shaped. One of the stinkhorn species is called *Phallus impudicus*, or impudent phallus. Another species, *Mutinus caninus*, looks just like a dog penis. And still another, *Dictyophora duplicata*, if picked in the young button stage, will likely develop an erection by the time you get it home. English maidens were warned about touching them, but the Chinese cultivate them—when the spore mass is removed, the mushroom is edible—and serve them braised in broth to foreign dignitaries. It's a symbol of power. When he was secretary of state, Henry Kissinger ate one.

the United States, bioluminescence, which is the result of a complex series of chemical reactions, is most commonly seen in the mycelium of the wide-ranging honey mushroom. Since mycelium doesn't produce spores, it may be glowing to attract the predators of the microorganisms that predate the fungus. (Foxfire, also known as will-o'-the-wisp or fairy fire, is the greenish glow produced by bioluminescent mycelium. It was used to illuminate instruments in the first battle submarine. There are anecdotes about troops in both World Wars fastening bioluminescent fungi on their helmets so they could spot each other in the dark without alerting the enemy.)

The bird's nest fungus, a cup-shaped fungus that contains a little clutch of spores that look like eggs in a nest, utilizes the energy of raindrops: When rain hits the cup, it splashes out the spores. The outer skin of puffballs, which hold all their spores inside, disintegrates or splits or is broken by mechanical forces like rain, hail, and small children, allowing the spores to blow out. Other mushrooms simply inundate the atmosphere with spores: The fairy ring mushroom releases millions of spores every minute.

Spores can't navigate themselves to a food source where they can safely germinate: They just have to be lucky enough to land in the right place, with some lying dormant for as long as 20 years, waiting, despite dehydration or extreme cold, for the right conditions. In order to increase their odds of success, mushrooms have evolved to produce lots and lots of spores. There are an estimated 1,000 to 10,000 fungal spores floating around in every cubic meter of air in the atmosphere, everywhere at any given time (which we constantly inhale but aren't usually affected by because our immune system keeps them from causing trouble), so many that they may influence the weather cycle by acting as nuclei for water droplets and ice crystals in clouds, fog, and rain.

The microbiologist Elio Schaechter wrote in his book *In the Company of Mushrooms* that a medium-size mushroom, one with a cap 3 to

4 inches across, can produce 100 million spores per hour. One wood decay fungus produces spores at the rate of 350,000 per second, 6 months a year. That's 5.4 trillion spores a year for as many as 10 years. Tom Volk, who loves a cheesy analogy, said that a single basketball-size giant puffball contains 14 trillion spores, and if all 14 trillion spores germinated and matured they would circle the Earth almost 85,000 times. In 2009, I attended a lecture by the mycologist Bob Mackler, whose delivery was weirdly mesmerizing: Mr. Rogers on spore. "I dreamt of what would happen if all the spores germinated at once," he said. "The mass of mushrooms they would produce would knock our planet out of orbit. It's lucky that it is rare a spore turns into a mushroom."*

Tom Volk was on the bus with me the next day to visit the White Cedar Swamp trail in Wellfleet. When I told him I was from New York, he said, "I heart New York," which took me a few minutes to digest because I knew he'd had a heart transplant in 2006. (In the beginning of his lecture he'd shown a slide of himself holding his heart. It looked like a glandy piece of veal in a Baggie.) When I gave him what I guess was a forced smile, he said the proper response to a pun was a groan.

The swamp trail is right next to Marconi Beach, and while on it I could hear the relentless ocean. There were a variety of habitats, but I kept returning to the rolling dunes sprinkled with pine trees twisted by the coastal weather like miniature fossilized tornados. Speckled over the surface of the dunes were earthstars, a strange little fungus that is composed of a center puffball with ray-shaped arms that open like the rays of a star or the petals of a flower, inverting enough to lift the puffball a few centimeters aboveground so the spores have better access to wind. I gathered a few of these for an artist friend who is inspired by

---

*Mackler's analogy might seem excessive, but massive spore production is consistent in nature: Human males produce, on average, 85 million sperm per day per testicle starting around age 13, and one ejaculation releases an average of 100 to 200 million sperm cells.

such things (they aren't edible), following what seemed like a path of them over a dune, a brown milky way in a white sand sky. Each of those earthstars was puffing out little brown clouds of spore, and each spore was hoping to land on a bit of real estate that would meet its requirements for germination. When it does, the spore swells up and then spits out a hypha, a cell surrounded by a tubular wall. The hypha uses up the scant food reserves stored in the spore to give it energy to probe for an outside source of nutrition. If the hypha finds some food—and this is why it is so important that the spore land in a food-rich environment—it grows one cell at a time from its tip, becoming a one-cell-thick string of cells that is nine times thinner than a strand of hair (depending on the fungus). In most hyphae (the plural of hypha), permeable cross walls divide the cells, allowing some of the cellular contents to flow between cells, but generally retaining each cell's genetic material. This string of cells is the fungus.

Plants photosynthesize their food, animals ingest their food, and fungi absorb their food. A fungus secretes enzymes to the outside through its cell walls, including the tip of its hypha, that predigest whatever organic matter the fungus is specialized to consume. It breaks down the organic matter into its component molecular parts, like water, sugars, amino acids, and so on, and then absorbs the molecules, which gives the fungus the nutrients it needs to grow. "Fungi are so tiny they can't eat their own food, so they basically have inverted stomachs," said the mycologist Amy Tuininga. "Imagine you are lying on a giant steak. Your stomach enzymes seep out to predigest the steak, and then you absorb the steak through your skin." Fungi actually live in their food supply, and as that supply becomes depleted, the fungus grows into the next food-rich environment, if one is available. And because fungi aren't dependant on light to grow, they can live in dark habitats, like underground or inside wood.

A fairy ring illustrates the spherical nature of fungus mycelium.

The hypha grows one cell at a time—but it doesn't grow in just one straight line: That wouldn't be a very efficient survival technique. Rather, the hypha branches, growing in three dimensions if that's where the food is and there is nothing in its way. Mycelium typically grows in a circular pattern to maximize its chance of finding nourishment. Starting from its food point of origin, the hyphae grow out in all directions, creating a ring of growing hyphal tips, sort of like the ripple wave created when you toss a pebble into a pond. This growth pattern causes the red ring you see when you have ringworm, the fungal skin disease. It is also the mechanism behind fairy rings, those mushrooms that grow in a ring on your lawn: The mushrooms indicate where the hyphae have grown.

These branching hyphae become increasingly meshed and matted, creating a spiderwebby substance collectively called mycelium. When you break up a rotting log and you see that cotton-candy-like stuff running throughout the wood, what you are seeing is the mycelium: thousands upon thousands of hyphal threads, each one a single cell thick, and each probing tip secreting enzymes that break down the food source, each one a food absorption point. As one purply mycologist described it, the mycelium is composed of "transparent tubes, branching and rebranching [and in each] a rushing torrent of the living contents, the protoplasm, pressing toward the ever expanding tip."

Mycologists have measured intense pressure inside those hyphal tips. Turgidity (the pressure inside the cell, usually from water) is essential for growth in the face of obstacles. The mycologist Nicholas Money has measured fungal turgidity at 1 to 10 atmospheres (for comparison, the air pressure in a car tire is 3 atmospheres).

Depending on the species, mycelia can grow into complex mats or ropey forms, and their size and density may be dictated by the available growing space and food supply—there can be as much as a ton of mycelium per vegetated acre. There is also some evidence that hyphae follow rules of predetermined growth like plants. There is a proscribed amount of space between the hyphal tip and the place where it branches, for example; but unlike the branches and twigs of a tree that grow smaller as the organism as a whole grows larger (there's actually a name for that—apical dominance), hyphae are thought to grow the same all over the organism.

You'd think that each individual hypha is after its own food, but actually, when one hypha comes in contact with a new food supply, the mycelium—the collective hyphae—turns its attention toward that new source and mobilizes its energy to grow toward it and exploit the new food. All the hyphae in a mycelial colony have the same set of chromosomes: They're not individuals in a genetic sense, but clones, like a grove of aspen trees. Some mycologists describe fungal mycelium as a single-minded organism, and plenty of mushroom enthusiasts talk about fungal intelligence. The evidence most often cited is a Japanese study that tested

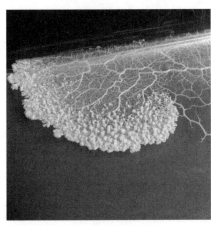

Slime mold on the move

the intelligence of slime mold by placing pieces of the mold in the middle of a 5-inch-square maze with a food source—a bit of grain—at the exit points. Since the hyphae of fungi grow in every direction at once in search of food, the question was whether the mold would overwhelm the maze as a strategy or show intent in pursuing the food source by solving the maze. Researchers were surprised when the mold actually stretched itself out into a thin line and negotiated the maze to find the food. (Slime molds have since been taken out of the Kingdom Fungi and are distributed among several other classifications.)

Given the proper and consistent conditions, there is no reason why a fungus couldn't live indefinitely, growing and storing energy as long as there was a food source and space to grow into. And indeed, a fungus was discovered that turned out to be the largest and one of the oldest living organisms on Earth, and it's still growing.

In 1998, forest service scientists discovered a giant wood-decaying fungus, the *Armillaria gallica* that produces the edible honey mushroom, living

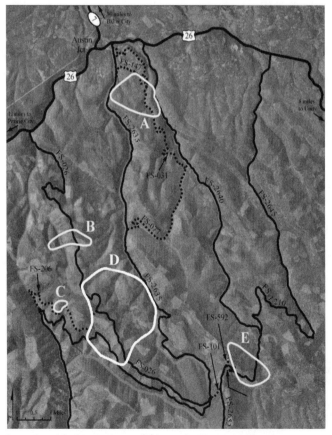

Large fungal bodies, the largest (D) being the Humongous Fungus.

in the Malheur National Forest in the Blue Mountains of eastern Oregon. The fungus spans 2,200 acres—the equivalent of 1,666 football fields—and is at least 2,400 years old. The fungus is largely composed of a type of mycelium called rhizomorphs (from the Greek, *rhizo* = root and *morph* = form), ropey bundles of hyphal strands with a protective melanized rind (melanin is the same stuff that protects you from UV rays by causing you to tan) that seek out new food sources, sometimes at great distances, even crossing over food-poor areas in order to find richer feeding grounds. In this way, the mycelium can and may live on and on, absorbing nutrients and growing ever larger. Because of the enormous size of what the newspapers dubbed "the humongous fungus," it's a bit hard to think of it as an individual, but it is. The Blue Mountain specimen has a single genotype. All its parts have the same set of chromosomes.

Mycelia (the plural form of mycelium) that have grown from separate spores can fuse together in a kind of nonfruiting joining. And one mycelium may be able to take advantage of the helpful genes it encounters in the mycelium it fuses with right away. Unlike animals, which transfer genetic material by inheritance, from parent to child, fungi can benefit from the useful genes of its partner immediately upon fusion. Once the two fungi have fused, they may be able to access genes they can promptly utilize, like those that may increase the fungi's ability to adapt to current environmental challenges, defeat a new threat, or digest something they haven't encountered before.

Sometimes, when two different mycelia from the same species encounter each other, they don't fuse but rather become hostile and compete for resources. Individual fungi can communicate with each other via pheromones, the secreted chemicals that trigger social reactions in animals, plants, and fungi. If they recognize a competitor, they can inject toxic chemicals into the substrate in order to repulse competitive species. They can even invade a competing fungus and suck its hyphae dry of nutrients.

In general, a mushroom grows when two primary mycelium, containing the genetic payload of two different spore sources, fuse to produce a secondary mycelium. It is the secondary mycelium that produces mush-rooms. There are a few factors involved in what triggers a fungus to fruit (and they vary in importance in different fungi), like when the second-ary mycelium reaches a critical mass, or a certain nutritional peak, or when it has to, because its environmental conditions degrade.*

For whatever reason that sparks the mushroom-making process, the hyphae wind around each other at a nexus, creating a dense node, like a knot in your hair. Selected hyphal threads, functioning cooperatively, pro-duce different parts of the mushroom. Different hyphae in the mycelium are specialized for different duties, like cap building or stem building. The nexus becomes a primordium, a dense little nubbin of preformed mush-room that (in many cases) contains all its cells, and the primordium devel-ops quickly into a proper mushroom. Then the reproductive structures of the mushroom produce spores with one set of chromosomes that reflect genes from both strains of the fungi that were involved in its making.

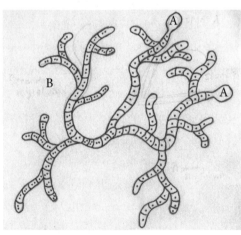

Two primary mycelia (A) fuse to produce a secondary mycelium (B)

If only that were all there was to it. The truth is, there is very little you can say definitively about fun-gal sex. Fungi don't even abide by the two-parent model. Scientists have counted as many as nine individual mycelial parents involved in the making of a single mushroom. And the primary/secondary mycelia

*There are also strange impetuses for mushroom fruiting: A Japanese study looking to reproduce a phenomenon observed in the field, that shiitake mushrooms fruited prolifically after the ground had been hit by lightning, has found that exposing the substrate of various species of fungi to an electrical charge of 50,000 to 100,000 volts for one 10-millionth of a second will double the volume of fruiting. This may be an evolutionary adaptation. Because lightning poses a survival hazard, and may deliver a dead tree for dinner, it leads to accelerated fruiting.

paradigm only applies to fungi that produce mushrooms. Other fungi produce asexual spores on single-celled spore-bearing structures, like the molds. Some produce spores on the hyphae. And many don't make spores at all. Some multiply by fragmenting—that's when a hypha breaks in half (either by accident or on purpose) and both halves go on to live. Many unicellular fungi (mostly yeasts) just pop off daughters like bubbly warts (it's called budding). It's kind of hard to wrap your mind around, and much is still unknown.

There was a pub attached to the pool area at the Four Points Sheraton, and over beers at the bar I became friends with Bart Buyck, the *Russula* expert. We played hooky from the foray one afternoon to visit the drizzly Wellfleet Oysterfest. He's Belgian-French, small and wiry and tough like a jockey, but also rather Euro chic: He wears his jeans tight and his hair long. While we slurped down oysters (raw, roasted with butter sauce, and Rockefeller), Bart pointed out a very important thing about mushrooms that I hadn't understood at all.

He explained that mushrooms grow two ways: indeterminately, meaning the mushrooms are producing new cells from a new growing edge all the time, their shapes influenced by grasses or whatever else is in their environment, and determinate, which are mushrooms that don't grow like a plant, but rather, they swell. When it rains, those little primordia of fused hyphae suck up moisture from the mycelium and enlarge, and as the mushroom expands it pushes up out of the soil. All the genetic material and the full count of cells that the mushroom will have upon maturity are present when the mushroom is a primordium. But while the number of cells doesn't change, the cells themselves get bigger, kind of like one of those superthin sponges that expand to enormous size. When a determinant mushroom, like a porcini, is mature, it is 90 percent water. (Humans, by the way, are 78 percent water.)

For this reason, mycologists don't call the mushroom stem a stem but rather a stipe. While it does support the cap, mycologists think the main reason mushrooms have stipes (which are composed of sterile hyphal tissue) is to elevate them higher, to better disperse their spores.

Likewise, the cap is not really called a cap, though most guidebooks and all restaurants use that terminology. The horizontal spore-bearing part of the mushroom is called the pileus. There are also plenty of mushroom species that don't have a stipe: They are simply all pileus, like oyster mushrooms, or spore-bearing structures, like truffles and puffballs. Some species expand slowly, over many days. Others can expand in a matter of hours; even expand, sporulate, and decompose in a day. This unusual quality of expanding, sometimes so quickly it seems sudden, has led to the use of the word *mushroom* to describe something that expands or swells, like a mushrooming debt, or a mushroom, the gang slang for an innocent bystander who pops up unexpectedly.

While some mushrooms seem to appear overnight, others grow for years, like the shelf mushrooms. Many polypores (also known as bracket or shelf fungi, and their fruiting bodies are called conks) are perennial. You will find them attached to the same dying or dead tree year after year, having fruited from mycelium living within the tree's carcass. They will continue to be nourished by the mycelium until it dies. Polypore is an umbrella term for a variety of mushrooms, usually tough, leathery shelflike mushrooms that grow on trees or logs or roots. Some are edible, some are used for medicinal purposes, and none are thought to be deadly poisonous (although many can cause GI upset). Many are rot resistant, and some species can live to be quite old.

They can also be huge, even becoming a platform for a mini ecosystem. *Bridgeoporus nobilissimus* is called the noble polypore. Only a handful of specimens of this huge, inedible mushroom, which can weigh more than 300 pounds and be more than 3 feet across, are known to exist, all in Washington and Oregon. It looks like the basin of a birdbath filled with furry organic matter, and grows at the base of old-growth noble fir trees. This rapidly disappearing species is capable of sustaining plant life like tree seedlings, ferns, moss, algae, and even other fungi on its pileus. The noble polypore, which typically lives for 25 to 30 years (that's the mushroom—not the mycelium, which of course can be incredibly old), is the first fungus to be listed as an endangered species.

The NEMF conference included a lecture on evolution by Gary Lincoff, dressed up like Darwin in breeches and vest; an extremely complicated board game that sought to introduce players to the fungal tree of life; and a vendors area that included the moody still lifes of a lithe, melancholic painter of mushrooms. There was also a mushroom cooking class that used all of the collected mushrooms, even the coveted matsutake, which grows on the Cape. This thoroughly pissed off the fellow who'd found most of them and clearly hadn't given his permission for his matsies to be eaten by the mob. I'd seen him a few times over the weekend, and he had impressed me as a very mellow, chai-tea kind of guy, but mushroomers can be bipolar when it comes to their haul. He certainly was: He stomped around the hotel in search of someone in authority to complain to, leaving indignant muddy boot tracks up and down the carpeted corridors.

I gave Bart a ride back to New York City, and he listened very patiently as I tried to express how excited I was about all the stuff I had learned at the foray. For 5 hours. At least, he seemed patient. It was sometimes hard to tell if his eyes were open behind his bangs.

In early December, the Mycological Society of San Francisco puts on their Fungus Fair, and the year I went it was held at the Lawrence Hall of Science, in the Berkeley Hills overlooking the bay. I'd never really spent much time in San Francisco before this trip, except for one weekend on the back of a college friend's Ninja motorcycle during which I had my eyes closed the whole time, but now I understand what the big deal is. This was the kind of place where even the most grody-looking off-the-grid type is quick to comment if the Chardonnay he is sucking through his teeth is overoaked or not. Once I saw the Berkeley Bowl grocery store, with its giant bins of cheap, fresh chanterelles, matsutake, and porcini mushrooms, I was a goner: just $3 million short of buying an uninsulated bungalow in North Berkeley. I mean, the Google map of the area actually has Chez Panisse on it, as if the restaurant were an airport or an auditorium.

After seeing all those good mushrooms for sale at the market, I decided to forfeit the walks in the University of California Botanical Garden and spend more time at the lectures. I ended up passing a lot of time in the gift shop, admiring the iridescent silk garments that were dyed with mushrooms—colors strange but natural at the same time, like the colors inside a mussel shell. They were dyed by Dorothy Beebee, a honeybee of a woman with a soft gray Gibson girl bun who wore a hand-knitted shawl composed of the most lovely, delicate mushroom-dyed colors: all shades of the shady woods. When she turned around to burrow in a bin of silken fabrics for me, her shawl made her look like a very fine hen.

Dorothy is one of the country's leading experts on mushroom dyes. She learned her craft from Miriam Rice, who, since the late 1960s, has been experimenting with mushrooms for color and is generally considered the mother of mushroom dyeing . . . in the United States at least. In 1974, Miriam published the first book on the subject, *Let's Try Mushrooms for Color,* and Dorothy did the illustrations. Since then, mushroom dyeing has grown, if not mushroomed. In 1976, the Mendocino County Museum in Willits, California, put up an exhibit called *Natural Dyeing with Fungi,* the "first known exhibit of mushroom dyed fiber art in the world," and thereafter, every 2 to 3 years, an International Fungi

& Fibre Symposium is held somewhere. There is almost always a mushroom dyeing class or lecture at mushroom fairs and festivals.

Records of mushroom-based dyes are sparse, but dyeing with lichens has a long history. The most famous example is orchil purple, produced from a rock lichen. Orchil purple was used as an underdye for Tyrian purple, a color produced from the secretions of a snail, and then as mollusk supplies dwindled, orchil became the primary dye. Tyrian purple has been associated since Biblical times with power, wealth, and royalty. (It went out of fashion around the 8th century.)* But by the early 20th century, pretty much all commercial dyeing utilized synthetic dyes— probably a good thing, as harvesting lichen means killing the organism, in contrast to harvesting mushrooms, where the fruit of the fungus is removed but the fungus itself stays intact to fruit again another day.

Strictly speaking, lichens are not fungi. They are a composite of a fungus or multiple fungi and a photosynthetic partner, primarily a unicellular green alga or a photosynthetic bacterium. The fungus enslaves the photosynthetic cells by merging with the cell at numerous points or swallowing it whole, in effect retaining the photosynthesizer as a kind of in-house food producer of sugars. The algae part of lichen is only 5 to 10 percent of the whole—most of it is fungus. Lichen can live in the most extreme environments—bare rock, hot deserts, the Arctic, the seashore, even in space (for 16 days in a European unmanned spacecraft). They grow, said the mycologist Bryce Kendrick, "wherever the air is clean."

If there are no lichens growing in your city, it is probably because of air pollution. They grow incredibly slowly, only 1 to 4 millimeters per year radially. Some lichen colonies are said to be 4,500 years old, and new lichen species are constantly being discovered. One, *Caloplaca obamae* found on Santa Rosa Island in 2007 in California, is named after President Barack Obama. The fungal partner in lichen creates a vegetative structure

---

*"Tyrian purple" is still made by some manufacturers, from another species of snail, *Purpura lapillus*. The secretions of 10,000 snails make 1 gram of dye.

of hyphae in which the algae live. It makes sexual and asexual reproductive structures and accesses water and minerals to feed the whole. A fifth of all fungi are in lichens.* But lichens get short shrift at the fungus fairs because they're not mushrooms, although they traditionally get a seat at the table.

All colors in the spectrum can be achieved with mushroom dyes, although most that Miriam tested produced yellows, golds, oranges, rusts, and into burnt sienna and various shades of browns, but some, from the (occasionally lethal) *Cortinarius* mushrooms, produce vivid rose, burgundy, and violet hues. There are organic compounds in some mushrooms called chromophores—molecules that absorb certain wavelengths of visible light and, when properly treated, those colors can be retained by fabrics like cotton and silk.

Next to the gift shop were the purveyors of mushrooms. The standout collections belonged to Todd Spanier, a work-the-room kind of guy who imports truffles. Todd sold hedgehogs and matsutakes, chanterelles and trumpets . . . the whole room was inundated in an earthy, woodsy aroma, made all the more intense when Todd ceremoniously uncovered an Italian white truffle wrapped in a paper towel, which drew a crowd in an instant, as if tugged by their noses. But most people hung out in the ID room, which was the most sciencey and what all the parents wanted their children to see, where long tables decorated with fanciful displays of a vast number of mushrooms amid bits of moss and leaves were manned by men in moustaches and khaki shorts that had the earnest vibe of middle school science teachers. We have lots of mushrooms in the East, but the splendor of the California collections was truly dazzling. I'd never seen so many different mushrooms in one place before.

Fungi are incredibly diverse and have found an ecological niche just

---

*Scientists name lichen for the dominant fungal partner, not the symbiotic photosynthesizer.

about everywhere. For example, they live within a range of temperatures from below freezing to over 150 degrees Fahrenheit. They grow in the dark and in the light, on shoe polish and ink pads and in paint, on the Mir space station (indeed, 250 species of microorganisms, including fungi and bacteria, lived inside the spacecraft during the 20 years it was in operation), in the desert (like the desert truffle of the Middle East, which grows in sand), inside the cooling water systems of nuclear reactors, on your scalp (also known as dandruff), and underwater, in streams and rivers, lakes and oceans, and as symbionts of algae and marine plants. Fungi love to grow on cotton shirts but are less likely to grow on a silk blouse. Lots of fungi grow on manure. (As the mycologist Tom Volk wrote in the voice of *Pilobolus*, a dung decomposer: "You should be so grateful for what I can do. Without me, good friends, you'd be knee-deep in poo.") The corpse finder mushroom grows on dead animals, including humans. In his book *The National Audubon Society Field Guide to North American Mushrooms*, Gary Lincoff reported that its presence has helped forensic workers locate human remains. Fungi grow on the body of mites,* on or between the cells of plants—*all plants*—in frozen Arctic tundra, on rocks (which may be residual from the days when rock was the primary substrate for ancient fungal lineages), on other fungi, inside insects, and in your lungs (for example, coccidioidomycosis is a fungal infection that attacks the lungs, spleen, kidneys, and brain in immune-deficient patients or immunocompetent hosts that have inhaled a sufficient number of spores). There are about a dozen reports of mushrooms, mostly *Schizophyllum* but also a few *Coprinus*, fruiting in the sinuses or soft palate of small children. There are fungi growing on the Lascaux cave walls in the Dordogne region of southwestern France, threatening the magnificent prehistoric paintings. (And have been since the early 1960s. Lichen are the reason why the caves

*The mycologist Roland Thaxter spent his life studying fungi that live passively on insects and identified 1,500 species.

were closed to the public in the first place.) There are also fungi growing on the prehistoric rock paintings in Australia, but in the case of the "Bradshaw art," as it is known, colored fungi have replaced the original paint, creating, in essence, a living canvas.

Throughout the Lawrence Hall event I'd seen big mountain men lumbering about, navigating around the sandwich boards with educational displays on medicinal mushrooms and microscopy, all of whom seemed to have copious amounts of hair wherever they could grow it and sporting plaid shirts and hiking boots. They were like bears trapped in the tidy halls of the Hall of Science, pacing about and looking for beer. But in the ID room they congregated. They were the fellows who had done most of the picking for the tables, and after exhibiting a serious interest in what they had to say about collecting mushrooms and mushroom habitats and the notorious Ranger Woody, whose specialty is handcuffing pickers in California's Salt Point Park for picking off-limits, I managed to get invited to Michael Wood's house that night for dinner. I was thrilled to be asked along.

When I arrived, the house was awash with chanting monks (on the stereo), and various members of the San Francisco Mycological Society were sitting around a long dining table, Michael at the head, a huge steaming platter of oxtails with mushrooms and open bottles of California wines of all sorts in front of him. As I sat down feeling very meek and grateful to be included, Britt Bunyard—the editor of *Fungi* magazine, a mix of highbrow and lowbrow mushroom business, and kind of a mix of highbrow and lowbrow himself; he's supersmart but not beyond revealing he watches tacky TV sitcoms—turned to me and said, "Everything you hear at this table from now on is off the record." (The admonition wasn't really necessary: They mainly drank wine and ribbed each other.)

I made a point of attending Britt's lecture the next day, which was called "Incredible, Edible Fungi" but mostly consisted of weird anecdotes like the time some audience members ate hallucinogenic laughing jims before his talk on the *Amanita* genera and couldn't stop cracking up, and how many mushroom-related car accidents there are each year due to people looking out their car window for mushrooms and hitting electrical poles. I went to Ken Litchfield's lecture as well: "The Domestication and Training of Native Mushrooms for Wildlife Stewardship, Companionship, and Fun" (the lecture where he freaked out the audience by chewing on a piece of death cap). Ken reminds me of Jed Clampett: He's skinny and sinewy and uses lots of colorful metaphors in his conversation. He roused the audience to think like a mushroom, and pointed out we live in a cubical world, except for the bowls we eat in and the bowls we defecate in, and finally suggesting we were very much like mushrooms, though at times it sounded like he was referring to ex-girlfriends: "Some are parasitic, and want you to give them things, some are saprobes—even vegans eat dead things—and others are opportunists where their thing is a hybrid thing." But of course he was trying to get us to understand how different fungi live and what kind of relationships they have with their environment.

Fungi live in their food. Their nutrition is their habitat, and the way they get nutrition defines their role in any given ecosystem. After the San Francisco foray, I became increasingly dedicated to the study of mycology, but I was hitting some serious snags when it came to fungal lifestyles. It seemed like fungi would live one way until they lived another way instead, which I found very confusing. It was as if a cow suddenly became a predator like a lion. It was clear I needed help, and so I signed up for the largest conference in the country, the North American Mycological Association foray in Colorado.

I also had a secret motivation for going to the NAMA conference: I was really hoping to reconnect with the amateur and expert mycologists I'd met in California. Indeed, my fascination with mushrooms had become a fascination with mushroom people.

Chapter 3

MUTUALISTS,
DECOMPOSERS,
AND PARASITES

The North American Mycological Association (NAMA) foray, which is held in early August, is like the NEMF foray in that it is a serious scientific conference for amateurs with great speakers and bad food. Before NAMA was NAMA, it was the People-to-People Committee on Fungi, affiliated with the People-to-People Nature Committee, a mid-'50s organization that tried to enhance understanding and friendship through education and cultural exchange. There are 69 affiliated member clubs, three regional clubs, six Canadian clubs, and one Mexican club, the Myco Aficionados of Mexico. NAMA is composed of toxicology, cultivation, education, mycophagy, photography, and dyeing and papermaking committees, among others. It publishes a newsletter, *The Mycophile,* and a peer review journal called *McIlvainea,* as well as indexes of all sorts on the Web. They are busy.

I attended NAMA's 50th anniversary foray at the Snow Mountain Ranch/YMCA Camp near Winter Park, Colorado, the summer of 2010, a collection of ski dorm/ranch-style institutional buildings plunked in a high, wide, treeless valley in the Rocky Mountains. It was like the landscape was nude: just rock and sagebrush and time on display. The camp is surrounded by the kind of lumpy mountains skiers love, and behind them, intense red rock peaks. There was a sign in front of the most picturesque vista that announced the view was Exclusive Photographic Property and those wishing a photo should contact a given phone number. But the forests on the ski slopes were very brown, dead from pine bark beetle infestation, which didn't bode well for either photographers or mushroom hunters.

I arrived at my dorm in the early evening. It looked like a big chicken coop, with exits at the ends. It took a while for me to finally realize the room numbers started at the top of the building, so mine, which was high digit, was on the ground floor. Considering this was a church camp, I guess counting from the top and working your way down had a sort of logic. My roommates had already arrived, their bags laying claim to the two beds against either wall. Mine, a bunk bed, was between them. About 200 members attended the NAMA event that year, and I was rather excited because by then I was feeling a bit less the outsider. When I stopped by the vendors area on the way to the opening program at the lecture hall (the usual fungal-themed T-shirts, mushroom-decorated coffee mugs, dried edible mushrooms, mushroom identification books), I saw Britt Bunyard, editor of *Fungi* magazine, whom I'd met in San Francisco. Behind his stacks of magazines, Britt was surreptitiously pouring plastic cups of sherry. I took one gratefully.

The opening ceremony of NAMA consisted of an introduction by the hosting club—this year it was the Colorado Mycological Association—and the usual round of introductions and volunteer thank-yous and tips about recycling and getting lost in the woods and reminders not to collect mushrooms growing on mining tailings. There were a number of mycologists in the audience, and the khaki-clad, hand-lens-wielding, middle-aged to senior group I'd encountered before, psychiatrists and schoolteachers, Wall Street biggies and grocers, half of whom started to nod off as soon as the lights dimmed for the slideshow presented by an earnest forest service officer in a crisp beige uniform. He stood up to describe the forest habitat we were in: Fifty percent of the region's 100- to 200-year-old lodgepole pines were dead, and he recommended we not park our cars under any of them. He also recommended we keep an ax or saw in our vehicles to remove fallen trees across the road. "You guys are so INTO this!" he said suddenly, and a half-dozen people abruptly lifted their heads off their neighbor's shoulder to look around and see what had happened.

Most people went to bed right after the introduction was over, but I headed to Britt's room, where I'd heard some folks were partying it up among the bunk beds. Britt had appetizers and dips and crackers and a wide selection of booze lined up on the windowsill, and he poured drinks and offered "snacky snacks" to the various people who wandered in. It was like boarding school, except everybody had a PhD (except me). Britt is something of a naughty Garrison Keillor. Just beneath his midwestern farm charm and humility, he's as feisty and sharp as a Manhattan real estate broker. When I arrived, Michael Beug, a legendary professor of mycology from Evergreen College, was swishing and sniffing and sipping his own Cabernet Franc from a paper cup. Elinoar Shavit, a well-respected amateur mycologist, who is compact and tidy in her person, self-assured and feisty, and her husband, Eyal, were engaged in animated conversation, half in English, half in Hebrew. I met Larry Evans, a kind of troubadour mushroom picker and expert amateur mycologist, who was trying to corral the women into singing backup while he rumbled the lyrics to his song "Chanterelle" ("No," he corrected us, "you sing it like this" and in a high voice he trilled "ChannnnteRELLE!"); and Denis Benjamin, a brilliant, prickly medical doctor and expert on medicinal mushrooms who sat stiffly on the edge of a bed, brandy in hand, and told me that people are susceptible to the claims of medicinal mushrooms because of fear of death. Others were there, too, presidents of mycological clubs elsewhere in the country; Virgina, a lovely young master's student prone to writing chivalrous poetry about mushroom hunting; and myself, all in black, as per my homeland. Everyone was very friendly toward me and extremely rowdy with each other. I felt like the new kid at school who'd finally penetrated the in crowd, and I was so eager to show my gratitude that I invited the entire group to stop by my cabin in Colorado on their way to the Telluride Mushroom Festival.

When I got back to my room, my roommates were asleep, their backs turned away, allowing me the only privacy I had. I silently undressed in the dark and slipped into bed. When I woke up the next morning, it took me a moment to figure out where I was. I looked up at the underside of the bunk above me at the scrawled adolescent graffiti. "I am gay," it read. "My name is Wan."

The programs held at the NAMA conference were a lot more technical than those I'd attended elsewhere. For example, "Laccaria in the Rocky Mountain Alpine Zone: Field Notes and an Introduction to DNA-Based Taxonomy," "*Cortinarius* Identification Basics and Note Taking," and "Proper Use of Microscopes and How to Keep Yours Clean" were among the offerings. I sat in on Michael Kuo's talk on morels. He prefaced his comments by stating he was "just an English teacher," which suggested to me he'd been reproached by some cranky pro. I learned that morels are living fossils, like horseshoe crabs, and so opportunistic they can lifestyle in vastly different ways. At the same time, some species are evolving so quickly, at least in terms of their DNA, that it begs the question of what constitutes a morel at all. I attended Michael Beug's—the winemaker—roundtable on toxicology, which mostly consisted of up-to-date news on poisonings: Barium in Chinese mushrooms may cause sudden cardiac arrest; people mistaking the deadly *Amanita smithiana* with the delicious matsutake mushroom; the feasibility of an icky-sounding procedure called bile duct drainage after amatoxin poisoning to remove the toxin before it is recycled back through the body; and the deaths of young men who were killed by police but designated as *Amanita muscaria* poisonings, in particular, a poor fellow who ate the mushroom and then jumped naked on a police car, whereupon the cops fired. In the evening, Gary Lincoff told stories of 50 years of NAMA pranks, like the time someone hung a foul-smelling stinkhorn outside his window, the year the camp was infested with chiggers, and the year a guy woke up dead.

But it was Tom Volk's lecture that I had really come to NAMA for: "Fungi of the Forest: The Good, the Bad, and the Not So Attractive," a review of the different lifestyles of fungi.

Fungi are everywhere and they figure prominently in the healthy functioning of plants and forests and ecosystems, but they are also seriously destructive agents to property, crops, and human and animal health. When I started to understand how fungi live, I began to appreciate that every single life, be it an insect or a mushroom or a tree, lives in a web of interdependencies with other creatures, and as a result, each was way more complex and much more beautiful than I had ever imagined. And fungi play a key role in it all.

Fungi function as links in the food chain of nature, supplying nutrients from the soil to the plant (and via plants to animals), and removing nutrients from dead plants, other fungi, and animals, and returning them to the soil. (Bacteria and mechanical forces like weather have a role in this, too, of course.) Other fungi perform important duties in terms of evolution (duties that are also performed by bacteria): Some weed out weak plants, fungi, and animals; others provide an evolutionary advantage, functioning as a virtual immune system for the host plant.

These functional descriptions are ultimately nutritional descriptions. Since fungi live in their food, their food is their habitat. Mycologists have organized the types of relationships fungi have with their food three ways: mutualists, which are composed of mycorrhizal fungi (from the Greek, *myco* = fungus and *rhizal* = root) and endophytic fungi (from the Greek, *endo* = inside and *phyte* = plant) as well as lichens; saprophytes (from the Greek, *sapro* = rotten and *phyte* = plant); and parasites (in Greek, *parasitos* is a person who eats at someone else's table). Mycorrhizal fungi live in and on the roots of 90 percent of all plants, helping them access nutrients from the soil in exchange for photosynthesized sugars. Endophytic fungi live in between the cells of the stems and leaves of all plants, possibly providing immune services to the plant. Saprophytic fungi feed upon dead, dying, or decaying organic matter. They are the scavengers and recyclers of their ecosystems. Pathogenic fungi are parasites. They are predators of other organisms. Most are too tiny to see but can cause great damage to crops and forests and people. Commensal fungi are parasites as well. They use other organisms as a leg up, but they aren't pathogenic: They don't seem to do any harm (although some, when the host is somehow weakened, can become pathogenic and raid the host for food). An example of a commensal fungal/host relationship is the strange little Laboulbeniales. These tiny fungi look like miniscule pins. They parasitize and feed on the chitin of arachnids (like spiders and beetles) but are considered by mycologists to be benign. They are host specific and very specialized, the most cited example being a species that grow only on the left side of a beetle's shell, having adapted to patterns of beetle mating behavior.

But these lifestyle descriptions are not hard and fast: Some fungi, like morels, seem to swing as saprophytes (decayers) or mycorrhizae of some sort (where the fungus and its host have a mutually beneficial relationship). Other fungi may combine lifestyles, starting out as endophytes and then switching to a saprophytic mode once the host starts to fail or dies.

You can't define a fungus exclusively by its lifestyle: Rather, the fungus determines the lifestyle, and an attempt to lock these organisms into tidy categories is crazy-making. "These are categories that we made up," said Volk. "But in actuality, there is a continuum among the lifestyles."

There are a number of fungi that live in mutualist relationships in which a balance of interests occurs between two organisms. Lichen has a mutualist relationship with photosynthesizing algae and bacteria (although it is rather hard to see how a fungus enslaving an alga cell to produce food is actually mutualistic—the fungi/algae relationship seems to me more like the rancher/cow relationship—but maybe the fungus provides the alga with a safe place to live). And there are also commensal relationships, where the fungus may not be doing the host any good or any harm, either—the raison d'être of some yeasts in our body, for example, is unknown and may be commensal. But mycorrhizal fungi are the princes of mutualism. "Fungi can't make their own food," said Gary Lincoff. "So they made a strategic choice to team up with plants."

Ninety percent of natural land plants are thought to have mycorrhizal fungi partners. It's a masterpiece of evolution: Mycorrhizal fungi break down nutrients like phosphorus, carbon, water, and nitrogen into a readily assimilative form and deliver them to the plant in return for sugar produced by the plant via photosynthesis. The fungus needs sugar for energy and to launch its spores, and the tree needs nutrients because (despite what I learned in school) tree roots don't do the job adequately. Tree roots primarily anchor the tree in the soil. While tree roots will absorb moisture if watered and nutrients if fertilized, it is the mycorrhizal fungus *growing on and in the tree roots* that provides the tree with the lion's share of its nutrition and water. Mycorrhizal fungi significantly expand the reach of plant roots, and by extending the root system, increase the tree's nutrient and water uptake.

In the wild, mycorrhizal fungi are key to not just the health of single trees but to healthy forest ecosystems. A single fungal genotype or clone can colonize the roots and maintain the nutritional requirements of many trees at once. And multiple fungi can colonize the roots of all or most of the trees in a forest. The hyphae, those threadlike strings of cells that are the fungus, function as pathways for shuttling nutrients, water, and organic compounds around the forest. The mycologist Paul Stamets believes that mycorrhizal fungi function as a giant communications network between multiple trees in a forest—he calls it "nature's Internet." Others have described this linkage as the "architecture of the wood-wide web."

Weaker plants are able to tap into this network, too, like hitchhikers on a nutritional superhighway. Young seedlings struggling to grow in the shadow of established trees tap into the larger, older tree's fungal network to improve their nutritional uptake. This network exists to benefit not only established trees and seedlings of the same species but also trees from different species, and at different stages of development. So one multitasking fungus, its hyphae attached to the roots of multiple trees in the forest, can simultaneously provide a different nutritional load as needed to different trees. It's a couture service.

The old trees in a forest function as hubs for these mycelial networks. "Like spokes of a wheel," said Suzanne Simard, a professor of forestry at the University of British Columbia who studies mycorrhizae. Rhizomorphs (ropes of hyphae) connect the foundation tree with other trees—like an express stop on a subway system where lots of local trains come through—and the bigger the tree, the larger the hub. That's because the largest trees have the greatest root system, and the more roots there are, the more real estate there is for the fungus to colonize. "In one forest, we found 47 trees linked by two species of fungi composed of 12 individuals," said Simard. (By individuals, she means two genetically distinct fungal entities.) "Talk about two degrees

Indian pipes

of separation!" Even nonphotosynthesizing plants take advantage of "the hub." Parasites like the Indian pipe depend totally on mycorrhizal fungi for its nutritive needs. It taps into the nutrients and water provided by the mycorrhizae and connects via the mycorrhizae to a photosynthesizing plant for sugar.

Despite the fact that fungi are microscopic organisms, the functions they perform are often on an ecosystem or landscape scale.* If you could take an x-ray look at the soil, you'd see that underneath the forest duff there is a layer of mycorrhizal mycelium running between, on, and in the roots of plants. It's like a stratum of life between the duff and the soil that holds water and nutrients in the ground. And when that stratum is disrupted, or not present, plants suffer. In fact, ecosystems with inadequate mycorrhizal fungi can experience catastrophic losses of plant biomass.

The rich diversity of plant life in the Amazon rain forest has nutritionally poor soil but survives in cooperation with a dense mat of mycorrhizal fungi. Decomposers like saprophytic fungi and bacteria recycle leaf litter so quickly there is little opportunity for soil to build up. Amazonian plant root systems need mycorrhizal fungi to help them absorb nutrients because they cannot process nutrients quickly enough on their own before rains wash them away. Logging and farming destroy this

*Because of this symbiotic relationship, it is very difficult to cultivate mushrooms that are produced by mycorrhizal fungi because you have to create an ecosystem: You have to grow the fungi on the roots of living plants. That's not an easy thing to do—and it's too bad, because some of the most delicious mushrooms are mycorrhizal: porcini, chanterelles, and truffles. Some species of truffles, however, have been cultivated in orchards.

crucial mycorrhizal mat. Recent evidence suggests that the Amazon basin may have been home to complex prehistoric societies, but the question remains: How were such large numbers of people fed?

The native people of the Amazon may have created orchards in the forest by clearing small plots and planting selected tree crops. Amazonian forests are characterized by widely dispersed species—two peach palms, for example, might be quite far away from each other. It is possible pre-Columbian farmers moved seedlings near an established tree so the young trees would be able to access the elder tree's established mycorrhizal hub, just as early truffle orchardists planted new tree seedlings next to truffle-producing trees to encourage the mycorrhizal fungi to spread to the new tree roots. The native people of the Amazon may have known better than to destroy an organism that sustained part of their food supply, and they may have even utilized it to increase the forest's edible yield.

When farmers till the soil, they break apart and kill mycelial mats belowground. Tilling breaks the old crop stubble into finer bits and compacts the soil, leading to erosion: It's the primary cause of agricultural land degradation. In the no-till scenario, the intact mycelium retains moisture and soil particles in its architecture and sequesters carbon contained in fertile soils. Additionally, crop roots colonized by mycorrhizal fungi are significantly longer and more robust. The benefit of utilizing natural mycorrhizae in crop management is significant enough to have the USDA recommend no-till agriculture over conventional plow tillage systems.

Despite their pervasiveness and adaptability, mycorrhizal fungi are sensitive to air pollution, acidization of the soil (through acid rain), and fertilizers. The fertilizer problem is particularly significant because when trees are exposed to nitrogen fertilizers, they no longer need mycorrhizal fungi to deliver nitrogen and other nutrients. The excess nitrogen also stifles fungal growth. It's a case of negative reinforcement: Fertilizers take the place of fungi in the tree's life. But then, when environmental conditions degrade, like during a drought, the fertilizers can't help the tree and the tree fails to thrive. Mycorrhizal fungi, in contrast, can survive drought conditions and will continue to distribute water or whatever the tree needs.

More and more agriculturists, particularly those in the business of planting trees and reforestation, are using mycorrhizal fungi as a pre-planting strategy. The process is simple and quite inexpensive: Seedlings are dunked in a slurry of mycorrhizal spores and water prior to planting. The slurry is called an inoculant. Currently, only a few mycorrhizal fungi mixes are produced commercially, but awareness of their effectiveness is growing. The USDA's Natural Resources Conservation Service recommends mycorrhizal inoculants on tree plantings, and some cities have gotten into the action. New York, for example, has tree-planting standards that describe the required mycorrhizal inoculant of both endomycorrhizal fungi, which live in the roots of trees, and ectomycorrhizal fungi, which sheath the roots of trees. Plants with mycorrhizal partners don't need as much fertilizer; withstand various pollutants better; are more resistant to disease; withstand drier, saltier, and more acidic or alkaline soils better; and survive transplantation more successfully. The lack of a fungal partner is one of the reasons that your nursery plants don't always do well. Without mycorrhizal fungi, a tree may persist for a while, but eventually it will die of malnutrition.

The other important mutualists are endophytic fungi, the microscopic fungi that live inside plants, *all* plants, including marine plants. Mycologists believe every wild plant has an endophytic fungus partner, if not many fungal partners. "You can put any leaf on a mushroom foray

ID table," said Tom Volk, "and we'd have to identify it, though it might take several months." That's because these fungi grow between the cells of the plant's leaves, stems, and roots. They don't produce macroscopic mushrooms—mushrooms you can see with the naked eye—but they are ubiquitous. What they are doing inside plants is mostly a mystery, mainly because the research is in its infancy.

"Maybe some are just in there incidentally," speculates George Carroll, an expert in endophytes. "Are they doing something? It's very hard to tell." James White of Rutgers University, who studies endophytes, suggests many in the field are of the opinion that endophytic fungi perform a defensive function for themselves that is at the same time a protective function for the plants. It's as if these tiny fungi have evolved to take over the duties of an immune system for the plant. And so far, they have been shown to protect plants (and, from the fungus's perspective, their home and food source) in two ways: Some endophytes shield plants from disease arising from environmental degradation like drought, and others help protect plants from predators through a kind of biochemical warfare.

According to research prepared by the mycologist Russell Rodriguez, endophytic fungi in plants help them become more heat tolerant, salt tolerant, and drought tolerant. The mechanism of how "symbiotically conferred tolerance" works is not yet known, but Rodriguez speculates that someday farmers could dust seedlings with the spore of selected endophytic fungi, and as the symbiosis between plant and fungi develops, so too will the environmental tolerance, allowing the plant a better chance of survival during difficult conditions. But the spore must be harvested from plants that already endure stressed conditions. So in order to confer heat tolerance to a wheat crop, for example, the fungi must be collected from wheat grown in superdry conditions. The same fungal strain, if gathered from a stress-free environment, will not confer tolerance.

Nursery seedlings are unlikely to come with their endophytic partners and the protections they provide. Likewise, the sterilization of seedlings to kill pathogens kills the endophytes, too. Preliminary research by James White suggests this may be happening with the agave plant in Mexico. Without their endophytes, the plants are less hardy and productive, which could in turn affect tequila prices. Wild endophytic fungal spores—and Rodriguez suspects that almost all endophytes can be grown in culture—can be literally sprinkled onto many different kinds of seeds, although spore and seed must be properly matched. "And we haven't found the limit to the host range," said Rodriguez, referring to these prospective matches. "The range is ancient and it's broad."*

The potential benefits of transferring endophytic fungi from wild to cultivated plants are myriad. "We could confer functionality to crop plants that couldn't be achieved any other way," said Rodriguez, "providing functions like metabolic efficiency, stress tolerance, and increased yield." Crops and reforestation projects planted with their endophytic partners "could sustain communities and support conservation biology."

Rodriguez's research suggests that without endophytes, there may be no hope for a plant in a high-stress location. "When a plant is under stress, it produces biochemicals that don't seem to help the plant. When the endophyte is there, the plant under stress doesn't produce those biochemicals," said Rodriguez. "We think the fungus is preventing the plant from initiating a stress response and as a result the plant is better able to deal with stress." It's as if the plant suffers a panic attack that the endophyte can suppress, like a tranquilizer on a hysterical person.

For the past 10 years, biologists have been trying to genetically modify food crops for stress tolerance. "But they don't perform well," said

*Another Rodriguez study, on tropical panic grass, showed that the grass better tolerates heat when inoculated with a particular fungus that in turn is the carrier of a particular virus! Turns out both endophytes—the fungus and the virus—must be present for the plant to become heat tolerant.

Rodriguez. Genetically modified strains are expensive to produce. They are proprietary, they reduce genetic diversity, and they have created a public backlash. "Endophytic fungi do the same thing [as GMOs]," said Rodriguez, "but faster and with more diverse applications." And without the baggage.

The other way endophytic fungi are known to protect their plant hosts is by repelling predators and disease. In the 1970s, George Carroll concluded that toxins produced by endophytic fungi killed insect larva on Douglas fir trees. In exchange for this service, the fungus receives nutrients from the tree (sugar from photosynthesis, and other nutrients that the tree got from its mycorrhizal partners). Indeed, he suggested that a range of endophytic fungi may be present in an individual host, providing a virtual pharmacy of toxins derived from fungal enzymes that deter or reduce a variety of insect pests.

Endophytic fungi with this pharmacological arsenal have been found in a wide range of plants, protecting against pests of all sorts. In one surprising study ("some years before endophytes were hot stuff," said Carroll) that asked why the fungal blight Dutch elm disease was not affecting trees in northern England as intensely as expected, scientists discovered that those trees hosted an endophytic fungus that produced toxins that inhibited not the spread of the fungal blight, but the fungal blight's vector, the beetle. Likewise, there are many fungal endophytes of grasses that are responsible for producing alkaloids that are toxic to grazing animals, like fescue grass, which is drought and pest resistant. But it gives the cows that eat it gangrene and leads to serious reproductive issues in horses. All this is horrid for animals and ranchers, but it is good news for the plant, as the fungus protects it from predators (both grazing animals and insects) and uses very little of the plant's resources to survive.*

---

*Fescue grass is obviously not a good food source for animals. However, for areas where grass is desired for nongrazing purposes, like golf courses, it is great because it needs few pesticides.

Endophytes may live in a mutually beneficial relationship with a plant, or they may be hitching a ride on a plant to get somewhere else, or they may just be temporarily endophytic, a contingent sort of thing that's simply opportunistic, a kind of farming of plants by forcing them to grow in a way beneficial to the endophyte. For example, James White and Patricia Alvarez at Rutgers University have studied an endophytic fungus living in a common tropical palm tree. If the seeds of the palm fall in the shade of other plants, the fungus remains a helpful symbiont and protects the seedling from insect pests. But if the seeds fall in the sunlight, the fungus becomes a pathogen and kills the palm seedling. This endophyte dramatically alters the ecology of the palm, forcing it to live as a forest understory plant. When it comes to endophytes, "there are a whole bunch of individual stories," said George Carroll. "And a lot of work to do."

Mutualistic relationships exist between a few species of fungi and various insects as well. A number of insects farm fungi for food. For example, leafcutter ants, which live in the tropical and subtropical Americas, forage for certain kinds of green leaves, which they cut up into bits, smear with digestive enzymes to speed up composting, and bring home to their nest. There, they add the leaves and their own feces to a compost garden upon which fungi grow. (And there is a third symbiont. The ants also spread an antibiotic secreted by a bacterium that lives upon them. The antibiotic controls fungal pathogens and weeds out competing fungi for space in the nest.) The fungi provide all the nutrition the ants need.* A species of termite gathers woody material that they masticate and then regurgitate back at the nest. Mycologists assume this woody material is

---

*The queen brings a bit of the fungus from her birth nest, which the mycologist Harold Brodie called "her dowry," and sets up a small compost operation to feed the fungus while she establishes her colony.

Termite mushroom (*Podaxis beringamensis*) growing from a termite mound

inoculated with the fungal spores of *Termitomyces*, or the termite mushroom. Nest workers create fungus combs with the regurgitated woody material. The comb is a kind of incubator for the mycelium, which quickly spreads, digesting the cellulose and lignin into a simpler form, and the termites consume this enriched mycelium.

In both cases, and others where insects cultivate fungi, the question remains: What's in it for the fungus? Some scientists have suggested that these fungi, protected in the insects' nests and carefully gardened, are relatively free of competitors and so they have evolved to be helpful to the insects. What's indisputable is these organisms have an ancient, unique, and complicated alliance—they are, in essence, mini ecosystems.

Saprophytes are the recyclers of nature. "The law of microbial infallibility," said Tom Volk, "says if a substrate exists in nature, there is a microbe that can degrade it." And some of the busiest microbes are saprophytic fungi. Saprophytic fungi—and this includes molds and yeasts—decompose organic matter, *all* organic matter, animal or vegetable, even organic matter that you didn't know was there. If you've ever seen mold in improbable places, like growing on a CD, it's because the fungus is finding something to eat. Some species of yeasts are part of your skin flora: They are breaking down and consuming oils produced by your skin. Other yeasts break down the sugars in fruit juice, producing alcohol. Some saps degrade rock: They produce and release oxalic acid, known to aid in weathering of minerals (and, in the process, increase the nutrient load of the soil).

It's even suspected that a saprophytic mold can break down radioactive particles and convert them into chemical energy that the fungi can metabolize. There's an extensive fungal growth thriving on the inside walls of the Ukraine's Chernobyl nuclear power plant's damaged, radioactive unit No. 4. The fungus has been exposed to annual radiation doses more than 10 times greater than what causes severe radiation sickness in humans. In 1999, a number of species were collected robotically—the unit is entombed in a sarcophagus of cement—and studied. Most of the fungi were found to contain melanin, the same pigment that we have in our skin. Melanin is typically found in fungi living in extreme environments, where it serves a similar purpose to ours: protecting against UV and solar radiation.*

"Melanin is an energy transducer," said Ekaterina Dadachova, an associate professor of nuclear medicine and microbiology and immunology at Albert Einstein College of Medicine of Yeshiva University. (Dadachova is right out of a Bond film: good looking, with blond hair, a heavy Russian accent, and a formidable mastery of nuclear chemistry.) She explained that just as the chlorophyll in plants converts sunshine into chemical energy to feed the plant, some fungi may convert subatomic particles into chemical energy to feed the fungus.

We already know for certain that saprophytic fungi can degrade toxic chemicals that are carbon based, like petrochemicals, dioxins, pesticides like DDT, dimethyl sulfide, and chemical warfare agents like sarin gas and VX. Fertilizers, munitions, and textile dyes are all susceptible to enzymes secreted by saprophytic fungi. The fungi break down

---

*There is paleobiological evidence that suggests ancient fungi may have used melanin to survive the Earth's geomagnetic reversal during the Cretaceous period. Many plants and animals died when Earth experienced a decline in magnetic field strength and an increase in solar radiation. But not melanized fungi.

these substances into their organic molecular parts (which is what has to happen for the fungi to feed on them), absorbing what they need for energy and liberating the rest back into the nutrient cycle. The way we make chemical weapons and plastics is by combining molecules that are not naturally combined in nature. Saprophytic fungi disassemble those molecules. Saprophytic fungi are opportunistic, said Tom Volk. "They have this battery of enzymes, and if they encounter something they can degrade, they'll do it."

White button mushrooms are saprophytes. So are cremini, portobello, oyster, maitake, royal trumpets, shiitake, enoki, and medicinal mushrooms like reishi—pretty much all cultivated mushrooms, because they are relatively easy to grow as long as they have their preferred organic matter to feed on. The yeasts and molds used in making beer, wine, cheese, and bread are all saprophytes. You could say that saprophytic fungi have been key to the civilizing process, if you consider good wine an indicator of civilization.

Yeasts are pretty remarkable: They can tolerate cold and heat, aerobic and anaerobic conditions. They can lay dormant for months, like the Fleischmann's commercial dried yeast you buy in the grocery store, yet have one of the fastest vegetative, asexual cellular division rates of any fungus (about 45 minutes). There are about 100 genera (with 700 species) of yeasts. But only one genus, *Saccharomyces*, is needed to produce bread, wine, and beer.

The yeast *Saccharomyces cerevisiae* degrades carbohydrates (simple and complex sugars and starches) in bread dough, grape juice, and malted barley and, in the process, converts the carbs into alcohol and carbon dioxide. In the case of bread, the yeast digests the sugar in the flour and produces gas as a result. The gas—carbon dioxide—becomes trapped in the dough, causing it to leaven. The digested sugar is converted to alcohol, which evaporates during baking. In pre-1866 winemaking, wild yeasts— preferably *S. cerevisiae,* as some wild yeasts make wine taste nasty—on the skin of the grapes were crushed with the grapes. The yeasts on the crushed grapes were then allowed to ferment the sugar in the grape juice. Post-1866 winemaking has seen the innovation of suppressing wild yeasts with sulfur dioxide in favor of the introduction of pure yeast cultures (yeasts that have been selected and grown in sterile conditions in a lab), which has allowed winemakers to improve their product by matching the yeast culture to the juice. (Although a California winemaker who surveyed her wine for yeasts after fermentation was complete found 25 species of yeasts in the wine beyond that which was put in.) Yeast is added to ferment the sugar in beer malt (*S. cerevisiae* for ale and *S. carlsbergenis* for lager—that's *Carlsberg* Latinized). Other foods and beverages that use saprophytic fungi for fermentation are whiskeys: bourbon (fermented corn), rye (fermented rye), and scotch (fermented barley). Rice wine and soy sauce (and other soybean-based fermented products), tempeh, miso, and marmite all utilize a variety of yeasts or molds.

There are two types of cheeses that benefit from saprophytic mold. Blue cheeses like Gorgonzola and Roquefort utilize *Penicillium roqueforti*. The curd is inoculated with the mold, which then grows throughout the cheese, adding flavor and fragrance. Camembert and brie-type cheeses are ripened with *P. camemberti*. The mold creates the thick white rind and digests the milk proteins—that's what creates the silky mouthfeel.

But above all, saprophytic fungi degrade the plant fibers cellulose and lignin, and in the process enrich soils. Indeed, fungi are the digestive organs of forests.* In the wild, it is the wood-decaying fungus's job to break down cellulose and lignin. Cellulose is the primary structural component of the cell walls of green plants, comprising almost half of the dry wood weight, followed by lignin, which adds structural stability to the cell

---

*Wood decayers specialize in many ways. When you see a tree that has fallen over in the forest, either snapped at the base or turned over and exposing the roots—barring a hurricane or tornado-type disaster—that is wood-decaying fungi at work. Fungi that consume heartwood (the old wood at the center of a tree) will cause a tree to snap because the structural interior of the tree has been undermined. Fungi that consume roots will cause a tree to fall over, exposing its rootball, because the roots are no longer strong enough to support the tree.

walls, mostly in woody perennials like trees. Lignin sequesters carbon and is very slow to decompose. Some wood-decaying fungi degrade lignin first, and then later will go after the cellulose and other parts of the wood cell, while others degrade just cellulose and don't even go for the lignin.

Saprophytic fungi can cause all kinds of damage, but if it weren't for the wood decayers and their ability to break down organic debris, we would be buried under miles of dead plants. The fact that during the Carboniferous period massive amounts of dead plants did accrue (and turned into the fossil fuels) suggests there may have been a lack of lignin-eating fungi at that time. "We speculate that fungi that degrade cellulose evolved first because cellulose is a simpler compound to degrade," said Tom Volk. "A period—a *long* period—passed before fungi evolved to degrade lignin, too, and all the while plants were protecting their cellulose with lignin. So, during the time after the introduction of fungi that decay cellulose, but before the introduction of fungi that can decay cellulose and lignin, only parts of plants rotted. The parts that did not rot became compressed into fuels. That's not going to happen again."

The dark side of all this wood eating is the destruction of wood products that we would rather fungi stay away from. Dry rot, which probably got its name for the crumbly texture of wood in an advanced state of decomposition, was a huge nuisance for the navy prior to the development of ironclad ships in the late 19th century. "But don't blame the fungi," said Volk. "They don't know it's not a tree." There are regular reports in regional newspapers about oyster mushrooms fruiting along the baseboard of homes, dock pilings decomposing, library books

Oyster mushrooms fruiting along the baseboard of a home

turning moldy. If you kept them around long enough, your dollars would decay (they are covered in mold spore). You've likely seen the paper sheath of Sheetrock walls stained with blotches of mold. Anything made from wood and exposed to water is an all-you-can-eat buffet for saprophytic fungi.

Two notable molds famous for the trouble they cause to property and food products while in storage are *Stachybotrys* and *Aspergillus*. *Stachybotrys*, known as "black mold," is the mold you see in pictures of postflood homes where big black blooms of the stuff cover interior walls like ominous polka dots. It can produce trichothecenes, a family of mycotoxins that can be harmful to humans and animals. *Aspergillus* is a genus composed of several hundred mold species, at least one of which produces the carcinogenic toxin, aflatoxin.

Except in rare cases, such as a farmer handling large amounts of contaminated grain in a closed environment like a silo, molds need to be either weaponized or swallowed (or inhaled in some cases) to cause serious health effects in animals or people. Molds do not produce these toxins to harm animals. Instead, mycologists think these toxins are produced to battle rival microbes, like other fungi, bacteria, and soil protozoa, for food. Animals and people just sometimes get in the way.

The third category of fungi are parasites. Parasites depend on living hosts for their survival, and a parasite that is consistently related to disease is called a pathogen. Pathogenic fungi affect humans in many ways. They are a scourge on human health, crops, and trees; they cause billions of dollars in damage worldwide—85 percent of all plant diseases are caused by fungi—and are responsible for countless famines recorded from Biblical times through today. Like an infectious agent, pathogenic fungi often kill their living hosts—animals, plants, and other fungi—or inhibit their ability to reproduce. Most are microfungi that, like other predators, do the job of natural selection, singling out the weakest organisms for destruction. The lobster mushroom (*Hypomyces lactifluorum*) is an example of fungus-to-fungus pathogenicity. An edible fungus parasitizes another fungus, usually either an edible *Russula* or an (otherwise) inedible *Lactarius*, deforming the host's cap, stem, and gills, and turning the fungus a bright orange. The lobster mushroom is delicious, but it can't reproduce.

Evidence of pathogenic fungi was everywhere at the NAMA foray in Colorado. The forests around Winter Park, once dark green and glorious, are now dead, devastated by a lethal infestation of fungi and its insect vector. It did not look mushroomy at all. But people were hunting mushrooms nonetheless.

I was, too. I took off with Larry Evans, who was selling his wild mushrooms in the vendors area, up into the crispy mountains. Larry is well known on the mushroom scene. He is tall and lanky and wears his hair in gray braids. When I met him, he was eating a raw porcini mushroom like an apple. He told me he eats mushrooms every day, often raw, so I imagine his digestive system is a bit like a bobsled track. When I got into his red Subaru, I noticed he'd decorated it with white refrigerator magnets so that it looked like an *Amanita muscaria*, and as Larry sped along, his exhaust pipe scraping the rutted dirt roads, the magnets kept flying off the hood and whizzing by my passenger window. Up, up, up we went, 10,000 feet high to look for hunting grounds with healthy trees. Larry pulled over at a spot that was so steep I had to go up on my knees and down on my bottom. But he was unfazed, and sang as he climbed from his CD, *Fungal Boogieman,* which features songs like "Breakfast of Champignons" and "Everything's Got a Fungus." Unfortunately, even at this altitude, the forests were dead: a dry reddish brown that seemed just

Old growth chestnut, Great Smoky Mountains, NC (ca. 1910)

a pack of matches away from an inferno.

Most of the plant pathogens we see every day are those that attack trees. Here in the United States we've lost, and continue to lose, vast forests to fungal pathogens. Mountain pine bark beetles in cahoots with fungi killed the forests surrounding the Snow Mountain Ranch, and so far around 3 million acres of Colorado pine forests have been affected. The mountain pine bark beetle is spreading the blue stain fungus, *Grosmannia clavigera*, among pine trees—mainly ponderosa and lodgepole. The fungus interrupts the tree's ability to conduct water and stains the wood blue. Some people choose this wood for furniture, calling it "blue pine." The American chestnut used to be known as the Redwood of the East, with trees reaching a circumference of up to 10 feet and a height of 120 feet—higher than a 12-story building. Chestnut trees ranged over 200 million acres of eastern woodlands from Maine to Florida until the chestnut blight *Cryphonectria parasitica* wiped out 3 billion trees in the first 50 years of the 1900s by rotting the cambium, the critical layer of living cells just under the bark that generates new wood. The fungus was spread by woodpeckers. Dutch elm disease, caused by a few species of fungi from the *Ophiostoma* genus, has had a similar devastating effect on the American elm tree (as well as the European elm). So far, 100 million trees have died in the Northern Hemisphere since the epidemic began around 1918. It arrived in the United States via infected elm burl logs that were imported for furniture manufacture. The fungus, transported by various species of bark beetles, attacks the tree's vascular system and renders it incapable of conducting water.

Those are the big die-offs. But in any given year, newspapers will publish stories about local threats to native species—dogwoods, oaks, beech trees, white pines—where trees stressed by drought or other environmental factors become vulnerable to fungi and their insect vectors.

Pathogenic fungi of crop plants are a major cause of famine worldwide and the single most important cause of plant disease. There are pathogenic fungi that grow hyphae, like the *Fusarium* genera. Species in this group are responsible for scab, a particularly devastating disease of wheat and barley, and the "H.I.V. of banana plantations" according to an Australian newspaper.* *Fusarium* also attacks chile seeds. In fact, the chile pepper produces its delicious heat as a strategy to repel the fungus.

Then there are the many smuts and rusts and molds that cause tremendous damage to a wide variety of crops, from grains to grapes, chocolate to corn, rubber (the nonsynthetic kind used to make, among other things, condoms) to rice, and they have been wreaking havoc as long as humans have farmed. The Federal Plant Quarantine Act of 1912, which has been amended many times, most recently in 1994, seeks to control the importation of plant pathogens. Unfortunately, it's hard to manage a microfungus.

Smuts—and there are about 1,200 described species—tend to replace the fruits in a plant, interfering with its ability to reproduce, causing the

*In 2010, Taliban insurgents and angry Afghan farmers accused the United States of dusting their poppy crops with *F. oxysporum*, affecting up to 50 percent of their opium crop. A program (funded by the USA) within the United Nations Office on Drugs and Crime did seek to develop *F. oxysporum* to battle pot and poppy fields, but the project was terminated in 2002 without ever being used, the result of warnings from scientists that the fungus could mutate into hardier strains that could attack nontargeted crops. The poppy crop failure was likely the result of a natural fungal blight, possibly *Macrosporium papaverus*, a type of root rot.

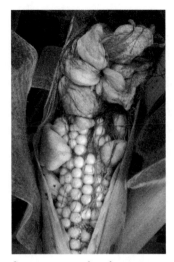

Corn smut causes fungal tumors on the ears of corn that taste delicious.

plant to grow galls or tumors, and costing millions of dollars a year in damage, mainly to cereal crops. But one man's tumors are sometimes another man's treasure. The corn smut *Ustilago maydis*, which causes fungal tumors on the ears of corn, is known in Mexico as *huitlacoche* or *cuitlacoche,* maize mushrooms, or Mexican truffle. The immature galls have been considered a delicacy since pre-Columbian times. It tastes delightful, of both mushrooms and corn, and is rather exotic, like a vegetarian foie gras. Four hundred to 500 tons of huitlacoche are sold annually in Mexico, and a few US farmers have gotten into the business as well, but while the fungus can be more profitable than the corn it grows on, marketing a product called smut has its challenges.

Rusts are so called because a leaf sprinkled with their reddish spores or small brown pustules looks like rust. They are pathogens of foliage, killing leaves and debilitating the plant. There are about 5,000 species of rusts and, like smuts, they can have a devastating economic impact. Rusts have plagued crops since the dawn of agriculture. The Romans conducted an agricultural festival on April 25, the Robigalia, where red-haired dogs were sacrificed in order to appease the personification of rust disease, Robigus. Of the many famines caused by rust, the most well known may be the Egyptian famine described in Genesis in the Old Testament (the one Joseph alleviated on behalf of the Pharaoh). Currently, a rust named Ug99—for where (Uganda) and when (1999) it was first identified—has already jumped the Red Sea and entered the wheat fields of Iran. It now seems poised to enter India. The worst rust outbreaks have been controlled for many decades through the development of rust-resistant wheat seed,* but 90 percent of the world's wheat has little or no resistance to this strain. Researchers are currently racing to develop a Ug99-resistant wheat ahead of the pathogen's migration.

Molds cause enormous crop losses as well. While some species of the *Aspergillus* genera are saprophytic in lifestyle—they feed on cereals that have already been harvested—others infect living cereals, spices, nuts, and cotton and can also produce dangerous mycotoxins, contaminating foods that can cause poisoning in the people and animals that consume them. For this reason, the USDA monitors peanuts and field corn for "unacceptable levels" of aflatoxin.

One of the most famous crop pathogens is *Phytophthora infestans,* which decimated Irish potato crops over a 5-year period in the 1840s. The potato was the staple food for one-third of the population; when the crops failed, approximately 1 million people either starved to death in the countryside or moved to cities in search of food, where they died of epidemics like typhoid, cholera, and dysentery. Another million emigrated to England, Australia, and the United States. Potato blight, which turns the tubers into stinky black slime, was long thought to be a mold. In the past 30 years, *P. infestans* has been reclassified a few times, and though it is still studied by mycologists, currently *P. infestans* is a member of a weird kingdom called Stramenopila, which some consider the sixth kingdom, home of organisms like giant kelps.

Farmers don't despise all molds, though: The noble rot, *Botrytis cinerea,* is a pathogenic mold that attacks fruit and consumes their water.

---

*The agronomist Norman Borlaug developed this rust-resistant cultivar and others. His high-yielding crop strains fed millions in Mexico, India, and Pakistan—known as the Green Revolution—and won him the Nobel Prize in 1970. The Green Revolution has come under recent criticism, however, as it has led to monocropping and related abuses by fertilizer, pesticide, and farm equipment corporations as well as the decline of family farms producing genetically diverse crops. Borlaug blamed the excesses of monoagriculture on the demands of the exploding world population.

It is bad news for strawberries, but if it infects the wine grape during wet conditions and if the weather then dries up, the resultant raisiny grapes produce some of the best wines in the world, including the Hungarian Tokaji Aszú, French Sauternes, German Eiswein, and Italian Amarone.

Many fungi are parasites of animals, keeping populations in check and ecosystems in balance. All kinds of animals, from nematodes ($\frac{1}{32}$-inch-long soil-dwelling eelworms) to humans, dogs and cats to oysters and sponges, fall prey to pathogenic fungi. Some fungi, given the right conditions, even threaten their host species with extinction. *Fusarium solani* is suspected of playing a key role in the decline of the loggerhead sea turtle. A virus and a member of the microspordia, a fungal parasite of animals, working together, may be behind the colony collapse disorder currently decimating the honeybee population. A chytrid fungus (belonging to a primitive division of the kingdom fungi) poses one of the biggest threats facing the amphibian species today, having hitched a ride on certain species of African frogs that were exported for use in pregnancy tests. The disease caused by the fungus, chytridiomycosis, is responsible for the decline or extinction of up to 200 species of frogs worldwide, and, according to the biologist Lee Francis Skerratt, "the

Bats infected with white-nose syndrome

most spectacular loss of vertebrate biodiversity due to disease in recorded history."

The bat story is similar. Bats across the eastern United States are dying due to a new fungus infection called white-nose syndrome (WNS). It has spread into at least a dozen

Cordyceps sinensis, a parasite of the larva of the ghost moth

states east of the Mississippi and killed more than a million bats to date. Researchers have estimated that North America's most common bat will be virtually extinct by 2026. The fungus, which is cold tolerant, grows on the bats' muzzles, wing membranes, and ears while they are hibernating, causing the bats to waste away, then wake up early from hibernation to forage in weather that is too cold for them.

Manipulating host behavior is definitely a survival adaptation for some parasitic fungi. For example, one species of *Cordyceps* attacks bullet ants. Hyphae infiltrate their bodies and their brains. The fungus infection induces a kind of mind control, because the ant is compelled to climb high into the foliage and then grip a stem with its mandibles, where it dies. If a member of the ant colony finds an ant infected with *Cordyceps,* it is removed far away from the colony. But if not, a fruiting body (it's not exactly a mushroom) erupts from the ant's head, growing like a slender worm as long as the ant itself, its tip packed with spores, which it sprinkles on the ants below.

The name *Cordyceps* refers to the morphology of the mushroom (from the Latin, *cord* = club and *ceps* = head), and they can look like miniature rubbery billy clubs. There are about 400 described species, most of which are exclusive to one or just a few hosts. The most famous is *Cordyceps sinensis* (from the Latin, *sinensis* = of China), a parasite of the caterpillar of the ghost moth. The infected caterpillar hibernates underground during the winter, and in early summer the fungus compels the caterpillar to crawl close to the soil surface. The fungus absorbs all of the worm's nutrients, replacing the insides of the caterpillar with mycelium, and a club-shaped fruiting body grows out of the insect's head and pushes up through the soil. The mycelium-riddled caterpillar carcass and the mushroom that erupts from its head have an ancient reputation as a cure for a number of ailments in traditional Tibetan and Chinese medicine.

Daniel Winkler is probably the leading expert when it comes to the ethnomycology and economy of the *C. sinensis* harvest in Tibet. Winkler is a long-haired, excitable German who first came to the USA to follow the Grateful Dead but who now makes a living being an expert on this particular fungus—no small task. According to Winkler's research, the appearance of *C. sinensis*, also known as the caterpillar fungus, sets off a regional harvesting rush that occupies up to 60 percent of the population in some counties of Tibet. In one county, Winkler found that a harvester's typical yield, about 10 specimens a day, is the cash equivalent of a week's wage in the region. (The sustainability of Tibet's high-pressure caterpillar fungus harvest is unknown, but the harvest has been going on for centuries.) Winkler has reported that Tibetans collected 50,000 kilos of caterpillar mushrooms in 2004, worth about $133 million. This sum is equal to 40 percent of the rural cash income nationwide, and 70 to 90 percent of incomes in production areas. Incredibly, this tiny parasitic fungus is the primary commodity of Tibet. The country is, as Winkler says, "a globally unique, fungally dominated rural economy."

In 2008, the fungus—always attached to the worm—was selling for $6,000 to $13,000 a pound in Mainland China, Hong Kong, and San Francisco, depending on the quality. The most valuable specimens are those with large caterpillars and young, presporulated mushrooms, as the healing power of the fungus is believed to be greatest in the mycelium-filled worm. The primary market for the caterpillar fungus are the Chinese, and when I suggested to Winkler only half-jokingly that the Chinese may have had the fungus in mind when they occupied Tibet, he just gave me a significant look.

Everything changed after I learned about fungal lifestyles and how key they are to the functions of nature. Now, when I look at anything—the walls of my house, the food I eat, the trees and parks, the potted orchids in the grocery store—I realize I am also looking at fungi. I'm seeing more than meets the eye. And while I know it is not a matter of faith, but science that has accessed this world to me, I nonetheless feel a kind of ecstasy in the knowing.

Chapter 4

HUNTERS, GATHERERS, AND THIEVES

T he most valuable culinary mushrooms—morels, chanterelles, porcini, truffles, and matsutake—are primarily collected in the wild. There is no mechanized harvesting, no union or contract employees, no dependable crop, and little oversight by the federal government. When you order pasta with wild mushrooms in a restaurant, you are eating a food that someone searched for, hand-picked, and carried out of the woods.

Morels are found in commercial quantities in many places in the United States, but in the western states, if there has been a forest fire in a national park during the summer and the following spring is wet, then fire morels may bloom in vast quantities—thousands per acre—amid the wreckage of the incinerated trees. Commercial pickers descend on these burn sites by the hundreds, and the forest service has to set up campsites to accommodate them. (Morel flushes on privately held burn lands, like American Indian reservations, are more likely to be picked by the owners or the picking is contracted out.) When my friend Andrew Geiger, a photographer based in Kalispell, Montana, called me one early May with word that the Flathead National Forest, just across the North Fork of the Flathead River from Glacier National Park, was awash with morels, I didn't hesitate. I was really curious about the roaming gypsylike culture of circuit pickers and fascinated by the idea of a fungal version of a gold rush.

Shortly before leaving for Montana, I had lunch with my tiny, beautiful sister Lisa. A choreographer and aerialist, Lisa worked in the circus for many years. When I told her about my upcoming adventure, she commented that she hoped I wouldn't get my period.

"Why not?" I asked.

"Because," she said, "aren't the parks in Montana full of grizzly bear?"

"I guess."

"Well, bear are just like elephants. I had an affair with an elephant trainer years ago, and his elephant charged me twice when I was menstruating. Of course, she was jealous. It was a complex relationship. Actually, she was just a 3-ton teenager. Anyway, I was asked to work as a sidekick in a bear act. I held off, hoping for a better opportunity than feeding jelly beans to a bear, but from what I understand, you will ruin the act if you have a surprise menstruation." Lisa is full of stories of this sort, and so once lunch was finished and we parted, I didn't really think further about the perils of one's period.

Until the day before my flight to Montana, that is, when I became victim of one of those peculiar moments of cosmic irony. (Despite the anecdotal opinion of certain circus folk to whom I am related, the hypothesis that bears are violently attracted to menstruating women is unproven, except in the case of polar bears, as put forth in an enlightening article, "Bears and Menstruating Women—Should You Camp?")

I knew this trip wasn't going to be like other mushroom hunts, and not just because there were bear in the mix. I was joining a commercial scene, and if the circumstances were right, there was going to be a lot of pickers in the woods. Three things are necessary for commercial picking: climate, habitat, and accessible territory in which to find mushrooms. The primo mushrooms are most plentiful in wet, 40- to 60-year-old forests, where the mycelial network is robust but competition from multiple fungi and other critters in the soil is still low. (Old-growth forests are packed with variety. They are key to fungal diversity, which is very important but not ideal when you are looking for large fruitings of a single species.) Forests in the Northeast, which have been cleared in waves for timber, agriculture, roads, and real estate development, are significantly less prolific—and mature trees tend to be on private property. The great picking in the USA happens in the northwestern states, starting with the morels in the spring.

There are two kinds of commercial mushroom pickers: those who pick in order to sell the mushrooms they find to restaurants or distributors and for whom it is a job, like logging; and those who hunt edible mushrooms as a paying hobby that also garners them mushrooms to eat themselves.

The first group is composed of circuit pickers, 1,000 or so transient people who travel the mushroom trail 6 to 10 months of the year. The route begins in British Columbia with the late summer harvest of matsutake, porcini, and chanterelles. They follow these mushrooms south through Washington and Oregon in September, October, and November and into northern California in December and January. In April, the morels come up in eastern Oregon and the pickers head farther north and east, and into higher altitudes, as the weather warms. By August, they may still be picking morels in Canada.

The circuit pickers are primarily Southeast Asians and white off-the-grid types, around 75 percent of whom came from outside the harvesting area. Together, they are what the author and mushroom expert David Arora called "the latest incarnation of a wandering community as ancient as humanity itself—one that is nature-immersed and moves with the seasons, dispersing and coalescing as conditions dictate."

The second picker group type is composed of an odd assortment of gourmands, amateur mycologists, wild food advocates, and people who just like to tromp around in the woods and call their day productive— people who will pick mushrooms to sell in order to supplement their incomes, but not as assiduously as the circuit picker. These autonomous pickers, who usually hunt solo, tend to be iconoclastic, prickly, and gossipy about the community of mushroom enthusiasts. They like their wine and are quick to warm up over a glass. Besides picking mushrooms for sale to distributors and restaurants, the really knowledgeable foragers, like Larry Evans of Montana, David Campbell of California, and John Getz of Oregon, lean toward public education. They lead instructional walks, head up local mycological societies, and guest lecture at forays on a variety of nontechnical subjects, usually surveys they've conducted in the field or cooking techniques.

My plan, or rather, Andrew's plan, was to camp in the commercial pickers' area to get a sense of their gypsylike culture, in the hope of finding a lot of morels.

In the little commuter plane to Kalispell I sat next to a huge mountain man in a plaid shirt, jeans, and jumbo hiking boots, who was mashed into his window seat like a raccoon stuffed into a too-small Havahart trap. He told me he'd found morels that weighed a quarter-pound each. "I stuff them with cream cheese, crab, and shrimp, and season them with Mrs. Dash Southwest seasoning and then slow smoke 'em over mesquite and serve 'em with elk," he said, red-cheeked and friendly. "Awesome."

Morels, fire or otherwise, are probably the most desirable of all the edible mushrooms, enjoyed by both the elite and the hoi polloi (they are sometimes called "redneck caviar"). Morels have a long tradition of inclusion in elegant meals, from the table of the Duke of Bolton in the 1700s, who enjoyed a "ragoo of veal sweetbreads, fat livers, mushrooms, truffles, morils [morels], artichoke bottoms . . . which you toss with a little melted bacon," to first-class passengers on the *Titanic,* who were served tournedos with morels on a bed of braised cabbage the night the ship sank. When you order a morel dish in a restaurant, it's hard to know whether the mushrooms came from a fire or from the banks of the Illinois River unless you can identify the species or taste the difference— which some people think they can. I once sat next to a very crabby Japanese woman at a New York Mycological Society banquet who told me in no uncertain terms that fire morels were not delicious and implied I was a rube to think they might be. Tom Volk thinks morels that grow under live trees are tastier because they contain a buffet of flavorful bacteria and yeasts and other symbionts—critters that would otherwise get cooked by a forest fire. If that is so, then a mushroom's symbionts are a kind of terroir, helping to determine its flavor like soil and yeasts do wine.

Wild mushrooms in America are a regional product that was first harvested by local people, beginning with Native Americans, and followed by European settlers who collected the mushrooms they recognized from their homelands. Then, in the 1980s and early 1990s, came the double whammy: recognition that Europeans and Japanese would pay good money for wild mushrooms that were in declining numbers overseas, and the American culinary awakening. Wild mushrooms had been diminishing in Europe and Japan for decades, due to aging forests and dying trees, soil chemistry problems arising from air pollution, and general habitat displacement. The international trade in American wild mushrooms was $5 to $10 million a year in the 1980s. A decade later, the industry was moving hundreds of millions of dollars worth of fungi each year, mainly morels, chanterelles, porcini, and matsutake. John

Getz was among the first generation of modern pickers to recognize the commercial importance of wild mushrooms in the Pacific Northwest. "One day in 1989 I was picking matsutake with elk grazing nearby," he said, "the next day there were thousands of people on every ridge looking for mushrooms."

At home, chefs and home cooks were waking up to the culinary delights of wild mushrooms. Loggers, who found themselves out of work due to attempts to save the habitat of the spotted owl in the Northwest, needed supplementary income, and they knew where the mushroom patches were. The Pacific Northwest has an abundance of mushrooms plus a good infrastructure that allows the fungi to get to foreign markets reliably. It took a while for other countries, China for example, to develop viable systems to get their mushrooms to market, but now they have and subsequently the US worldwide share of the wild mushroom market has dropped by about 50 percent.

Between supplying local markets and overseas sales, the wild mushroom industry in the United States is probably pretty stable right now, in the low hundreds of millions of dollars a year. Professional pickers aren't making as much money as they did during the heyday of wild harvesting, and there are fewer of them—only about 15 percent of the former picker population is still active—and those who are still picking do so for a number of reasons, not least because they like the lifestyle.

Andrew and I bought our commercial licenses at the Hungry Horse Ranger Station, where we joined a small group of Asian and Latin men, who, by their big smiles and nods, led me to believe none of them had a good grasp of English. A Rubenesque ranger in tight khakis and mascara ran through a quick chart of poisonous mushrooms (noting especially the deadly death cap mushroom, which has been mistaken for the delectable paddy straw mushroom of Southeast Asia). She pointed out we'd be hunting in grizzly bear country, and that to avoid an unpleasant confrontation, we should bury our waste, discard our garbage in designated containers, and not walk around with open soda cans. She played us a video of a grizzly dismantling just such a garbage container, warned us that grizzlies can pull the door off a car, showed us a 4-inch bear claw, and told us to have a nice day.

Most prime edible American mushrooms are found in great abundance on federal lands. As a result, the forest service has had to get involved in the management of the resource, the forest, and the pickers. For much of its history, the forest service's primary focus was the management of the timber harvest and fighting forest fires (almost half of the forest service budget goes to fighting fires). The forest service had to get up to speed quickly when, in the late 1980s, the demand for edible wild mushrooms exploded. Almost thirty years later, they've developed a grab bag of state and federal regulations that determine the limitations of mushroom gathering. These regulations seek to discipline foraging behavior by controlling foragers' access to the forest and its products, a system that was developed with minimal input from the pickers.

A national forest may require noncommercial mushroom pickers to procure a free license, or require pickers to mutilate their mushrooms in order to render them commercially unmarketable. It may limit the number of commercial licenses it sells (or not: All fees remain local for use by the forest management in their programs) or define the territory in which a picker can harvest mushrooms. It may limit a picking area based on such factors as wilderness area, research area, active timber sales area, wildlife protection, areas of safety concern, and soil erosion. Idaho requires harvesters to obtain a contract to harvest that includes $1 million in liability insurance, which may explain the dearth of mushrooms coming from that state. Most forests require commercial pickers to purchase a camping permit and camp in designated areas, to avoid overwhelming recreational campgrounds.

There were a few fire sites to choose from that year. We decided to go to the Wedge Fire, which was located on the western bank of the North Fork of the Flathead River. As Andrew and I drove north, climbing to about 3,000 feet through spring's lukewarm woodlands and towing a tidy little camper, I asked him about this bear business. I had a pile of pamphlets on my lap: "Enjoy Them at a Distance: Park Bears Are Dangerous!" and "Living with Grizzlies," which warned that if I encountered a bear, I should drop my hat and back away, speak in soft monotones, and avoid eye contact. My options seemed to look worse from there. I'd done a little bit of research on the plane, and it wasn't comforting. Stories of bear mauling abound; from the dreadful dismemberment of Timothy Treadwell and his girlfriend Amie Huguenard in Alaska, to books like *Danger Stalks the Land, Killer Bears, Bear Attacks,* and *Night of the Grizzlies,* in which a pair of bears killed two women in Glacier National Park.

"Look," Andrew said. "Just to make you feel more confident, I have some bear spray for you." The effective ingredient in the spray is capsaicin or hot red pepper. The main difference between bear spray and the mace women carry in their handbags is that bear spray has been tested to ensure it is humane to the animal. Most sprays have an effective range of 30 feet. The one Andrew bought for us had an effective range of 10 feet, close enough to smell the bear's breath. "But the spray is awful," he continued. "It maddens the bears, makes them bash their heads against the rocks and tear at their muzzles." I detected a note of ursine sympathy. Andrew is a peaceful soul, which is kind of easier to be if you aren't emitting a pheromone that may attract 500 pounds of 4-inch-clawed appetite.

"I want a gun," I told him, and in fact, Snappy Sports in Kalispell had .44s on sale for $99, but Andrew laughed me off. He had me pegged: I couldn't really defend myself with a handgun. In the face of such a confrontation, I would probably just try to run away.

Not too far into the forest we found our campsite, a slovenly acre or two of gravel studded with portable toilets and trash bins. Blue plastic

Commercial mushroom pickers' camp in Montana's Flathead National Forest

tarps sheltered dirty canvas tents, and smoky campfires and cook-stoves smoldered before the dark entrances. It smelled like a cold fire-place. There was one large tent that blared Chinese pop music and turned out to be a makeshift casino and noodle house. Someone exited the casino, dumped a wok full of grease into the brush by the door, and reentered. I immediately thought of the grizzly lecture we'd heard hours before. There were a few beat-up trucks covered in mud, most of them with California plates, all of which were being tinkered on by men completely blackened by charcoal, cigarettes hanging from their mouths and pistols hanging from their belts. I could guess their race by their body types: sturdy, big-headed Mexicans and slender, petite Asians. There was a smattering of Caucasians. We unhitched our camper smack in the middle of the camp, where it stood out like a shining sore thumb. Except for the men maintaining their trucks, all the pickers were on the burn.

Depending on whom you talk to, there are either a few or a lot of different species within the genus *Morchella*. The taxonomy is, as Tom Volk said, "a mess." But the most common burn morels—the ones we were after in the Flathead Forest—are the black or burn morel, the *Morchella conica*, and the gray morel (actually immature specimens of the blond or yellow varieties). The latter is large, heavy, and durable, which makes it more valuable, as morels are sold by weight, and these travel well.*

Morels are native to temperate forests—forests that endure a winter snow—across the Northern Hemisphere (though introduced morels grow in the Southern Hemisphere as well) and in a range of habitats from dunes to dumps, bomb craters to basements—really, as David Arora said, "wherever they please." The forest mycologist David Pilz dubbed them the "weeds of the mushroom world" for their ability to pop up in disturbed environments like logging roads, animal tracks, and roughed-up terrain of all sorts. There are dozens of names for morels from countries spanning both the globe and the millennia, and an estimated 50 million people pick them worldwide.

Fire morels were actually cultivated by 18th-century German peasants, who set fires in the forest in order "to favour their propagation" (the practice was shut down by the authorities). The huge fire in Yellowstone National Park in 1988, which burned 36 percent of the park's 2,221,800 acres, produced an immense morel fruiting, as did the Mount Saint Helens eruption, where thousands of gritty morels came up in the ash. The Flathead Fire was a relatively small one. More than 500 commercial licenses were sold (and 1,500 personal-use licenses distributed) by mid-June, with a peak commercial volume of around 10,000 pounds a day.

Why morels are so prolific after a forest fire is a matter of dispute. Some scientists have suggested that since fire neutralizes organic acids, it might reduce the number or growth of microorganisms that compete with the morels. Another suggestion is that by clearing groundcover, the morel has a better chance to develop its sclerotia—the lump of mycelial matter from which a morel fruits. A third idea has it that fire releases

*Grays may or may not be the *Morchella esculenta*, *M. deliciosa*, or *M. crassipes*; the work of sorting out the morel genus is ongoing. There are also blonds, yellows, tans, pickles, blushing, and half-free morels, as well as others that grow in nonburn habitats.

mineral nutrients from the organic matter and the morels take advantage of the bounty. Maybe the morels flush as a result of the destruction
of their host trees. Whatever it is, fire morels tend to come up only for a
year or two, whereas morels that grow in nondisturbed areas will come
up for many years.

It is incongruous to regard this tremendous flush of fungal life in the
midst of the devastation wrought by a forest fire. When Andrew and I
drove the muddy logging road deep into the Wedge Fire burn, we could
see nothing but miles of burnt timber and stump holes littering the
ground. Many trees remained upright, black and unstable. There was no
animal life: no squirrels, no chirping birds, just the moan of wind
through dead limbs and the creaking of standing snags. The devastation
was at once glorious and horrible: glorious in the hugeness of the event,
the phoenixlike power of nature to destroy itself in order to renew, and
horrible, too, because of the utter Biblical totality of the destruction.
Witnessing this forest was like watching a nature film of lions taking
down a young antelope: splendid in the innocence of its brutality.

A lot of heat is produced in a forest fire, as much as 575 degrees
Fahrenheit (about the temperature you need to leopard the bottom of
a pizza). Forest fires play an important role in the forest ecosystem. In
nature's scheme, fires were started by lightning and were relatively frequent and low to the ground, taking out the underbrush and leaving
the canopy intact. A century of fire suppression has led to an overgrowth of underbrush—bushes, saplings, and accumulated detritus—
which in turn sets up a ladder effect, allowing the fire to climb up
trees. This creates a bigger conflagration. Hot, intense fires cook the
soil. They kill the microorganisms that keep the soil fluffy, in turn
inhibiting the absorption of moisture. Morels survive because their
sclerotia, the prefruiting body of the fungus, can tough out the heat.
Today, forest managers consider controlled brush fires to be the best
solution for the long-term health of forests and are setting controlled

burns fairly routinely, especially around towns, buildings, and in productive timber areas. Fire morels prefer to grow in areas littered with
dead conifer needles—ideally the reddish needles of a moderate burn—
along the path of tree roots, and in shady dips and boles in the earth.
But walking around in those blackened woods, it was hard to pull my
eyes away from the long view. The destruction stretched as far as I
could see, plus I was keeping an eye out for bear. When I finally did
cast my eyes down, I had to freeze. All around my boots—and probably
even under them—black and brown morels poked their brainy caps up
through the pine needles. There were hundreds of them, like sentinels
of the forest's robust return to life (or its last gasp). I gathered quickly,
cutting the morels and tossing them in my bucket, all the while playing
a loop of bear advisories in my mind: Stay calm. Don't climb a tree.
Don't run. Don't look a bear in the eye. I was torn between wanting
dreadfully to return to the truck and roll up the windows—no protection from a bear attack anyway—and my gluttony.

Every few minutes I'd look up for Andrew. If I didn't see him, I'd call
for him anxiously, and when I found him, he'd be casually swaying his
bucket as he walked, looking for new patches and calling out to the bear
almost playfully, "Hey bear. Hey bear." I couldn't help but think he was
yanking my chain a little and letting my fears run rampant. After all,
Andrew was so organized about the camper and everything it was
almost sporty, and yet *he did forget the bear spray back at the camp.* Once
I thought I saw a bear in the distance between the trees, and I sprinted
back to the truck, completely forgetting the soft monotone and all the
other bear encounter instructions, but it turned out to be a pair of pickers: hooded men bent low to the ground, humping blackened laundry
hampers filled with mushrooms.

The circuit pickers are primarily legal Southeast Asian immigrants:
Laotian, Cambodian, Hmong, and Mien. The buyers who purchase their
mushrooms frequently refer to them as the "tribes," and indeed, most of

them harvest in family groups or crews.* There are some Latin American pickers, many of whom are probably illegal aliens. The people in both these groups have limited job skills and a minimal mastery of English, and harvesting mushrooms is work they can do. Experienced morel harvesters can earn more than $1,000 a day if the morels are abundant and the competition low, though the majority of pickers probably earn much less.

The lifestyle has its trade-offs: Pickers can't depend on a steady income, but there's no boss telling them what to do. Picking is a cash business, but there are no benefits. The only rights pickers have are the same that every American has in the forests. They do have some representation—there's an organization called the Alliance of Forest Workers and Harvesters (AFWH) based in Albany, California, that works to preserve prime mushroom patches from logging (which can be detrimental to both the fungus and mushroom fruiting) and helps forest services develop protocols for handling commercial pickers. But it is not like their $10 membership dues pay for a union. Mother Nature doesn't negotiate. The AFWH is more of an advocacy group that provides pickers with translation, ethical harvesting guidelines, and support in the face of racial profiling by local law enforcement. A relatively new safety issue for pickers is the increase of marijuana plantations hidden in national forests, particularly in California and Oregon. This has opened the potential for violence as pickers wander onto pot plantings.

Wild mushroom harvesting, which has been going on in earnest for 25 years, is loaded with stories of migrant Asian pickers and local whites staking out and defending territory in national forests with automatic weapons, robbing each other of their mushrooms and robbing the mushroom buyers of their cash. ("I have never heard of one instance of robbing a buyer," said the forest mycologist David Pilz. "They *all* carry

*David Arora reported that seasonal mushroom pickers are "an incredible mix of men and women," listing races, genders, and ethnic groups from a range of lifestyles as diverse as rocket scientist to refugee, belly dancer to congressional candidate. Personal experience and all other reports I have read, however, suggest most circuit pickers are Asian.

firearms.") There are tons of rumors: that loggers determine the picking area (they don't); that pickers will despoil one another's campsites by dumping bacon grease near their tents, which attracts bear and leads to fines; that the "Camboes" cordon off areas with fake forest service tags to discourage competitors from picking; that circuit pickers start forest fires in the summer in order to create morel grounds for the following spring; that the Asians have Uzis and the whites carry machine guns. Most of this is nonsense. Here is a more typical scenario: In the parking lot of a market in town, a couple of belligerent locals pick a fight with a circuit picker, who then stands up for himself by shooting a few rounds in the air. Later, the locals gather some friends, have several drinks, and hunt down the circuit picker for a proper assault. They either beat up one or two people or find themselves facing a camp full of nervous, armed Laotians. The forest service police breaks it up and arrests the locals on a malicious intimidation charge or the like, and there is grumbling and uptightness all around.

The racial profiling that worries the AFWH has more to do with accusations of circuit pickers abusing the forest. Circuit pickers are thought to be reckless harvesters who damage the fungus and pack the earth hard by trampling, and some are. They are accused of overharvesting, and some do. But while the pickers may indeed take every single mushroom they can find, it has not been shown that harvesting wild mushrooms affects the ability of the fungus to fruit in future years. "We don't have evidence that says there's no impact from harvesting, but we don't have evidence of any negative impact, either," said David Pilz.

The question of whether mushrooms can be harvested sustainably is difficult, since so many factors go into a fruiting (like moisture, temperature, soil conditions, and the condition of their symbiotic plant partners), and so little is known about how many mushrooms are necessary for spore dispersal and reproduction to sustain a healthy fungal community. According to Pilz (*Pilz*, coincidentally, is German for mushroom), "the only way to reasonably monitor production is on the scale of forest stands or landscapes and over periods of decades or centuries." In the interim, the forest service does err on the side of caution, and areas with sensitive or rare plant species, despite the fact that those areas might be productive edible mushroom patches, may be off-limits.

In the end, the racial profiling and rumors have more to do with a divide between circuit pickers and local white pickers; the result of differing attitudes toward the forest that are rooted in cultural traditions, including ideas about ownership, rights, and livelihood, even spiritual connections with nature. And this divide can cause dangerous misunderstandings. In 2001, for example, Flathead National Forest rangers had to contend with the "mushroom wars," when vast amounts of morels came up on the Moose Fire burn. The forest was full of Asian circuit pickers who would signal to each other by shooting in the air. Local pickers thought they were being shot at, and they started shooting back blindly into the woods. Fortunately, the shootings were resolved without any fatalities.

Those differences are amplified when there is competition for limited resources, as in the case of morels on a burn. Part of the problem, suggested John Getz, is "white boys resent good pickers, and Asians respect good pickers." Locals also harbor resentment against those whose sole interest in a place is in the wealth that can be extracted from it. "Migratory labor," wrote Paul S. Taylor in a post–Depression-era paper, "slips through stable and often rich communities, of which it is never an accepted part." A conflict is inevitable when multiple groups have the same rights to a wild place but only one group calls that place home. But according to David Arora, "to say that these mushroom pickers do not 'belong,' that they do not have as much stake in a place as its permanent residents, is like saying that migrating geese do not belong to the lakes to which they flock in winter. . . . " But the fact remains: Gypsies are never welcome.

After an hour of labor, Andrew and I had collected about 10 pounds of morels. All along the road back to camp, we saw the tents of morel buyers. The buyers tend to be independent contractors who work for one or more wild mushroom distribution companies. These companies may front substantial amounts of cash to the buyers who purchase mushrooms directly from the pickers, but most buyers finance their purchases independently. It is not uncommon for buyers to purchase tens of thousands of dollars worth of mushrooms a day. Prices depend on species; demand in the United States, Europe, and Japan; quality; and availability. If mushrooms are scarce, then the price goes up; if the mushrooms are prolific, then the price will be lower, but more mushrooms are purchased. Indeed, wild mushroom transactions may be the largest legal cash-based commerce in the USA. That doesn't mean Uncle Sam doesn't get his piece of the action. Distribution companies do send 1099s to the buyers, though the pickers usually don't get one. Many pickers' incomes probably fall beneath the reporting minimum anyway.

Outside the Wedge Fire burn, just about every buyer's tent had a truck pulled up to it, with pickers unloading crate after crate of morels. The buyers rendezvous with field managers to deliver the mushrooms, which are then shipped to warehouses for processing and distribution. Morels are sold fresh or dried, from a few pounds to a restaurant, to shipments of tons overseas.* We stopped at the tent of Jay Southard, who was buying mushrooms for Alpine Foragers Exchange of Portland, Oregon. (Buyers must purchase permits for operating a buying station in the forest.) It was a pretty humble setup; he had a table, a scale, and a few dozen plastic crates. Jay is an amiable fellow, a white guy with long ties

---

*Although the topic is beyond the scope of this book, the international commerce in morels is huge. India and Pakistan each supply one-third of the global morel commerce, which is in the millions of pounds for fresh morels. The fall of the Berlin Wall in 1989 opened the Eastern European and Russian mushroom markets to the rest of the world. It also cut deeply into American international sales. The Pacific Northwest, the USA's most prolific mushroom region, provides less than 10 percent of the global wild mushroom market.

to both Asian and local pickers. He was paying $3 a pound, of which his cut was 50 cents per pound, no matter the paying price. That evening he was hoping to buy up to 1,000 pounds of morels.

Before 2009, harvesters did not require certification. The quickie review of poisonous mushrooms that we received at the Hungry Horse Ranger Station was all the info we got regarding which mushrooms to pick and which we should stay away from. Nonetheless, most problems brought on by misidentification tend to self-correct. Buyers favor harvesters who have a track record of picking the right mushrooms, just as distributors favor buyers who have a track record of providing the right mushrooms. It is very much a business built on personal reputation rather than regulation. That doesn't mean mistakes aren't made. Gary Lincoff told me there are misidentified mushrooms in nearly all the market bins in New York City, though not dangerous misidentifications, more like mixing up chanterelles and hedgehogs (both are delicious). Some states are seeking to rectify this. Iowa and Minnesota require wild mushroom harvesters to be certified, mainly to distinguish between true morels and false morels, which can make you extremely ill. Maine is developing a certification law. The New York State Department of Health requires that wild mushrooms be approved by a certified mushroom inspector. To date, however, there are no standards in New York for certifying these inspectors.*

There is no real accounting of the wild mushroom harvest, either in volume or in dollars, and though many states require buyers to keep records of whom they purchased products from, and the species, volumes, and values of the products purchased, whatever information might be gleaned from this reporting just isn't. "In 18 years, nobody has ever asked to see my records," said Jay. While Alpine Foragers told me

*In France and Switzerland, pharmacists are required to be certified in mushroom identification. It is their job to verify species before sale in local markets.

that they bought 200,000 pounds of morels out of the Flathead Fire dur-ing the 2004 spring season, most mushroom distribution outfits tend to be very secretive. David Pilz estimated the commercial morel harvest in Oregon and Washington in 2005, half of which was shipped overseas, was over 770,000 pounds. At today's retail prices, that's over $300 mil-lion. (And of course, there is no accounting for the volume of mush-rooms gathered by recreational pickers.)

Closer to camp, we stopped at the tent of a Laotian couple, David and Alune. The Asian pickers had been selling to them: Their worksta-tion was crowded with crate upon crate of fragrant morels. Long-haired and silent, Alune hovered over the mushrooms protectively, removing the rotten specimens, snipping the dirty ends. David, with a long Fu Manchu moustache that started at the corners of his mouth, smoked constantly and fingered through a thick wad of bills. They were from Washington State and were paying $3 a pound until they realized the Asian pickers were favoring their station, at which point they dropped their price to $2.75. Truck after grimy truck pulled up to unload their morels, pouring them like gravel into David's white plastic crates, weigh-ing them off, separating the gray morels, which sell for a dollar more a pound. Many of the mushrooms were swollen with rain, and David mumbled something about wet mushrooms to legitimize his price drop.

By 7:00 p.m. the pickers were off the burn and the smoky camp was full of people, all of them sticky with charcoal and pinesap. The Latinos congregated near their trucks, beers in hand, asking each other if they'd seen bear and hitting on the occasional Latina woman who mistakenly wandered into their sights. Over smoldering campfires built just outside the entrance of their tents, the Asian women cooked—I caught a glance of chicken livers and fiddlehead ferns from the forest frying in a wok of bubbling oil. When I asked the cook if she ate morels, because Andrew and I had big plans for ours later in the spanky little camper kitchen, she shook her head no. I don't know if it was because she wouldn't eat what she could sell, or if she just didn't like them. It was very hard to make friends with the Asians, although they were always polite-ish.

Andrew and I decided to stop in the blue tarp casino tent for a little cheer. Inside were a half-dozen wobbly plastic-covered tables with squeeze bottles of sriracha hot sauce and chopsticks in cans. A wood-burning stove warmed the place, and a generator powered a karaoke machine boasting Indian music videos with Laotian subtitles. A fierce-eyed Laotian lady in her sixties peddled Budweiser beer and Marlboro cigarettes for much more than they cost in town, and served up tasteless noodles in broth. The crowd—small, sooty men slurping soup, rolling dice, and smoking cigarettes—was decidedly not merry, and none of the men acknowledged my presence. Even Joi, a stoned 18-year-old Laotian from California, directed his answers to my questions to Andrew instead. "I make more money babysitting, man," he complained in his homeboy patois. It turned out that Joi left his glasses in Sacramento, and the profits of what few mushrooms he did see to pick were promptly lost in a dice game an hour before we arrived.

Pickers described their work as "gambling" and "like playing the slots." Charles Novy, who founded Fresh and Wild, one of the first wild mushroom companies to exploit the early days of the mushroom boom, described it as "hope springing eternal. It's like the gold rush miners. They're looking for the spot loaded with morels when the price is high." Pickers have to make investments in licenses, transportation, and camping equipment, but there is no guarantee that they will turn a profit. They pay taxes, maybe, but if they did and submitted their deductions, "they'd be getting a tax refund," said one pickers' advocate. But many of the pickers don't have that kind of business savvy—they function outside the system, and seem to relish the independence that wild crafting affords. "Once you're out here, it's freedom, man," said Linda, a Californian I met in the camp, who showed me a picture of herself before she'd had her stomach stapled. "Just you, God, and the bears." But while the Asians will nod in assent when the white folks' discussion comes round to freedom and self-reliance and general avoidance of federal conspiracies like the Internal Revenue Service, they don't really say anything about it themselves. Rather, they give yes or no answers, or, more often, simply walk away.

The pickers I did talk to were the most upset by park rangers who they said raided their camps for signs of food that had been left out, and even entered their tents while they were on the burn to confiscate food in the name of bear control. Not only are campers fined for leaving food around, but the pickers resent anyone entering what little property they've staked out. While this kind of policing may be necessary for the safety of all people in the camp, the current disciplinary system is not one that seeks to change the pickers' attitude toward the forest and nature, to make them more responsible and sensitive to the forest environment and safety issues. I heard complaints of the Big Brother–like attitude of the forest service when I spoke to the white, more politicized pickers in the camp.

For example, Wally Johnson, a morel buyer from California, came by our camper while I was cooking dinner (risotto with ground pork and sautéed morels). A Vietnam War veteran who "fought to free these people," Wally said he heard I was asking questions about what life was like for the picker, and he wanted me to understand the racism the Asians endure. "The white camps don't get hit by the forest service," he complained, referring to the food raids. "They'd get shot at if they did anyway. The service just hits this camp, takes their food, and threatens to throw them off the fire. All these people are funneled into one camp, just so [the service] can watch over them." Wally felt the white pickers had another camp that was much nicer and roomier, and maybe there was a harvesters' camp where white people congregated. But no campground was off-limits based on race. Personal-use harvesters were allowed to camp in smaller campsites, and the one I saw was definitely tidier, probably because only a few people were camping there. I told Wally I'd seen someone dump a wok of grease outside the casino, which is exactly the kind of thing that pisses off the forest service. "The truth is," he replied, "snags are more dangerous than bear."

Wally said the problems the forest service complains of, like garbage, are the results of pickers being crammed into designated campgrounds. "Open the fires to commercial pickers and they'll spread out," he said. "The truth is, this shantytown freaks out the tourists. It boils down to two things around here: racism and garbage," he continued with increasing heat. "Instead of these costs [for campsites and licenses], pickers should have a license like a fisherman!" When Andrew mentioned he had paid a $400 photography fee to shoot in the forest, Wally got so upset his stomach ulcer acted up and I had to give him a Pepcid.

For 20 years, Billy Stewart patrolled about 4 million acres in northwest Montana, including the Flathead Forest. He supervised 10 people whose jobs consisted of a variety of responsibilities, from domestic disturbances in campgrounds to fish and game violations like poaching, and boundary encroachments like riding snowmobiles in the designated wilderness. Stewart's job got more complicated when there was a burn on his beat. In general, a burn is a headache for the forest service. Mushrooms can eat up all of their time, especially if there aren't a lot of spring burns to pick elsewhere in the West. "But luckily, the vast majority of pickers are pros," said Stewart. "They're pretty good about getting permits and following the law."

The forest service has to make sure the pickers don't drive into areas where the fire has weakened the soil. They have to check the pickers' and buyers' permits, usually by hanging around the buyers' tents at the end of the day. There was no violence on the Flathead burn, but competition between the different ethnic groups can become a law enforcement issue, Stewart said, when pickers looking for better grounds harvest off-limits burns or get into fights with locals. "The locals think it is their forest and they should have the best spots. The Asians tend to be territorial, too, but it only becomes a problem when there is crowding." But by closing much of the burn to pickers, the forest service actually encourages competition. On the other hand, the understaffed service can better handle pickers on a smaller burn. And it's not just handling them from a policing perspective but also from a public service perspective. Rangers resolve disputes, help with injuries and disabled vehicles, and look for pickers who've gotten lost in the woods.

If, like Wally suggests, the pickers were allowed to scatter throughout the forest, they would tend to congregate near fresh water—this has happened in the past—where they are rough on the environment and leave behind large amounts of garbage. Of course, littering isn't unique to migrant pickers. As Kalispell's own bearded Reverend Reginald Duncan of the Universal Life Church told me, "there are buttheads everywhere." The regulations seek to mitigate problems like these and improve the service's ability to get their job done. In the long run, the compromises pickers have to make is deemed necessary for the benefit of all who have a stake in the national forests. What makes the forest service jittery is the fact that most pickers are armed—though mainly for signaling when they are lost, or for defense against bears. In fact, around camp they said you need five bullets in your gun: four for the grizzly and one for yourself.*

*The circuit pickers who hunt nonfire morels, chanterelles, porcini, and matsutake are similarly controlled, though their numbers are relatively steady year after year, as they return annually to check the patches they know can be productive. But there can be dramatic swings in mushroom production, and when there is a particularly large fruiting, public land agencies and local communities have been caught off guard by the sudden flood of circuit pickers who need adequate lodging, camping, sanitation, and garbage facilities. As in the case of fire morel pickers, they can be good for the local economy, but they can be hell on the forest.

I had my bear spray with me the next morning when we headed out to an especially devastated area. The going was rough. Huge burnt trees had fallen over, creating massive obstacles to a clean getaway. I watched carefully and noted fallen trees that I could scramble under should a bear suddenly appear. A low mist hung in pockets between the downed timber. I climbed up a hill of new bear grass, the first green thing I had seen all morning, following a set of muddy elk hoofprints, a pair of blond morels growing in the cup of each one. And then I heard it: a tremendous crashing sound just beyond my sight line. The crashing grew closer, definitely heading my way, and in a split second I made the decision to run. I rushed back down the hill, slipping in the dead pine needles over the slick gray mud, sliding, finally, on my rear, and the whole time I was freaking out, thinking, "He smells me! He smells me!" Brittle branches exploded into cinders as my shoulders ripped past them, tearing off my hat, poking holes in my new Patagonia windbreaker, all the while the crashing sound growing louder. I hit the road at the bottom of the hill with a thump, then jumped back to avoid being run over by a grody truck bristling with a half-dozen pickers, all as muddy as I was, tearing around the corner, having just descended at top speed from the logging road at the summit of the hill. I was bruised and shaken and mortified for having mistaken what was very obviously a truck for a bear. But I was still holding my bucket of morels.

Autonomous wild mushroom hunters make up a much smaller part of the mushroom economy but are significant on a local level. They may have relationships with distributors to whom they can bring their goods, but often they will act as distributor as well, driving their product to the nearest town where they will sell to the markets and restaurants. Restaurateurs can't depend on what they call "back door" or "kitchen door" sales, but they love it when the pickers come around.

When in Colorado, I often make a pilgrimage to Six89 in Carbondale. The chef, Mark Fischer, is one of the best in the state, and his crazy menu always surprises. I've had his yummy crisp gnocchi and roasted wild mushroom salad many times, and when I asked where he got his fungi, he rolled his eyes and grinned. "Buying from the mushroom pickers is definitely one of the more amusing aspects of the restaurant business," said Fischer, who buys about 100 pounds of fresh wild mushrooms a year from pickers. "Five minutes before dinner service some grubby guy in a Ford Taurus with mismatched wheels that's been dragged through the mud shows up and says he's got mushrooms like porcini and chanterelles in his trunk. The conversation is typically, 'Where'd you get those?' and he'd say, 'Oh, you know. My spots. McClure Pass.' They aren't really forthcoming about their spots," said Fischer. "So then we negotiate. For us, the price is based on what we pay our regular distributors, like Fresh and Wild. It's pretty competitive when the mushrooms are in. I mean, when Joe is at the back door, Jim is right around the corner waiting for him to leave."

It's a feast-or-famine business, because when the mushrooms are up, they are up suddenly and everyone's prices drop precipitously. But if there are a lot of mushrooms, restaurants like Six89 will buy a large quantity and dry, freeze, or otherwise preserve them. "The pickers are antisocial and entrepreneurial," Fischer continued. "Ted Koczynski comes to mind. I haven't come across a well-groomed forager yet. Oh, and they prefer to be paid in cash." When I asked Fischer for some names, he said, "I mainly know them by their vehicles. Like, 'The guy in the Taurus is back.'"

Not all regional pickers are so rough. David Campbell, who led the WAM foray I attended, differs from the circuit picker in many ways. Regional commercial pickers know their territory very well and will control their mushroom patches by "keeping it clean. I'd go in and make sure the mushrooms are picked. I tended my places regularly to keep other pickers off scent." In this sense, circuit pickers cannot compete with a local.

Campbell also described his days of picking commercially as being more opportunistic than speculative. If the circumstances were right, he'd collect mushrooms. If not, he'd scope for habitats. During the summer of 2010, when the porcini were fruiting in Colorado like they hadn't in 30 years, David gave me a call at my cabin and said he was on his way from California to the West Elks for some picking. And indeed, within a few days he showed up in a van loaded with empty, eager coolers and was up in the mountains within a few hours of arriving. Circuit pickers' success is much more of a gamble. Far from home and incurring operating costs, they never know how successful they might be. But their communication networks are, according to David Pilz, "robust," and they will go where the action is. Campbell later told me that within the first few weeks of the porcini flush in the West Elks, 10,000 pounds of porcini had been harvested commercially. I never once saw a commercial picker, though. "You won't," he said. "It is in their best interest to stay low-key."

In the early days of the American wild mushroom scene, chefs didn't know much about mushrooms. "They'd say, 'Oh, I'll take a half pound'— so a big part of it was educating them," said Campbell. He considered 5 to 10 pounds of mushrooms to be the minimum amount that a solo hunter could sell to a chef and make it profitable. Campbell had to find the mushrooms, then cull them (discard mushrooms with insects or bruises, and waterlogged specimens, and "separate out the top 5 percent and bottom 5 percent for myself") and clean the mushrooms. He'd find out what the going wholesale price was from sources like Fresh and Wild, and then call his list of chefs. As time went on, more chefs became interested in including wild edibles on their menus—pretty much concurrent with the rise of Chez Panisse, the restaurant from which Alice Waters and company launched their regional food movement—and more pickers got into the woods. Eventually, Campbell aged out of the business, as did his contacts in the restaurant world, "and I got into other stuff, like the WAM forays." Today, regional pickers will also use the Internet to advertise: "Dried Mushrooms by Scott," "Deb and Andy's sand-free morels," and "DAL's *Sparassis crispa*" from locations all over the country.

Making money is not the sole motivation of many commercial mushroom pickers. There is "the freedom thing," but just as compelling is the excitement of discovery. Whether they were professional or recreational, pickers told me over and over that the thrill of finding a patch of mushrooms never dims. When a mushroom is found, "it's not an abstract reward," said Campbell, his eyes glittering. "They're like an Easter egg. When you find it, it's yours and it's valuable." That's an analogy I heard frequently.

Social attitudes toward pickers are not unlike attitudes toward treasure hunters. Both are considered rogues, people who avoid what the Calvinists considered the necessity of hard work (although you'll hear pickers talk about what backbreaking work mushroom picking is—but there are degrees of exertion). And that's not just an American phenomenon. In Italy, the owner of a Tuscan trattoria told me that all *tartufatti* (truffle hunters) were bums and scallywags who don't want to get a real job, though most were actually retired grandpas augmenting their pensions.

In the USA, the ultimate booty is the matsutake. In the late 1980s and early 1990s, the matsutake, or pine mushroom, fetched hundreds of dollars a pound, the highest market price of all wild mushrooms harvested commercially in North America. Many pickers I spoke to said that John Getz was "legendary" in the picking scene in general, and the matsutake

Matsutake are highly valued by the Japanese and often given as gifts.

scene in particular, a fact he credits to having noticed a plant that he said "seeks out" the matsutake mycelium, *Allotropa virgata*, known as the candy-stick. Since then it has been established that *A. virgata* does indeed have a parasitic relationship with matsutake mycelium that in turn has a mycorrhizal relationship with the pine tree.

Matsutake fill the same niche in the Japanese market as truffles do in the European market. They have both culinary and cultural value, with the most splendid specimens given as corporate gifts. In 1992, the *New York Times* reported that Japanese businessmen spent as much as $240 for a box of three or four mushrooms. In 2007, the North Korean leader Kim Jong II gave President Roh Moo-hyun of South Korea 500 such boxes equaling 4 tons of matsutake mushrooms prior to a summit meeting.*

Native Japanese matsutake has been in decline for the past 50 years for many of the same reasons the truffle has declined in Europe, including the decimation of the mushroom's symbiotic partners due to infestations of the pine wilt nematode. Of the 3,000 tons of matsutake consumed in Japan in 1996, two-thirds were imported. The majority of exported wild American mushrooms are matsutake sold to the Japanese. In the past decade, however, Korean and Chinese sources for matsutake have

---

*In North Korea, the government controls the matsutake harvest. According to an article in the *Daily NK*, an online news site dedicated to democracy in North Korea, farmers will sometimes risk punishment and sell their matsutake to Chinese smugglers, who pay more than the government does. The smugglers work in concert with border guards who, according to one smuggler, said smuggling pine mushrooms was a lot less risky than smuggling people.

opened up, while the Japanese demand has decreased as a new generation without the same reverence for the mushroom has come of age. As a result, the price of American matsutake has dropped—in 2010, American matsutake were selling in Japan for $17 to $53 per pound wholesale—and stories about matsutake-related violence in national forests (one man shot through the heart, his mushrooms missing; five dead in a prime matsutake patch, etc.) have receded into legend.

In December 2009, wild mushroom distribution companies were selling fresh matsutake for about $49 a pound online. When I stumbled across the matsie bin at the Berkeley market where they were selling for $19 a pound, I just about had what the husband calls a sporgasm.

The matsutake is all about the aroma. It is powerful and distinct like a truffle, but different, like a funky Red Hot, and in fact, the cinnamon smell is one of the ways this mushroom is identified in the field. It's not the easiest mushroom to cook (based on my experiments), but when you find the right combination—nanoslices floating in consommé, cooked with steamed eggs, or baked in parchment—the taste truly transports.

The American species, *Tricholoma magnivelare*, tastes much the same as the Asian species, *T. matsutake*, and both use the same common name, although the Oriental species fetches about twice the price of its American cousin. Matsutake grow all over the country (as well as a commercial harvest in the Quebec region of Canada) but they are most prolific in the Pacific Northwest. However, unlike the bright orange chanterelles or the king bolete, matsutake are not easy to spot.

"It takes extreme prejudice to find matsies," said David Campbell, who was in on the matsutake boom early on. Although they are big white mushrooms with caps and gills, they do most of their growing (or swelling) underground, and as they are most valuable when young, sometimes the only indication that they are there is a bump—or mushshrump, as pickers say—in the soil at the base of its partner tree. Matsutake have less commercial value when they are cut, so harvesters must carefully wiggle the mushroom free of the mycelium. David Campbell developed carpal tunnel syndrome from picking matsutake.

Unfortunately, many harvesters tend to rake for them under the trees, which damages the mycelial mat that connects host trees—known as the shiro (which means "white castle" or "place")—and generally wreaks havoc on the soil and its living community. Taking care of matsutake grounds is something John Getz, who lives in Florence, Oregon, cares a lot about. Early in the matsutake rush, he alerted the forest service to matsie patches in an effort to initiate resource control. "I took a lot of heat from locals, but I thought if we leave this wide open with no one to look out for the resource, we are going to be in trouble."

Raking is also a technique used by harvesters in search of Oregon's truffles and the pecan truffle, which grows in a mycorrhizal relationship with pecan and other trees. It is a stupid harvesting method for many reasons, not the least because raking uncovers immature truffles that have not yet developed their flavor, giving rise to the fallacy that American truffles are tasteless. It's bad for nature, bad for truffles, and bad for business. Worries that raking negatively affects mushroom yields and causes environmental degradation have resulted in the forest service restricting harvests in some areas.

Because they harvest the same limited number of patches year after year, regional pickers have a vested interest in ethical harvesting. For them, ethics have an economic component. Unethical harvesting like raking damages the fungal organism, which in turn undermines the health of trees, which affects the well-being of a forest ecosystem.

The primary rule of picking is to not disturb the fungal organism. From there, the best pickers harvest cleanly by cutting the mushroom with a knife and replacing the covering duff. Most commercial pickers use plastic buckets, but they drill holes in the bottom so spores can shake

out. "I often use a basket," said Connie Green of Wine Forest Wild
Foods, a distribution company, "and I like to picture myself as the Mor-
ton Salt Girl of the mushroom world as I go walking through the woods,
shaking out spores with every step I take."

In general, conscientious pickers advise against picking immature
mushrooms, especially those that take a long time to mature, like morels
and chanterelles. While the science is not clear on the importance of this
prohibition for the long-term health of the fungus (mycologists still don't
know how fruiting is initiated in most species, or how mushrooms are
distributed in time or space), it may undermine the gene pool and reduce
future harvests. It makes sense commercially, too, because, according to
Connie Green, "the communal agreement of 'thumb-size' (meaning pick
no mushrooms smaller than your thumb) serves everyone's interests.
The pounds harvested from a good area can literally double and triple if
everyone respects this." Plus it's just considered tacky and lowbrow to
pick immature mushrooms. "There is tremendous peer and financial
incentive to leave the babies," said Green. Commercial buyers don't like
to buy undersize mushrooms anyway.

The other rule of picking, according to David Campbell, is don't
crowd a hunter's space, meaning if you see someone picking mushrooms,
don't run over and start picking from the same patch. On the Flathead Fire
burn, you might have found a gun pointed at you, but most of the time it
is simply considered bad manners. What determines a patch, though, can
be a bit ambiguous. Campbell said, "It is the eyes that take possession."

"No trespassing" is the final rule of picking, as it is for hunters and
fishermen. It's a rule I have broken unintentionally and intentionally. To
this day I cringe at an act of thievery I committed on Long Island. I was
driving home from an unsuccessful hunt for oysters (the bivalve, not the
mushroom) and feeling very unfulfilled and annoyed when I spotted a
bright orange chicken of the woods mushroom growing on a tree in

someone's yard. I pulled over, left the car running, dashed onto the property in my flapping waders, ripped the mushroom off the tree, ran back to the car, and took off with a screech. When I ate the mushroom (sautéed in garlic and butter, finished in white wine and parsley, and served in an omelet) I got what I deserved: an allergic reaction that left my lips puffy and tingly for hours.

In some countries, commercial pickers have foraging rights that may supersede private property laws. In Tuscany, for example, my cousin Mario trespasses every day during the season. He told me that truffle spots are passed from father to son, and the Italians, rather than see the supply of white truffles diminish in any way, quite sensibly allow the *tartufatti*—truffle hunters—free rein over private lands. In Sweden, the *allemansrätten*, or the right of public access, allows anyone to walk, bicycle, horseback ride, or ski on any noncultivated land and private roads; to recreate on somebody else's waters; and to pick wildflowers, berries, and mushrooms.

In the United States, if you are hunting in a state (not national) forest or on private land with permission, then you are okay. But if you hunt anywhere else, you may be trespassing, and local police can be aggressive about enforcing the law. "I was busted once," said Campbell. "They held me with the shoplifters." Hunters who wander into national parks to hunt mushrooms can incur huge fines, regardless of whether they were lost or not. The year I was on the Flathead burn in Montana, there was also a lot of burn territory in Glacier National Park, where commercial hunting is prohibited. Nonetheless, pickers looking for noncompetitive hunting risked the $5,000 fine.

Poachers target private land. For more than a decade, poachers, who maintain detailed maps and GPS records of private mushroom patches, have plundered ranches along central California's coast, returning every season to pick, even at night. The ranchers know the patches as well, and find their main recourse is to pick the mushrooms on their property themselves, and as quickly as possible. But the poachers are effective harvesters and hard to arrest.

A gang of three poachers of Eastern European origin, known for years around the Santa Barbara Rural Crimes Department as "the Czechs," was finally busted in 2006 and arrested for grand theft (of a crop) because they had $10,000 worth of mushrooms in their trucks. Sergeant Rob Wright, the rural crime coordinator for the Santa Barbara Sheriff's Department and the arresting officer, told me the police patrol the ranches looking for out-of-state license plates. They tracked the poachers back to their motel, where the officers found records documenting $20,000 worth of mushrooms that they'd just shipped that day to distributors.*

Setting aside outright thievery, picking etiquette is variously observed. The English introduced a 30-point code of conduct for mushroom harvesting 10 years ago, but we have no such conventions in the United States. It seems to me, though, that the more a picker knows about fungi in general, the better he or she behaves in the woods. It's certainly made me a more conscientious mushroom hunter, although I have to admit, it is hard not to pick the small ones.

---

*In France, organized crime is in on mushroom poaching. Gangs from the cities, particularly Marseilles, have been hunting on private property in southern France with less-than-eco-sensitive methods, like hunting in a line, raking, and stomping on tree seedlings, and confrontations have ensued, even some gunplay. In response, the French government is developing mushroom hunting licenses and with the fee money will hire officers to guard the woodlands and scare off the thugs.

Chapter 5

THE EXOTICS

L ike most people, when I saw bins of specialty mushrooms at my
market, I assumed they were wild harvested. But since I started
hitting the mushroom festivals and forays, I've learned that lots
of the mushrooms I thought were wild are not. I mean, just about every
mushroom foray or amateur conference has an oyster mushroom kit-
making class—a buoyantly sloppy procedure wherein a table of sterilized
straw, hot and wet as rough spaghetti, is tossed with oyster spawn (*Pleurotus eryngii*–inoculated barley), packed vigorously into plastic bags,
stabbed all over with a penknife, fastened with a twist tie, and then
brought back to the student's car or luggage or left in the conference
area, tucked under a folding chair like a forgotten loaf of bread. It's one
of those anybody-can-do-it projects, but the truth is, mushroom growing is a complex task.

Most of the "wild" mushrooms you see described on menus or in the
market these days are saprophytic mushrooms. Because saprophytes
grow and feed on hosts that are dead or dying, the grower can inoculate
a compatible host like hay or wood with the germinated spore of a particular species and, if the right environmental conditions are created, the
fungus will fruit. (Mycorrhizal fungi are a different story. Since they

grow in or on plant roots, and are dependant on live plants for part of their food, such fungi can only be cultivated in association with a host. Without the host, there will be no mushrooms. So growers of truffles, for example, which are mycorrhizal, need to inoculate trees and plant an orchard. But more on that later.)

The forces that spurred the American culinary awakening—the back-to-nature movement of the 1960s, the acceptance of the ethnic kitchen in the 1970s, the fascination with regional foods in the 1980s, and the advent of the locavore movement in the 21st century—have propelled "wild" mushrooms into the American consciousness. No longer is the white button mushroom the only game in town. Today, farmers cultivate oyster, shiitake, enoki, maitake, royal trumpets, beech, and other mushrooms.

The first brown mushrooms to enter the stage were the crimini and portobello. (The spelling for these mushrooms varies. My preferred spelling for crimini derives from a seminal Italian grower, Crimini, whose name was printed on his box of brown mushrooms, but you'll also see cremini and cremino. Portobello is also a made-up name. You may see portabella and various other spellings. It's called *fungo prataiolo* in parts of Italy.) In the early 1980s, the restaurant critic for *Gourmet* magazine, Jay Jacobs, raved about Felidia, a tony Upper East Side restaurant in New York owned by Lidia Bastianich, and its radical inclusion of a grilled portobello cap entrée on the menu (radical for New York at the time. Bastianich ate the dish as a child in the Friuli region of Italy, where she is from). The portobello cap as a substitution for meat took off and, with the advent of the portobello burger, is now firmly established in the mainstream food culture, albeit with the predictable caloric adaptations, as in the blue cheese portobello burger.

Today, only restaurants catering to the uninitiated would put crimini and portobello forward as wild mushrooms; not only are both cultivated, they are the same species as the common cultivated button mushroom. The crimini mushroom is simply a young, nonselected for whiteness *Agaricus bisporus*, and a portobello is a mature crimini. This distinction is smaller than a species differentiation. It's more like the difference between people of different skin color. But the brownness is what makes the mushroom seem wild and indeed, in its wild aspect, *A. bisporus* is brown, cream, or grayish. Typically, food stories in newspapers and magazines will describe the crimini as "rustic" and "woodsy," which it may be, but not much more so than a white button mushroom. But public misperceptions of this sort are tolerated by the food industry, even encouraged, as such misunderstandings can be a marketing gift horse. A good parallel would be the assumption that a brown chicken egg is more "natural" than a white egg, when it is simply the egg of a different breed of bird and can be produced under conditions equally horrific as a white egg. Likewise, the difference in flavor between crimini and white button mushrooms are minute. Psychologically, however, the introduction of the crimini in the late 1980s was huge. Mycophobic Americans began to show an interest in purchasing mushrooms that *looked* wild.

This, in turn, has led to a boom in commercial "wild" mushroom cultivation. In general, smaller mushroom operations are more likely to take on specialty products that distinguish them from the megamushroom outfits, although there are large operations, too, like Phillips Mushroom Farms, in Kennett Square, Pennsylvania, that cultivate specialty or exotic (meaning other than white button) mushrooms. Phillips produces more nonwhite mushrooms than any other farmer in the USA: portobello, crimini, shiitake, a variety of oysters, maitake (also known as hen of the woods), beech, enoki, and royal trumpets (also known as king oysters), which are sold under their own and their clients' brands, like Mr. Mushroom, Publix, and Wegmans.

When Pete Gray married Jill Phillips in 1990, he married into mushroom aristocracy. The Phillips family has been in the business since 1927. Jill's grandfather William made a significant contribution to the industry when he developed the use of ice for temperature control during the summer months (mushroom farming was a cool-weather operation prior to this innovation), allowing mushrooms to be grown year-round. Gray is a lanky, low-key guy, a Grateful Dead fan, and one of the farm's grower/managers. He took me on a tour of the farm's two campuses, including the doubles (traditional Pennsylvanian-style mushroom houses) where the crimini and portobello are grown, Quonset huts that house the specialty mushroom growing rooms, the lab, and packing plant. All told, the farm is composed of about 50 structures.

More and more, the landscape of mushroom farming in Pennsylvania is looking like the Phillips operation, which employs 300 workers and produces 45 million pounds of mushrooms a year. Gray says the smaller mushroom farms—those with four or five doubles—have a hard time coming up with the capital to finance the changes they need to meet regulatory standards. For example, workers need to have places to eat and put their belongings, and Phillips had the resources to build a lunchroom and locker room. Some of their competitors did not. Nor are the profit margins for smaller operations high enough to finance expansion. The technology that makes mushroom farms efficient is unaffordable on a small scale. Buying compost is steep; marketing is expensive; and it is very difficult to expand because purchasing zoning permits to build doubles, in Pennsylvania anyway, is costly.

The crimini and portobello house at Phillips is warm and humid and smells like food. These mushrooms are grown in the same way the farmers cultivated carnations 100 years before: in wooden beds filled with compost. The room is large, with 8,000 square feet of growing area, and dark, with only thin fluorescent tube lighting to help the humans navigate the space. Contrary to myth, mushrooms don't grow only in the dark; they just don't need sunlight to grow because they don't make chlorophyll. Keeping mushroom houses dark uses less energy and prevents the rooms from heating up, which in turn reduces the need for expensive air-conditioning. The space houses seven heavy wooden beds filled with 200-plus tons of steamed compost, known in the industry as substrate (to avoid the stinky connotation), that has been inoculated with germinated mushroom spore, or spawn. The mycelium grows for about 2 weeks, after which a layer of peat moss is applied to the surface. Four days later, the mycelial network is complete. Fresh air is introduced and the temperature drops to about 60 degrees Fahrenheit. Thereafter, the mycelium forms thick strands that coalesce into primordia, which then develop into mushrooms. *Agaricus bisporus* is a determinate mushroom, meaning at its most tiny beginning stage all the cells it will ever have are in place. The mycelium feeds water to the growing mushrooms and they simply expand.

Crimini of all sizes pop from the dark, sweet casing soil, from just-emerging baby crimini the size of pearls to market-size crimini, round as Ping-Pong balls, creating a bubbled landscape of fleshy spheres. On the sides of the bed I saw the tangle of mycelium threaded through the soil. It looked light and fluffy as cotton candy, but when I touched it, it was surprisingly dense and stiff: like cotton threads chaotically intertwined and knotted into a gigantic pale gray dreadlock.

Thirty days after the spawn has been mixed into the compost beds, the first flush (also known as a break) occurs and is picked. Two more flushes follow. Each flush is less aggressive than the previous one as the nutrition in the substrate becomes depleted. As a result, there is less competition among the crimini for space in the beds. But that is a good thing, because it creates the room necessary for some of the crimini to develop into the wide-capped portobello.

All mushrooms have their own specific needs in order to fruit, and the challenge for mushroom growers who are producing more than one genus of mushroom is ensuring that, beyond the perennial issues of pathogen-free spawn and substrate, they provide the right environment for each. Enoki like it cold, around 47 degrees Fahrenheit, and grow in bottles; shiitake like it warm, about 67 degrees; maitake like it supermisty—so much so that when I gazed into the maitake room, it was almost impossible to make out the hushed, feathery mushrooms through the warm fog.

My personal experience with mushroom growing is limited to a steamy bag of oyster spawn–inoculated straw that we made at SOMA camp in Sonoma, California. I traveled back to New York with my plastic bag of inoculated straw in my carry-on luggage. It was surprising how much warmth the straw kit generated. My whole duffel was heating up like a menopausal woman, and the smell, when I opened the overhead compartment to retrieve my bag, was strong enough to cause me to glance sideways at my fellow travelers: a kind of hot, sweaty smell—not a foul odor, but a sublimely living one, like a vegetable version of the smell of skin under a Band-Aid. As it wasn't something I could explain with a glance and a shrug, I kept my head low and exited the plane as quickly as possible.

At home I was challenged with where to house my kit. I live in an old loft building, where a system of overhead steam pipes creates a dry, hot environment, especially in the winter, and oyster mushrooms like cool, wet places. I ended up placing my kit in the broom closet on top of the water heater and gave it a periodic spritz from the sprayer I use to dampen the ironing. It only took a couple of days for the bag to become very hard—like a roll of toilet paper—and white with growing mycelium. Then, about a week later, the heads of tiny mushrooms appeared through the holes I'd stabbed all over the bag; little bouquets like white-headed craft pins with a lovely, clean mushroomy smell.

My oyster log developed tiny primordia (baby mushrooms) in the cuts in the plastic. A few began to form under the plastic, and I liberated them with an X-Acto knife. The smell was marvelous, clean, and woodsy. I also enlarged some of the other slits, as per the instruction page I was sent home with. Then I moved the log to a table near my west-facing windows. I created a rather unstable tripod by sticking some Chinese take-out chopsticks into the bag, as air is supposed to circulate around it, and misted as frequently as I could remember to. Within about a week, the primordia darkened to a pale gray and sprouted beautiful oyster mushrooms about the size of quarters.

My oyster mushrooms continued to enlarge over the next week, but something was wrong with them: They began to warp, twisting in on themselves in a kind of slow-mo torture. My teenage children advised me many times that the mushrooms looked repulsive, and indeed they did. I thought it had something to do with the light, or the fact that my chopstick tripod kept falling over, or that the cat had become infatuated with the log and had taken to jumping on the table and rubbing her whiskers against it. Anyway, after about 9 days the log began to smell very nasty, like a large, dead insect. It started to embarrass the teenagers (what doesn't?), and even my husband, who generally encourages home projects like sauerkraut and yogurt making, suggested my oyster log was stinking up the house. It became clear that the mushrooms were putrid and unharvestable. Indeed, when I took it in the elevator to dispose of, one of my neighbors, who joined me on the way down, glanced surreptitiously at my malodorous bag. I pretended to smell nothing, which is the usual protocol in New York when you are caught with garbage that should have been tossed days before. It turns out, of course, that my oyster log had become infected with something.

When there is a glitch in the system—a microscopic bit of contamination gets into the substrate, for example—disaster can hit, as it did for Phillips a couple of days after I visited the farm. A routine food safety

Enoki grown in jars

quality assurance test revealed the presence of the bacterium *Listeria monocytogenes,* which can cause food poisoning. *Listeria* is widespread in nature—but out in the wild it faces competitors that restrain it. In the enoki rooms, it is too cold for many of those competitors to survive, and *Listeria,* which likes cold temperatures, can thrive unchecked. Phillips voluntarily recalled 7,000 pounds of enoki mushrooms that had been distributed around the East Coast, discarded 300,000 fruiting bottles, shelled out over $50,000 to clean up the enoki house, lost up to 3 months' worth of production, and ended up ditching the whole enoki operation. In the end, nobody reported getting sick.

When Phillips started to diversify their mushroom production in 1980, they were the first in the country to do so on a commercial level, and shiitake mushrooms were key to that diversification. Shiitake are prized in Asia for both their mild, nutty flavor and medicinal properties, but Americans didn't get to taste them fresh until after 1972 because the USDA used to quarantine shiitake spawn imports. It seems the agency had confused the shiitake's Latin name—*Lentinula edodes*—with the Latin name of a fungus that attacks railroad ties, *Lentinus lepidius.** Today, shiitake constitutes 2 percent of the American mushroom market. Shiitake are wood decayers in nature and can be grown outdoors on logs, but that technique is not economically viable on a large scale.

Lentinus lepidius owns some of the blame for the South's defeat during the Civil War. In her book *Mushrooms, Molds, and Miracles,* Lucy Kavaler reported that many of the trains sent to support General Robert E. Lee's troops never made it due to rotten railroad ties.

For a millennium, the Japanese collected shiitake in the wild. The fungus grows on the dead wood of shii trees—an evergreen related to oak, and hence the name: *Shiitake* means mushroom of the shii tree. By 1943, the Japanese had figured out how to make spawn plugs by inoculating wood chips and inserting them into holes cut in shii logs. Some shiitake growers bang on their inoculated logs in order to stimulate fruiting. Shiitake fruits on a fallen branch because once the branch is off the tree, the food supply for the fungus is suddenly restricted. It's possible that banging on inoculated logs simulates the moment in nature when the branch falls to the ground, which is maybe a signal of some sort to the mycelium. (I couldn't find anyone who thought much of this idea. I realize I am kind of assigning consciousness to a fungus. But this is what happens when you become a mycophile. You think the mushrooms are listening.)

After many failed attempts, Phillips, in conjunction with Lambert Spawn, developed a sawdust bag for growing shiitake mushrooms.* The spawn is mixed with a combination of sawdust, wheat bran, millet, or rye grain; chalk; and water in gallon plastic bags. In a matter of weeks, the mycelium grows and binds the substrate in a kind of log that is dense but light, sort of like peat. These logs are removed from the bag and allowed to harden for a couple of weeks, then soaked in water. Within a matter of days, pins begin to form and push their way through the "bark," and eventually the mushrooms mature, up to 2 pounds per bag. Phillips produces 7,500 shiitake bags a day, 6 days a week. They call the bags logs, a reference to the traditional method of cultivation. The shiitake house is an eerie, misty place, where 10,000 logs covered with mushrooms sit on shelves that climb to the ceiling eight levels high. It was uncanny. The place felt more like an animal mill than a plant nursery.

*At one time, all shiitake spawn grown in bags of sawdust (versus on wood logs) in the United States came from a single strain that originated on an outdoor shiitake farm in Virginia and was cultured by the mycologist Mark Miller, Lambert's spawn maker, though lots of other strains have been imported since then.

There was something almost conscious about all those mushrooms. They emitted a keen life force, like a very ancient tree that has been around long enough to gain some sentience.

w

Megaproducers like Phillips are not the only game in town. There are a host of other producers, from businesses like Fungi Perfecti, which, among other ventures, grows medicinal mushrooms like turkey tail for processing into supplements, to monks selling oyster mushrooms grown in their monastery in Charleston, South Carolina; from BTTR Ventures, a company in Berkeley, California, that sells shiitake growing kits on spent coffee grounds supplied by a local roastery, to subsistence farmers like Open Minded Organics on the east end of Long Island, New York.

David Falkowski, in his mid-thirties, wears one gigantic knit hat to hold his copious dreadlocks off his face. He is a third-generation farmer in Bridgehampton—a meaty, handsome Polish American. His grandfather planted row crops, his father planted landscaping trees, and, since 2003, Falkowski has taken over the farming of this 10-acre piece of family land. The setting is pristine. The rich alluvial soil is 12 feet thick in places, and the weather is moderated by the Atlantic Ocean less than 5 miles to the south. Typical of the ritzy Hamptons, Open Minded Organics is hemmed in on all sides by huge, bonus-financed mansions. In the flat landscape, they look like stranded, shingled ocean liners.

Falkowski farms yellow and blue oyster mushrooms, shiitake, and sometimes royal trumpet mushrooms. "I got my start from Paul Stamets's workshop on mushroom cultivation. I was very interested in the idea of a specialty market that had a healing form to farming. We use organic by-products [like straw] and turn it into food and compost." The spent compost from his mushroom operation goes onto the fields, which he is slowly transforming from a tree farm back to row crops. As of 2009, his mushroom business has been self-sustaining, but the challenges are great. As a boutique business, he's had to work hard at marketing; he's contracted respiratory illness from the spores; and there is always the threat of catastrophic contamination from molds or pests.

Even though Falkowski's growing room is significantly smaller and lower tech than Phillips's, the space is filled with the unmistakable sentience of mushrooms. Four-foot-tall bags of oyster mushroom substrate colonized with mycelium (Falkowski makes his own spawn in the attic of his farmhouse) hang from steel bars like clear punching bags filled with clotted cream. I noticed that "love" was written on each bag. "It's from *The Hidden Messages in Water*," said Falkowski, sheepishly scratching his dread cap. "Since mushrooms are 90 percent water, we think it makes them happier."*

Spawn makers are busy creating cultures from an ever-widening variety of saprophytic mushrooms. Morels, which can be saprophytic in lifestyle, have been grown successfully, though on a limited scale and with diminished flavor. Morels are difficult to grow because they have a kind of extra stage in their life cycle. Before its fruiting stage, morel mycelium forms a sclerotium, a bulblike fungal mass that is capable of surviving tough natural conditions like a cold winter and forest fires. In the spring, the morel sclerotium forms new mycelium that may form a mushroom. A collection of circumstances are necessary for the mycelium to produce a mushroom—temperature, moisture, carbon dioxide quantities, nutrition in the soil—and to make it more complicated,

The Hidden Messages in Water is a book of photographs of frozen water crystals by Masaru Emoto. Emoto claims the crystals are ugly or beautiful depending on the words or thoughts that were directed at the droplets before they are frozen. His claims have been endorsed (Yoko Ono) and challenged (most notably by Kristopher Setchfield of Castleton State College). To my mind, Emoto's ideas are cool but kooky. On the other hand, what's not to like about writing "love" on every bag of mushrooms you grow?

those circumstances change as the mushroom grows. It turns out it is easier to get the sclerotium to produce mycelium than mushrooms. Indeed, morel mycelium can survive in the sclerotium/mycelium cycle for decades without producing a mushroom, and as mentioned earlier, their preferred habitat is very hard to pin down. According to Tom Volk, there are scientific reports on success with growing morels as early as 1883. But Ronald D. Ower, a San Francisco State University master's student, is credited with producing the first cultivated morels in a "walk-in growth chamber" (although there are also tales that he grew morels in a box in his San Francisco kitchen). He published his results in *Mycologia* in 1982. Ower discovered that the sclerotium doesn't develop unless the nutrients in its environment have become depleted, so he needed to start the mycelium in nutrient-poor soil, surrounded by rich soil. The mycelium quickly consumed the nutrients in the poor soil, and then went after the nutrient-rich substrate. This stimulated the formation of the sclerotium, whose job it is to retain nutrients for wintering over. With correct temperature and high yields of water (simulating spring rains), the sclerotium produced mycelium that formed primordia, baby morels.

Ower went on to develop protocols for cultivating morels with two Michigan State University scientists, Gary L. Mills and James A. Malachowski. The technique, to put it simply, consisted of the following steps: 1) Produce a spawn culture of the morel. 2) Mix the spawn culture in a nutrient-poor soil that is laid on top of or near nutrient-rich soil. 3) Water well. The species they cultivated was later identified as *Morchella rufobrunnea,* common to California, which some people think are bland in comparison to other morel species.

Ower and his partners received funding from the Neogen Corporation, a Lansing, Michigan, company founded by the nonprofit Michigan

Gary Mills' morels

State University Founda-
tion as a vehicle to exploit
innovations emanating
from the school.* Neogen
was assigned a patent for
the Ower, Mills, and Malachowski technique in 1986.
(The scientists were the
inventors, but as employees
of Neogen, not owners of the technology.) Tragically, Ower never got to
see the fruits of his discovery. He was murdered in San Francisco in a
gay-bashing incident a few weeks before the patent was granted.

Ultimately, Neogen was assigned three patents for growing morels.
The morel-growing patents and technology were resold a few times
over the next 8 years, and each company that owned an interest had a
go at growing morels for sale. Domino's Pizza was in the game for a
while, as they were interested in developing a morel topping for pizza,
and Terry Farms, a grower of button mushrooms, invested millions—
with help from the city of Auburn, Alabama—in the first commercial
morel cultivation plant. Terry Farms grew and sold morels for about
5 years. At its peak, they produced 1,300 to 1,400 pounds a week, but it
wasn't a profitable venture, and by 1999 the plant was abandoned.
When Mills went to check on the farm 4 years later, it was gutted of all
its equipment.

Although the patents have expired, according to the *Mushroom
Growers' Newsletter*, no one has been able to produce morels by the
instructions. "I don't know why people can't figure it out," said Gary
Mills from his office at Diversified Natural Products, an industrial

---

*Neogen developed Agri-Screen, an inexpensive diagnostic kit to screen grain used in animal
feed for the carcinogen aflatoxin—a mycotoxin caused by a fungus.

biotechnology company in Scottville, Michigan. "It's snowing outside and we are harvesting morels right now."

As far as Gary Mills knows, no one else is producing morels commercially (his cultivated morels can be found on the Internet: Chris Matherly in Georgia sells them through his Morel Mushroom Hunting Club). Otherwise, hopeful home cultivators can buy morel cultivation kits with ready-to-go spawn or inoculated trees. In 2005, Stewart C. Miller patented a process for inoculating seedlings with morel mycelium, a process by which the mycelium is allowed to produce sclerotium and then the seedling is killed to induce the sclerotium to fruit.

Based on the failure of my oyster log, I think I am pretty unlikely to get into any more mushroom cultivation projects; however, the mycologist Mark Miller told me that if I ever wanted to grow morels, he'd send me all the spawn I needed.

"Rake it in some ashes from the fireplace and you might get them— I've done it by accident."

Chapter 6

TRUFFLES

ycorrhizal species are the holy grail of mushroom cultivation: the porcini and chanterelle, neither of which has been successfully cultivated, and the truffle, which has been cultivated to a limited extent. Unlike mushroom farmers who are growing saprophytes, the challenge of mycorrhizal fungi farmers, or, in most cases, hopeful or potential mycorrhizal mushroom farmers, is to create a living ecosystem. "It's really terraforming," said David Falkowski of Open Minded Organics. That's not an easy task, because living ecosystems are very complex—as any aquarium or zookeeper will tell you. You can go into business hoping to recreate an ecosystem, but the chances that you know everything you need to succeed, especially about these microscopic systems, is pretty slim. Nonetheless, there is a cadre of American truffle growers out there, planting truffle groves and orchards and trying to coax nature into producing the most coveted foodstuff in the world.

Years ago, I went to Tuscany with my parents to truffle hunt for the *Tuber magnatum pico*, the white truffle, with my father's cousin Mario. A retired barber, Mario and his cronies, all grandpas with perennially sunburned necks, spend their days in November trespassing on private property with their little truffle hunting dogs called *lagatti*, checking the spots under scrubby willow that the men in their families have checked for generations. The *tartufatti* found quite a few white truffles that foggy morning and gave a small one to my father. It looked like a tiny hepatic turd, but the smell! As soon as the dog scratched up the truffle from its hiding place in the earth, the immediate area was flooded with an intoxicating aroma: intensely pleasurable, gamey, and sweet, like the smell of a lover. My father kept the truffle in the breast pocket of his aging leather bomber jacket, and throughout dinner that evening in Florence he kept opening his jacket to sniff. Indeed, as we crossed the Ponte Vecchio on the way back to our hotel, my father stopped a pair of tourists from Wisconsin. "You wanna smell something special?" he said, opening the flap of his jacket. "Smell this!" He demanded. "Come on, SMELL IT!"

Although they didn't seem keen to stick their noses into my father's sleeve, the Wisconsinites could smell the truffle's aroma from 3 feet away. At first timid, they were soon sucking the air around them hungrily. Humans are smitten with truffles, and they will spend hundreds of thousands of dollars to buy one. It's one of the ultimate symbols of wealth. A luxury apartment building in lower Manhattan even calls itself Truffles Tribeca (which sported a sign with an Edward Albee quote during construction that read, weirdly, "You gotta have swine to show you where the truffles are."). Restaurants lock truffles in safes at night. In fact, Italian white truffles are the most expensive food in the world. Retail prices have averaged around $3,000 a pound for the past few years. Usually about the size of a Ping-Pong ball, the largest found was 3.3 pounds and sold at a charity auction in 2007 for $330,000 to a casino owner in Macau after a bidding war with the controversial English artist Damien Hirst. (The truffle subsequently spoiled. Undaunted, the same casino tycoon matched that record price in 2010, when he bought two white truffles totaling 2.8 pounds.)

Should you be so lucky as to eat a very fresh Italian white truffle or a *Tuber melanosporum*, France's black Périgord truffle (they both have expensive sounding monikers, like the diamond of the kitchen, the black diamond, the white diamond, etc.), you will understand what all the hubbub is about. Lots of language has been used to describe the truffle flavor: mold, garlic, soil, onions without heat, meat, sweet body odor. None does them justice. Unfortunately, access to truffles of this sort is limited to season, regionality, and how much money you are willing to spend on your belly.

Truffles are hypogeous fungi: fungi that live underground. There are many different species of truffles (more than 60 species have been described, 20 of which are found in Europe), and about 10 species are of culinary interest. The edibility of the rest is mostly unknown. Of the preferred edibles, some taste like cheese, others like garlic, some are fruity, many are mild flavored, a few will knock you out with the power of their flavor, to the extent where your whole body will reek deliciously of them for hours after consumption. If you look at a map, the tastiest and most celebrated truffles grow in a belt along the upper half of Spain, the lower half of France, and the upper third of Italy and Croatia. The belt no doubt continues straight through to the southern coast of China. (There is some evidence that truffle habitats are shifting into latitudes farther north, possibly the result of climate change.)

But edible truffles grow all over the world. There are truffle mines in the Kalahari Desert in Botswana (in mycorrhizal association with desert plants), truffles to be found in Slovenia, Sweden, China, the Himalayas, New Zealand, Australia, Syria, and North America. Our knowledge of the distribution of truffles, however, is limited to those places where they have been traditionally collected. For all we know, there could be truffles growing in New York City's Central Park.

Theophrastes (372–287 BC), a Greek philosopher and author of *Enquiry into Plants*, described truffles as a plant but grouped them with plants "with smooth rinds . . . the mushroom, the fungus, the geranium," and described them as having the smell of meat. Fungal taxonomists divide truffles into six genera. The *Tuber* genus (as in potato tuber) is the one associated with the best-tasting truffles and is in the class Ascomycota, meaning fungi that form spores in sacs, like morels.

It is hard to understand how a morel, which is a cup fungus—an aboveground mushroom shaped like a cup, or with cuplike features—can be related to a subterranean truffle, until you imagine its morphological evolution. Over time, the cup fungus became increasingly convoluted, its spore-covered cups becoming wavier and wavier, creating, in the process, a greater surface area for spores. Eventually the sides of the cups pressed together, encasing the spores inside. If you cut a truffle in half you can see the wavy lines that were the rims of the primeval cup fungi that is the ancestor of the truffle. This adaptation has evolved in other genera as well.

The wavy lines in a truffle are the rims of an ancestral cup fungus.

For example, *Boletus* (the genus porcini comes from) has an underground relative. Historically, the "true truffle" belonged to the genus *Tuber*, and other, non-*Tuber* evolutionary cousins were known as false truffles.

There may be multiple evolutionary reasons for the truffle's descent belowground, but the prevailing hypothesis holds that the fungus became subterranean in order to survive the stresses of environmental factors like drought or frost. The diversity of truffles that live in arid environments supports this theory. In fact, truffles are prolific in the Middle East and are considered a delicacy there.* Desert truffles are wild crafted—cultivation attempts have not been successful— and they are large and prolific. Preferred by the ancient Romans, desert truffles are thought by some academics to be the "manna from heaven" referred to in the Old Testament. The amateur mycologist Elinoar Shavit, an expert on Middle Eastern truffles, described them as having "the texture of a crisp potato, the smell of a bee's wax candle just snuffed out, and the flavor of macadamia nuts." They are prepared numerous ways. The traditional method is to roast them in the embers of a fire, but they are also cooked with rice, with stewed meat, and grilled like a shish kebab.

When truffles went belowground, they gave up the most common method of fungal spore dispersal: wind. They may be simple morphologically—they're just lumpish little clods of fungal material—but ecologically truffles are quite complicated, as they depend on animals to distribute their spores. When ripe, the truffle produces volatile chemical compounds that mimic mammalian reproductive pheromones and are irresistible to some mammals, particularly swine (hence the tradition of putting pigs to work hunting truffles). Animals dig for the truffles and either eat them and distribute the spore in their scat, or just generally disperse the spore as they disturb the ground with their digging. The California red-backed vole is an obligate truffler—which means it has coevolved with the truffle and depends on it for food. The northern flying squirrel is a preferential truffler, which means it prefers truffles. Humans are preferential trufflers, too.

Truffles have long been considered an aphrodisiac. Brillat-Savarin,

---

*These are not species from the genus *Tuber* but species from two genera, *Terfezia* and *Tirmania*, that live in a mycorrhizal relationship with *Helianthemum*, a flowering bush related to the North American rock rose.

in his *Physiology of Taste* (1859), wrote, "The truffle is not a positive aphrodisiac, but it can upon occasion make women tenderer and men more apt to love." And stories abound, from those who tried to keep truffle-liberated libidos at bay (like the Vatican and Islamic Imams, who denied their followers truffles because of their supposed power to corrupt the pure) to those who wished to release the libido from its bindings, like the Marquis de Sade, who reportedly used truffles to soften up his victims. As John Davenport rather curiously wrote in his book *Aphrodisiacs and Antiaphrodisiacs* in 1869, "The erotic properties of truffles and mushrooms are considered by most writers as better established than fish."

These suggestions are not totally anecdotal. One of the components in the odor of truffles is a steroid that is also found in the saliva of rutting boars, the armpit perspiration of men, and the urine of women. The chemical substance alpha-androstenol is currently being added to colognes like Lure for Him and Lure for Her.

It is that sexy, gamey aroma that makes or breaks a truffle, as the taste of the truffle itself is actually rather bland. In 2000, I attended a dinner party in Memphis, Tennessee, at which the very New Yorky Max Frankel, the former executive editor of the *New York Times,* and his wife, reporter Joyce Purnick, were guests. He complained to me that he'd had truffles before but they simply didn't taste like much and, frankly, he didn't understand what all the hoopla was about. The problem, I think, was the great man had been served either an inferior species of truffle or truffles whose perfume had in great part dissipated due to age. My cousin Mario, the white truffle hunter, told me that the scent, and therefore the taste of truffles, starts to disappear after 4 days. It's downhill from there, so folks who buy a truffle and save it for a special occasion may find themselves sorely disappointed. It's better just to gobble the thing up right away. The season for Périgord truffles and white truffles is approximately November through March, though like all fungi, their quantities are affected by rainfall and other environmental factors.

Truffles are sold buried in oil, butter, salt, rice, or flour, even held in a bag with raw eggs—all in the expectation that those mediums will absorb and retain the elusive truffle aroma. Some of them sort of do, but as soon as the truffle or the truffle-aroma-soaked medium hits the heat, those volatile chemicals that create the aroma are rendered inert and the flavor disappears. Furthermore, rice, salt, and flour draw moisture out of the truffle, leaving behind a dried-looking little scab of a thing that smells like it once smelled like a truffle. Likewise, the truffle aroma dissipates when exposed to air.

Almost all truffle oil, that staple of gourmet stores and ever less-fancy restaurants, is flavored with a synthetic petroleum-based chemical, not truffles. This is common knowledge to most chefs, although maybe it is not in their best interest to share that knowledge, as truffle oil is popular with diners. The food writer Jeffrey Steingarten made that revelation in *Vogue* magazine in 2003, but either not many people read it, or few cared, as truffle oil sales remain robust, especially around the holidays.

The "truffle" smell in truffle oil is created by a combination of olive oil and bis(methylthio)methane, among other chemicals. There may be some bits of dried truffle in there, but they are not really lending any flavor. According to the Italian chemist Sandro Silveri, who worked for Urbani Truffles for many years, "all truffle-aromatised foods have the same terrifying stink of hydrocarbon and sulphur-based substances. No one can now afford to say that the substances used to aromatise vegetal oil seasonings and several other foods have a natural origin or come from vegetal or animal raw materials without saying something hypocritical or mischievous." In fact, truffle oil flavored with bis(methylthio)-methane has a slight metallic aftertaste.

You can spot a fake truffle oil product easily. Labels on the bottles

list truffle aroma and truffle essence as an ingredient. Those terms refer
to the chemicals: "Aroma" and "essence" are not USDA-approved food
descriptions. Rosario Safina, who sells a truffle oil that he says is not
made with synthetic chemicals, has been trying to get the FDA to pay
attention to fake truffle oil (which would be very good for his business),
"but they asked me, 'Do you know any rich people that have gotten sick?'
Truffle oil is pretty low on the FDA's list." (Rosario claims his oil is made
using a pharmacological extraction process where "truffles are put into
a patented extractor chamber that takes all of the truffle's volatile molecules . . . a connecting chamber transfers the molecules and infuses
them into certified organic extra-virgin olive oil.") When I told some
friends in Berkeley, California, about the truffle oil scam, they were out-
raged. "That's the kind of issue Berkeleyites can really get behind," joked
my dinner companion.

The way truffle oil is sold to the public is simply not legit. Truffle oil
is very pricey—$8 an ounce is not unusual, but in actuality the glass and
bottle cap cost more than the flavoring and oil. One teaspoon of "truffle
aroma," the amount typically used in an 8-ounce bottle of white truffle
oil (black truffle oil is made with a lesser quantity of the same chemical),
costs about 40 cents. This is typical of the shysterish atmosphere that
pervades the world of truffle oils—and truffles in general—and has
since the beginning. The naturalist Pliny the Elder reported on a Roman
official in Spain who broke a tooth biting into a coin that had been
embedded in a truffle—possibly to increase its weight, and hence its
cost. Indeed, the truffle industry is rife with chicanery. For every straight
shooter I met, there was also someone who was, upon further research,
tweaking the facts. There are a great many disputes in litigation regarding payment for trees and truffles, and grudge matches between competitors are *de rigueur.*

There are really only two ways to enjoy fresh truffles: Go to Europe during the season (the fall truffle festivals held in the Piedmont region of Italy are on most mycophiles' bucket list), or buy one from a reputable retailer. You might be best off ordering truffles at a restaurant. A fine French restaurant will serve Périgord truffles with classic dishes like Chateaubriand truffé, and a proper Italian joint will show you the white truffle you are buying—indeed, the maître d' will carry the truffle on a plate through the dining room so everyone gets a whiff. Half a dozen shavings of raw white truffle on your pasta, from the size of a nickel to the size of a quarter, can set you back an additional $100. If you buy a fresh truffle at a gourmet shop, you can store it in your fridge in a paper bag, and it can be frozen in a glass jar, but it's best to eat it right away.

Gourmands have enjoyed truffles for a very long time. "To write the history of the truffle," wrote Alexandre Dumas in his *Dictionary of Cuisine* in 1873, "would be to undertake a history of civilization. . . . " Indeed, there are references to enthusiastic truffle eating in the Old Testament, in Egyptian, Mesopotamian, Babylonian, Chinese, Greek, Roman, Japanese, and Islamic texts. European references declined during the superstitious Middle Ages, probably because of the notion that the truffle was created by unholy lightning and whipped diners into sexual frenzy, but post-Renaissance, the mycophagy of truffles was reinvigorated. By the end of the 19th century, as much as 1,000 to 2,000 tons of truffles were supplied annually from France, and recipes from the turn of the 20th century call for wanton usage. Dumas's turkey was stuffed with 4 pounds of truffles (40 francs' worth at the time, but at today's price of $63 an ounce, it would cost you over $4,000 to make this recipe). Dumas described truffles as the "*sacrum sacrorum* [holy of holies] of the gastronomes."

The desire for truffles has continued unabated ever since, although the harvest has decreased substantially. Multiple factors may have been at play, but ultimately, truffle production has declined, said the plant pathologist Tom Michaels, "due to interactions between people and the fungus."* James Trappe, a mycologist at Oregon State University who specializes in truffles and is revered in the field—he's kind of the Obi-Wan Kenobi of mycology—suspects the decline in truffles, both French and Italian, is related to the decline of habitat, either from development or overgrowth of woodlands, and the loss of expertise in the management of that habitat. Likewise, Ian Hall, author of *Taming the Truffle*—the bible for hopeful truffliers—suggests that knowledge of wild truffle grounds died with many soldiers during the two world wars. Rosario Safina, who worked for the truffle distributor Urbani for 23 years, adds that ground and air pollution may also be culprits in diminished yields. "I'm surprised there are any truffles at all," he said from his office in Long Island City, New York. "And believe me, I am not an environmentalist," he continued. "I mean, I used to sell caviar."

The cultivation of truffles has a short history, probably because it is a capricious crop to grow. The fungus is difficult to fruit and, when it does, the yields are low. The Périgord and the white truffle are mycorrhizal partners of various species of oak, hazelnut, poplar, beech, willow, and sometimes fruit trees. The white truffle is exclusively wild crafted, although there are truffle farmers that are trying very hard to crack the mystery of what makes them grow. But the black Périgord truffle, as well as numerous other species, is cultivated in Europe, Oceania, and the United States. And it all started in France.

In the Provençal town of Saint-Saturnin-lès-Apt there is a statue of Joseph Talon, considered the first person to draw a connection between truffles and specific trees when he stumbled upon a cache of truffles growing in a grove of oak trees. In 1810, he planted acorns at the base of truffle-producing trees, then replanted the seedlings and managed to

---

*Truffle production in France spiked at the beginning of the 20th century. Acres of grape and mulberry crops were lost due to disease and insect epidemics during the latter part of the 1800s and truffle trees were planted in the available land. Truffle production peaked right around the turn of the century, but then underwent a decline.

harvest truffles from the transplanted trees. Within 35 years, the practice was widespread if not very dependable. In 1855, the possibility of truffle farming became official when jurors at the Paris Exposition gave a medal to M. Rousseau, a truffle merchant from Carpentras, France, in recognition of his success in cultivating truffles (although the prize was officially for the preserved truffles he brought).

Mr. Rousseau was likely motivated by the same dream that motivates truffle orchardists today: the incredible profit to be had. In year four, Rousseau found a few truffles, but by year eight, he had harvested 30 pounds off his 3½ rocky acres of trees. But the mother lode it was not: In his essay "Oak Truffles," M. de Gasparin, one of the jurors at the Paris Expo, broke down the costs associated with the truffle orchard and came to the conclusion that "if the future does not render him larger profits, and the quantity of truffles does not considerably increase, M. Rousseau will have made some curious experiments, but not attended with any remunerative return. He can only look forward in the distance to any fall of wood." After that, there was little development in truffle cultivation until the 1970s, when Jean Grente and Gérard Chevalier developed the technique for inoculating seedlings with the mycelium of truffles and subsequently patented the process with the National Institute for Agricultural Research (INRA). After the mycorrhizal association is established, the seedlings are transplanted to orchards. INRA licensed this technique to two French nurseries, Agri-Truffe and Robin Pépinières, both of which are still in business. Other nurseries are reproducing this technology and, in some cases, improving upon it. But while you can prove truffle mycelium has colonized the roots of your seedlings, you cannot be assured that it will produce fruiting bodies. As a result, truffle cultivation falls in a unique place between farming and wild crafting.

Pinning down the amount of wild versus cultivated French truffles on the market is not easy. INRA reports that 80 percent of all Périgord truffles are cultivated, and that 400,000 truffle-inoculated trees have been planted every year for the past 20 years in *truffières*—orchards or plantations—and onto state property in wild form, mainly in the traditional truffle-producing regions of France. But other sources suggest that cultivation in orchards accounts for only 35 to 40 percent of production. (Rosario Safina said that large numbers of truffles come from wild crafters who planted inoculated trees in the areas where they gather in the wild, on their own property, or on the property of other people, a sort of unofficial cultivation practice.) Truffle-inoculated trees are producing from New Zealand to Sweden, and thousands of acres of trees have been planted in Spain. The world's largest single truffle plantation, with 150,000 inoculated oaks on almost 1,500 acres of land, is in Navaleno, a village north of Madrid. Other black truffles are grown as well, including the inferior *Tuber brumale* (sometimes called the musk truffle), harvested between December and March, and *T. aestivum* (which, when harvested in the summer, has an incipient flavor, but when harvested in the fall is more robust).

In the mid-1980s, Americans imported over 68,000 pounds of fresh truffles from Europe, primarily France. The US Department of Commerce, which compiles truffle import statistics, does not designate what kind of truffle was sold, only the country of origin. But by 2008, French imports had diminished to a mere 60 pounds.

That number may be slightly increased when one considers nonreported truffle sales. It is not illegal for truffle retailers to bring a suitcase of truffles that were paid for in cash at the French truffle markets into the United States, and there is a reason why they might not want to report their importation of European truffles. Since 1999, the USA has enforced a 100 percent tariff on truffles in retaliation for the European Union's ban on hormone-riddled American beef, a campaign led by the French. China is currently a large on-the-books exporter of their much cheaper and inferior-tasting truffles. Croatia and the Ukraine exported 5,200 and 7,400 pounds of truffles, respectively, in 2008. It is possible they are reselling French truffles. (Italy and France dominate the exportation of prepared truffle products, however, which are not subject to the tariff.) The bulk of European truffle production stays in Europe. Aside from North America, the future of non-European truffles may be in the Southern Hemisphere, particularly Australia, which was set to produce 6,600 pounds in 2011 and has been harvesting since the mid-1990s.

International truffle commerce is expected to exceed $6 billion within the next 20 years, but that's really a guess. The industry is rife with secrecy and misleading information. True to the hidden nature of the truffle, those who trade in them are unwilling to share specifics, and they like to be paid in cash. Unfortunately, fraud is rampant. Unripe white or gray truffles may be darkened with substances like walnut stain. Products stating they contain truffles may indeed, but the producers take advantage of the mycologically unsavvy by packaging species with no flavor or value.

Last year, I bought a jar of Italian black truffle "carpaccio," thinly sliced and preserved in oil, for a supergood price. I had a houseguest at the time, the mycologist Bart Buyck. He looked at my jar, then me, like I was an idiot. "I think," he said in his Belgian accent, "that if I look at those mushrooms with the microscope, they will not be the kind of truffles you think they are." I tried to talk my way out of total embarrassment. "But I bought the truffles from a reputable guy," I said. "He said they were great." Bart shrugged the shrug of someone who absolutely knows better. Later I made a pasta dish with them that was so tasteless I threw out the whole bowl and dumped the remaining truffles as well.

They were likely the inexpensive Chinese truffle, *Tuber sinensis* or *T. indicum* (both names apply). They have almost no flavor but look a lot like the Périgord truffle or the mild *T. aestivum* (also known as

T. uncinatum; again, both names apply). Unsuspecting truffle product buyers are easily duped because all these truffles except the white truffle look the same: a black, scaly ball that can vary from the size of a marble to a golf ball.*

There are a variety of Chinese truffles, but the one known in China as the pig snout fungus because it was traditionally used as pig feed and not eaten by humans is a particular problem. Spores of the pig snout (and a few other problematic species) find their way into inoculants for trees and rapidly colonize the roots, potentially displacing native European species. Similarly, truffle orchardists fear that the Chinese truffle could crossbreed (or hybridize or both) with European truffles and possibly undermine the flavor of the native truffles. A kind of fungal xenophobia has taken root, with some advocates of native truffles campaigning to "send those Chinese blacks back where they came from."

It's happened in the USA as well. A huge truffle operation in Texas, the T-Bar Ranch, put in 44,000 trees that were supposedly inoculated with Périgord mycelium by the Urbani operation. Years later, the plantation produced only *Tuber brumale*, whose odor, according to the author Ian Hall, is "similar to tar." (The mycologist and trufflier Tom Michaels said 1 percent of *T. brumale* spores are all it takes for you to harvest 100 percent *T. brumale* truffles.) The entire plantation was abandoned.

There are efforts under way in the United States, and laws are already in effect in Europe, that seek to penalize those who sell Chinese truffles and truffle products as other species, whether intentionally or not. Australia has banned the importation of Chinese truffles altogether. Many truffles look so similar that they have to be examined under a microscope to verify their species, based on spore morphology. Still, exact identification can be tricky, so the Europeans have created a molecular

---

*Chocolate truffles, a French confection invented in 1895, are called truffles because they are usually about the same size, shape, and color of the Périgord truffle.

test that can identify the truffle via DNA in about 48 hours—which I think is proof of how seriously the Europeans take their truffles. After all, next-day paternity tests can cost you about $1,000.

I was surprised to learn that Périgord truffles have been cultivated in the States for over 20 years, although the volume has been too small to impact prices or access; and I was very curious to see what a truffle orchard looked like, and what kind of person would invest their time and fortune on this highly speculative agricultural dream. It does sound glamorous to own a truffle orchard, like having a vineyard or growing lavender, but the most basic understanding of mycorrhizal biology is enough to know that growing truffles is a very hard thing to do. A few people have had success, and lots of growers are hoping they'll get a harvest eventually, but it's really a tricky proposition.

There are about 300 "serious" truffle orchards in the United States, according to James Trappe, only a few of which are headed up by trained mycologists. But growing truffles is about more than mycology. "It's a well-established art and science combining mycology and horticulture, and after planting, you should know entomology, nematology, soil science, and prayer," said the mycologist Mark Miller.

Truffles from southern Europe can be grown in North America in the southern parts of the Midwest, northern parts of the Southeast, parts of the Mid-Atlantic states, and a long strip along the West Coast in California, Oregon, and Washington. Other areas may be suitable, including parts of Texas, Oklahoma, Idaho, and southwest British Columbia. The folks who are starting orchards are, according to the mycologist Charles Lefevre of New World Truffieres, the same kind of people who pioneered the wine industry in the USA: professionals looking for a lifestyle change.

American truffles are cultivated in the same way as European truffles. In fact, the American truffle industry started with a Frenchman,

François Picart, whose Agri-Truffle was a subsidiary of the French company Agri-Truffe (which licensed the truffle cultivation technology from INRA). During the 1970s and '80s, Picart sold Périgord-inoculated hazelnut seedlings from a nursery in Santa Rosa, California.*

The pioneering American truffle orchardists bought their hazelnut seedlings from Picart. William Griner, Don Reading, and Bruce Hatch, partners in an orchard in Mendocino, California, and Franklin Garland in Hillsborough, North Carolina, all planted orchards within the first few years of the 1980s. Griner and his partners found their first truffles in 1991, 9½ years after they planted the orchard, and continued to harvest until Griner's death from pneumonia in 2008. Franklin Garland's first truffles appeared in 1992, and the orchard produced until 2002, when his hazelnut trees were decimated by eastern filbert blight (filberts and hazelnuts, same thing). Griner was reportedly very secretive about his orchard, and much of his knowledge died with him. Garland, on the other hand, has become active in promoting truffle farming in his state as well as in his own role as the father of North Carolina truffle farming.

Franklin and his wife, Betty, operate Garland Nursery, which sells by-order Périgord-inoculated hazelnut and oak seedlings in the thick woods of North Carolina. In 1980, inspired by a *Wall Street Journal* article about Picart and the potential profits to be had from truffle farming, Garland planted 500 Agri-Truffle hazelnut seedlings and 250 oaks (although the oaks didn't survive—Garland says they were ill suited to North Carolina's climate). Once the orchard got going, Garland says his trees produced about 50 pounds of Périgord truffles a year for a decade. When I made my appointment to visit the nursery, Betty

---

*Quite the enterprising Frenchman, he also farmed snails and at one point owned a truffle orchard in Dripping Springs, Texas—the home of record-setting mold-infestation litigation. His American businesses have been dissolved. He is also the author of *Truffle, The Black Diamond*, an 89-page trade paperback that costs at least $245 on Amazon.com, and a paperback called *Escargots from Your Garden to Your Table.*

Garland was at her hairdresser's, and through the sound wall of hair dryers she warned me their place wasn't so easy to find. Indeed, my rented car's GPS had me turning down dirt roads and zigzagging through housing developments. When it finally informed me I had reached my destination, there was no sign, and the driveway was a gravel road lined with downed timber and underbrush, the kind of road that, after you've driven almost a mile, you start to wonder whether you might be about to get into trouble. But when I arrived, Franklin Garland, a lean, weathered man in overalls, assured me that the incessant honking of my car security system that I was desperately trying to turn off wasn't annoying at all, and that I was indeed where I wanted to be: a property cut out of the woods, isolated from prying eyes, with the sound of Interstate 40 roaring in the background and large greenhouses plunked near the ranch-style house. As we toured the greenhouses and their occupants (hundreds of skinny hazelnut tree seedlings), and later during a lunch where Franklin served up chopped frozen Périgord truffles in an omelet, he explained that his learning curve, and that of all truffle growers' for that matter, is in the details. "There was a lot of trial and error," he said, "but I've learned a lot in 30 years."

During what he likes to call the first generation of American truffle farmers, "plenty of people just stuck the trees in the earth and expected truffles in 8 to 12 years." But truffles are particular. They prefer soils with a high pH—7.9 to 8.1, about the same pH as an egg—and need lots of water. They need the soil to be a certain temperature at a certain point in their growth, which means access to the right amount of sun. A root colonized with the mycelium, which in the case of the Périgord truffle is composed of superminiscule hyphal threads that even at full maturity are no longer than ½ inch, must meet and engage with other colonized roots in order to merge in a kind of tangle that leads to the formation of a nascent truffle.

The specifics are still unknown, but once the truffle is established, it grows until it reaches, well, a point of maturity, then detaches from the mycelium. "Then it just sits there underground, going through its metabolic changes," said James Trappe. It develops its spores as a free entity. And of course, if you have truffles, once ripe, they have to be found. Which means dogs have to be trained to sniff them out. The first generation truffle orchardists—around a dozen people from North Carolina, California, and Oregon—figured out a lot, and some have truffles to show for their efforts.

One of the great success stories of cultivated American Périgords is Tennessee Truffles. In the 2006–07 season, Tom Michaels harvested his first Périgords from a 6-year-old hazelnut orchard he'd planted behind his house in Chuckey, Tennessee. ("I can see Davey Crockett's homestead with my x-ray vision, just beyond a hill," he said in a phone conversation.)

"When I went to visit him," sighed Jack Ponticelli, a truffle orchardist from North Carolina, "his fridge was stuffed with truffles. His freezer was stuffed with truffles. The whole house smelled like a gigantic truffle." Tennessee Truffles claims to be the first truffle orchard to produce commercial quantities of truffles—enough "to pay Uncle Sam." The amount of truffles Michaels's 2,500 trees produce varies. In the 2008–09 season, he picked over 200 pounds. "Truffle growing makes you humble," he said. "We really only control the process during the first year in the nursery. Otherwise, Mother Nature calls the shots." Michaels doesn't describe himself as successful because of his techniques but because he is simply a few years ahead of the curve.

There are at least four suppliers of oak and hazelnut seedlings inoculated with Périgord truffle mycelium, but the dominant suppliers are Garland Truffles and New World Truffieres. In 1998, Garland licensed the method for producing inoculated hazelnut seedlings from INRA in France (and eventually produced his own inoculants from truffles he grew on his farm), and he began selling the seedlings. In the beginning, he sold to anyone who wanted them—growers Garland refers to as the second generation—but there was a 50 percent rate of failure due, he said, to maintenance issues, divorce, and so on. In 2004, Garland said, he became more selective about his customers—a group he calls the third generation of truffle growers: entrepreneurial types and those with postretirement ambitions—and took an active interest in their orchards, helping them with planting and irrigation advice and, in some cases, going into business with them. He said he stopped taking small orders for trees, as he believes it takes four trees to support a single truffle. (He recommends about 500 trees per acre—in his opinion, lower density plantings take a longer time to produce.) He also grew hazelnut seedlings with an immunity to eastern filbert blight, which kills trees in 5 to 12 years, just about the time they should start producing truffles. Garland and Betty, a rather formidable woman with tiger-striped hair and a husky Carolina accent, conduct educational presentations for the serious and curious alike, replete with a truffle omelet and champagne, but they don't share his technology, "although the only people who are capable of industrial espionage in this business are academics." Yet Garland is clearly proud of what he describes as the small improvements he continues to make on his truffle cultures.

New World Truffieres in Oregon's Willamette Valley near Eugene was founded by Charles Lefevre in 2000 while he was still a graduate student at Oregon State University pursuing his PhD in mycology. New World Truffieres produces hazelnut and two kinds of oak seedlings inoculated with a variety of their own Périgord truffle spawn strains "in order to maximize strain diversity in the hope that one set of strains might be more adaptable to other soils," he told me. New World tests all their seedlings for colonized truffle mycelium on the rootstock, and they've sold about 100,000 bareroot trees, with their sales trending up. Currently, there are trees from Lefevre's seedlings growing in California, Idaho,

North Carolina, Tennessee, Virginia, Oregon, and Washington, but he couldn't say how many orchards, because "that would depend on what you count as an orchard—I have lots of customers with a couple of trees."

On the Garland Truffles Web site there is a page called "the Bottom Line." According to it, 4 to 12 years after planting, an orchard on 1 acre with 500 trees will produce 50 pounds of truffles over a 3-month period annually for about 20 years. At a minimum wholesale price of $300 per pound, that is $15,000 per acre per year. But it's not those kind of minimum projections that have seduced growers like Jack Ponticelli to go into partnership with Garland. It's the more generous projections of up to 200 pounds of truffles annually per acre, at $800 per pound—the 2009 wholesale price for Périgords set by the French. The problem, however, is in the waiting, and how long a farmer must wait for truffles is a matter of some dispute in the truffle community.

Jack Ponticelli has the easygoing, free-spirited quality of other balloonists I've met (oddly, I know several). He doesn't bother too much with the science. He sees himself more as a man of the land. His Black Diamond Farm has 15,000 trees of combined hazelnut and oak planted on 30 acres. The 5-year-old orchard nearest the family home looks bushy and untreelike to me, but Jack showed me where the mycelium creates the brûlé, a circle of pale, sandy soil around the base of most of the older trees, where no grass is growing. This impoverished soil has been "burnt," nutritionally and minerally depleted by the truffle mycelium. It is the telltale sign of the fungus's presence. "We're waiting," he said and gazed at the trees. "Hope it happens soon, because the balloon business is bust."

It took 6 years for Jane and Rick Morgan Smith of Keep Your Fork Farm (the smallest farm on the tax records in Stokes County, North Carolina) to harvest their first Périgord truffles: 5 pounds in 2006. Like most other orchardists, Jane Smith believes that in the near future many orchards are going to come online. For the Smiths, who are 60 and 65, respectively, the orchard—600 Garland-inoculated trees on 2½ acres—is a postretirement business. Jane thought other farmers would be interested in the orchard, especially considering the hit small tobacco farmers have endured since the tobacco industry meltdown. "We thought we would have lots of inquiries from local farmers, but that has not been the case. They are sitting back and watching."

But both private and public institutions are doing more than just watching. The North Carolina Tobacco Trust Fund Commission is one of three groups that make grants to persons who suffered as a result of the federal government's settlement with Big Tobacco in 1998, including former tobacco growers. They authorized a $235,000 grant in 2003 to supply 50 farms growing 1 to 20 acres of tobacco with the stock, supplies, and expertise (from Garland) to each plant 200 inoculated truffle trees, part of a program to test the feasibility of new crops to replace tobacco (a medicinal herbs grant was issued as well). Another truffle orchard, a collaborative research project between North Carolina State University and the North Carolina Department of Agriculture and Commerce, is under way. These projects hope to add to the body of knowledge about cultivating truffles.

Each truffle orchardist has tweaked the basic recipe for growing truffles in their own way, and to a man (and woman) the growers I met were steadfast in the conviction that their small manipulations of spacing, liming (to increase the pH of the soil), soil aeration, pruning, thinning, weed control, and irrigation will yield the mother lode. Someday. Hopefully soon.*

"Look, the industry is in its pubescence," said Betty Garland. "It's becoming professional and has dropped from extremely high risk to, well, just risk." The shares of other truffle farms that Franklin Garland owns, as

---

*One of the more famous orchardists is Prince Philip, the Duke of Edinburgh (the Queen of England's husband). He planted 300 inoculated hazelnut and oak seedlings in the Royal Fruit Farm at Sandringham in 2006. He was reportedly disappointed there were no truffles as of 2009. An estate source told the *Daily Mail* that year, "He is now beginning to realize why truffles are so bloody expensive." There were no truffles in 2010, either.

well as his own orchard, amount to his retirement scheme. Garland is counting on a lot of truffles coming in around 2011–12, and he estimates that he can move between 500 and 1,000 pounds of truffles a week. Indeed, he adds, "even the French will buy from the Americans if we have truffles to sell. As we start producing more in this country, demand will increase." Tom Michaels agrees. "Even if every tree in the USA produces, we still won't meet the demand."

Today, there are numerous businesses associated with the American truffle industry: nurseries, mycorrhizal assessment operations (that check the roots of trees for the presence of the microscopic fungi), and truffle dog trainers. One needs a pig or a dog to find truffles. (Although in France, one can look for the truffle fly, the *Suilla gigantean*, which lay their eggs in the dirt above the truffles so that the hatched larvae may find and eat them. Truffle hunters sweep the ground around a prospective tree, which disturbs the insects. Their flight patterns are distinctively heavy and lethargic.)

Most of the truffle orchardists I met are dog lovers who admitted to dreams of tromping the orchards with their pets as much as they do the potential payola. But since truffles are not game for dogs like they are for pigs, they must be trained. The Oregon Truffle Festival provides a truffle dog-training seminar for those who prefer to train their own animals. The balloonist Jack Ponticelli told me he trained his dog by hiding truffle-oil-saturated rags—but wished he'd trained for multiple targets. "He'd find one truffle and then would be ready to go home and take a nap." He got help from Lisa Kennel of Gleaneagle Farm, a retired canine law enforcement officer for US Customs and the Department of Homeland Security. "The dogs need to have a continuous search pattern," she said from her farm in Virginia. "I can scent associate any dog. A Pekinese? Sure, I can do it. But the dog needs a search-and-hunt drive." Lisa is training more and more dogs as orchardists are expecting to see their truffle orchards come on.

According to Oregon's Trifecta Training Center, which specializes in truffle-hunting training, any species can be trained to hunt truffles, although there is a traditional Italian truffle-hunting breed, the Lagotto Romagnolo, or the Romagna water dog. The Lagotto is an ancient water retriever breed that has been around since the 16th century in the Comacchio valleys and the Ravenna lagoons, east of Bologna on the Adriatic Sea, and then spread, after the 19th century, west and north into the plains and hills of Emiglia-Romagna. My cousin Mario had a Lagotto (he said the females were better diggers), and Tom Michaels uses this kind of dog to harvest his truffles as well.*

There are currently two established truffle societies in the United States: the North American Truffling Society (NATS), which is based in Oregon and headed by Charles Lefevre, and the North American Truffle Growers Association (NATGA), which was founded by the Garlands. While the interests of both groups are the same—the health and well-being of the American truffle industry—the original purpose of NATS was to deal with wild-crafting issues, like indiscriminant raking of soil beneath truffle-producing trees, which leads to the unearthing of immature truffles. NATGA is more of a trade organization. It is hoping to ban the Chinese truffle, which Franklin Garland believes undermines the market potential with its disappointing flavor.

The nascent American truffle industry is somewhat split between orchardists who depend on farmers' intuitive and observational clues and orchardists who depend on the science of mycology to unravel the mysteries of growing truffles. Either way, a good measure of optimism seems to be a necessary quality in this business. Indeed, hopefulness has many

---

*Truffle Hunting Dogs, a kennel located in Los Angeles and North Carolina, prefers German shepherds because of their "reliability as working companion." These dogs, one of which will set you back about $12,500, are trained for hunting truffles using the same techniques used to train drug-, bomb-, and cadaver-detection dogs. For an additional $400 per mushroom species, they'll train the dog to hunt morels, porcini, and chanterelles, too.

truffle farmers looking to expand their orchards, and in their search for investors, there is plenty of overstating the financial potential of an orchard, from the projected value of truffles to the projected yield per acre. One truffle orchard in North Carolina, which I didn't visit, was cited by numerous truffle growers as circulating pictures of truffles harvested from the orchard that had not actually been grown there. (Not that this is such a surprising agricultural ploy: The farm stands in the glammy Hamptons have a tremendous you-pick pumpkin business in October, but a reporter turned up evidence that at least one farm was purchasing pumpkins elsewhere and then "planting" them in the field.)

All truffle orchardists are stymied by the same problems—they need to create a complete ecosystem in order to succeed, and everyone I spoke to was proprietary about their system. Indeed, no one would say anything exactly, not how much irrigation water they used, or how they limed their soil, since it has not yet been revealed whose tweaks will produce the most predictable crop. When it turns out the choices one farmer made were the right ones, then I think it is pretty unlikely he will be broadcasting those particulars anytime soon, if indeed any of those particulars actually matter. "All of this proprietary behavior is an impediment to the growth of industry," said Lefevre. "We're facing challenges we don't even understand."

"You just have to keep the faith," said Jack Ponticelli.

For those to whom the truffle fantasy has taken hold but the reality is impractical, one can always adopt a truffle-inoculated oak from the Truffle Tree Ltd, a UK truffle business operating in southwest France. For $299 and an annual fee of $69, any truffles found underneath "your" tree are yours.

Chapter 7

ALL ABOUT BUTTONS

T he heart and soul of the American button mushroom industry is Chester County, Pennsylvania, located in the southeast corner of the state, about 30 miles west of Philadelphia. Horse farms proliferate in the bucolic, rich farmland. William Penn, who was granted the land by Charles II of England in 1680, originally held the parcel that comprises the Township of Kennett Square, named for the Kennett River in England and because the township is a mile square. Penn was the founder of the Province of Pennsylvania—hence the name—and, as its "proprietor," set up a constitution that inspired the writers of the United States Constitution. Like Penn, most of the early settlers of Kennett Square were Quakers who worshipped at the Old Kennett Meetinghouse, a 1710 stuccoed fieldstone building, simple to the point of austerity and surrounded by mature trees.

Today, Kennett Square is a lovely little town with narrow three-story buildings that kiss one another along State Street. It has something of the urban density of an English village, but with a distinctly Pennsylvanian aesthetic. Stone facades and early American decor— what antiques dealers call "American Fancy"—prevail. It is a dressy town: There is a ladies' day spa and a snazzy gourmet shop with $8 bottles of ranch dressing. Kennett Square has its own symphony (in fact, Kennett is the smallest town in America with that distinction) and a Brandywine Valley wine tasting room (Pennsylvania ranks seventh in the nation for production of wine). And certainly aspects of its heritage linger: I noticed an antique bookshop had a flier in the window that said "Visit Quaker Meetings." But what drew me in was a mushroom-themed shop called the Mushroom Cap that sells everything the mushroom lover and her codependents might desire: dried spicy mushroom snacks called Snack N Shrooms, truffle oils, mushroom-themed playing cards, fly agaric refrigerator magnets, mushroom dolls, identification guides and cookbooks, and T-shirts that say "shiitake happens." It feels like one of those stores that sell Christmas ornaments all year-round. In 2009, Kathi Lafferty, the store's owner, organized the Kennett Square 24th Annual Mushroom Festival.

"It was probably the best attended festival we've had, about 80,000 people," said Lafferty. "Although the mushroom bobbing didn't happen."

I went to Kennett Square to attend the mushroom festival because it is *the* event celebrating the white button mushroom. Most festivals are about wild mushrooms: finding them, identifying them, and cooking them. This festival is about an industry. It's about jobs, marketing, and regional pride, and Kennett Square, according to *The Mushroom Festival and Visitors Guide,* is the "mushroom capital of the world." The USA is the world's second largest producer of mushrooms, following China, and Chester County is its largest mushroom-producing region. The total volume of mushroom sales in the US in 2008–09 was 817 million pounds, with the white button accounting for 802 million pounds. Almost two-thirds of all white button mushrooms are produced in Chester County, within 50 miles of Kennett Square, where the first mushroom farm was started.

But Pennsylvania's small mushroom farms are in decline, particularly in Chester County, and fewer farmers are producing more mushrooms. "We're losing farms every 5 years or so," said Chris Alonzo of Pietro Industries, which grows 2 percent of all US mushrooms. "We had 400 farms about 50 years ago. Now there are only 70." And those 70 farms constitute about 70 percent of the total number of mushroom farms in the USA, all of which are family owned and operated.

The Swayne family is among the oldest in the area. The founding member, Francis Swayne (1660–1721), was an English Quaker who immigrated to Pennsylvania in 1710 with his family and a 6-foot-tall grandfather clock. He purchased 425 acres of rolling hills in Chester County, land originally owned by William Penn. For almost 2 centuries, Swaynes farmed the land. The seventh-generation Swayne, William (1851–1950), was a "florist under glass" according to the language of the time, growing carnations and roses in a greenhouse (a specialized agriculture that flourished in Kennett Square in the latter part of the 19th century). William Swayne is generally credited as the father of US mushroom growing, although he may be more of a figurehead for an industry that has had numerous fathers (and mothers). For example, in 1891 William Falconer, a mushroom grower from Dosoris, New York, compiled the (then) current thinking about growing mushrooms in *Mushrooms: How to Grow Them; A Practical Treatise on Mushroom Culture for Profit and Pleasure*. In it, Falconer recommended florists look into mushroom growing, as the conditions in greenhouses were ideal, and he cited the first mushroom house—a dugout cellar in 1881. John Bancroft Swayne III told me it was actually William's son J. Bancroft Swayne (the first) who began growing mushrooms in the space under his father's elevated carnation beds in the late 1800s or early 1900s, using mushroom mycelium he bought from England. To this day, mushrooms fall under the USDA's nursery-greenhouse-floriculture-sod category.

⚜

The Mushroom Festival celebrates Kennett Square's historic role and traditional dominance of the mushroom industry. The festival ran along State Street, with some activities on side roads, like a Ferris wheel, a cooking demonstration tent, the EMS team, and the guys who sat around in folding lawn chairs teasing each other and who signed you up for the farm tour. The festival also had an educational tent. That's where I met Mark Miller of Lambert Spawn over his stacks of petri dishes of *Agaricus bisporus* and Steve Regester of Regester Mushrooms over the compost bins.

Mark Miller looked at me over the rim of his glasses. "Lambert produces 45 percent of all spawn in the USA, Canada, and South America," he said. "And I've possibly produced more spawn than anyone in the world."

Miller, bantamweight, smart, and feisty, is a spawn maker. Every day he drives through the verdant Pennsylvania countryside, past the stone houses decorated with iron Union stars, the tidy fields, and schmoozily smooth roads, to his lab at Lambert Spawn where he makes commercial spawn, a fungal starter composed of living mycelium from which the common white button mushroom is grown. Lambert Spawn was originally the American Spawn Co., founded in 1902 by a Belgian mycologist, Louis Lambert, in Minneapolis. It is the oldest spawn-making company in the US.

Mark explained to me, and to a couple of freckled, restless children whose parents had nudged them into the festival's education tent, that there are two distinct aspects to mushroom farming: spawn making and mushroom growing. Most growers are not spawn makers as well, because spawn making requires controlled laboratory conditions, starting with the selection of the mushroom strain. When you see those ubiquitous plastic cartons full of white button mushrooms in the grocery store, what you are looking at are clones of one mushroom; one perfect, creamy, pathogen-resistant strain that has been selected for those characteristics, because it meets a kind of marketplace fantasy, like a perfect red apple or an ideally formed rose. What Miller does is ensure that's the strain the mushroom farmer gets when he orders his spawn from Lambert.

Mark's display in the education tent consisted of dozens of stacked petri dishes, their lids secured with clear tape and scrawled with numbers in indelible pen: #901, #950, #805. Inside each was a delicate web of mycelium, its radial growth starting from a single grain of rye and extending to the perimeters of the container. The growth pattern of the captured mycelium had a kind of natural geometry that I found beautiful and rather uncanny, like a motile spiderweb. Many of the dishes had small cores removed. From one of those cores, no bigger than a watch battery and weighing about as much as a housefly, Miller will inoculate 1 gallon of rye or millet grain—called the master bottle. It takes up to 3 weeks for the fungus to colonize the entire master spawn bottle, and each week he makes about 500 such bottles, which are refrigerated and remain genetically stable for up to 6 months. One master bottle is enough to inoculate 5,000 to 7,000 pounds of millet or rye, or a synthetic substrate like vermiculite amped with nutrients. And from that 5,000 to 7,000 pounds of spawn,

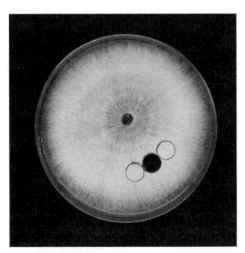

Petri dish colonized with mycelium

about 280,000 pounds of mushrooms can be grown. "That's what makes spawn work," explained Miller. "You are exponentially increasing the spawn."

Here's what happens: When a hyphal thread is broken, the broken end kicks into rapid regeneration and grows in two directions: not only from the lead end of the broken thread, but from the rear end as well. No surprise, then, that the word *spawn* is derived from the Old French verb, *espandre*, to expand. "Seriously," said Miller, "one petri dish could produce and often will produce about 1 million pounds of mushrooms."

Miller makes spawn in a sterile lab, controlling every aspect of the process. But the early days of spawn making were a much messier affair. Spawn making began in France sometime between 1550 and 1707. Some historians say French farmers discovered mushrooms growing in their spent compost from hot beds used to grow melons. Others have reported the *Agaricus bisporus*, commonly called the white button mushroom, champignon, or, as the mycologist Tom Volk calls it, "the pizza mushroom," was first cultivated in caves and quarries outside Paris. Still other histories suggest that mushroom cultivation was the innovation of agronomists employed by the court of Louis XIV (1638–1715).*

Regardless of the seminal scenario, through the 1800s mushroom growers gathered virgin spawn in the wild. They watched for flushes of *A. bisporus* in nature, usually on manure, then dug up the associated mycelium—not the mushrooms—and transplanted it into beds of composted manure. The fact that the button mushroom is partial to manure may be the reason why some people think mushrooms are dirty. They're not. There is no poop in a mushroom because the fungus breaks down the organic matter into its molecular parts, and unless you pick it off a pile of manure, the mushroom is clean. Button mushrooms like dung because it generates heat and retains moisture as it decomposes.

Richard Kerrigan, who works for Sylvan Inc., another major spawn operation, once wrote that the most reliable places to find spawn in the 1800s were in the mill tracks that surrounded horse-powered grinding

---

*A parallel arc of cultivation breakthroughs existed at about the same time in Eastern Europe, and the Chinese have cultivated mushrooms for centuries. The writer W. P. K. Findlay stated that ancient Greeks and Romans grew the poplar fungus by placing small pieces of poplar wood on land that had been covered with manure that was inoculated naturally.

stone mills. As the horses trudged along its circular track, they left behind "a massive accumulation of their rich, fragrant calling cards." Hence the name of the first spawn to be advertised in England: "mill-track spawn."

But success was spotty. The substrate material—be it earth or animal waste—is loaded with pathogens from the natural environment. In every ounce of soil, for example, you'll find several million hungry parasites including live bacteria, protozoa, fungi, algae, nematodes (microscopic worms), and other tiny organisms, all of which are competing in the microbial arena. Wild-gathered spawn easily succumbed to these pathogens (we're talking 25 to 50 billion bacteria per gram of wet spawn) during the stress of travel and transplantation.

In time, more reliable forms of spawn substrate were developed, like the rather colorfully named French flake and the English brick spawn. French flake (also known as flake spawn, French spawn, or Parisian spawn) was dried mycelium-colonized compost that was pulled apart and flaked, and English brick (also known as brick spawn or English spawn) was composed of compressed bricks of compost and horse or cow manure colonized by mycelium. The term *spawn,* then, came to refer not just to the mycelium but also to the substrate upon which the mycelium had been colonized. Dried brick spawn—essentially, preserved spawn—was less fragile than the fresh stuff and easier to transport. By the late 1800s, more than 147 metric tons of brick and flake spawn were being exported from France and England to the United States annually. Still, the imported spawn often died en route.

There are native strains of *A. bisporus* in North America, but due to the importation of brick spawn, by the early 1900s the European fungus had found its way into American manure piles in the wild via discarded compost. American spawn makers gathered the mushrooms in the wild to make their own spawn; fungi that likely had their origins in Europe. You won't find feral *A. bisporus* anymore, although there are other wild

American species of *Agaricus*, like the pink-gilled, almond-scented *A. subrufescens,* for example, which tastes pretty fabulous.

Because the failure rate of brick spawn was high but the market was promising, the USDA was motivated to produce pure culture brick spawn for the home market in association with the American scientist Benjamin Duggar (1872–1956). Spawn is known as pure culture when it is free of any microbial hitchhikers, including other fungi, and the only way to ensure that is to grow the mycelium under laboratory conditions from a piece of mushroom tissue or a germinated spore. In 1905, Duggar produced healthy *A. bisporus* mycelium on a sterilized medium from a bit of mushroom tissue. This was a huge advantage to growers, because for the first time they could know exactly what species they were growing (brick spawn, which is made from collected mycelium, could easily include any number of other fungal species).

Benjamin Duggar's pure spawn cultures opened the door to large-scale commercial farming. By 1914, 4 to 5 million pounds of mushrooms were grown in the US, mostly in Kennett Square. (By 1917, however, spawn makers had forgone Duggar's tissue-culture technique and instead were starting spawn from germinated spore.)

Different species in the *Agaricus* family have different colorations, and different strains of those species also show variation, based in part on environmental conditions. The first pure white mushroom, known as the 'Snow White' or 'Alaska', may have been discovered growing spontaneously in a bed of cream-colored *A. bisporus* in Chester County, Pennsylvania, in 1926, or the USDA Bureau of Plant Industry may have cultured the white button 20 years earlier. Either way, the commercial white mushroom industry today is a monoculture.

Virtually all white button mushrooms today originate from the same single spore, the U1 hybrid, discovered by a Dutch scientist, Gerda Fritsche, in 1980. "It was a fluke that she found it," said Miller. "That spore has never been found again. But its discovery was not a statistical anomaly. I mean, that's how nature functions. Every baby is different." This superspore was selected and continues to be preferred because it produces a high yield of disease-resistant mushrooms with good flavor.

Cultured spawn, whether produced by tissue culture or germinated spore, cannot be considered pure unless the substrate (the millet or whatever the mycelium is grown on) is sterilized, too. Likewise, planting new spawn in old, microbe-riddled compost beds puts it in danger of disease. In the early 1930s, the four major spawn-making companies in business at the time—Lambert, Swayne, Mushroom Supply, and the Mushroom Grower's Cooperative Association—began producing spawn on a substrate of sterilized grain that could be easily raked into the compost beds on the farm.

Starting with the initial jar of spawn growing on millet grains that comes out of Miller's lab, every pound of millet that is inoculated, bagged, and allowed to become thoroughly colonized has to be sterile. A bag of spawn can be ruined if a problematic mold or bacterium finds its way in (in fact, 2 percent loss is common), so any innovation that can reduce the spawn's exposure to contamination is financially important. Sterilization, usually in an autoclave, is key to a business like Lambert staying in business. After that, the plastic bags of sterilized, cooled, inoculated grain are transferred to temperature-controlled growing rooms, breezy cool spaces where the tagged bags of mycelium develop like fertilized eggs, silent but busy. Once the bag is thoroughly colonized into a solid futonlike mass, it is sold on a preorder basis to mushroom farmers all over the country (and the Americas and Europe, too).

I continued to ask Miller questions and he was very nice about it, although he kept glancing nervously at the small crowd of people who had piled up behind me. The way the education tent was set up, you were supposed to just look at the displays and keep moving. Finally, someone behind me interrupted and, holding up a petri dish, asked, "What's this?" I nodded my thanks and good-byes to Mr. Miller, and as I moved on I heard him start the whole story over again.

After Miller's table came Steve Regester's. Regester looks like a tough from a comic strip: He's a big burly guy with biceps and a crew cut, but he was good natured and easygoing about explaining to the curious how *A. bisporus* mushrooms grow. There are good reasons why Kennett was attractive to the early mushroom growers, he explained: the proximity of spawn manufacturers; the region's proximity to markets like Philadelphia, Washington, DC, and New York City via rail; and the plethora of manure produced by neighboring farms. Additionally, Pennsylvania State University established a mushroom research center in 1925 that is still a source of research, development, and distribution of new technology in the mushroom industry.

The horse farms and fields of Chester County are the source of straw-bed manure, and fresh-cut dried hay that is the medium upon which the mushrooms are grown. The manure and hay blends are combined with nitrogen supplements, like chicken manure, and thoroughly mixed with water and gypsum to initiate a controlled fermentation process. Composting is done outdoors or under roofs on concrete pads, collectively called wharfs. After 2 to 3 weeks, the compost is moved to wooden beds in the mushroom houses to complete the composting and kill off all potential pathogens. "We pasteurize the compost in 6 days using a natural cook-out method," said Regester, versus heating the entire mushroom house to temperature—an expensive proposition (indeed, heating and air-conditioning can cost up to $10,000 per mushroom crop per standard-size mushroom house).

Decaying organic matter is packed with microbes of all sorts, and as the microbes feed on the compost, they grow, generating heat. As long as food and water are available, the microbes will continue to multiply, eating up the materials that create the ammonia smell that comes off compost and killing off insect larvae. Eventually the compost reaches

pasteurization, or 140-plus degrees Fahrenheit for a sustained 4 hours.*
At the end of fermentation, these heat-tolerant bacteria convert the compost into a medium that, once it cools down to about 90 degrees, is perfect for growing *A. bisporus.*

The way the festival was set up, you educated yourself with the help of Mark Miller and Steve Regester, and then you took a farm tour. I was signed up by a young woman in New York Yankee regalia: her sweat suit, cap, even her gold jewelry carried the baseball team's insignia. I was half expecting one of the gentle people, the Society of Friends, but this gal had a distinctly Bronx vibe. "Mushrooms," she announced as our bus lurched into traffic, "is a family-oriented business." She turned out to be of Italian descent.

This is less surprising when one realizes the labor-intensive mushroom industry has relied on the immigrant Italian laborers who came to work in the flower business, the quarries around Avondale, and the DuPont gunpowder mills on the Brandywine over a century ago. Today, Italian families run about 90 percent of all mushroom farms in Kennett, many in the second and third generation of operation. The first Italian mushroom farmer in Kennett Township was Bernard Cordivano. He had immigrated to the US to work in a stone-cutting mill in Toughkenamon, but he learned the mushroom trade from J. Bancroft Swayne, son of William. J. Bancroft built the first modern mushroom house in the country: a specialized building where temperature, humidity, and ventilation could be controlled, and he expanded the business into canning and spawn making. He built Bancroft Manor in 1909, a 4,200-square-foot Queen Anne–style house across the street from his father's greenhouses and florist shop, his home for 16 years. (The manor

---

*The spontaneous combustion of haystacks—a phenomenon noted by farmers and naturalists since at least Pliny, who wrote about it in 60 BC—is similar. Microbial activity, in combination with moisture, heats the hay to autoignition temperatures. Likewise, hay and straw piles, waiting to be composted, have attracted arsonists in Kennett. They burn for weeks.

has been a bed-and-breakfast since 2000, and the area has been designated a national historic district. I had planned to stay at the manor during the festival, but the owner, who is not a Swayne, developed a sinus infection and had to cancel my reservation. I mollified myself by hanging out on the empty front porch of the house for a half hour or so, peeking through the windows and imagining what it looked like at Christmas, as the B&B is a two-time first place winner in the Victorian category of the town's Christmas decorating contest.) J. Bancroft started a family, producing, among other children, another J. Bancroft. His father, William Swayne, continued to grow carnations until he sold the business in 1940 to Roland Barber, whose descendants still run the florist shop today. William lived to be almost 99, outliving an insurance policy that had been in force for 51 years. He credited his long life and good health to fishing.

The Swayne family stayed in mushrooming for about 2 centuries. There was a period when Proctor & Gamble owned the companies, but they were bought back by J. Bancroft III. For 20 years he ran his family spawn company, but as neither of JB's children were interested in the family business, he sold it to Sylvan in 2001. "And that's the end of the era," he told me over the phone. I asked if he knew anything about his ancestor Francis's grandfather clock.

"I'm looking at it right now," he said. "And it's still running."

The basic techniques of mushroom farming today are largely the same as they were at the turn of the 20th century. Our bus pulled up to the doubles—the classic Pennsylvania mushroom house built into the side of a hill like a root cellar—at Pietro Industries.* There was some confusion as to who would give the tour, and finally a young man with a

---

*There are all kinds of mushroom houses: from 300-feet-belowground limestone mining tunnels in southwestern Pennsylvania (which are now all closed) to former nuclear missile silos in Hungary to abandoned rail tunnels in Australia.

predilection for the word *stuff*, as in "This is where we grow the mushrooms and stuff," took on our group. We had to put on blue bouffant
hairnets, "Penn State Blue" pointed out one young woman, and another
woman giggled at the sight of her husband in his net. A teenage boy
resisted, wondering why his cap, brim turned to the side, wasn't adequate, and a new mom adjusted one on the bald head of her baby, asleep
and slumped in a Snugli like a sack of big soft tomatoes.

We lingered in the parking lot as our guide explained how the
mushroom spawn is mixed or "broadcast" into compost beds and stuff;
how the mycelium grows for 2 weeks and then a ¼-inch casing layer is
added; how the casing is a soft, wet peat moss mixed with limestone
and water. And then how the baby mushrooms push through the peat
moss, growing until they reach harvest size. (No one knows exactly
what initiates the pinning stage, said Mark Miller when I asked him
later. "But it's likely a combination of bacteria in the casing combined
with changes in gases and temperature.") Pietro Industries was
founded in 1938. They grow 18 million pounds of white button mushrooms a year and have 150 employees. We begged for more statistics
from our reluctant and self-conscious guide, but he preferred to shep-
herd us into the mushroom houses to see for ourselves what I suppose
was obvious to him.

The doubles looked like horse stables, clean in a functional agricultural way. The standard for doubles in Pennsylvania is 60 feet long, with
8,000 square feet of growing space. There was a central hall, where various other tour groups collided, separated, and then reorganized. Along
the hall, wide doors opened into the mushroom rooms. These were
dimly lit spaces, cool and humid as a fall night, with four shelves stacked
six beds high, like bunk beds in a navy ship, each containing rich compost studded with tiny mushrooms as small as baby aspirin. "The mushrooms. When they are young and stuff," said our guide. The casing layer

was very damp and black, with white mushrooms scattered across the dark surface like stars. In the next room, we saw mushrooms the size of grapes, clustered now in cauliflower-like bouquets of fluorescence, and in another room, Latin American men were cutting mushrooms and gently placing them in plastic boxes. The flush of grown mushrooms can last from 3 to 5 days, followed by another flush a few days later. A mushroom farm, according to Peter Gray of Phillips Mushroom Farms, has to produce 8 pounds of mushrooms per square foot in order to succeed. "You break even at 6½ pounds." Losses can be the result of many factors, but pests are a big one.

In the mid-1950s, a nationwide virus, La France disease, devastated the button mushroom crop. In agriculture, a disease is anything living or nonliving that causes a loss in yield. In mushroom growing, a pathogen is a disease-causing organism, like certain species of flies. In the past, pesticides were used to control pathogens. But while button growers were (and are) good at growing lots of pounds of mushrooms from a couple of strains, their understanding of fungal pests was on a slower learning curve. "In the early 1980s, the flies got really bad," said Mark Miller. "You'd walk into a double and see them everywhere." The flies were able to resist chemical pesticides by mutation. In essence, the fungal pathogens evolved faster than the evolution of the chemicals. "Resistance," said Miller, "is an evolutionary, continuous adaptation to the environment."

Cultivated mushrooms can be infected by fungal, viral, and bacterial diseases. Farmers usually deal with pests by avoiding them in the first place: clean environments, proper CO_2, air circulation, and the like. Currently, the trend is away from pesticides. That's because pesticides aren't as necessary due to improved hybrids and cultivation techniques, aren't as effective due to pathogen resistance, aren't as cheap, and aren't as available as they once were. The status of the most effective fungicide, Topsin, is in limbo, as it exceeds the EPA's safety threshold for human exposure.

Cost-effective biologicals are preferred, like entomophagus nematodes—which are insect larvae–eating microscopic roundworms—or fermented bacteria, neem oil, and rosemary oil. And peat moss, when used as topsoil for growing, is so clean there are no pathogens in it to kill.

Mushroom farming is a labor-intensive business. The mushrooms must be selected for size, cut, and trimmed, each one by hand. Forty years ago, mushroom growers and pickers contracted a pulmonary disease called mushroom grower's lung, but proper compost pasteurization, good air circulation, and the use of face masks have all but eliminated the condition. Mushroom houses are generally kept in a pressurized lockdown during cropping, and afterward the white button spores and all pathogens in the air and compost are killed using steam and chemicals.

The Italian laborers from a century ago were replaced with Puerto Rican laborers in the 1970s, who in turn were gradually replaced by Mexican workers. Today, approximately 98 percent of the labor force is Mexican. Whether the Mexican community will continue to supply the mushroom farms with labor into the next generation continues to be a worry for many farmers, and some, like Phillips Mushroom, are using agencies to find workers. These days more and more of those workers are Indonesian.

It takes about 8 weeks to produce a crop of mushrooms, from preparing the compost to picking the mushrooms. At the end of a harvest, the mushroom houses have to be emptied of the spent compost. This is one of the big problems of the commercial mushroom industry: What to do with all that compost? Spent compost must be pasteurized to eliminate any pathogens and weed seeds before it can be used as mulch (mushroom compost supports a variety of plant growth like corn, pumpkin, tomatoes, and potatoes); for roadside landscaping; in coal mine reclamation ("They dump tons of the stuff in old mines," said Pete Gray); or for tamping down artillery fungus, a pest to car owners and homeowners nationwide. The artillery or cannonball fungus ejects a sticky spore sac for a distance of as much as 18 feet and 14 feet in the air, where it adheres to whatever surface it comes into contact with.* Since the artillery fungus is common in wood chips and other landscaping material, homeowners are constantly battling this gummy goo that

Artillery fungus globs stick to siding.

is spattered all over the sides of their house and cars. (And if the house siding is wood, the spore will germinate and grow mycelium.)

The mushroom industry produces about 2½ billion pounds of spent compost annually—and sometimes farmers have to pay to have their compost hauled away. As Pete Gray said, "We've already pretty much covered the whole state." Our tour guide at Pietro Industries summed up our visit to the mushroom houses by saying, "Never dump spent compost on your yard or you'll be mowing the grass for, like, twice a week and stuff."

Up until the 1970s, 80 percent of the American mushroom crop was canned. That changed when the Taiwanese, and later the Chinese and other countries, started shipping canned mushrooms to the United States, forcing the mushroom growers to produce a better product for the fresh market and to produce those mushrooms year-round.

In 2003, the USDA did a mushroom consumption survey (they

*The mycologist Tom Volk made this analogy: "For a 6-foot-tall person to accomplish the same relative feat, he would have to throw a baseball nearly 1½ miles high, and the ball would fall almost 2 miles away."

actually call it food disappearance data, since there is no way to know how much of that package of mushrooms was actually eaten versus how much was left to go bad in the fridge) that suggested, in general, more Americans are consuming fresh mushrooms than they have in the past, with the concentration of consumers being men and women 20 to 36 years old, in suburbia and in the West. The increases are in part due to mushrooms appearing on more restaurant menus, particularly fast-food joints and ethnic take-out, and to immigration trends: Asians and non-Hispanic whites were dominant consumers, with African Americans the least likely to eat mushrooms.

The report also suggests a correlation between income and the consumption of fresh and processed mushrooms. Households in the highest income bracket (income exceeding 350 percent of the poverty level) ate the most mushrooms, with the inverse being true of the lowest income level. The authors suggest the increase in per capita consumption of mushrooms is likely the result of the appeal of newer varieties like the portobello; a strong national economy (remember, this was 2003); and, to a lesser extent, public awareness of the health benefits of mushrooms. They also credited better marketing and promotion on the part of the industry. That's where organizations like the Mushroom Council and the American Mushroom Institute and events like the Kennett Square Mushroom Festival come into play.

The Mushroom Festival's mandate is "to promote the mushroom, educate consumers about the health benefits of mushrooms, and to promote tourism in Southern Chester County, all while financially supporting local and regional charities through a grant process." The festival certainly did not neglect eaters. There were dozens of food stands promoting imaginative ways to eat the white button. The year I attended, there were wonderful hot, creamy mushroom soup stands, each distinguishing its product by the addition of paprika or sherry or tarragon;

stands selling mushroom risotto, mushroom crepes, mushroom spring rolls, mushroom garlic rolls, elk mushroom chili, and mushroom-filled potted bread. La Michocana, the Mexican food stand where all the teenagers were hanging out, sold homemade mushroom ice cream bars that, though wonderful in concept, tasted more like plain vanilla bars to me. I sampled them all, including the "original breaded mushroom," which mostly tasted of fried bread served with ranch dressing, and then surveyed the usual, nonmushroomy enemies of our waistlines: crab cakes, funnel cakes, cupcakes, and the ubiquitous Italian sausage-and-peppers stand, where a pear-shaped police officer jumped the line to get a sandwich and, when he rather limply gestured to pay, was offered his hoagie free of charge.

Former contestants from the TV show *Top Chef* were in attendance, one from a recent season whose demo clocked in at well under 30 minutes, and another from a season a few years back who hung around onstage, his mushrooms long since stuffed, complaining about not being famous anymore. He offered to take pictures and sign autographs, finally lingering outside the tent to chat with a gaggle of culinary students in their chef's whites. (I felt bad for him, but this is the reality-star syndrome—it's the saltpeter of celebrity. One's status burns out more quickly than a Camel cigarette.)

There were loads of retail vendors selling quilts and hula hoops, candles and signage, lots of signage, like the welcome signs and funny aphorisms that hung on every doorknob of the B&B where I stayed. At various posts along the road were Mushroom Council booths selling overpriced locally grown white buttons and shiitake, oyster, crimini, and portobello mushrooms, the proceeds earmarked for scholarships and other good causes.

I didn't buy any, and felt kind of cheap that I didn't, but I did take all of the printed matter they provided. Back at my B&B, as I gobbled down a large cup of congealing mushroom soup, I went through it all. In it, the council was promoting mushrooms as the new superfood. I grew up loving mushrooms, but always assumed they had the nutritional value of iceberg lettuce or celery. Now they're considered a superfood? And the button mushroom, no less! I used to think of the button mushroom as a kind of lowest common denominator mushroom: inferior in nutrition and taste to other mushrooms. I never cooked with them, preferring wild fungi or exotics. But now I realize I was just being a snob, due to a combination of my own ignorance and a knee-jerk reaction to the button mushroom's industrialization. After all, industrial food is something I had been brought up to disdain. But I've developed a new respect for the humble *A. bisporus.* I recently saw a Jacques Pépin cooking show where the great chef sautéed button mushrooms, which he called *champignons,* and spooned them into ramekins. He broke an egg on top, added a bit of cream, salt, and black pepper, and then baked the eggs in a *bain marie.* It looked so good I made the dish the next day. It was earthy and yolky; rich, creamy, and comforting. And the mushrooms, those modest buttons, were absolutely delicious.

Chapter 8

THE NEW SUPERFOOD

S hortly after we'd met at the Kennett Square Mushroom Festival, Mark Miller and I struck up an e-mail friendship, and he came to visit me in New York, and to Christmas-shop for the ladies in his family. Mark loves fine things and cheerfully allowed me to steer him toward this shop and that. He was just generally game and didn't even peep when the dim sum place we went to, which had changed management since the last time I had been there, proved to be manky in the extreme.

But my friendship with Mark was not my only one. By this time, I had introduced myself to just about everyone at every festival and foray whose book I had on the shelf above my desk. The truth is, I'd become a bona fide mycology groupie. At one of the business meetings of the New York Mycological Society, I heard some concerns about the cost of housing visiting lecturers and I promptly offered my place—actually my husband's and my place—to the mycologists that Gary Lincoff booked to speak at our lecture series. I told him they could stay in the city as long as they liked, and I promised to cook a dinner in their honor with plenty of pomp and Pomerol.

For those dinners—and I am still doing them—I served mushrooms.

But I was using fungi for flavor and to show off my stash of foraged mushrooms, which had begun to dominate the space in my freezer: frozen sautéed porcini and chanterelles, dried and frozen candy caps and morels; hedgehogs and fairy clubs and hawk's wings. I cooked the mushrooms all kinds of ways, to get a feel for what methods and ingredients worked best together. Gypsy mushrooms, for example, make the otherwise pedestrian chicken fricassee divine. I love quick-pickled black trumpets in a tuna and potato salad, beef chunks rolled in dried porcini powder before being cooked in a stew, cannoli cream flavored with mapley candy cap mushrooms, and delicate yellowfoot mushrooms and fillet of sole cooked together in parchment with white wine and thyme. But until I started to read about mushroom nutrition on the mushroom industry Web sites (organizations like the Mushroom Institute finance much of the current research), I never thought once about cooking mushrooms for nutrition.

Like most people, I didn't give mushrooms much cred when it came to health. When I asked a nutritionist I met at a Christmas party about the nutritional value of mushrooms, she said, "Nada" and pointed out that mushrooms were mostly water. And prior to 2010, most nutritionists seemed to agree. There is historic prejudice regarding mushroom nutrition. As far back as the 2nd century, the Roman physician Aelius Galenus declared mushrooms "very cold and moist and therefore do approach unto a venomous and muthering faculty and ingender clammy and cold nutriment if eaten."

In the 1930s, Otto Carqué, at that time an eminent authority on natural foods, wrote in his book *Vital Facts about Foods*, "The general composition of the various fungi shows that they have not a high nutritive value. The average amount of protein they contain is 3.5 percent. The mineral matter consists mostly of phosphoric acid and potash." And the trend continued. In 2008, a study revealed that less than 40 percent of dietitians recommended mushrooms to their clients. By 2010, more than 50 percent of nutritionists were recommending mushrooms.

Within 2 years, mushrooms went from being the nutritional version of an icicle to what the industry now describes as a superfood. That's because mushrooms have been found to have a specific role in nutrition and have weight-management benefits. Mushrooms are cholesterol free and low in sodium, yet they provide several micronutrients, including potassium, the B vitamins riboflavin and niacin, and selenium, which are typically found in animal foods and grains. Fungi are the only non-animal food that naturally contains vitamin D. And because they are mostly water and fiber, mushrooms are very low in fat. A cup of uncooked white button mushrooms yields about 21 calories.

The upshot is you'd have to eat a lot of mushrooms to meet daily caloric requirements. An average sedentary male would have to eat 17 pounds of mushrooms cooked without oil a day in order to meet his necessary 2,000 calories. Paul Sadowski, John Cage's longtime nota-tionist and the secretary of the New York Mycological Society (NYMS), told me that at one point when Cage's finances were particularly low, he took to foraging for wild mushrooms. After one week of subsisting on mushrooms, he found himself unable to muster the energy to walk the half mile to a friend's for lunch.

So the superfood tag needs to be taken with a grain of salt. It's ulti-mately a marketing ploy. Blueberries are a superfood, too, but you need to eat 2 pounds of them a day to get their super benefits. The same goes for mushrooms. But that doesn't change the fact that mushrooms have recently been liberated from their bad reputation and acknowledged as a healthy, low-fat food.

Mushrooms "occupy a place somewhere above vegetables and

legumes but below the 1st class protein in meat and fish," writes Denis Benjamin in *Mushrooms: Poisons and Panaceas.* That's pretty impressive, considering the fact that most people consider mushrooms more of a garnish than a primary ingredient—about as important to one's overall health as curly parsley. "But what consumers think does not reflect the true potential of mushrooms," said Mary Jo Feeney, who coordinates the nutrition research program for the Mushroom Council. The same characteristic that makes mushrooms low in calories—that they are 90 percent water—is what keeps them from scaling the peak of the food pyramid. However, they are clearly an optimal food for desk jockeys: You can stuff yourself with mushrooms, get lots of good nutrition, and the only way they will make you fat is if you drown them in butter sauce.

Simply put, mushrooms represent a distinct and unique food group that adds a great deal to a healthy diet, and they should be eaten enthusiastically.

In the winter of 2010, I had just hit another weight plateau. Since my children were born I have put on a couple of pounds every few years, and every time it happens, I get uptight about it. Over the years, I've tried tweaking my eating habits to lose the weight without heartbreak. I went through the shake thing (filling but depressing), the no-carb thing (my tongue felt greasy all the time), and the just-have-a-cigarette-instead thing (absolutely ran me down). And then I read a study conducted by Lawrence Cheskin, MD, of Johns Hopkins Bloomberg School of Public Health in Maryland.

Dr. Cheskin conducted a 2-week trial comparing the palatability and the effect on appetite of using mushrooms as a replacement for meat. The study was financed by the Mushroom Council, a research and promotion organization that was mandated by Congress in 1990.* Two groups of people took turns eating otherwise identical recipes featuring either meat or mushrooms (meat or mushroom lasagna, savory napoleon, sloppy joe, and chili). The meat entrées averaged 783 calories each, the mushroom entrées averaged 339 calories. The subjects were randomized to consume all four meat entrées or all four mushroom entrées in the first week, and then ate the alternate mushroom or meat versions of the same entrées in the second week. Substituting mushrooms for meat in four meals out of eight resulted in subjects consuming about 1,485 fewer calories over the 4-day mushroom portion of the test than they did over the 4-day meat test period—an unsurprising result.

What *was* surprising was the palatability ratings, which in this test described how full the subjects felt. The results were similar for meat and mushroom recipes. According to the study, "There were no significant differences in ratings of appetite, satiation or satiety between the meat and mushroom condition . . . despite the sizeable reduction in fat and energy content it produced." The subjects who ate mushrooms instead of meat consumed an average of 420 fewer calories per meal but didn't need to compensate for the diminished calorie intake by eating more food later in the day. The study suggests that eating mushrooms in place of foods like ground beef could be a strategy for controlling weight gain without sacrificing satisfaction.

A follow-up trial commissioned by the Mushroom Bureau of the UK, and conducted by Sarah Schenker, a British dietitian, had similar findings. At press time Dr. Cheskin was conducting a long-term trial with 80 subjects, in hopes that beyond establishing the dietary significance of

---

*The Mushroom Council is a checkoff organization. They collect funds from producers and use those funds to research and promote the commodity. It's the same kind of organization that exists for beef, eggs, pork, and milk, among other foodstuffs, and produces slogans like "Beef. It's What's for Dinner" and "Got Milk?" The Mushroom Council's slogan is "Fresh Mushrooms—Nature's Hidden Treasure."

mushrooms, he may also be able to determine the metabolic benefits of eating lots of mushrooms—in other words, how mushrooms can contribute to our overall health.*

I decided to test the mushrooms-for-meat idea on myself.

I changed none of my habits beyond replacing meat and poultry—which I usually ate about four times a week—with mushrooms in my dinner recipes. I continued to eat fish or eggs at the remaining dinners, worked out three or four times a week at the gym, still ate cereal in the morning and cheese and vegetables at most lunches, and drank a glass or two of wine every night. I also liked a little sundae a few nights a week (vanilla ice cream, Kahlua, ground-up amaretto cookies). I started at 127 pounds on February 21 (a few defiant pounds over my normal weight) and ate three meals a day with a snack (sometimes a handful of nuts, other times a yogurt). For 3 weeks I pretty much stuck to it, although one of those nights I entertained Daniel Winkler, the cordyceps expert, who was in town to lecture to the NYMS, and I was showing off, so we definitely overate: spaghettini cooked in chicken stock and garnished with sautéed hedgehog mushrooms, then bollito misto with pickled chanterelles (beef ribs, cotechino sausage, chicken thighs, parsnips, carrots, and potatoes), and panna cotta with candy cap mushroom sauce. A couple of martinis were consumed during those weeks as well (my son got a day's suspension from high school, my daughter decided she hated college and took a bus home). Overall, I lost a little under 2 pounds a week and never felt it.

Now, when I think about what to serve for dinner, I consider

---

*There is a fungi-based diet supplement called chitosan, which is derived from chitin, the primary component of fungi cell walls. Chitin supplements are often made from shrimp shells—fungi is the only "vegetable source." Chitosan supposedly binds to fat in your digestive system—it is sometimes sold as a "fat attractor"—and, because it is indigestible, carries that chocolate croissant you ate earlier out of your body. In response to an FDA warning, at least one producer of chitin supplements has dramatically toned down their claims, suggesting the product may have benefits but results are best obtained with a low-fat diet.

mushrooms as an option on par with meat, poultry, and fish. And as a result, I'm making a little dent in the chest freezer trove.

Take away the 80 to 95 percent of water in mushrooms and the remaining 5 to 20 percent is composed of protein, carbs (which includes fiber), sugars, vitamins, and minerals. It should be said that the bioavailability of the vitamins and minerals in different mushrooms—how much nutrient is actually absorbed by digestion—is not well known. However, there are a few standout nutritional aspects of mushrooms. They contain the essential amino acids, the building blocks of protein; they are a good source of fiber; and they are an unusual source for some important vitamins and minerals.

The Greeks believed mushrooms gave warriors strength in battle.* That notion may be rooted in their history, but it's not without some truth as well. The greatest challenge in meeting human nutritional requirements is supplying adequate amounts of protein. Mushrooms contain all nine essential amino acids, which are needed to produce high-quality protein. No feeding trials have been conducted, but researchers have judged the nutritional value of mushrooms through analyses of these essential amino acids. (Mushroom nutritional values change from species to species, sometimes quite a bit, but for the sake of simplicity, the values in this chapter refer to *Agaricus bisporus*, the white button mushroom and the crimini.) So mushrooms provide high-quality protein, but in low volume. A middle-aged woman my weight needs about 21 grams of protein a day. An 84-gram serving size of

*The word *mycology* is thought to have derived from the Greek *mukes*, which in turn may be derived from the Greek place name Mukanai, otherwise known as Mycenaea. There, the hero Perseus lost the hilt of his sword, which looked like a mushroom cap.

mushrooms—four or five white button mushrooms—offers 3 grams of protein, about 7 percent of the Daily Value (DV). In order to fulfill my protein requirement, I'd have to eat about 60 mushrooms.

However, when mushrooms are eaten in conjunction with other foods, they can lift those foods nutritionally. For example, cereal protein is characterized by a low level of the amino acid isoleucine. According to a Polish review of research on mushroom nutrition, "The consumption of mushrooms with cereal products [like a mushroom barley soup] is recommended for balancing the level of essential amino acids in the diet." So for vegetarians and vegans who do not eat the more common sources of amino acids, mushrooms should be a key food. Likewise, in developing countries, mushrooms can be an important protein source. According to Denis Benjamin, "Mushrooms utilize otherwise unavailable organic material and convert it into protein." Or to put it another way, mushrooms turn poop into protein in a matter of days.

Mushrooms are a good source of fiber. Half of the dry weight of mushrooms is composed of carbohydrates. Mushroom carbohydrates are primarily made up of long chains of sugar molecules called polysaccharides. Polysaccharides include glycogen and indigestible forms of fiber. Glycogen stores energy as a modified form of glucose in most animal and mushroom cells—it's the equivalent of starch in plants. The fiber content in mushrooms comes from the chitin in their cell walls. (In plant foods, that fiber is often cellulose, found in plant cell walls.)

Chitin is cited as a potential prebiotic food source. Scientists G. R. Gibson and M. B. Roberfroid describe prebiotics as a "non-digestible food ingredient that beneficially affects the host by selectively stimulating the growth and/or activity of one or a limited number of bacteria in the colon." A prebiotic has to be indigestible, otherwise it will be digested in the upper GI tract before it has time to get down to the colon and stimulate the growth of probiotics, the bacteria necessary for digestive health. They found that the definition of *prebiotics* more or less overlaps with the definition of dietary fiber, except for its selectivity for certain species of bacteria. More specifically, chitin in mushrooms is being explored for its capacity to stimulate the growth of good bacteria like *Lactobacillus, Bifidobacterium,* and *Enterococcus faecium* in the colon.

Mushrooms contain an array of interesting minerals and vitamins, a few of which are particularly significant. Minerals are essential inorganic chemicals that are required to run the cells' metabolism, and mushrooms are loaded with them. Minerals in mushrooms tend to be concentrated in the pileus (cap), rather than the stipe (stem). The most abundant minerals are potassium and phosphorus, followed by selenium and copper, with lesser quantities of zinc, iron, and magnesium. (Wild mushrooms can also accumulate heavy metals from the soil, sometimes to an unhealthy degree.)

It's not a big deal that mushrooms contain potassium and phosphorus. Potassium, a type of salt essential for the function of all living cells, and phosphorus, a component of all living cells, both as a structural element in DNA and RNA and lipids (fats and fat-soluble vitamins), are ubiquitous in nature. We get them from many food sources, and deficiency is unlikely in a well-fed person (although short-term potassium deficiency can occur when you drink heavily).

More interestingly, mushrooms are an excellent source of selenium. Selenium is a naturally occurring solid substance found widely but unevenly distributed in rocks and soil. Plants and mushrooms draw selenium from the soil. Mushrooms provide 31 percent of the current Recommended Daily Intake (RDI) in one serving of four or five button or crimini mushrooms. Only garlic provides more of this nutrient per gram. (In fact, in the rare case of a selenium overdose, excess selenium, when excreted by the breath, smells garlicky.) Selenium is toxic in large amounts—some plants accumulate selenium as a defense strategy—but the daily requirement is necessary for the healthy function of cells, as it induces the action of antioxidants and other enzymes.

Mushrooms are also a great source of copper, which is necessary in trace amounts to the action of a variety of enzymes in humans, like those involved in repairing connective tissue, as well as facilitating the body's absorption of iron and zinc. Some studies suggest that the typical American diet is low on copper. Copper is bioaccumulated from the soil by mushrooms. A serving of four or five mushrooms provides 20 percent of the recommended Daily Value, 10 times more than carrots.*

Mushrooms contain trace amounts of zinc, iron, and magnesium. A serving of four or five dry-cooked button mushrooms contains about 3 percent of the recommended DV of zinc. Three-quarters of a cup of dry-cooked oyster mushrooms provides around 8 percent of the DV for iron, and about half that for magnesium. It is estimated that up to 20 percent of American women suffer from iron deficiency anemia. However, because the body lacks a regular process by which it can excrete excess iron in the body, iron supplements have to be taken with caution. Iron toxicity can damage components of cells, particularly in the heart and liver, and in therapeutic doses causes constipation. Food sources like mushrooms are best. (Plus, you can provide your body with additional iron by cooking iron-rich foods in an iron skillet if you use acid like lemon juice in the cooking process to release the iron.)

Mushrooms contain fatty acids, with unsaturated fatty acids like those in oily fish, walnuts, and flaxseed occurring in greater concentration than saturated fats, like those found in lard, butter, milk, cream, eggs, red meat, and chocolate. One of those fatty acids in mushrooms,

---

*Copper bracelet advocates, who believe wearing them can relieve joint pain, may find satisfaction in the fact that copper does assist in the regeneration of connective tissue; however, no studies—and there have been a few—have found evidence that copper bracelets affect connective tissue. Copper does have a germicidal effect, however. A pure copper tabletop will disinfect itself of various bacteria in as little as 45 minutes, depending on the temperature.

linoleic acid, is essential: Humans do not naturally produce it. Fatty acids are necessary building blocks in the manufacture of hormonelike substances that regulate a variety of human functions, like the immune response and blood pressure.

Vitamins are chemical compounds that cannot be synthesized in the human body in sufficient quantity and so must be obtained from outside sources, like diet. Mushrooms have lots of vitamins, and are particularly rich in the B group and vitamin D.

Vitamin B is actually composed of eight water-soluble vitamins, of which mushrooms contain five, that are necessary for immune and nervous system function, increasing metabolism, preventing anemia, and possibly reducing the risk of some cancers. Vitamin B_{12} is not available in plants, so vegans should take note: Mushrooms are the only food source of B_{12} acceptable to their diet.

Probably the biggest news in mushroom nutrition is the discovery that mushrooms contain ergosterol, the biological precursor to vitamin D_2. Vitamins D_2 and D_3 (D_3 is synthesized in our skin when exposed to sunlight) are the two physiologically relevant forms of vitamin D. Vitamin D can be obtained through sunlight; supplements; foods that are fortified with vitamin D_2 and/or D_3, like milk; and very few, rather strange foods, like some fish liver oils, the liver and fat from aquatic mammals like seals, and egg yolks from chickens that have been fed vitamin D supplements. And mushrooms.

Vitamin D is crucial for activating the immune system (it triggers T cells—the immune system's killer cells—into action) and is necessary for bone growth, among many other benefits. Vitamin D deficiency is considered widespread throughout the industrialized world, most likely because of sun avoidance, whether intentional or due to smog or office jobs. About 9 percent of the American population is vitamin D deficient, according to the National Institutes of Health. Other researchers suggest that number is seriously low. As many as half of all older Americans who break their hip are vitamin D deficient (it gets harder to synthesize vitamin D from the sun as you age). Vitamin D deficiency causes soft or brittle bones; fatter, weaker muscles; liver and kidney disorders; and, by some reports, depression. It's been linked to a host of diseases, from cancers to autoimmune diseases, MS to TB, as well as schizophrenia and seasonal affective disorder (SAD).

I attended the 51st Annual Pennsylvania State Mushroom Industry Conference to hear the maestro of vitamin D advocacy, Dr. Michael Holick of Boston University School of Medicine, deliver the keynote speech. The conference took place on a beautiful September day at a swanky golf club in the town of State College, and while I waited for the session on dietary health to begin, I ate a club sandwich on the patio and watched the golfers bump about in their buggies, and, after a few moments of confusion, discovered the Frank Sinatra tunes I was hearing were emanating from a nearby speaker camouflaged as an ornamental rock.

Dr. Holick's bio is reminiscent of a yearbook overachiever: PhD, MD, professor of medicine, physiology, and biophysics, director of the General Clinical Research Unit, director of the Bone Health Care Clinic, director of the Heliotherapy, Light, and Skin Research Center at Boston University Medical Center; diplomat of the American Board of Internal Medicine, fellow of the American College of Nutrition, member of the American Academy of Dermatology and American Association of Physicians; recipient of many awards including the Linus Pauling Prize for Human Nutrition; author of over 300 peer-reviewed papers and two books, *The UV Advantage* and *The Vitamin D Solution*. Dr. Holick is on a mission to wake the American public up to the importance of vitamin D, and the path he has chosen to take—jazzy, sensationalist, and straight to the people—has put him on a collision course with the dermatological community.

Michael Holick is an impish man with a hank of white hair over his forehead. In contrast to the pedantic style of the other speakers, whose talks had most attendees nodding like dahlias, Holick woke everyone up. He sped through a lecture laced with puns and darted through slides that somehow included images of Darth Vader. There's a fine line between presenting material entertainingly and allowing it to seem dubious, and Holick's lecture rode that line. After a few minutes, I gave up trying to take notes.

But the chain of his thinking about vitamin D and mushrooms is compelling. Holick proposes there is widespread vitamin D deficiency in this country and that deficiency is connected to a host of problems, starting in the womb with vitamin D–deficient pregnancies. For years the Institute of Medicine (IOM) recommended a daily intake of 200 IU (international units) for males and females from childhood through middle age, then 400 IU in older age (the American Academy of Pediatrics recommends children take 400 IU). But recent research has generated new values: The IOM now recommends 600 IU of vitamin D per adult per day—three times the former recommendation—and 800 IU per day for persons 71 and older. Holick thinks the IOM number is still too low. He points out that 15 to 20 minutes of sunlight on Cape Cod in summer at midday is the equivalent of taking 20,000 IU of vitamin D orally, and he suggests a preferable value is 1,000 IU a day taken orally plus a multivitamin that includes 400 IU of vitamin D. He's not alone. The Harvard School of Public Health also recommends 1,000 IU, as do many other authoritative sources. When I asked my doctor about vitamin D and mentioned the IOM recommendation, he pooh-poohed it. "Forget about that," he said, "1,000 IU a day, minimum."

On the other hand, a report issued by the Institute of Medicine in 2010 suggested that high levels of vitamin D are actually harmful and stands by the current recommendations. If you live below 42 degrees latitude, a line running approximately from the northern border of California to Boston, then the UVB radiation wavelength from sunlight is insufficient for your skin to make vitamin D during the four months of winter—and that stretches out to 6 months the farther north you go. South of 34 degrees latitude, a line running approximately from Los Angeles to Columbia, South Carolina, adequate exposure is possible year-round.

Dr. Holick has his detractors. One of the most influential is the former chair of the dermatology department at Boston University School of Medicine. Barbara Gilchrest, MD, an authority on melanoma, the deadliest form of skin cancer, flipped out when she read his first book on the subject, *The UV Advantage*, which stated the warnings about sun exposure were exaggerated and should be reconsidered in light of the curse of vitamin D deficiency. This is not the message supported by the dermatological community: UV radiation is a carcinogen responsible for most of the estimated 1.5 million skin cancers and the 8,000 deaths from melanoma that occur annually in the United States, and lifetime sun exposure also contributes to cosmetic changes like wrinkling. Holick announced his book's publication in 2004 at an Indoor Tanning Association meeting in Nashville—he says you can also visit a tanning salon and lie in a UVB bed to get your vitamin D dose, as does the National Institutes of Health—a move that led Dr. Gilchrest to question Holick's integrity and proclaim his book "an embarrassment for this institution and an embarrassment for him." She went as far as to call for his resignation from the dermatology department, which he did, though he remains a member of various other departments. Holick wasn't the only one talking about the benefits of UV. Richard Hobday, PhD, published *The Healing Sun* in 2000, and James Dowd, MD, published *The Vitamin D Cure* in 2009. In 2010, Holick came out with another: *The Vitamin D Solution*.

The most bioavailable way to get vitamin D is from the sun, according to Dr. Holick. After that, assuming you aren't vitamin D deficient

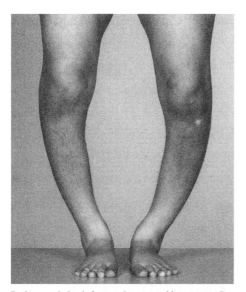

Rickets, a skeletal abnormality caused by vitamin D deficiency

and need massive doses of supplements to bring your serum level up to normal, the best source is food, and in this lecture, he discussed irradiated mushrooms. Irradiating sounds creepy, but it's been going on since 1923, when a University of Wisconsin researcher, Harry Steenbock, demonstrated that irradiating certain food with ultraviolet light increased vitamin D, which in turn could eliminate the disfiguring childhood disease of rickets, a skeletal abnormality in children. Fortified foods, *irradiated* foods, provide most of the vitamin D in the American diet. In the 1930s, the United States implemented a milk fortification project to combat rickets, and the disorder was virtually eliminated. The vitamin D precursor, ergosterol, found in supplements and vitamin D–enhanced milk, comes from dried *Saccharomyces* yeast.

Irradiation is like putting the mushroom onto a tanning bed. Energy comes from the sun, and there are different types, like ultraviolet light, radio frequencies, and gamma rays. Trees absorb radiation that stimulates photosynthesis. UVA, UVB, and UVC rays are ultraviolet radiation. UVC rays are capable of destroying pathogenic bacteria on and in foods (and, according to the FDA, USDA, and WHO, are perfectly safe). In the case of irradiated mushrooms, the fungus is exposed to a UVB or UVC light that stimulates the ergosterol in the fungus to synthesize into vitamin D_2 (ultraviolet light is the same trigger our skin uses to synthesize vitamin D_3).

A serving of four or five white button mushrooms contains about 6 IU of vitamin D_2. Expose mushrooms to sunlight for 5 minutes and, according to preliminary research, the vitamin D is boosted to 400 IU. But after blasting them with high-intensity UVB light pulses, the mushrooms' vitamin D_2 values can go up to 8,000 IU. That quantity of vitamin D is achieved because mushrooms have a lot of ergosterol in them, and the more ergosterol there is, the more potential vitamin D there is. Exposing sliced mushrooms produces more vitamin D than whole mushrooms because the light can hit a greater surface area. The converted vitamin D in mushrooms may degrade about 25 percent within 3 days, but then it levels out for the next 10 days. Vitamin D in mushrooms remains stable after cooking.

"D mushrooms" have got the industry in a tizzy, and as many as a dozen American companies are producing or planning to produce vitamin D–enhanced mushroom products, including the California giant, Monterey Mushrooms. Dole, the world's largest producer and marketer of fresh fruit and vegetables, is now selling whole and sliced portobellos that have been exposed to UV light/simulated sunlight to the full daily nutritional requirement—which won them a Good Housekeeping Research Institute award as one of the top 10 innovative products of 2009.

Not all mushrooms that are consumed are stir-fried. Somewhere between functional foods—eating for health—and taking medicines are nutraceuticals,* a combination of the words *nutrition* and *pharmaceutical.*

---

*Nutraceuticals are not to be confused with homeopathy, which is an alternative medicine based on an 18th-century concept called the Law of Similars; it's kind of like the idea that eating the heart of a lion will make you brave. Homeopathic remedies typically won't hurt you, but their efficacy is unsupported by any scientific or clinical evidence.

There are a host of powdered mushroom supplements, extracts, and teas that fit the nutraceutical definition.

Officially, nutraceuticals are dietary supplements and fall under the Dietary Supplement Health and Education Act (DSHEA) of 1994. The FDA regulates dietary supplements under a different set of rules than those covering "conventional" food and drug products. Under DSHEA, the supplement manufacturer is responsible for ensuring their product is safe before it is marketed. Other than that, they aren't regulated. They don't need to register their products with the FDA nor get FDA approval before producing or selling. As of 2007, the FDA amended DSHEA and instituted manufacturing protocols for nutraceuticals in order to ensure the supplements don't contain contaminants or impurities, and are accurately labeled.

There is a spectrum of nutraceutical mushroom products. At the low end are products with no proven health benefits, like kombucha tea, brew fermented by various yeasts and bacteria living in symbiosis, and credited with benefits like increased sexual drive, increased energy, and increased stamina, even youthfulness. I put kombucha tea in the same it-can't-hurt category as kimchi and other probiotic fermented foods, although it actually can harm you if not properly made: According to the mycologist George Hudler, "many of the molds likely to contaminate kombucha are producers of life-threatening mycotoxins." My husband went through a kombucha tea thing in the early 1990s— it seemed like everyone we knew in lower Manhattan had sour-smelling crocks dominating their teeny apartment kitchen counters.

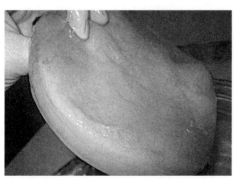

A kombucha culture

But the American love affair with the drink is only the most recent man-
ifestation of kombucha's 2,000-year-run of global popularity.

On the other hand, red yeast rice, which is the filamentous yeast
*Monascus pupureus** grown out on rice, then dried and powdered, is a
very effective nutraceutical. It has small amounts of compounds called
statins, one of which is lovastatin. In purified, derivative form, lovastatin
is the primary component of the cholesterol-lowering drug Mevacor.

So here's the difference between what Dr. Andrew Weil calls "green
medicine" versus "white medicine," or a nutraceutical and a prescription
drug. Mevacor and other patented statin drugs are intense, fast acting,
and effective, but come with an array of potential side effects, some very
serious. Ron Sabourin, a biologist formerly with Sylvan in Pennsylvania,
which produces red yeast rice, explained to me that when "the active
ingredient [used in patented statin drugs] has been removed from the
natural matrix, the other active ingredients of the green medicine, which
can potentiate the beneficial effects *and* attenuate side effects, are now
missing." The nutraceutical supplement red yeast rice will also lower
cholesterol, but it is much slower acting, with fewer side effects. Statin
drugs, whether white or green, are known to cause muscle and liver
damage, and those side effects are quantified in a prescriptive setting.
For example, if you are taking Mevacor, your doctor may check your
liver enzymes regularly. In contrast, you can buy red yeast rice at your
local GNC and administer it yourself but you could cause harm if you do
so without the supervision of a doctor. So some nutraceutical mushroom
products can pose a risk, but they also offer an opportunity to improve
health. In traditional Chinese medicine, a doctor or practitioner may
prescribe nutraceuticals like red yeast rice. In the USA, it's harder to get

*This is the same yeast that is used to make Peking duck red.

a doctor to prescribe a nutraceutical because there isn't definitive research on the products' efficacy. But maybe that will change: "My guess is," said Sabourin, "eventually the FDA will develop some standard between food and pharmaceuticals for nutraceuticals."

ω

Mushrooms make sense as a part of our daily diet, particularly for vegetarians and overweight people. But few people seem to know about them. Part of the reason why is because the government has been slow to embrace mushrooms. The USDA published its first food guide in 1916, which established dietary standards in five food groups: milk and meat, cereals, vegetables and fruits, fats and fat foods, and sugars and sugary foods. Over the next 70 years, a number of different guides were instituted: the standards for 12 major food groups to be eaten weekly (1933), the Basic Seven (1942), the Basic Four to be eaten daily (1956), and, in 1979, the Basic Five, which were published in 1980 as the *Dietary Guidelines for Americans* and advised on the consumption of sugars, fats, and alcohol. Each guide reflected the current science, trends, and influence of industry food groups. In fact, in 1979 the influence of industry groups was considered controversial enough to produce another version of the guidelines, this one developed with more input from the scientific community.

In 1990, Congress directed the Department of Agriculture and the Department of Health, Education, and Welfare to issue dietary recommendations every 5 years. The third edition of the *Dietary Guidelines* was produced that year. The fourth edition, published in 1995, included the commonly known food guide pyramid and established nutrition facts labeling. None of these guides mention mushrooms in any significant way.

According to a paper published by the Harvard School of Public

Health, the *Dietary Guidelines for Americans* is important because it sets
the standard for all federally financed nutrition programs, including
school lunches, and presumably influences what foods consumers purchase. This can affect the bottom line of sectors in the food industry.
They have a vested interest in the content of the guidelines. Indeed, the
guidelines, concludes the report, "continues to reflect the tense interplay
of science and the powerful food industry."

I asked Laura Phelps, president of the American Mushroom Institute, a national voluntary trade association representing the growers,
processors, and marketers of cultivated mushrooms, what kind of pressure her organization was bringing to bear on the guidelines process.
"The best way to lobby is from a factual standpoint," she said. "We send
comments to the committee and provide them with updated information." But Phelps explained the process is slow, and there is a lag time
between what the science has to say about mushrooms and what gets
into the guidelines.

In 2009, the USDA dumped the old pyramid model from 1995 and
created a new one, MyPyramid, based on 2005 guidelines, which encourages the user to personalize eating plans based on the *Dietary Guidelines
for Americans*. MyPyramid, unfortunately, perpetuates some of the same
nutritional misinformation as previous pyramids, like suggesting that
nutritionally poor refined starches are an acceptable form of grains.
And, of course, mushrooms—categorized under "other vegetables" on
the ChooseMyPlate.gov Web site—are virtually ignored. Dried beans
and peas made it into the protein group, but not mushrooms. MyPyramid misses many good opportunities to exploit the new science regarding mushrooms, and particularly surprising is the lack of mushroom
information in the dietary sections of the Web site.

There are other food pyramids, most of which are mushroom blind as well: The Mayo Clinic's Vegetarian Food Guide Pyramid has no images or mention of mushrooms in either the vegetable or the protein categories, nor does the Vegan Food Pyramid issued by the University of Chicago's Vegan Society. There are, however, mushroom icons on the Mediterranean Diet Pyramid, the Asian Diet Pyramid, and the Vegetarian Diet Pyramid promoted by Oldways, a nonprofit education organization.

In an issue of *Fungi* magazine, the editor, Britt Bunyard, explained the conundrum of determining what food group mushrooms belong to. "Their chemical makeup would likely favor them being placed with vegetables as they are mostly water and fiber (albeit different from plants'), plus some important nutrients. But their reason for being would make one want to place them with fruits, as they are devices for the purpose of sexual reproduction, as are true fruits of plants. But, evolutionarily speaking, fungi are more closely related to animals like us (than they are to plants) so does that more correctly place them in the meats group?"

The official acknowledgment of mushrooms and nutrition may be lacking because mushrooms are hard to categorize, or because they are a relatively small food group (there are lots of fungi, but not so many commercial culinary mushrooms), or maybe because the word just hasn't gotten out. It takes a long time for the bureaucracy to accept, digest, and apply new information, so there is a delay between what the scientists are finding out about the nutritional value of mushrooms and what the public hears. Indeed, there is a gap between nutritional scientists, who conduct the scientific investigations, and nutritionists, who use summaries of those studies in their practices. In many ways, the issue is communication. "It is extremely difficult to saturate a market with information," said Laura Phelps. "And at the same time, the market is too saturated with information. Everybody has something positive to say about their product."

The most mushroom-oriented pyramid I found was Dr. Andrew Weil's Anti-Inflammatory Food Pyramid, which, according to one nutritional scientist I spoke to, "goes overboard into kookiness, then comes back, then swings out again." Besides giving pasta a place in the pyramid, specifically "al dente" pasta, Weil places cooked Asian mushrooms between whole soy foods and other sources of protein, and recommends "unlimited amounts."

He's right. You need to eat a lot of mushrooms in order to reap their benefits, but if you do, "Nutritionally-speaking," wrote the nutritionist Mary Jo Feeney, "mushrooms are in a class of their own."

Chapter 9

FUNGI THAT MAKE YOU WELL AND FUNGI THAT MAKE YOU SICK

T he mycologist Paul Stamets's name came up at every foray or conference I have attended in the past 5 years. Stamets is well known because his books and lectures inspire people to think about mushrooms in ways they hadn't considered before. His business, Fungi Perfecti, supplies organic culture to mushroom-growing operations, produces mycorrhizal fungi inoculants, and sells an array of medicinal mushroom supplements (in essence, nutraceuticals). Stamets has acquired patents and trademarks for his various fungus-based products, and his ideas, what he calls the "Stametsian Vision," regarding the applications of the degrading, forest-sustaining, and medicinal properties of fungi have influenced a generation of environmentally conscientious people. Knowing who Paul Stamets is will pretty much guarantee you entree into any coffee bar in the Pacific Northwest.

Fungi Perfecti's medicinal mushroom supplements, what Stamets has trademarked as MycoMedicinals, are made on his farm in Washington

from tissue cultures he collects in the wild or from mushrooms grown in
his own doubles. The mycelium, which many alternative medicine pro-
viders believe has stronger medicinal aspects than fungal fruiting bodies,
is harvested when the fungus is at its "most hungry," a sort of enzymatic
peak, then dried and powdered into supplements. Fungi Perfecti's catalog
opens with an index of mushrooms and their putative therapeutic effects.
For example, according to Stamets, *Cordyceps sinensis*—the Tibetan caterpillar fungus—is antibacterial, antioxidant, antitumor, antiviral, good
for moderating blood pressure and blood sugar, good for cardiovascular
and respiratory health, a cholesterol reducer, an immune system enhancer,
a kidney, liver, and nerve tonic, a stress reducer, and a "sexual potentia-
tor." And there are similar claims for many other fungi.

That was my motivation for signing up for Stamets's seminar
"Mycelium Running" at the Hollyhock Educational Retreat Centre on
Cortes Island in British Columbia, Canada. I wanted to know more
about medicinal mushrooms. There is a breach between those who prescribe and use medicinal mushrooms in the United States and the medical establishment. A conversation on the medicinal value of mushrooms
often degrades into antagonistic camps of belief or skepticism. I've seen
it occur between mycologists, doctors, and neighbors. But, of course,
the truth lies somewhere in between.

The beach at Hollyhock

Hollyhock is located on the coast of the island facing the cold Strait of Georgia. It is composed of lovely hobbity wood buildings nestled among huge pine trees, with tidy pine needle-carpeted paths outlined by stones, lots of quiet nooks for reading, yoga classes at dawn, meditation, kayaking, and a bodywork spa. Almost all the staff was female. Hollyhock is an all-natural, antiallergenic, vegetarian-verging-on-vegan environment (spelt-speckled breads, porcini stroganoff, yam soup, nutty grains topped with beet greens, and salads tossed with a yeast dressing that the gal who motored me over from Vancouver Island warned made you fart). It's a no-shoes-in-the-dining-hall, recycle-all-your-bottles-and-cans, brown-sugar-for-your-coffee sort of place. Also on the program that October weekend was an oddly matched couple (she was a giantess, he a tightly wound, bald fellow) presenting a seminar titled "Getting the Love That You Want."

I arrived late in the day, with time only to unpack and eat dinner. Stamets wasn't around, but I got a look at some of my fellow seminar mates, a mix of Canadians and Americans, mostly young men and women who wanted to grow gourmet or medicinal mushrooms for their own pantries and pharmacies, and some myconauts. (Myconauts are devotees of magic mushrooms. Stamets also wrote a book called *Psilocybin Mushrooms of the World*.) One ornery little fellow with pierced eyebrows, rife with conspiracy theories about Canada's nefarious neighbor to the south, was on the lookout for *Amanita muscaria*. "I will *pay* anyone that finds one," he announced early on.

The next morning, Stamets made his appearance. He is a stocky, bearded man with an ivory turtle amulet on a leather thong around his neck and a BlackBerry in his pocket. He seemed to have so much passion for mushrooms that there was enough for us *and* the future audiences he was booking. Indeed, in every free moment, Stamets worked his phone like a teenager between classes. After a brief introduction, he took us out on our first foray. We carpooled into a forest filled with old-growth,

Nonpsychedelic *Psilocybe* mushrooms growing from deer dung

moss-covered stumps as big as Volkswagen Beetles and second-growth trees that were the largest I had ever seen. There were no birds; indeed, there seemed to be no wildlife: The forest was deeply silent, and the only movement I noticed was the slow oozing of giant slugs consuming the bright red lobster mushrooms that grew among the glowing green ferns at the base of the trees. The ground was soft and pillowy underfoot and the air was cool and damp. It made my skin feel creamy.

As is my habit, I didn't range far, as I am afraid of getting lost, and anyway, I'd foolishly brought a pair of new boots that, while very fashionable, were not waterproof. Even though I didn't do any bushwhacking, my toes were wet the entire trip. When our time in the woods was up, I was among the first to arrive at our rendezvous, and I leaned against the car next to Stamets, watching as he texted. Within a few minutes, other hunters emerged from the woods. One young lady presented her find of ten thin mushrooms, no bigger than toothpicks, each one growing from a deer dropping the size of a peanut M&M.

Stamets went ballistic.

Whoever he was texting was promptly cut off as he bent to inspect the find. "This is incredible!" he gushed, and he gave the gal a bear hug.

"I want Paul Stamets to hug me, too," said another woman standing nearby with a red lobster mushroom in her hand.

Stamets got so excited about those scrawny mushrooms because they were growing from dung, and that suggested the mushroom, actually a nonpsychedelic *Psilocybe* species, contained antimicrobial properties with potential medicinal value. We all clustered around as he laid out the mushrooms and photographed them, then carefully wrapped them up.

We ended up hanging around the cars for quite a while because one of our party was missing. I'd sat next to her on the ride to the forest: a compact Asian woman who was very chatty and seemed extremely knowledgeable about mushrooms. She kept asking me if I'd ever picked this mushroom or that, the *Calvatia rubroflava* or the *Macrocystidia cucumis* or *whatever*, and when I asked her the common names, she'd repeat, with a triumphant little smile, the Latin. But the delay turned out to be a blessing in disguise, because everyone used the downtime to display their finds on the hood of the car: bits of bark covered with lovely strange witch's butter, which looks like salmon caviar and can be eaten raw; big floppy orange chanterelles; fleshy mauve pig's ears. And then Stamets pulled from his trunk a mushroom he calls the agarikon, large as a Thanksgiving turkey. It was *Fomitopsis officinalis*, a perennial polypore that grows only in old-growth forests, mainly on mature Douglas fir and larch. It can live to be 50 years old, but due to diminishing habitat, is extremely rare in the USA and practically extinct in Europe.

Stamets handled the mushroom, which had died and fallen from its perch high in a Douglas fir, with a kind of awed gravity, like a curator handling a Leonardo da Vinci drawing. It looked like a hanging wasp nest made of solid papier-mâché and was hard to the touch. Stamets also called it the Venus de Milo mushroom, I guess because it was white like marble with feminine curves, but maybe more so because he saw the mushroom as a kind of goddess. We each took a pinch to taste. It was chalky and had a menthol-like quality, like an aspirin that wished to be a cough drop.

Fomitopsis officinalis (from the Greek, *fomes* = tinder, *officinalis* = pharmaceutical) is also known as the quinine fungus, and although it does not contain quinine (an antimalarial compound), according to Stamets, it does contain "significant antiviral and antibacterial effects against tuberculosis and *E. coli*." The Greek pharmacist Dioscorides (c. AD 40–90) attributed an array of efficacious characteristics to the agarikon (or agaricum or agarick) and recommended it for a wide range of complaints, from hysteria to fractured limbs to kidney disease. No one knows for sure what the agarikon of antiquity is, though many people believe it is *F. officinalis*.

The English herbalist John Gerard (1545–1611 or 1612) recommended "agaricke" as a treatment for a wide variety of ailments, including lung conditions. The key pharmaceutical compound in *F. officinalis* is agaricin (agaric acid), which in 1901 was recommended by the American Medical Association for treating night sweats. *F. officinalis* was also an ingredient in Warburg's Tincture, a concoction of powdered *F. officinalis*, quinine, aloe, and spices, and was used to treat malaria and a variety of other ailments in Europe and the United States until the early 1900s. A century later, the mushroom is getting another look. Scott Franzblau, director of research at the University of Illinois Institute for Tuberculosis Research, suggests *F. officinalis* may "possibly contain novel anti-TB active compounds" and is studying its effects on tubercle growth.

Stamets continued to pick through our finds, identifying what he called "the silent citizens": a gypsy mushroom, which he said had antiviral qualities and was good for herpes ("It's edible, and it can be boiled and made into a salve"); a cauliflower mushroom ("antifungal, antibiotic"); turkey tail ("Good for hepatitis C," he noted). Stamets makes these statements based on studies that suggest the potential of these mushrooms to support health.

He also looks to traditional Chinese medicine and folk practices for hints as to a mushroom's medicinal properties, as do others. Companies like LifePharms Inc. are in the business of collecting and analyzing mushroom samples from the wild in search of various compounds that could be used by them and their collaborators, and they look to traditional uses for clues. After all, although Alexander Fleming was the first to figure out the mold *Penicillium notatum* was an effective agent against some bacteria, he wasn't the first to recognize the correlation. Moldy bread was used to treat wounds and infections since antiquity, and the practice was recommended in the English herbalist John Parkinson's 1640 book on pharmacology, the *Theatrum Botanicum*.

In the West, folk uses of mushrooms ranged from real effects, like the penicillin in moldy bread, to utter fantasies. *Daldinia concentrica,* also known as the coal fungus or cramp balls, were carried around by the British as protection against leg cramps. Some mushrooms were hailed as universal panaceas. Pliny recommended *Suilli* (*Boletus edulis*) for pimples, dog bites, diarrhea, rheumatism, and "fleshy excrescences of the anus," probably hemorrhoids. Others were assigned very specific attributes. Gerard mentioned *Auricularia auricula-judae* as good for sore throats, and indeed, the mushroom is high in soothing mucilage. Mushrooms have been used as folk medicine for decreasing inflammation, as cauterizing agents, cathartics (purgatives), and styptics. For example, Native Americans used puffballs as styptics to staunch bleeding.* Ötzi the Iceman, a 5,300-year-old mummy found in 1991 in a glacier in the Ötztal Alps on the border of Austria and Italy, was carrying two species of polypore (shelf fungi): the tinder conk, which is an effective fire starter (indeed, it can be hard to extinguish a lit tinder polypore), and the birch polypore, which Gary Lincoff described to me as "practically a first-aid kit." In traditional medicine, apparently going back at least 5 millennia, the birch polypore was used to staunch wounds and for its antimicrobial properties.

---

*On the modern front, chitosan, made from chitin, the material from which the cell walls of fungi are made, is utilized as a blood-clotting agent in superbandages, currently employed by the US Armed Forces.

Midwives in 18th-century Germany and Italy used ergot, from the sclerotium, the wintering-over structure of the fungus *Claviceps purpurea*, to induce labor (it causes uterine contractions), and rural populations in Europe used chaga (*Inonotus obliquus*) to treat digestive ailments. "Steroidal compounds and antioxidants," said Stamets.

After about 30 minutes, the final member of our group appeared, unapologetic and smiling, and we loaded into the vans. That night in my room I slept with the window open even though it was chilly outside. A few times I was awakened by the scent of pine trees and mushrooms riding the puffs of night air into my room. It was like being visited by ghosts.

I went to yoga just after dawn the next morning. It was wonderful climbing the piney hill to the yoga studio, the deep bay silent, gray, and smooth as an ice rink except for the boil and huff of a black killer whale. The class was full, and I was slightly late, which meant others had to shift their mats around to make room for me, and then more people came even later, and with the same sigh of annoyance I moved my mat, too. Maybe because there were so many of us, there wasn't much actual stretching. We spent a lot of time listening to our glands, something that was beyond my sensitivity level, especially since I was blocked up with a nascent cold. By the time we were released, the sun was high and the water sparkling and the air was squawking with birds.

At breakfast, I sat with a collection of people from the seminar, all younger than me, many hoping to start either culinary or medicinal mushroom businesses, mostly Canadian. It was a bit of an eye-opener, listening to the litany of conspiracy theories about the USA: that the US government bombed the World Trade Center (I tried to explain I'd seen those planes fly into the towers, but they were adamant); that Congress had to choose between bailing out failing American banks or martial law. According to the sallow, jumpy fellow who was hot to find and consume *Amanita muscaria,* as of that morning there were riots at the gas pumps in Florida. I was really bewildered by the looniness, but then I realized these conspiracy buffs represented yet another category of mushroom enthusiasts, joining Masters of the Forest, World's Leading Experts, Off the Gridders, and Belly Feeders like myself.

These are pretty disparate groups, but we all have a few things in common: We all seem to feel humbled by nature (to varying degrees), and we all seem to regard establishment notions with skepticism, also to varying degrees, ranging from a general suspicion of corporate patriotism to total rejection of certain Western traditions. Indeed, when my cold kicked in during breakfast, one lovely young woman with dark blue eyes and long brown hair offered me a hit of Fungi Perfecti's G5 tonic, "for supporting your immune system," she said. "Forget the drugstore drugs." I took a swig. It tasted like vanilla extract, without the vanilla.

The decline of medicinal mushrooms in the West, what used to be known as "simples," or herbal cures, reflects the economic imperatives fueling the rise of synthesized drugs. You can't patent a mushroom species, but you can patent a synthesized drug. Western medicinal practices are based on scientific studies with clear goals—is this particular medicine effective as a treatment against that particular ailment?—goals that have been evaluated using standards like the double-blind test. The Western approach to medicine is based on the notion of the silver bullet, the one shot that cures the disease, either by eradicating or relieving illness surgically or chemically. It is, according to Dr. Denis Benjamin, a "reductionist" approach.

In contrast, Asian medicine promotes health, including improvements of a more general sort, like immune system enhancement and increased vigor. You could say the definition of Western doctoring is to respond to disease and the definition of Eastern doctoring is to avoid disease.

In traditional Chinese medicine (TCM), mushrooms are prescribed and prepared as teas or powders or extracts. The TCM approach is to create a synergy of several components rather than a single active chemical, a practice known as polypharmacy. That's what Fungi Perfecti's G5 is: a formula composed of five species of *Ganoderma* mushroom extracts from mushrooms grown on the farm. (*Ganoderma* species are known in TCM for fortifying the immune system, as well as providing anti-inflammatory and antiallergenic effects.) In TCM, small amounts of therapeutic agents like mushroom extracts are taken over long periods of time, often in combination with foods and other therapies like acupuncture, all specifically tailored to the individual. What happens in the West is we cherry-pick remedies like G5. Without the whole package of individualized wellness therapies as prescribed in the East, it's questionable how effective, even by TCM standards, the mushrooms can be.

Lots of different mushrooms are used in TCM, but those that have predominated in Asian studies are shiitake and reishi (aka lingzhi), both saprophytic fungi: the first, a fleshy gilled mushroom, the second a polypore.

According to the Ming Dynasty physician Wu Juei, shiitake (*Lentinula edodes*) preserves health, improves stamina and circulation, cures colds, and lowers blood cholesterol. Modern studies suggest it may lower serum cholesterol levels and provide immunological effects that are linked to preventing or shrinking tumors. The mushroom contains two important extracts. Lentinan is a polysaccharide that is thought to enhance the immune system by activating killer cells and stimulating the body's natural production of interferon, and in the process slowing or arresting the growth of tumors. Lentinan has been approved as a drug in Japan and is prescribed to support immune functioning in cancer patients undergoing chemotherapy. (Another study suggests, however, that the interferon effect of shiitake is not due to compounds in the mushroom but to a virus that lives in the mushroom.) The second extract is LEM (*L. edodes* mycelium), a more complex polysaccharide prepared from the mycelium of the fungus, credited with stronger antiviral rather than immune-stimulating features. In studies it has been shown to enhance the effects of AZT (azidothymidine—an antiretroviral drug that inhibits the reproduction of viral replication in patients with HIV). But according to Memorial Sloan-Kettering's Cancer Center, "large scale studies are needed to establish shiitake as a useful adjunct to cancer treatment."

In TCM, reishi (*Ganoderma lucidum*, the "herb of deathlessness" or the "10,000-year mushroom") has been credited with ameliorating a wide variety of ailments, from cancers and heart disease to hepatitis and hypertension. The many active compounds with potential medicinal applications present in reishi—more than 100 distinct polysaccharides and 119 steroidal triterpenoids—have attracted the interest of Western scientists. Most studies on the medicinal properties of reishi have been limited to the laboratory and animal models, and as a result claims regarding the mushroom's effects on humans are anecdotal only. But Asian clinical studies with humans have suggested that reishi can relieve many symptoms, from those associated with anorexia and muscular dystrophy, to insomnia and liver failure. Though these trials don't meet Western standards, as Denis Benjamin writes, "it is clear that the mushrooms [in the *Ganoderma* complex] contain compounds with potent physiological effects." Indeed, reishi is in clinical use in the East.

Turkey tail (*Trametes versicolor*) is another very important Asian medicinal mushroom. In terms of the quality of the scientific research that has been done, turkey tail, along with shiitake, is "the most credible of them all," said Christopher Hobbs, an herbalist and author of *Medicinal Mushrooms*. Turkey tail is used in TCM to treat pulmonary disorders, and two polysaccharide compounds from this fungus, PSP and PSK, are used as standard adjuvant cancer therapies in Japan and China, respectively, as immune stimulators. Gary Lincoff has a story about a pharmaceutical company that asked him for an exciting new mushroom they should explore. He pointed them toward the turkey tail. "In fact, it's growing in your parking lot!" he told the executives, which seemed to turn them off. "I guess they wanted to go to Papua New Guinea," sighed Lincoff.

Other important Asian medicinal mushrooms include the oyster mushroom, which has been used to control high blood pressure. Studies on animals have shown that an oyster mushroom extract may decrease serum cholesterol levels, and studies on human breast and colon cancer cells have shown oyster extract can halt the growth of these cells. *Grifola frondosa* (maitake, or hen of the woods) is used in TCM for tumor regressions and to reduce symptoms of breast, prostate, and colorectal cancer. Zhu ling (*Grifola umbellata*) is used as a diuretic and a treatment for edema and diarrhea, the earthstar (*Geastrum triplex*) as a tonic for the lungs and throat, and the honey mushroom (*Armillaria gallica*— same as the humongous fungus) is used to affect the nervous system as an anticonvulsant. Chaga (*Inonotus obliquus*) was traditionally used to treat TB; ulcers; digestive, heart, and liver cancers; and was actually approved as an anticancer drug in Russia in the 1950s. (There is a chapter about chaga in Alexandr Solzhenitsyn's *The Cancer Ward* called "The Cancer of the Birch Tree.") There are many others.

The most expensive of the medicinal mushrooms is *Cordyceps sinensis*, the Tibetan caterpillar fungus. It is venerated by the Chinese, and costs about half the value of gold. In TCM, this insect parasite is used to improve liver and kidney functions, rebuild the body after illness, and enhance stamina. Indeed, during the Beijing Olympics in 2008, three female Chinese athletes set world records for the 1,500-, 3,000-, and 10,000-meter races. The Chinese coach explained the swimmers were taking *C. sinensis* (though they ended up testing positive for other drugs and were stripped of their medals). A slew of in vitro and in vivo studies have been done on *C. sinensis*, and these have revealed the

Bundles of *C. sinensis* with caterpillars for sale

fungus to have potential therapeutic value in a variety of aging disorders and sexual dysfunction.

The Asian case for the effectiveness of medicinal mushrooms, however, is flimsy by Western medical standards. While the use of medicinal mushrooms in TCM has inspired many modern scientific studies, the herbalist Christopher Hobbs pointed out that most of the human trials on record are Chinese studies that are "more like clinical reports," he writes in *Medicinal Mushrooms,* "in that a group of researchers give mushroom extracts to a number of patients . . . and the overall results are noted," or in vitro studies (studies using bacterial or animal cells in a lab environment) or in vivo studies using animals, primarily rodents, the results of which are hard to extrapolate to human use.

That said, more than 4 decades of scientific studies have been conducted on a wide range of mushrooms and are ongoing, with some researchers searching for novel compounds and others looking for an explanation for the prevalence of mushrooms in the Asian pharmacopoeia. One can't help but think there is something to be said for 5,000 years of practical knowledge. On the other hand, "the mere fact that the Chinese believe in them has as much currency as their belief that rhinoceros horn is an aphrodisiac," said Denis Benjamin, "or that cigarettes were once a tonic for breathing problems."

The compounds of medical interest in mushrooms are polysaccharides, glycoproteins, ergosterols, triterpenes, and antibiotics. Some of these compounds, like antibiotics, have been effectively harnessed and make a substantial impact on human health. Others are very interesting to Western medical science but haven't yet proven to be medically viable, despite claims to the contrary.

Fungi capable of producing antimicrobial substances are widely distributed in nature. Mushrooms protect themselves from microbial rivals with a range of chemicals that are antibiotic, antiviral, and/or antifungal. Because animals, like us, and fungi share common microbial antagonists, the strategies fungi have evolved to combat their competitors and predators can benefit us as well. (The flip side of this is the medicines that kill fungi can harm us, making fungal disease hard to eradicate.) Isolating and synthesizing fungal chemicals has led to a collection of powerful drugs.

The antibiotic penicillin is one, and there are many other important antimicrobials derived from fungi that are effective against different bacteria, viruses, even other fungi, and combinations of these microbes. For example, cephalosporins are a family of compounds derived from the fungus *Acremonium* that are active against all sorts of bacteria, including *Salmonella typhi*, the cause of typhoid fever. Indeed, fungi have provided the majority of agents and lead compounds currently used against bacterial infections.*

Some immunosuppressant drugs are derived from fungi. Fingolimod, which was approved by the FDA in 2010, is an oral medication for patients with multiple sclerosis that works by preventing immune system cells from attacking the protective covering around nerve fibers. It is derived from a fungus, *Isaria sinclairii*, a parasite of a cicada from East Asia. (The fungus has long been part of the Chinese traditional pharmacopoeia.) Cyclosporine, which Tom Volk takes so his body doesn't reject

---

*As antibiotic-resistant strains of bacteria evolve, scientists are looking farther afield for new antibiotics. One company, Aloha Medicinals in Nevada, has pursued the reanimation of archaic strains of penicillin found in ancient coal deposits more than 8 million years old, under the expectation that from them antibiotics might be made that no modern bacteria can resist. But as Denis Benjamin says, "Every antibiotic we have used merely produces resistant strains within months. Bacteria evolve far too fast and too effectively for us to ever win this battle."

The scarab beetle was the ancient Egyptian symbol for rebirth.

his transplanted heart, is derived from a *Cordyceps* fungus that is a pathogen of one insect, the scarab beetle. It's quite a coincidence: The drug that has given Volk a second chance at life is a parasite of the ancient Egyptian symbol for rebirth.

All sorts of interesting isolates found in mushrooms are available commercially. Grisovin (the generic name is griseofulvin) is used to treat ringworm, a fungal infection of the skin. It is derived from a fungus in the *Penicillium* genus. The steroids in birth control pills are derived from a fungus, *Rhizopus nigricans.* So are the steroids in cortisone and prednisone. Ergot derivatives from *Claviceps purpurea,* particularly ergotamine tartrate, are used to induce abortions, decrease postpartum bleeding, and to treat migraines. (Cafergot is a migraine medicine combining ergot and caffeine.) Two fungi in the *Mortierella* genus are used to make arachidonic acid, a fatty acid necessary for brain development in babies. It is added to commercial bottle formulas. The statin drug Zocor is derived from *Aspergillus terreus* and used to lower cholesterol. Beano, which helps diners control farting, contains an enzyme from *A. terreus.* Right now research is at work on a fungal metabolite (isolated from an endophytic fungus collected from an African rain forest) that reduces blood sugar levels but is safe to ingest, suggesting that people with diabetes may one day have an oral alternative to the dismal chore of injecting insulin.

These are a few examples of common drugs derived from fungi that have powerful medical (and in the case of Beano, social) implications.

And research is ongoing to develop new medicines aimed at the more intractable diseases of our time, particularly cancer.

One of the most provocative areas of study is the action of fungal beta-glucans, chains of polysaccharides that may act as antigens to provoke immune responses. Proponents of the healing properties of mushrooms have suggested that our bodies are adapted to respond to fungal beta-glucans with an immune reaction. Here's the theory: Our immune systems have evolved to fight off the airborne pathogenic fungi that are ubiquitous in our atmosphere. When we are exposed to the beta-glucans in those pathogenic fungi, our immune system kicks in. However, when our bodies are exposed to the beta-glucans in nonpathogenic fungi, like shiitake mushrooms, it also triggers our immune system, which may offer an advantage in fighting off disease.

Many, if not all, higher fungi in the Basidiomycota phylum contain biologically active polysaccharides. In the past 20 years, some studies have suggested these polysaccharides may be effective in retarding the progress of various cancers through immune stimulation and in alleviating the side effects of chemotherapy and radiation with cellular regenerative effects, although these studies have not included human trials in the USA. According to a review paper in the *International Journal of Medicinal Mushrooms,* fungal polysaccharides "prevent oncogenesis, show direct anti-tumor activity against various synergetic tumors and prevent tumor metastasis" by activating the killer cells and chemical messengers that trigger the immune system. They do not, however, directly affect tumors (as surgery or chemotherapy do), so their benefits are expected to be effective in conjunction with more aggressive forms of therapy. But the majority of studies have been conducted in vitro, and in vivo on mice, and effects accomplished in a test tube or a discrete cell don't necessarily translate to humans.

So as far as the elusive cure for cancer is concerned, no fungal compound or collection of compounds has been proven to cure, manage, or prevent cancer in humans. This is not to say there is no connection between the two, but that the connection is made of loose links. For example, white button mushrooms contain flavones. Flavones have been shown to inhibit aromatase. Aromatase can effect estrogen production. Estrogen is a factor in breast tumor growth. The subsequent headline "White Button Mushrooms May Cure Breast Cancer" is inaccurate but not without basis. Yet the overhype breeds confusion and mistrust among medical professionals.

Nonetheless, medicinal mushrooms are a rapidly developing area of research for cancer therapy and other bioactivities. Researchers from Indiana University found that a dietary supplement known as Myco-Phyto Complex inhibited cell proliferation in invasive breast cancer cells. Studies are under way on the ability of oyster mushroom extract to cause apoptosis, sudden cell death of cancer cells; the ability of *Trametes versicolor* (turkey tail) to slow the growth of cancer cells in women with breast cancer; and whether white button mushroom extract can stop or delay the development of recurrent prostate cancer. But other studies have proved disappointing. Contrary to anecdotal evidence, shiitake mycelium extract is totally ineffectual against prostate cancer. Irofulven is an antitumor drug candidate derived from *Omphalotus olearius*, known as the jack-o'-lantern mushroom because it is bioluminescent. The drug, which decreases tumors, was granted fast-track status by the FDA and made it through Phase II (human trials), but was then abandoned because it showed no greater benefit than standard therapy and, ironically, had terrible visual side effects, damaging the retina. There are many other examples.

These studies, and others into antiviral and antioxidant substances in mushrooms, are very preliminary. A potential drug has to travel a long and expensive road before it becomes available to doctors to prescribe. But there is no lack of anecdotal evidence that such studies are indeed warranted. In June 2009, Paul Stamets's 84-year-old mother was

diagnosed with an aggressive form of breast cancer that had metasta-
sized into her sternum and liver. She was not a candidate for a mastec-
tomy or radiation and was given 3 months to live. Then her doctor asked
her if she would consider taking the medicinal mushroom turkey tail
(*Trametes versicolor*). Not only would she take it, she replied, her son
Paul grows it. He prescribed four of Fungi Perfecti's turkey tail caps in
the morning and four in the evening for 6 weeks. Stamets declared,
"Today [August 2010] her 5.5 centimeter tumor is gone, and she is still in
remission." A story like this is very hard to qualify. For Stamets and his
family, the proof is indisputable. But for the rest of us, anecdotal stories
can bring as much heartbreak as hope. Just as no two patients are alike,
no two cancers are alike, either. The most honest statement that can be
made from a Western medical point of view *today* about the claims of
most medicinal mushrooms is only that they hold significant potential
for rigorous research.

   Christopher Hobbs, who treats some of his patients with medicinal
mushrooms, believes they have an important role to play in modern
health. But as Denis Benjamin, the skeptic, says, "Despite all the basic
research and the description of many interesting molecules, there are pre-
cious few, if any, decent clinical studies that supports their use, efficacy, or
value. Medicinal mushrooms will not become mainstream until decent
clinical trials are performed and reported in widely accepted peer reviewed
literature. That being said, many people are easily seduced by hype and
hope, which accounts for the massive trade in food supplements, unproven
nutraceuticals, and the entire vitamin industry. All it has done for the
population is produce the most expensive urine in the world."

   The second and final day of our seminar with Paul Stamets
included a search for *Psilocybe* mushrooms, particularly liberty caps

A collection of *Psilocybe* mushrooms

(*P. semilanceata*). We cara-vanned to the interior of the island and parked beside a green horse pas-ture, soupy with white wet fog. Stamets explained the mushrooms are just a few inches tall; delicate, grey, and gilled, and the ones that are psychoactive stain blue and have a purpley brown to black spore print.

A few of us lingered while he described their habitat—they grow mainly on horse and cow manure—but most of our group, the younger members anyway, were off, seemingly well acquainted with the mushroom's biology. Stamets made reference to the "*Psilocybe* stoop," and indeed, scattered across the pasture were people bent at the waist, walking in small meditative circles, staring at the ground. I looked and looked, my back becoming increasingly achy, my crappy boots wet, my socks soaked from the tall dewy grass, and my resolution withering. Tired and discouraged, I sat down and promptly my eyes fell on a tremulous little mushroom growing tentatively out of a fist-size hunk of dung.

In the end, I gave the *Psilocybe* to Zack, a young man who had patiently explained the erotic applications of his tongue and genital piercings in the car drive over, and who thereafter became my friend, like a stray dog with which you've shared your sandwich.

Stamets's final evening lecture followed an oyster BBQ on the beach. I shunned the beautifully crisped oysters, their shells brimming with buttery hot sauce, and manfully slurped down a half-dozen Jurassic-size specimens raw. It was a little like swallowing a chicken cutlet, and filled me up instantly, as if I'd pumped a gallon of Gatorade into my belly. But they were delightful: briny and sweet and plentiful, the three essential ingredients of a proper oyster orgy. Oysters sloshing around inside me, I settled into the lecture hall with the rest of the audience, on the carpeted floor, cross-legged, slippers on, lights low.

Stamets ranged over many subjects: harnessing the decompositional power of saprophytes, the nutritive power of mycorrhizae, and the medicinal power of fungi's biochemical pharmacy. He more than venerates the fungus, he's personally grateful for it. He revealed that *Psilocybe* mushrooms had cured him of a lifelong stutter.

Psilocybin is a chemical present in a wide range of mushrooms, but half of all species in the genus *Psilocybe*—about 190 species—are psilocybin producing, though why psilocybin exists in these mushrooms is a mystery. Psilocybin is an indole alkaloid related to bufotenin and serotonin. When ingested, psilocybin metabolizes to psilocin, which resembles the chemical structure of serotonin. Psilocin may simulate serotonin and stimulate serotonin receptors in the brain. The action is similar to psychopharmaceutical drugs that treat patients by altering serotonin levels. Wrote Andy Letcher in his book *Shroom,* "It is rather as if a new, alien but curiously compatible piece of software is thrown into the brain's computer, disrupting its normal operations in novel and unexpected ways."

Basically, psilocin causes all kinds of hormones to fire off and affects a range of biological and neurological receptors in the brain, although this is a simplistic view: "There are subreceptors on the receptors and subreceptors on the subreceptors, and so on," said Charles Grob, MD, a professor of psychiatry and pediatrics at UCLA School of Medicine, who has studied the medical applications of psilocybin.

Psilocybin research is controversial, to say the least. In the late 1950s, Dr. Albert Hoffman (the scientist who first synthesized LSD from ergot—the fungus *Claviceps purpurea*—at Sandoz Laboratories in

Switzerland in 1938) extracted the active ingredients in a *Psilocybe* mushroom and synthesized the compound psilocybin.

In the years following its discovery, psilocybin was tested in a variety of psychiatric applications. In 1960, Timothy Leary, a young lecturer in psychology at Harvard University, administered psilocybin (the drug, not the mushroom) to 32 prison inmates to see if the drug would help lower their recidivism. (It only delayed their return to crime.) There were studies on its effect in treating alcoholism,* as a tool in therapy (to help "open up and discuss problems," wrote Christopher Hobbs in *Medicinal Mushrooms*), and as a mechanism by which the terminally ill might better cope with despair. All this, because, as Gary Lincoff wrote in *Toxic and Hallucinogenic Mushroom Poisoning,* "divorced from the crippling anxieties of the present, the patient can look dispassionately on his condition, perhaps come to understand it, and possibly learn to accept or correct it."

Interest in the medicinal value of psychoactive mushrooms, and in financing those studies, dwindled at about the same time psilocybin entered the mainstream as a recreational drug and was classified as a Schedule I substance, the same category as heroin. But now, 3 decades later, psilocybin is being reexamined for its medical applications. Doing this kind of research is no longer a career liability, and a handful of studies are currently under way, much of it building on the work of scientists 30 years ago.

In 2006, the University of Arizona conducted a study on the effects of psilocybin to modify obsessive-compulsive disorder. The study found

---

*Charles Schuster, professor emeritus of psychiatry and behavioral neurosciences at Wayne State University in Detroit, wrote, "It is entirely conceivable that psychotropic agents that produce [religious] experiences may have a role in the treatment of addictive states. Spirituality has long been a major component of the 12-step approach to the treatment of alcoholism and other forms of drug addiction. Although the investigations of LSD for the treatment of alcoholism failed to show any clear-cut significant beneficial effects, the possibility that a spiritual experience . . . might be useful cannot be discounted." Indeed, William Griffith Wilson told Huston Smith (an early colleague of Timothy Leary's) that his experience with LSD had led him to found Alcoholics Anonymous.

that several subjects within their control group experienced acute reductions in their core symptoms. That same year, the American Academy of Neurology issued a report based on interviews with 53 patients suffering from cluster headaches who had been using psilocybin (or LSD; ergot is also used as a migraine medication) to self-medicate this notoriously horrid syndrome. The researchers found that psilocybin was the only medicine known to abort the headaches.

Indeed, I met a young architectural historian in New York, Ralph Ghoche, who suffered from crippling cluster headaches for years. He went to numerous doctors who put him on analgesics and steroids, but they acknowledged there is no cure, no accepted treatment. On a Web site devoted to the syndrome, www.clusterbusters.com, Ghoche read a testimonial about the effectiveness of psilocybin. "So I got some mushrooms—I don't know what kind they were—and took the small dose recommended on the Web site." Ralph's trip was barely on the radar: "It was boring," he said. The next day, he felt the premonition of a headache coming on. "I thought, fuck, the mushrooms didn't work, and then I felt something *occurring* in my brain and the headache was blocked. The same thing happened the next day, and then that was it. I've been 3 years without a headache."

Since 2008, Roland Griffiths and his colleagues at the Johns Hopkins University School of Medicine have been studying psilocybin and patients dealing with cancer and depression. In 2009, Johns Hopkins Medical launched their Psilocybin Cancer Project, a study of states of consciousness brought about by psilocybin and their impact on psychological distress and spirituality. New York University is currently sponsoring a double-blind placebo-controlled study of the effects of psilocybin on patients suffering from cancer and associated anxiety, as are other research groups at Yale, UCLA, and MAPS (Multidisciplinary Association for Psychedelic Studies—not as goofy as it sounds).

Dr. Charles Grob completed a study in 2008 of psilocybin treatment for anxiety in patients with advanced-stage cancer. (Psilocybin was selected because it is less intense and paranoiac than LSD and carries less cultural baggage.) He and his colleagues found that patients exhibited "a significant reduction in anxiety at 1 and 3 months after treatment . . . and improvement of mood that reached significance at 6 months."

The study suggests that patients seemed to experience a reequilibration, where they acquired a perspective on their lives that helped them come to terms with their fate. "The universal fate," said Dr. Grob. "These are potent compounds in regard to their action on the brain and our sense of who we are."

ⱳ

Within a few days of leaving Cortes Island, my weekend of wet toes caught up with me. My feet were itchy and hot, and I woke up the first night home to find myself rubbing my feet together. A sniff inside my hiking boots, which were still damp 36 hours later, gave me all the information I needed.

For all the wonderful medicinal attributes of fungi, there is a dark side: a slew of mycoses—infections or diseases caused by fungi—that are usually just a nuisance but can sometimes make us sick. And occasionally, very sick.

Most of the time when you get sick from fungi, it is either because you have picked up one of the very common fungal infections, like athlete's foot, or because you are immunocompromised. Additionally, lots of people describe getting sick from moldy environments in homes, but they aren't actually succumbing to disease. They are more likely suffering from an allergic reaction.

Eventually, most Americans will encounter an infection caused by

dermatophytic fungi (from the Greek, *dermo* = skin, *phytes* = plants)
that feed on keratin, a protein on the skin, hair, and nails. Some live on
dead skin and others on live skin, and they tend to be contagious. Fungal
infections of the skin are known as ringworm infections (it was once
thought to be a parasitic worm). The ring, if it is even evident, is caused
by the outer edge of the radially growing fungus, like a fairy ring of
mushrooms in your yard. Athlete's foot is ringworm of the foot, and
many other locales on the body are the specialty of different species of
dermatophytic fungi.

While dermatophytic fungal infections can constitute disease, especially if allowed to proliferate, it's pretty unlikely you will die or become
infertile due to athlete's foot or a fingernail fungus (though you may be
disadvantaged in finding a partner). However, the more debilitated the
host, the more invasive fungi can be. For immunocompromised patients,
there is no such thing as a nonpathogenic fungus (except for fungi that
can't grow at body temperature). AIDS patients, for example, often deal
with fungal infections, as do those on immunosuppressant drugs or
antibiotics. Spores of potentially infectious fungi are widespread in the
atmosphere, and everyone inhales them with every breath. A fungus like
Aspergillus fumigatus (a ubiquitous, soil-based mold) is easily overcome
by a healthy immune system, but *A. fumigatus* can cause a range of pulmonary diseases in immunocompromised people and is the leading
cause of death by infection in leukemia and bone marrow transplant
patients. About 83,000 life-threatening fungal diseases are diagnosed
annually, and care for those patients costs as much as $2.6 billion a year.
And not just people: Livestock and farmed fish are also vulnerable to
fungal pathogens if their immune systems are stressed.

Mycoses are characterized by their location on the body. Superficial
mycoses are infections of the hair shaft or dead outer layer of skin.
Cutaneous mycoses are infections like athlete's foot and ringworm.

Subcutaneous mycoses are chronic, localized infections of the skin and tissue, some of which are nasty and disfiguring. One of the most common is "rose grower's disease," where the prick of a thorn, for example, allows the fungus *Sporothrix schenckii* access to tissue, where it grows and develops a pustule ulcer. During a New York Mycological Society morel walk one year, I got lost in the underbrush and, in a burst of adrenaline-fueled panic, charged through the prickers in search of the trail. A thorn branch grabbed my lips, and for days afterward I was constantly touching my mouth, paranoid that I'd managed to contract rose grower's disease. (I hadn't.)

Systemic mycoses are either fungal diseases of the body caused by common fungi that become pathogenic when the patient is immuno-compromised or otherwise debilitated, or fungal infections of the body caused by fungi that can affect a healthy person if they receive a large enough dose.

The most common systemic mycoses (the opportunistic type) is caused by *Candida albicans*, a yeast that lives in the skin, guts, and mucosae of 40 to 80 percent of all normal humans. A yeast infection is an overgrowth of yeast, and it can occur under different circumstances. But typically, people get yeast infections when they take antibiotics, which destroy both pathogenic bacteria and the "good bacteria" in our bodies that control yeast colonies. Occasionally, rarely, *C. albicans* can go systemic and even result in death.

The other important opportunistic fungal pathogens are aspergil-losis, a common respiratory infection by fungi from the genus *Aspergillus,* that can cause pneumonia in the immunocompromised, and cryptococcosis, caused by inhaling dust that has been contaminated by species in the *Cryptococcus* genus. There used to be signs all over New York City that said "Do Not Feed Pigeons" because their droppings were carriers of this disease. Cryptococcosis is fatal: One hundred percent of patients die without treatment, but it is very rare and is unlikely to affect people with healthy immune systems.

The deep mycoses, caused by true human pathogens, meaning anybody can get sick if they are exposed to enough inoculant, usually enter through the lungs as well. There are a few pockets of these fungal diseases in the United States, and lots of people who live in those regions are exposed to the pathogen, but they usually don't get seriously sick.

Some do, however. Coccidioidomycosis, also known as valley fever or desert rheumatism, is what Tom Volk calls the "dirty secret of Arizona." An estimated 600,000 people were infected in 2010, and Volk suggests that 90 percent of the population has been exposed to the airborne spores of the fungus *Coccidioides immitis*, which can cause pulmonary disease. While *C. immitis* is a true pathogen, it can also act opportunistically if the patient is immune suppressed. Sixty percent of those exposed are asymptomatic, or have very mild symptoms, but 5 to 10 percent are severe cases that present so much like TB it's often misdiagnosed. There are others. In 1997, Bob Dylan came down with an acute case of histoplasmosis, caused by the fungus *Histoplasma capsulatum*, which grows in soil and is associated with bird manure (a typical way to be exposed is by spreading chicken manure on a garden). Dylan was so sick, he said, "I really thought I'd be seeing Elvis soon." While histoplasmosis can be deadly if not treated, most people, including the musician, enjoy a complete recovery.

I have Internet alerts for "mushrooms" and "fungi," and I'd say about 25 percent of the items are about fighting nail fungus and yeast infections. But not so far behind are indoor mold complaints.

Molds are ubiquitous. Like other fungi, they grow wherever there is moisture and a food source. Most of us are familiar with them as competitors for the food in the refrigerator, but there are thousands of known molds, and probably many thousands unknown, and they consistently freak people out. Whether they experience real or fantasy mold infestations, people like to blame mold for all sorts of health problems, from autoimmune diseases like lupus and MS to cancer.

But the science has not been able to conclusively prove that airborne mold spores cause any disease. "The medical information on mold symptoms is abysmal," said Denis Benjamin. Mold spores have only been identified as possible allergens responsible for a variety of respiratory ailments in susceptible patients, like allergic asthma and pneumonitis.

In 2001, a Texas family won $32 million against their insurance company for mold damage to their 22-room house in Dripping Springs, Texas. This led to the "mold rush." About 38 percent of homes in the USA are contaminated with mold, and about 10 percent of the population demonstrates a significant response to mold. Following the Dripping Springs judgment, mold-related litigation tripled in some states. As one national legal group advertised, "If mold or fungus problems are in your home or condo, you need to make sure that you don't allow these issues to get worse. Contact a lawyer today."

There were big bucks in mold. Ed McMahon, Johnny Carson's straight man on *The Tonight Show*, successfully sued several companies, including his insurance companies, for $7.2 million for allowing mold to infest his home, sickening his family and killing his dog, Muffin. Bianca Jagger went on rent strike at her Park Avenue apartment due to "toxic mildew." And Michael Jordan sued the manufacturer of the synthetic stucco that clad his mansion in Chicago for $2.6 million. In response, insurance companies have adapted their rating schedules to include mold remediation limits.*

Mold contamination causes $3 to $5 billion in insurance claims a

---

*Molds can grow in air-conditioning systems and disperse spores through individual units. This has been cited as a cause of sick building syndrome (SBS), where building occupants experience acute health and comfort effects that appear to be linked to time spent in a building.

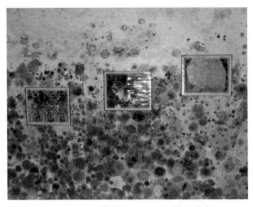

Mold damage in a post-Katrina home in New Orleans

year. It's hard, however, to determine what the mold remediation industry is worth annually, or to gauge how successful mold remediation actually is. That's because the industry is unregulated and lacks a professional advocacy group, and all kinds of mold remediation businesses have proliferated (like "Mold Mutts," a canine mold detection service). Unlike other biohazard remediation efforts, there are no established procedures for remediating mold.

Part of the furor over molds, I think, is psychological. Mold is the symbol of devastation, decay, disaster, and doom, and like death it spares nothing. It causes a rather uncanny fear in us: Horror movie set decorators use mold to make abandoned buildings look more frightening. One author suggests the Old Testament associated black mold with leprosy. But the truth is, if molds were as life threatening as some seem to think, pointed out Mark Misner, a remediation expert, "we'd see hospitals overflowing with sick and dying patients."

The other way people get sick from fungi (besides eating a poisonous mushroom) is when they are exposed to a mycotoxin, usually a chemical produced by a fungus to protect itself from competitors. We ingest them (as do our livestock) through contaminated food products like grain. As a result, over 100 countries regulate mycotoxins in crops.

Of the fungi that produce mycotoxins that affect humans, the big three are *Penicillium*, the primary mold group you see spoiling foods, which produces a number of toxins, from very weak ones to a neurotoxin that can cause seizures; species from the genus *Aspergillus,* which cause lots of common food spoilage, and some produce aflatoxins, which are highly carcinogenic to humans; and *Fusarium,* a group of grain pathogens that produce, among other nasty mycotoxins, the trichothecenes family of toxins. These have been explored as a biochemical weapon because they can act through the skin. During the Reagan era, Secretary of State Alexander Haig accused the Soviet Union of weaponizing one of the trichothecenes and supplying it to the Vietcong in Kampuchea and Laos in the mid-1970s to spray on the Hmong, the insurgent combatants and our allies in that war. In 1983, those charges were refuted and the "yellow rain" that Hmong refugees described was determined to be largely digested pollen in bee feces, from what Tom Volk rather vividly described as a "communal cleansing flight."

Probably the most infamous mycotoxin is ergot, the fruiting structure of *Claviceps purpurea,* a pathogen of various grasses, like rye. Today we use its chemical derivatives to make medicines and LSD (the ergotamine in ergot is metabolized in humans to lysergic acid), but for many centuries ergot caused acute poisoning.

There are two types of ergotism, possibly the result of two different strains of *C. purpurea*: gangrenous, where victims lose parts of their extremities like fingers, toes, and earlobes; and convulsive ergotism, which is characterized by hallucinations and awful self-destructive behaviors. Both

The black growths are ergot.

forms have a long history in Europe, known during the Middle Ages as St. Anthony's fire. A French nobleman and his son believed a relic attributed to St. Anthony had cured them of the poisoning and founded a hospital in the saint's name to treat other victims.*

But calling ergotism "fire" goes back hundreds of years earlier and refers to gangrenous ergotism, which causes burning sensations of the limbs before the gangrene sets in. (In 1940, E. C. Large wrote, in *Advance of the Fungi,* "Ergot, through its constrictive actions on blood vessels, not only caused abortions in women, it cut off the blood supply to the extremities of the body; hands and feet became devoid of sensation and then rotted most horribly away. In the process of the ergot gangrene whole limbs fell off at the joint, before the shapeless trunk was released from its torments.") Outbreaks of ergotism are found in the earliest written records, and thousands have died from the poisoning.

The cultural biologist Linda Caporael has suggested ergot poisoning was responsible for the insanity of the Salem witch trials in Massachusetts in the 1690s, and based on reports of convulsions and hallucinations suffered by people and animals, along with other circumstantial evidence, it was likely convulsive ergotism. Ergot poisoning may also have been behind the Old World witch persecutions that occurred periodically throughout the Middle Ages. Another author has suggested ergot poisoning as the source of Joan of Arc's "voices."

An outbreak of convulsive ergot poisoning in France offers the only modern record of the disease. Over the course of the summer of 1951, hundreds of townspeople in Provence were poisoned by bread made from contaminated flour. They felt chills, followed by severe stomach upset, nausea, vomiting, and diarrhea. Within 24 hours, some began

---

*Anthony (c. 1195–1231) was a Spanish-born Franciscan monk whose inspirational sermons earned him sainthood. Tradition has it that when his tomb in the Basilica of Padua, Italy, was opened 30 years after his death, his body had disintegrated but his tongue remained fresh.

suffering from convulsions, claiming their legs and arms were on fire, and town doctors reported their sweat smelled like dead mice and stale urine. Others became sleepless and wandered the streets night after night, talking ceaselessly in groups. Their moods alternated between elated and invincible and depressed and suicidal. Many experienced hallucinations, self-mutilation, and obsessive behaviors like counting sets of numbers over and over for days without sleep, and the fantasy that one could fly, leading to tragic falls, as well as other uncontrollable psychoses. Some saw the world as beautifully colored, found the meaning of life in common objects, and experienced mystical revelations. But most did not, and a few people died of heart failure.

Someone found grasses infected with *C. purpurea* at the NAMA foray in Colorado, and I saw it on a paper plate on the specimen table. To think the messenger of so much medieval suffering was happily growing on the lawn of a Christian summer camp in Colorado! And it was an odd thing to examine. This tiny bit of elongated mass on the tip of a blade of grass was so unremarkable, yet I knew it was incredibly potent. But that's what I was beginning to realize about fungi in general: that although the organism is very small, that doesn't mean it isn't mighty, and perfectly capable of benefiting or harming us in profound ways.

Chapter 10

SHROOMS

A s my obsession with fungi grew, I increasingly felt the pull of psychedelic mushrooms. Though never the topic of a lecture at the forays and conferences, they came up in casual conversation over and over again. People discussed them in the coded language of the myconaut, and indeed, I discovered that about 25 percent of the mycologists I talked to had at least tried psychedelic mushrooms. Slowly but surely, I came to realize that experiencing the mushroom was an inevitable part of my fungal journey. On a deeper and more personal level, I was kind of in a rut. I don't want to say I was going through anything heavy like a midlife crisis; it was more a kind of nostalgia. It seemed like I was past the exciting part of my life. Taking the mushroom interested me intellectually and excited me personally.

That doesn't mean I wasn't concerned. Addiction didn't worry me— hallucinogens are not considered drugs of dependence—and I wasn't totally unfamiliar with psychedelics. I'd taken LSD a couple of times in high school (though I mainly endured the experience, as it made me feel paranoid, queasy, and unmoored, much like a very bad airplane ride), but that's where my comfort zone ended. How was I going to get them? How do I make sure what I get is actually a *Psilocybe* mushroom? How

236

do I dose myself? How was I going to clear the house of kids, telephones, the FedEx guy? What if I freaked out? What if I was arrested? I'd spent most of my adult years trying to control the circumstances of my life. The thought of intentionally giving up that control, even for a few hours, made my stomach churn with nervousness.

I kept putting the adventure off.

But eventually, like all things, the moment arrived. I made arrangements to get some wild psychedelic mushrooms from someone I thought would identify them correctly and I packed my bags for the 30th annual Telluride Mushroom Festival, which is held in Colorado at the end of August.

The festival was started by a Denver-based group called Fungophile in 1980 and is now operated by the Telluride Institute. Typically about 200 attend, mainly hippies young and old, New Agers, "trustafarians," and other counterculturists. Most mycological forays and festivals are prudish about psychedelic mushrooms. I sensed they were an embarrassment; the black sheep of the mycological world. The fact that the Telluride festival celebrates psychoactive mushrooms has led to its characterization as the psychedelic festival.

Vehicles at the Telluride Mushroom Festival

In my conversations about psychedelic mushrooms, I often heard people talking about the importance of "set," meaning one's frame of mind, and "setting," the environment in which the tripper will trip. In his book *Psilocybin Mushrooms of the World,*

Paul Stamets lends some advice. Regarding mind-set, Stamets recommends that people who are mentally disturbed, violent, or ill, or who suffer from heart conditions and other disorders, should avoid taking the mushrooms. He suggests users remind themselves that regardless of any horrors they might experience on the mushroom, it will be over in a matter of hours—4 or 5 seemed to be the going rate. "Trip with someone you love," wrote Stamets. This was a bit of a worry, as I was planning to trip with people I hardly knew.

And have someone accessible whom you can count on to take care of you should something go wrong, he continued. Also problematic: The only person I knew in Telluride was my high school boyfriend, and nice as he is, the friendship is still laden with dramas of the distant past. (Actually, is there any better way to ensure a bad trip than revisiting 12th grade?) And Stamets recommended the setting be familiar, appropriate, and safe. I didn't know for sure if the Telluride festival was going to meet any of the criteria.

On the plane, I looked up the mushroom we were going to take. *Psilocybe cyanescens* is a species native (in the United States) to the Pacific Northwest and southern California. A saprophyte, it prefers woody debris and sawdust and mulched gardens, particularly under rhododendrons and roses. Paul Stamets reported that on the "psilometric scale of comparative potency," it gets a rating of moderately to highly potent. (Detection of psilocybin in a mushroom is determined by chromatography.) Psilocybin is, according to the author Andy Letcher, "about a hundred times less potent than LSD, but about ten times more so than mescaline."

I knew the psilocybin in the mushroom would metabolize in my body into psilocin, and the psilocin, carried in my bloodstream, would activate receptors in my brain normally affected by serotonin. But ultimately, what is happening to the brain on mushrooms is a mystery. Some have speculated that psilocin amplifies sensory experiences, even latent sensory abilities, not normally accessed by serotonin. For example, it has been reported that psilocin seems to boost the number and intensity of scents that can be experienced and increases the brain's ability to perceive visual detail. It also has reportedly launched personal epiphanies and spiritual experiences, and I wondered: Could spiritual feelings be stored in our cortical cells, as processes that may be amplified by the chemical? There's actually a name for it: neurotheology, the neurology of religious experience.

Maybe, I thought, looking out my airplane window at the great red continental collision that is the Rocky Mountains, I would have a personal epiphany when I took the mushrooms. My commuter flight from Denver to Grand Junction was flying like a bee in a windstorm, changing altitude constantly as we were buffeted by updrafts: the kind of flight that tempts you to write a good-bye note on the back of the seat in front of you. Oddly, I was less nervous about that bumpy plane ride than I was about taking the mushrooms, even with the possibility that I might have some kind of revelation that would, I didn't know, make me decide to start farming beets or something. I was relieved to learn that psilocybin is not particularly toxic. ("*Psilocybe* mushrooms?" laughed David Campbell when I expressed my worries. "Safe as milk.") There has never been a fatality reported from *Psilocybe* mushroom poisoning, although there have been plenty of cases of teenagers high on mushrooms walking into freeway traffic and other such tragedies. The mushrooms may not be poisonous, but that doesn't mean taking them is safe.

Other mushrooms produce psilocybin or analogous mushroom alkaloids. A major one is ergot, the fruiting body of the grain pathogen *Claviceps purpurea*. Ergot can be synthesized (or metabolized) into LSD and, when ingested, can affect the same serotonin receptors in the brain as psilocin. But LSD also affects dopamine receptors, which psilocin does not. High dopaminergic transmission has been linked to psychosis and schizophrenia. While there are psychoactive substances in the *Gymnopilus* (laughing jims), *Panaeolus, Pluteus, Conocybe,* and *Inocybe* genera, 80 percent of psilocybin-producing mushrooms are in the *Psilocybe* genus, well over a third of which are from Mexico. *Psilocybe* are similar to an untold number of LBMs (little brown mushrooms), but they have one defining but not absolute characteristic: They stain blue. Blue stain is an indicator of the presence of psilocybin, and in general the more blue stain, the more psilocybin is present.* A great deal of the biology of *Psilocybe* mushrooms was first described by the Mexican mycologist Gastón Guzmán, whose work *The Genus Psilocybe: A Systematic Revision of the Known Species Including the History, Distribution and Chemistry of the Hallucinogenic Species* is still the definitive text. He discovered and authored works on half of all known species.

Psilocybe mushrooms are widely dispersed and are opportunistic, rather like morels. They sometimes even produce a sclerotium (known as the magic truffle), presumably to withstand environmental challenges like fires. *Psilocybe* grows in grasslands, on dung (the nutritional makeup of the dung and soil may affect the potency of the mushroom), and in man-made habitats like mulched corporate parks, golf courses, and gardens. Paul Stamets said he likes to look for them in the landscaping around Google and Apple headquarters and that he's also found them on college campuses and in the landscaping outside courthouses and police stations. *Psilocybe* mushrooms are found in floodplains, in woodlands, and to a lesser degree on burns. They are ubiquitous in the Pacific Northwest, throughout the southwestern United States, in the tropics (there is a *P. cubensis,* first found in Cuba), in temperate forests across Europe, and in the subtropical Far East, for starters. Weirdly,

---

*Other mushrooms stain blue, too, and not because of the presence of psilocybin. There are boletes that stain blue as a result of oxidation. Psilocybe can be confused with other LBMs as well, like the deadly Galerina.

there are none in Colorado. Well, one, once. In 1993, after years of searching, *P. telluridensis* was "discovered" in the high alpine wilderness above Telluride. Never found again, it was likely a prank.

I was keen to go to Telluride because for the first time I would actually know a fair number of people, new friends I was hoping to know better. I felt like I was moving away from being just a witness to the mushroom community and with the advent of these blossoming friendships, I was on the cusp of joining the community. The mushroom subculture is very large, of course, but I was definitely finding my particular niche: the hipster mycologist, foodies with PhDs. And many of them were attracted to the merry capriciousness of the Telluride festival.

I'd become friendly with Daniel Winkler, the vivacious *Cordyceps* expert, and Larry Evans, the picker mycologist, who had both stopped by my cabin in Crawford, Colorado, on their way to the festival. (That summer, there was a foray in Eagle just prior to the Telluride festival. My cabin lies between the two towns, more or less.) They dumped their duffels in the driveway, so eager were they to get into the mountains for what turned out to be the best mushroom hunting season in decades (it was the wettest August on record: 3.5 inches). They brought back many pounds of porcini and then spent 2 days in my kitchen cleaning, slicing, and dehydrating. One night, as my husband, Kevin, and I soaked in the hot tub listening to Daniel and Larry carry on in the kitchen about the specifics of this species or that, Kevin observed that mycologists were the most obsessed people he'd ever met. "They wear mushroom T-shirts, they talk mushrooms, they eat mushrooms, they study mushrooms, they even recreate mushrooms." We tried to think of another group so single-minded but couldn't. The next morning, Daniel and Larry took off in Larry's red Subaru, the one decorated with white refrigerator magnets to look like a mobile *Amanita muscaria*. Tied to the roof was a huge net bag stuffed with porcini mushrooms, which they were planning to air-dry en route.

Tom Volk stopped by the cabin, too, and we picked lots of mushrooms together. (I had to keep calling for him in the woods because there were so many mushrooms he was only moving about a yard every 10 minutes.) Tom helped us stuff a pig with porcini stems, garlic, and branches of thyme and sage from the garden. We wrapped it like a mummy in cheesecloth and buried it in a hot fire pit. The next day, when we dug up the pig, it smelled like a giant bacony mushroom. I'd corresponded with Elinoar Shavit, shared recipes with Denis Benjamin, drank beers with David Campbell, provided a home base for Michael Wood's Colorado wine country expeditions, and befriended Britt Bunyard, who attended the festival as well. I'd teased him about his taste for sherry at the North American Mycological Association (NAMA) foray, and he'd e-mailed me saying he was going to "Man up on the booze" and was bringing . . . gin. Compared to what I was expecting at Telluride, NAMA was way more conservative: "I love them dearly," said Gary Lincoff about the NAMA crowd, "but I would have loved Ike Eisenhower, too. The Telluride festival is about orientation and reorientation."

Socked in the San Juan Mountains, Telluride is a pretty Victorian town of 3,000 crowded into a box canyon, with a waterfall at one end and a scandalously short airstrip at the other. The north-facing fields on the mountain above town, known as the sheep meadow and once owned by Greek sheep ranchers, are home to McMansions with their wide, river-stone chimneys and satellite dishes. Night and day, a gondola crawls to the top of the ski mountain where, if you take a connecting gondola, you can continue on to the spiffy Mountain Village and, beyond that, the silent, isolated townlette of Ophir. I'd visited Telluride once before and been shown around by a puckish English woman whose idea of a tour was to drive slowly by the little gingerbread houses and call out how many millions each had sold for.

I got into town a little late, mainly because I'd been cleaning up after the mycologists, and then driven from Montrose. (The route took me past Ralph Lauren's ranch, the Double RL, which is so huge, it's like an opera. You can take a nap and then wake up and still be driving by his property.) But I made the festival's introductory lecture that evening: Paul Stamets's "Psilocybin Mushrooms of the World, a Taxonomic & Historical Voyage." The house was full, crowded mainly with eager dreadlocked hippies and aging hipsters. But Paul was beat—it was obvious. His voice was hoarse, like an overworked pop star who's been on the road too long. After thanking Art Goodtimes, the festival's wizardy organizer and county commissioner, Paul thanked the mushroom itself, which to my ears set the tone for the entire festival.

The lecture was on entheogens: psychoactive substances used in religious or spiritual ritual for purposes of healing, revelation, and transcendence. *Entheogen* means "creates God within" (from the Greek, *en* = within, *theo* = god or divine, *gen* = creates or generates), the invention of a Greek scholar, Carl Ruck, as an alternative to the terms *hallucinogenic* and *psychedelic* to describe the mushroom's more profound aspect. Non–Native American exposure to psychoactive mushrooms is only about 50 years old, but the practice of using these substances to seek the divine may be ancient.

Ethnomycologists, who study how people use fungi, see mushrooms in many prehistoric images. The mushrooms themselves haven't turned up in the archaeological record, for the same reason they are rare in the paleontological record: They decompose quickly and thoroughly. But if one agrees the images cited do indeed represent mushrooms, it is utterly a matter of speculation as to what purpose those mushrooms were put. An example of this is amateur archaeologist Reid Kaplan's '70s-era hypothesis about a mushroom cult in prehistoric Sweden, Norway, and Denmark based on Bronze Age petroglyphs of what may or may not be mushrooms. Another very speculative theory says the ax engravings at

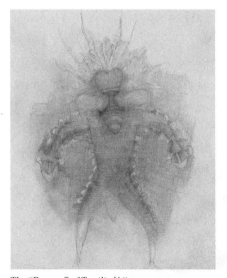

The "Beeman" of Tassili n'Ajjer

Stonehenge actually depict mushrooms, and the megalithic stone monument itself represents a mushroom fairy ring. But the most famous example is in the Tassili n'Ajjer ("land of many rivers") mountain range in the Sahara Desert of southern Algeria, home of beautiful and important groupings of prehistoric rock art. A UNESCO world heritage site, the paintings depict daily scenes of "a verdant Sahara teeming with life." The paintings are attributed to four chronological periods or traditions, and one painting, from the Bovidian tradition (4000 BC), has captured the imagination of ethnomycologists in particular: a bee-faced man bristling with tiny mushrooms . . . or arrows, or something else. Some have declared this image a depiction of a mushroom shaman. Stamets calls him a "shamanic figure . . . the bee-like face may relate to the preserving of mushrooms in honey." (The potency in *Psilocybe* mushrooms can be effectively preserved in honey.)

The other significant archaeological artifact is the mushroom stones of about 1000 BC, an enigma of pre-Columbian Central America. Carved in stone, they depict figures with heads topped with mushroom caps. Mainly Mayan and found in the Guatemalan highlands, about 200 of them reside in various museums and private collections. Although some of the stones resemble a metate, the traditional stone used to grind corn, many ethnomycologists believe the mushroom stones had ritualistic significance. The first to advance the theory that mushroom stones may be related to "the divinatory rite of the inebriating mushrooms of Mexico" were R. Gordon Wasson and Valentina P. Wasson. The Wassons were amateur mycologists who participated in and wrote about *Psilocybe* ceremonies in a 1957 *Life* magazine story called "Seeking the Magic Mushroom" (*Life* coined the term "magic mushroom"), in an issue Gary Lincoff said was full of ads for "cars and refrigerators, and about how to be a good workaholic American."*

The Wassons had studied and accumulated a huge collection of mushroom lore and published a very expensive limited-edition book, *Mushrooms, Russia, and History*, in 1957. According to the author Andy Letcher, they were set on proving the theory that "the human religious impulse itself had been awakened by a paleolithic mushroom cult," and they searched for a vestige of that cult in what was then perceived as primitive cultures. The use of psychoactive mushrooms in Central America had been reported on and off for centuries, notably in the *Florentine Codex*, a study on Aztec culture by Bernadino de Sahagun. A Spanish missionary who served in Mexico from 1529 to 1590, de Sahagun described the *teonanactl* ceremony (*teo* = God, *nanactl* = mushroom, or possibly flesh) in which the people drank chocolate and ate the mushrooms with honey. "And when the effects of the mushrooms had left them, they consulted among themselves and told one another what they had seen in vision." During the 1930s, anthropologists witnessed the mushroom ceremony in Oaxaca, Mexico, and in his book *The Ancient Maya*, published in 1946, Robert Sharer reported that "dictionaries of highland languages compiled immediately after the Spanish Conquest mention several mushroom varieties whose names clearly indicate their ritual use," like the "underworld mushroom" and the "lost-judgment mushroom."

But contemporary use of the mushroom was news. In his article,

*The subhead of the *Life* article is irresistible: "A New York banker goes to Mexico's mountains to participate in the age-old rituals of Indians who chew strange growths that produce visions."

Gordon Wasson described his encounters with a Mixtec *curandera*, a shaman, in Oaxaca state. The ceremony combined elements of Christian and indigenous pre-Christian religion and was conducted in the Mixteca language, the Mixtec being one of the great pre-Columbian civilizations. The mushrooms were used as an augur, providing an answer to questions regarding health, missing persons, and crimes. Wasson achieved access to the shaman and her mushrooms by stating he was concerned about his son. He described his trip as starting with graphic visions (seen whether his eyes were closed or open) that evolved into vivid landscapes. He pointed out that the effect of the mushrooms brings about "a kind of schizophrenia, with the rational side continuing to reason and to observe the sensations that the other side is enjoying." He reported that the Indians said the mushrooms "carry you there where God is," and speculated the mushrooms "stir depths that are truly the Unknown."

The Wassons' report in *Life* introduced psychedelic mushrooms to mainstream America. Previously, psychedelic substances had been limited to academics and the military, which tested LSD for a variety of unsavory applications. For example, in the early '60s, the US military strove to weaponize LSD in order to produce mass derangement (the term "to trip" was originally coined by army scientists). LSD was tested on military personnel as well as incarcerated persons, academics, and students, and it was through these guinea pigs that LSD entered the mainstream culture. Hallucinogenics were in the air, so to speak, and the Wassons' article on psychedelic mushrooms piqued the curiosity of many. (Including the CIA, which planted an operative, James Moore, in Wasson's 1956 trip to Mexico, in order to obtain samples of the mushroom for testing as a truth drug.) Some of the primary characters of the counterculture revolution of the 1960s were introduced to psychedelic drugs by *Psilocybe* mushrooms or synthetic psilocybin. What the author Don Lattin calls the "Harvard Psychedelic Club" included

Timothy Leary and his colleague Dr. Richard Alpert (who traveled to India and thereafter became known as Baba Ram Dass). They started the Harvard Psilocybin Project in 1960, where the drug was used in a series of psychology experiments. The "club" also included the holistic medical doctor Andrew Weil, a student at Harvard at the time, and Huston Smith, a professor of philosophy at MIT. Andrew Weil has written prolifically on the subject of psychoactive plants and chemicals. His book *The Natural Mind* (1972), which promoted mushroom- and plant-based psychedelics, was a bestseller. But his most notorious piece was an article in the *Journal of Psychedelic Drugs* in 1975 in which he revealed he had eaten 25 *Psilocybe* mushrooms—an insane amount. Dr. Weil even has a *Psilocybe* mushroom named after him: *Psilocybe weilii*. Huston Smith was older than the others and interested in the links between psychedelic drugs and religious experiences throughout the world, but he dropped out of the scene once Leary took his politics of psychedelia on the road.

Harvard shut down Leary and Alpert's project in 1962, when the administration decided their experiments, which increasingly involved students and were conducted without a medical professional in attendance, were potentially unsafe and crossed the line between scientific investigation and personal experimentation. Leary thereafter became a controversial—and some say irresponsible—advocate of hallucinogen use by youth.*

Psychedelic use in the United States exploded in the mid- and late 1960s, spread by word of mouth and by the intentional advocacy of a few, like Leary, the poet Allen Ginsberg, and the authors Ken Kesey and Carlos Castaneda. Psychedelic drugs, particularly LSD that was produced and distributed on a large scale, seeped into popular culture, influencing music,

---

*Leary died in 1996 and his cremains, at his request, were shot into space, where they are presumably orbiting the globe to this day.

fashion, and art. When the federal government clamped down on psychedelics in 1968, the less frequently used psilocybin got swept up as well.

The co-opting of the sacred mushroom as a countercultural party
tool upset the Wassons deeply. They had and would continue to spend
many years studying mushrooms in folk culture and, in the process,
basically created the field of ethnomycology. But the *Life* article made
magic mushrooms infamous. Rock stars and hippies flocked to the small
Oaxacan village in search of Wasson's shaman and her mushrooms. It
made Gordon Wasson famous and left the illiterate shaman, Maria
Sabina, whose village life and reputation were shattered by the inunda-
tion of American trip seekers, destitute.

Ethnomycologists study all kinds of human uses for mushrooms—and
not just entheogenics. In North America, a variety of mushrooms were used
for medicinal purposes, and some were venerated, and carved into beads
and totems. *Fomitopsis officinalis* (agarikon) played a role in the mythology
of the indigenous people of the Pacific Northwest. Puffballs were burnt as
incense to ward off ghosts in some native cultures. The ash from a polypore
mushroom, *Phellinus igniarius,* was used by others to freebase tobacco and,
before the introduction of tobacco, indigenous plants. (The alkaline fungus
enhances the kick of the alkaloid tobacco. The practice is still in use today
by the Yup'ik Eskimos in the Yukon-Kuskokwim Delta.)

Probably the most studied fungus from an ethnomycological perspective is *Amanita muscaria*, the iconic red mushroom with the white
polka dots that is depicted on Christmas tree ornaments and teapots and
in illustrations in children's books like Lewis Carroll's *Alice's Adventures
in Wonderland.* Whether *A. muscaria* is an entheogen or not is controversial. The mushroom, which grows wherever there are birch and conifer trees, causes a variety of pharmacological reactions. Some reports
compare it to being drunk, wild, and reckless, others say it is like taking
opium. Daniel Winkler says that eaten raw, it makes your body feel so
crummy your mind leaves for a while.

Amanita muscaria is also known as the fly agaric (a translation of the Latin) for its purported effects as a pesticide. It is generally described in guidebooks as poisonous to human beings, as are *Psilocybe* mushrooms. It used to be thought that *A. muscaria* caused muscarine poisoning (the poison is named for the mushroom, not the other way around), but it doesn't. The mushroom contains only traces of muscarine.* The active chemical in *A. muscaria* is ibotenic acid and its derivative, muscimol, a psychoactive alkaloid in a different class from psilocybin. Ibotenic acid is a neurotoxin that causes effects described in Gary Lincoff's book on poisonous mushrooms as "inebriation, derangement of the senses, manic behavior, delirium, and a deathlike sleep, from which all but a very few persons recover rather quickly." Muscimol, which is many times more potent than the ibotenic acid it derives from, is excreted in urine.

From the 18th century on, travelers in Siberia have described indigenous use of *A. muscaria*, both for shamanistic and recreational purposes, as a "sacred and a secular intoxicant," wrote Lincoff in *Toxic and Hallucinogenic Mushroom Poisoning*. The native people of the Kamchatka Peninsula, the Koryaks (or Koriaks), a non-Russian ethnic minority, were observed eating it and experiencing cheerfulness and inebriation, followed by passing out, then waking up, drinking one's pee, and starting all over again, as the ibotenic acid passes through the urine and the muscimol can be harvested through as many as five distillations. Another version of this has the rich Koryaks eating a broth made with dried *A. muscaria* and the less wealthy Koryaks drinking their urine. An early 19th-century traveler wrote, "Their passion for strong liquors, increased by the difficulty of procuring brandy, has led them to invent a drink equally potent, which they extract from a red

*Muscarine stimulates the parasympathomimetic nervous system, which controls unconscious activities in the body like salivation, urination, and digestion—hence all the drooling and GI problems that occur when you eat certain *Inocybe* and *Clitocybe* species and get a proper dose of muscarine.

mushroom." According to Gordon Wasson, even the Koryaks' reindeer were mad for *A. muscaria*, and their meat made you high, too.

One of the effects of *A. muscaria* inebriation is it causes objects to appear much larger than normal, a phenomenon called macropsia (suffered by Alice when she ate from the caterpillar's mushroom). Inebriated people will leap over a twig or step ridiculously high to climb a curb. There are also reports of visionary dreams during the coma-like sleep. Gary Lincoff visited the Koryak and Even tribes in 1994 and 1995 and observed their use of the mushroom. The Even shaman (named Tatiana Urkachan, who died in 1996) used the mushroom medicinally, to help the elderly sleep at night and increase their energy during the day, as a poultice to treat wounds, as an anti-inflammatory and analgesic, and entheogenically, on herself in order to access the spirit world. (Similar practices were reported by the late ethnobotanist Richard Evans Schultes [1915–2001] among the Dogrib and Athabascan people of northwestern Canada.) Evidently the practice of eating *A. muscaria* for ritualistic purposes continues, albeit in isolated regions of the world.

The Even shaman Tatiana Urkachan

Paul Stamets's lecture on ethnomycology was a liturgy of sorts: The crowd seemed thoroughly in his camp, even when he spun out some of the nuttier theories regarding the role psychedelic mushrooms may have played in human culture. I'd read them. In his

1968 book *Soma: Divine Mushroom of Immortality*, Gordon Wasson built a proposition that Soma, the divine god/plant mentioned frequently in the Rig Veda, the 3,500-year-old Indus scriptures, was *A. muscaria*. Another theory came from the Biblical scholar John Allegro, who was a member of the 1953 international team invited to study the newly discovered Dead Sea Scrolls. His 1970 book *The Sacred Mushroom and the Cross* used philology to prove that an ancient fertility cult inspired by *A. muscaria* evolved into the Judeo-Christian tradition, and "mushroom-worshipping Christians became the Church of later times."*

Gordon Wasson, in association with Albert Hofmann, the scientist who synthesized LSD and psilocybin, and Carl Ruck, published *The Road to Eleusis: Unveiling the Secret of the Mysteries* in 1978, which proposed that the visions achieved by initiates at Eleusis, the site of Ancient Greek ceremonies held for the cult of Demeter, were derived from a potion composed of ergot. In 1986, Wasson, Ruck, the ethnobotanist Jonathon Ott, and Stella Kramrisch, an authority on Indian art, wrote *Persephone's Quest: Entheogens and the Origins of Religion*, a grab bag of entheogenic mushroom theories, including the suggestion that the cow divinity in India may have arisen from the *Psilocybe* mushrooms that grew from its dung; that the ancient Roman cult of Mithras and their ritual meals were actually a psychedelic mushroom-eating sect, the remnants of which persist in secret societies today, like the Freemasons; that the Maximon deity of the Maya in Guatemala receives his powers from *A. muscaria*; that the Tree of Life, a notion that recurs in many cultures, is actually any tree that has a mycorrhizal entheogenic partner, particularly *A. muscaria*, where the fruit of the tree is the mushroom; and more.

Wasson thought that the psychoactive mushroom may have been

---

*The book ruined Allegro's academic career. Sometimes called the Liberace of Biblical studies, Allegro ended his life "dressed in white robes and leading a mushroom cult up in Maine," said Stamets.

a "detonator of ideas" for primitive man. That concept was taken further by the author Terrence McKenna, who wrote that plant hallucinogens are the source of the oldest human religions, that small amounts of psilocybin increased ancient man's visual acuity and that led to success as hunter-gatherers, that psilocybin was a catalyst for the human development of language, and that hallucinogenic compounds catalyzed the emergence of human self-reflection. Examples of other authors in this vein are Andrija Puharich, a parapsychologist who brought the psychic Uri Geller to national attention and wrote about the links between ancient Egyptian religion and *A. muscaria* (based in part on the claims of a clairvoyant), and the doomed late James Arthur, author of *Mushrooms and Mankind* (2000), which explored the "hidden meanings of Christmas" (the round, red-and-white-clad Santa Claus as a proxy for *A. muscaria*, the Christmas tree with presents underneath representing the pine tree under which the mushroom grows, and Santa's flying reindeer derived from the *A. muscaria*–eating reindeer herders of Siberia), an idea first bandied about by the poet Robert Graves.*

For those who are attuned to it, every mushroom-shaped, red-and-white image in folk or ancient art, every reference to divine fruit, is proof of a foundational *A. muscaria* mushroom cult from which later religions evolved. Mycology's archivist David Rose—he has the quiet, dry palms of someone who handles paper all the time—told me when I visited him at his cozy Victorian home in New Rochelle, "the biggest problem with [these authors] is they went overboard in interpreting everything in terms of the mushroom. But mushrooms are a window into the imagination," he said. "I think because they are hidden in plain sight."

---

*Arthur died in 2005 at the age of 47 of an apparent suicide. He was in a Madera County jail awaiting a hearing on charges of sexual misconduct with children. Arthur had a history of sex crimes in California.

ധ

Unlike other forays I'd been on, the Telluride Mushroom Festival didn't have a hotel that we all booked into, or even a meal plan. Festival attendees made their own arrangements, and the mellow town seemed content with turning over its identity to the mushroom crowd for a weekend. The bookstores displayed mushroom books and the restaurants advertised mushroom specials and the fellows that operated the gondola wore mushroom hats. We took our meals at restaurants all over town. When I say *we*, I mean the amateur and professional mycologists I'd hoped to befriend. Somehow the fact that we were all at the Telluride festival together locked me into the group. I got the message where and when people were meeting for dinner. I saved seats at lectures, and had seats saved for me. I attended talks by my dinner companions: Elinoar Shavit spoke about "Lebanese Viagra" (which grows on the plant *Ferula hermonis*), a mushroom that is caught up in Israeli–Lebanese border issues, and Britt Bunyard spoke on *Amanitas*. Disguised as a Soma talk (no doubt to accommodate the trippy inclinations of the audience), it was actually a very sciencey species roundup.

But some of the lectures pushed my bullshit meter into the red, particularly a panel on "Entheogens as Mind Medicine," the seriousness of which was undermined by a reporter who couldn't stop laughing and a therapist whose use of neologisms like *herstory* made it difficult to take her logic seriously. There was lots of talk regarding what the ancients knew about mushrooms, which also set off my bogus alert, because while we have inherited important themes, like ritual use, restrictions on use, and reverence, it's tricky to cast the ancients as role models. As Roland Griffiths, professor of behavioral biology at Johns Hopkins University School of Medicine wrote, "some of these cultures also engaged in practices considered unethical in our culture." Like human sacrifice and slavery.

I was trying to learn as much as I could from these lectures, but I admit my mind was preoccupied with the trip, which was drawing very near. So the segment in Gary Lincoff's lecture on "Magic Mushrooms: Mushrooms That Heal Body and Soul," which focused on what you should look for in a trip and what you should avoid, was particularly germane.

"Read the book!" said Lincoff and he waved a copy of Timothy Leary's *The Psychedelic Experience: A Manual Based on the Tibetan Book of the Dead* in the air. *The Tibetan Book of the Dead* is a manual for dying and being reborn, and it's the model Leary used to track the course of a psychedelic trip. Leary's book, which, true to the beneficent spirit of the transcendental experience, is available as a free download on the Internet, points out that "the drug does not produce the transcendental experience. It merely acts as a chemical key."

Leary describes the first stage, ego-loss (with the symptoms that herald transcendence: pressure in the head, tingling sensations, nausea, body pressure, trembling, etc., and he recommends you "accept them, merge with them, enjoy them"), followed by a period of hallucinations, then "re-entry," a return to normalcy, accompanied by a sense of mental liberation. Leary recommends dosages for psilocybin—the drug, not the mushroom—that are significantly higher than the 10 milligrams Jonathon Ott once suggested was an entheogenic dose—meaning enough to have a religious experience. Leary recommends 2 or 3 days be set aside for the experience, a day to prepare, meditate, and take care of your body, a day to trip, and a day to recover. Music, lighting, food, and drink "must be considered beforehand." A guide or ground control person is recommended for first-timers, and when doing it with a group, it's important to trust your "fellow voyagers." Finally, Leary recommended for first-time users that married couples do it separately.

Andrew Weil wrote that psychedelics can cause "heightened perceptions, increased awareness of one's surroundings, tremendous insights into one's own mind, accelerated thought processes, intense religious feelings, even extra sensory phenomena and mystic rapture." But he also pointed out the dangers. "It's not a good idea to take them near a railroad track, or climb to the top of a building," said Lincoff, who was wearing a red Dr. Seussian top hat covered in white polka dots. (While there are reports of people jumping off buildings when poisoned with ergot, the death of Art Linkletter's daughter Diane widely publicized the notion that psychedelic drug users will jump to their deaths—although an autopsy revealed Diane, at the time of her suicide, was sober.) "Psyche-delics are not a party thing," warned Lincoff and he looked at us gravely from under the brim of his big hat. The majority of *Psilocybe* dabblers and users I talked to were quite sincere and rather sober about using the mushrooms. "I'm horrified with people who use *Psilocybe* mushrooms as a party compound," said Paul Stamets. "I think the use of this mush-room should be done carefully and with enormous respect."

That was a lot for me to think about. "When mushroom use is ritu-alized," wrote Stamets in his chapter "Good Tips for Great Trips" (from *Psilocybin Mushrooms of the World*), "guided by veteran users who can help orchestrate the necessary variables with careful attention to set and setting—an extraordinarily gratifying cerebral adventure can unfold." When I asked how our trip was going to proceed, my shaman guide, who procured the mushrooms, told me he wasn't going to be much help. He was planning on taking an entheogenic dose, and just so I knew, in case something went wrong, his safety word was "popcorn."

The Telluride festival wrapped up with a parade and a party. The parade took place in the early evening, and started at the west end of town and carried on about a third of a mile to a park at the end of the box canyon. About a hundred people were in the parade—anyone with a costume was welcome—and there were about twice as many onlook-ers taking pictures. In fact, the whole event was like a gigantic photo op. Most costumes were haphazard and wacky—silly ears or painted faces—but one large fellow was impressively outfitted as the bee man shaman from Tassili n'Ajjer. There were a couple of women dressed as

Ernest Bloch's 1912 photo of the mushroom lady

Amanita phalloides, angels of death. They wore little feathery wings and a deathly pallor, and Gary Lincoff was there in his *A. muscaria* top hat with his petite wife, dressed like a pixie. There were lots of psychedelic outfits that might have been recycled from Grateful Dead concerts, and Claudia from the Missouri mycological club had somehow fashioned a headdress that trailed white curling hyphae. I had planned ahead and joined the ranks dressed up like Ernest Bloch's 1912 photo of the Swiss mushroom lady. I was sure the reference would be instantly recognizable, but unfortunately no one got it, and so, a bit humiliated, I had to pin a photocopy of the original picture to my chest. We followed Art Goodtimes in his pointed hat and staff, who kept yelling, "We want mushrooms!" to the accompaniment of a bagpiper and a truck full of bongo drummers. As we headed down the road, a rainbow came on suddenly and seemed to push lots of people into ecstatic giddiness. I think the mood was the result of a young man dressed in druid robes who carried a honey bear packed with crumbled *Psilocybe* mushrooms and doled out little droplets onto the tips of the revelers' index fingers. I didn't partake. I was too shy to stick my finger out, and since I was planning to trip the next day, I wanted to stay sober. After all, this was supposed to be my day of meditation and reflection and taking care of my body. When we arrived in the park, the bongo players assembled themselves and there was a lot of twirling and stomping and wild dancing going on in the big pasture into the evening. Britt Bunyard told me that if I returned to the pasture early enough the next morning, I'd find people crashed out all over, just asleep where they fell, sprinkled with dew. But when I showed up around 9:00 a.m., they were all gone, disappeared like morning glories in the afternoon.

I had to wonder, where was law enforcement? It's true that I didn't see any aggressive or disruptive behavior, but I did see a lot of people with pupils the size of black olives. "There were probably more drugs at the Phish concert," said Seth Cagin, publisher of the *Telluride Watch*. "And anyway, local people love the festival because it keeps Telluride funky." But he admits the use of psychedelics would be more difficult to sustain if this were a more "dialed in" event.

It's hard to determine psilocybin usage because reporting is an issue. Nonetheless, in 2009 a national survey of drug use sponsored by the US Department of Health and Human Services determined that the number of first-time users of hallucinogens was about the same as first-time users of marijuana, and has been for years. The Web site www.Erowid.com, which collects data on psychedelic substances, reported that as of 2001, somewhere between 3 to 10 percent of people under age 40 in the United States, Britain, and Canada had tried psychoactive mushrooms.

I asked my cousin Buddy Mancinelli, a Connecticut state crime scene detective, about psilocybin—also known as boomers, caps, shrooms (which actually made it into the very respectable *Oxford English Dictionary*), sherms, silly putty, simple simon, God's flesh, sacred mushroom, and, of course, magic mushrooms. "For a cop, it's hard to detect, other than the dilated pupils," he said. "But most of what we see is kids in their early twenties, late teens, usually high-end consumers. The guy that robs and shoots up a liquor store is not doing shrooms."

While psilocybin is a Schedule 1 drug, the mushroom itself falls in a more gray area. During the Convention on Psychotropic Substances at the United Nations in 1971, the signatories agreed to prohibit synthetic psilocybin. But the Mexican government pressured the convention not to prohibit the mushroom itself. Indeed, the mushroom enjoys a legal loophole, or at least, it has. The spores of *Psilocybe* mushroom are legal in most states—they don't have any psilocybin in them—which is why you can buy them on the Internet. But of course, *Psilocybe* spore sales are unregulated, so unscrupulous sellers may proliferate. Every state has psilocybin listed in its controlled substance acts but not the mushroom, *Psilocybe*. To address that, most state courts have determined the mushroom is a *container* of a Schedule 1 drug and so illegal. (For that matter, as Richard Glen Boire reported in his book *Sacred Mushrooms and the Law,* our heads could be considered containers of a Schedule 1 drug, too, as DMT [dimenthyltryptamine] is both scheduled and naturally occurring in humans.) Possession of psilocybin is a federal crime. A first conviction for possession is punishable, depending on the state, by a mandatory $1,000 fine and a maximum of 1 year in prison, with jail times and fines increasing as convictions are acquired.

The French mycologist Roger Heim was the first to cultivate *Psilocybe* mushrooms on horse manure, from samples he collected with Gordon Wasson in Mexico. In the 1960s, brochures began to circulate describing the growing methods, and in the late 1970s, two books were published with sufficiently reliable techniques to make cultivation widely available. The first book, *Psilocybin: Magic Mushroom Grower's Guide* (1976) was published by O. T. Oss and O. N. Oeric, now thought to be Terrence McKenna and his brother Dennis. The other book, *Magic Mushroom Cultivation,* was written by Steve Pollock, who owned a spawn-making company, Hidden Creek. Pollock was shot in his home in Texas in 1981. Gary Lincoff told me the story. "I think the problem was that he was writing prescriptions for 'drugs' (Pollock was an MD) and interfered with a local cartel's business monopoly, but this is hearsay. Steve Pollock was an amazing character, closer to an R. Crumb illustration than any human I've ever known." In 1991, another cultivation manual was published, *The Psilocybe Fanaticus Technique* with simplified techniques, and then in 1996, *Growing Mushrooms the Easy Way,* which featured using hydrogen peroxide as an agent for maintaining a sterilized substrate. Other handbooks for cultivation have been published subsequently, including a popular one by Paul Stamets, and information has proliferated on the Internet.

At the Galaxy Theatre, where most of the festival lectures took place, there was a table of printed matter. The festival's inherent conflicts were summed up in one document, "Warnings About Magic Mushrooms." On the one hand, it warned that "Magics" are illegal everywhere in the United States to grow, possess, give away, or sell, and federal penalties are severe, "so only an outstanding fool would get himself involved here." But in the next breath, it explained how to have a good trip. I especially liked the advice that raw mushrooms take 10 minutes to set a trip in motion, mushrooms in tea or juice take 15 minutes, and mushrooms cooked in an omelet, an hour.

I planned to trip with three other people—"Popcorn" and two women—and we decided to take the mushrooms shortly after the festival wrapped up on Sunday morning. I'd slept well the night before, drunk no alcohol, taken care of all my e-mails and phone calls, and had hot chocolate for breakfast, as I remembered Bernadino de Sahagun's text that said the Aztecs drank chocolate before eating the mushroom. (I later found out that chocolate contains a mild MAO inhibitor that can lengthen and intensify the trip.) We met in my hotel room. The mushrooms were dried and there was a lot of crumbled material, but those that were intact were a couple of inches high, pearl gray with brown gills and blue stains on the stems that looked like a ballpoint pen had exploded in the Baggie. I sampled the mushroom, and it was tender for a dried product, kind of like eating a piece of brown paper bag, and tasted mildly bitter and mushroomy. I loaded up with chocolate bars and water bottles, an extra sweater and a camera, a notebook and pens, and then I rode the gondola up to the top of the mountain. It was a classic blue Colorado day, dry and cool, green forests and red rocks and purple mountains, but I hardly paid any attention at all to the landscape—I was listening closely to my body, alert to any change.

Dosing is risky. The quantity of psilocybin can vary within a single species. And since a baby mushroom can contain as much psilocybin as a fully grown mushroom, a gram composed of small mushrooms could be significantly more potent that a gram composed of large mushrooms. Add unknowns like one's metabolism and maturity and the potential for danger increases. I was timid and ate only a tiny amount. I was also lucky. I expected to experience only enhanced hearing, giddiness, colors that would seem more intense, but no hallucinations.

Trails headed in every direction at the top of the mountain, and since they all looked good, we took the nearest. It seemed like we walked for a long time, and finally we had to lie down on the trail in exhaustion, amazed at how many miles we'd trekked, but when a storm blew up and we dashed back to the gondola, it turned out we were only about 30 yards away. Popcorn got unnerved and cold and returned to the hotel, but the gal I'll call Bonnie and I stayed behind, hiding under the eaves of the nature center and watching the raindrops, silver and dense as mercury, and could not pull our eyes away. The storm blew over fast as they do in Colorado, and we took the gondola down through a thick rainbow. Actually, we took the gondola up and down quite a few times. I felt like I had my own private 3D glasses on: Everything I looked at was extra vivid and detailed. At one point we checked in with Popcorn, but we were too restless to stay in the hotel room, like birds fluttering around in a kitchen, and we headed up the mountain again. I usually am very nervous about getting lost, about unwise decisions in the woods in general, but I seemed temporarily to have shed that particular inhibition and encouraged Bonnie to join me on a power walk down the mountain to the village—how far could it be? It looked very close. (Obviously, one's judgment can be seriously altered by the drug.) But then we hit a T and became flummoxed and, after a brief conference, turned around and jogged back up again.

We spent a couple of hours outdoors, and then, as the effects gently began to wane, returned to town for good. Back at the hotel, Popcorn was in cocoon mode, cozy under the covers, listening to the Flaming Lips and watching the visions behind his eyelids. I took a hot bath. For a moment I thought that might be a bad idea, as bath time is when women my age tend to be very self-critical and unforgiving. I'd had quite a few personal revelations on the mountain, about how I perceive myself and how I think others perceive me, but I will share this one with my lady readers of a certain age: While in the bathtub, I stopped feeling guilty about growing older and regretful about losing my looks, and then I realized my body was a vessel, like a ship that was taking me through life, and it functions well, and that made it beautiful, and I felt grateful. It was a tremendous relief that I still feel today.

After that I was well into "reentry." I went to a nice restaurant and had a good coq au vin and a nice glass of Syrah, and went to bed and dozed all night. I enjoyed the company of my fellow trippers, but in the end it turned out I didn't need them. The kinship I felt was more like befriending someone when traveling. The shared experience is unique and bonding, but it's temporary, and you always part ways. Aldous Huxley said as much when he described his trip on mescaline: "We live together, we act on, and react to, one another; but always and in all circumstances we are by ourselves." I felt mostly functional throughout. I could have gone to a café and ordered a cappuccino, but I couldn't have read the newspaper, and I definitely couldn't have driven a car. In real time, the experience was about 1 hour coming on, 4 hours on the mushroom, and 1 hour coming off. In perceived time, it seemed like the afternoon was many hours longer, but that is because I remember every moment in detail. As Wasson reported, one's memory is sharpened, but one loses all sense of time. The next day, I felt more aware and peaceful about my identity and definitely in love with the grand Colorado landscapes to a degree I'd never experienced before.

But I was very tired: not sleepy, more of a sensory and mental exhaustion. I didn't have an entheogenic experience. That would entail a large dose, and the subsequent increased risk. I had hoped someone at the festival would talk about what is physically happening in the brain that causes an entheogenic experience. Terrence McKenna wrote "nature communicates in a basic chemical language that is unconscious but profound." I was hugely curious about this idea of the perceived divine as a biochemical reaction, but when someone asked what entheogens can teach us, Gary Lincoff, who was on the entheogen panel, pretended his mike was turned off.

But I did have revelatory experiences that were significant to me. Solomon Snyder, MD, of Johns Hopkins University School of Medicine, wrote that "as the boundaries of our sense of self, our ego, are determined by the integration of sensory perception, it is conceivable that changes in serotonin systems mediate the diffusion of ego boundaries that underlies the transcendent merger of 'self with universe' that is reported consistently by mystics of all religious persuasions and occurs often under the influence of psychedelic drugs." Or, as my friend Marilee says, and she is a gal who tends to cut to the heart of the matter, "when you trip, you experience ego death and that allows you to be one with the universe."

The notion that psilocybin could induce a religious experience was first explored in 1962, but scientific interest withered in the ensuing decades. However, research into the entheogenic properties of psychedelics was renewed in the early 1990s and has accelerated in the 21st century, focusing on cognitive neuroscience and perception, time perception, hallucinogen pharmacokinetics and metabolism, model psychosis, and the facilitation of spiritual experience. A study published in the journal *Psychopharmacology* in 2006 showed that psilocybin-induced experiences were similar to spontaneous mystical experiences. The researchers, Roland Griffiths, et al., determined this by using questionnaires and scales developed for their study, as well as established measures developed for use in the field of the psychology of religion, among other disciplines. A follow-up report showed that 14 months later, 58 percent of the subjects rated the psilocybin-occasioned experience as being among the five most personally meaningful and spiritually significant experiences of their lives. Griffiths wrote that the results suggest that mystical or spiritual experiences "relate to the pharmacology of these agents rather than being based entirely on cultural suggestion."

I don't know if an entheogen provides actual transcendence or just the feeling of transcendence. It may depend in part on whether one describes transcendence as the result of encountering the divine or if it is described simply as a condition that is experienced (however achieved). People pursue meditation and fasting to get to a transcendent place, and maybe these disciplines alter the body's chemistry in a way that allows the brain to meet the requisite conditions for a spiritual experience that is similarly accomplished with psilocybin. "The observation that psilocybin reliably elicits a transcendent, mystical state tells us that investigations of these drugs may help us understand molecular alterations in the brain that underlie mystical religious experiences," wrote Solomon Snyder. "Religious sensibilities are increasingly prominent throughout the world and often involve 'born again' ineffable experiences analogous to psychedelic drug effects. Thus, seeking the 'locus of religion' in the brain is by no means fanciful."

What is so provocative about Griffiths's work is that it suggests the ability to experience transcendental feelings may naturally reside in our brains: literally, the God within. "Personally," wrote Charles Schuster, professor emeritus of psychiatry and behavioral neurosciences at Wayne State University, "I also believe that these drugs have a role in discovering the brain mechanisms underlying feelings of spirituality and that such understanding may lead to our investigation of nonpharmacological means of engendering such states."

I was skeptical when people at the festival talked about the "mushroom spirit" and personified the mushroom as a "teacher." More than skeptical; I thought it was nonsense. But since experiencing the mushroom myself, I am a bit more sympathetic. I understand why some folks are rhapsodic about them. The effect of this innocuous little mushroom on human physiology and perception seems supernatural, but in fact it is utterly natural. Ultimately, an appreciation of the psychoactive mushroom is as much about recognizing the capability in us to experience the profound as it is about a blue-staining fungus.

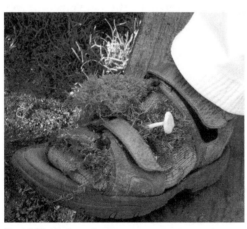

Daniel Winkler's mushroom man costume

Chapter 11

MYCOTECHNOLOGIES

"W e are being inundated with requests and cannot individually address all of the questions we have received. We are in direct dialogue with the EPA at the highest levels, and are teaming to implement solutions to this huge disaster." This statement appeared on Paul Stamets's Fungi Perfecti Web site during the April 2010 Deepwater Horizon spill, when a failed blowout preventer, combined with human error, led to an explosion of a British Petroleum oil drilling rig in the Gulf of Mexico. For months the rig leaked oil, up to 2.5 million gallons a day, and estimates regarding the environmental impact were dire.

The Fungi Perfecti site was inundated with calls because in his 2005 book *Mycelium Running: How Mushrooms Can Help Save the World*, Stamets described a demonstration project his team had performed in the late 1990s on the ability of mushrooms to remediate oil-polluted soil. It was the first time many people had heard of mycoremediation. At first glance, mycoremediation sounds like the answer to all our environmental problems. Fungi are, along with bacteria, nature's decomposers. Anything carbon based, and that includes oil, can be degraded by fungi.

I logged on to Fungi Perfecti's Web site when I read about the spill, too.

I had read *Mycelium Running,* and I was frustrated that mycoremediation was not being applied to the problem or at least being discussed in the media. I was convinced this was because of a corporate conspiracy or a willful disregard of an all-natural solution. If *I* knew about mycoremediation, why didn't BP? But I was quickly disabused of that notion the week that Tom Volk, who was on sabbatical from his teaching position at the University of Wisconsin, came to New York to speak to the New York Mycological Society and stayed at my place for a few days.

I had promised to make a special dinner for him the night before his lecture, and, of course, mushrooms figured prominently on the menu. Gary Lincoff and his wife, Irene, joined us, and we started the evening with a glass of sparkling wine. Gary lifted his glass. "To Wisconsin, the first to name an official state microbe," he said, referring to Wisconsin's recent anointing of *Lactococcus lactis,* the bacterium used to make Cheddar cheese. During the course of dinner (spaghettini cooked in steamed mussel stock and garnished with sautéed chanterelles; flounder cooked in parchment with maitake, leeks, and asparagus; and sheep's milk ricotta with candy cap mushroom sauce), I launched into a passionate Chenin Blanc–fueled speech about the power of fungi to remediate soil and water, and a condemnation: Why wasn't BP getting with the program? After all, fungi disassemble molecules in order to feed. They have unique enzymes that they use to digest their food before absorbing it, and those enzymes can also break down different pollutants as well.

In mycoremediation, a substrate colonized by mycelium is introduced to a polluted site, whereupon the mycelium grows into the contaminated substrate, secreting enzymes that break down the pollutants into nontoxic compounds. Research to match fungal enzymes to specific contaminants is ongoing, but so far, the heavy hitters seem to be saprophytic fungi, like oyster mushrooms, that degrade the lignin and cellulose in wood. These fungi are called white rot fungi because they eat the lignin first, leaving the white cellulose for later. Both lignin and petroleum are composed of hydrocarbon molecules. Because they have similar bonds, both types of molecules are vulnerable to the enzymes that white rot fungi excrete. Many pollutants (like diesel, motor oil, benzene, ethylene, and crude oil) are composed of hydrocarbons. Fungal enzymes—often multiple enzymes working in concert—essentially disassemble a product like petroleum into its molecular parts: primarily carbon, water, nitrogen, and oxygen. Those liberated elements then return to the natural system. When a white rot fungus encounters a hydrocarbon molecule in, say, petroleum, as far as the fungal mycelium is concerned, it's dinner. So why can't this process be deployed at will, and on a large scale?

Tom and Gary, who seemed to be enjoying their meal and so maybe weren't disposed to be too tough on me, gently explained that it was one thing to observe the decomposing power of mushrooms in nature, or even in a lab or limited test study, and quite another to apply the results to a large-scale environmental disaster like the BP oil spill.

Chastised, I realized that once awakened to the depth and breadth of fungi's impact on human life, I had come to indulge in fantasies about the ability of this organism to solve all our problems. That does the truth a disservice, because the truth is, fungi are of significant importance in industry, and their *potential* industrial importance as biomediators is huge.

Fungi are used to make all kinds of bulk enzymes and acids, and in fermentation processes, from the production of pigments to vitamins. A new technique has been developed to replace eggs with white button mushrooms in vaccine production. The process calls for inserting a gene that produces a vaccine into a bacterium that is in turn inserted into *Agaricus bisporus* mycelium. The mushrooms that produce the needed chemical are cultured to produce strains that carry the chemical, and the chemical is harvested for use in vaccines and other therapeutic drugs. It's a manufacturing platform for growing drugs called pharming, and it allows for large quantities of vaccine to be produced quickly—up to 3 million doses of vaccine in 12 weeks. (Unfortunately, you can't simply eat the mushroom in lieu of a vaccination, as the dosage in any given specimen is unknown.) Compared to other processes, utilizing mushrooms as a host for growing chemicals is easy, fast, and inexpensive, all key to producing affordable drugs. Due to this and other uses, the Department of Energy Joint Genome Institute considers the economic footprint of fungi to be "enormous."

But as in the case of medicinal mushrooms, much of the research going on in the headline-generating areas of mycoremediation and biofuels is in the discovery stage. Many surprising findings and encouraging projects and studies have been done, and more are under way. The tendency to conflate propitious early results into news copy like "Newfound Fungus Makes Better Biofuel" is misleading. I needed to separate the fact from the fiction.

While huge slicks of crude oil made their shimmering, iridescent way toward the fragile Louisiana and western Florida coastlines, the US government and BP grappled with how to deal with the disaster. The question on many mycophiles' minds was, could mycoremediation help?

There are two parts to cleaning up a marine oil spill: separating the oil from the water, and disposing of the oil. British Petroleum used two techniques to separate the oil from the gulf waters. They used booms and skimmers that collect the oil floating on the surface of the water, and chemical dispersants, which are sprayed on the oil slicks and break the large areas of oil into smaller parts that are more easily degraded by marine bacteria. (In his *New Yorker* magazine piece "The Gulf War," Raffi Khatchadourian made this analogy to describe how dispersants work. "Imagine a cake the size of a house, and a hundred thousand people trying to wolf it down at once; then imagine that cake cut into slices and passed around to the same crowd.") Oil that has been collected rather than dispersed must be disposed of. That's where mycoremediation may one day play a role.

Paul Stamets tested one of his oyster mushroom strains on diesel-saturated soil on the grounds of the Washington State Department of Transportation's maintenance yard, a project undertaken in conjunction with Battelle, a contract research and development laboratory in Columbus, Ohio. The test pile of contaminated soil had up to 2 percent diesel and oil contamination (which Stamets estimated was about equal to the concentration of oil measured on the beaches of Prince William Sound after the Exxon *Valdez* spill in 1989). Oyster mushroom spawn equivalent to 30 percent of the volume was layered throughout the pile, and the inoculated pile was covered with shade cloth. Within 4 weeks, the treated soil was covered with oyster mushrooms. By the 9th week, vascular plants were growing, and other mushrooms appeared, as well as insects and birds. "The pile's biosphere diversified," wrote Stamets. The hydrocarbon load in the pile decreased from 20,000 parts per million to 200 parts per million in 8 weeks, making the soil acceptable for highway landscaping. Remarkably, they also found that the oyster mushrooms contained no detectable petroleum. It was gone.

Stamets is not the only one exploring the bioremediation capacities of fungi. For at least 40 years, private research and development labs, university teams, and government agencies like the EPA and the US Department of Energy have explored the action of fungal enzymes on pollutants. Interest in and study of mycoremediation has come in waves. In 1969, the first patent for using fungi to bioremediate hydrocarbon-contaminated soil was granted; in the mid-1980s, a white rot fungus was reported to degrade DDT; and a decade later, other scientists discovered white rot fungi could degrade polyaromatic hydrocarbons, which are mostly pollutants from the petroleum industry but also include pollutants from coal processes, auto engine exhaust, sewage sludge, creosote, and fly ash.

Bacteria have long been used to bioremediate contaminated water and soil, but bacteria are very specific about what they eat, down to the size of the molecules of their food. Fungi, on the other hand, are capable of breaking down multiple pollutants at once, and pollutants with large molecules to boot (after which bacteria can join forces and finish off the smaller molecules).

Mycoremediation has implications beyond oil-contaminated soil. An array of fungi can degrade pretty much all industrial chemicals, even chemicals like PCBs that were designed *not* to be degraded by microbes. In laboratory studies, fungi have been found to degrade hydrocarbon compounds like chloroaromatic compounds (PCBs and dioxins like the horrific Agent Orange), nitroaromatic compounds (explosives, dyes, herbicides, insecticides, solvents), and polyaromatic compounds (oil, coal, and tar). Basically, any carbon-based product is food for fungi: pesticides of all sorts, nonylphenols (a precursor of certain detergents), phenolic compounds (phenol is the preferred chemical for embalming bodies), tannins in acids, cyanide compounds, chemical warfare agents like VX, fertilizers, and estrogen-based pharmaceuticals, along with many dozens more chemical derivatives and chemical precursors of products. As Dawn Stover wrote in an article in *Popular Science* 2 decades ago, "fungi [are] not picky eaters."

All of which makes fungi of strong interest to corporate America. Organisms cultivated from the wild cannot be patented, but once they are selectively bred, they can be patented, as can genetically modified organisms. So can some methods of application. (And where patents lead, dollars follow.) Many species of fungi are under investigation to determine which specific pollutants they can degrade, and the subsequent pairing of species to chemical is patented. There are patents for the remediation of pesticides and preservatives, for oil, tar, gasoline, diesel, dyes, paints, chlorine bleach, and a hodgepodge of chemicals.

Theoretically, fungi can degrade these pollutants on land and in freshwater as well.* But there's a stumbling block. It's easier, quicker, and cheaper to haul contaminated soil away and dump it somewhere else, or incinerate it onsite. "You know where the Alaska oil spill is right now?" asked Howard Sprouse, president of the bioremediation company, The Remediators, Inc., the first in the USA to utilize mycoremediation in a commercial capacity. "In a landfill in Oregon."

Unlike bioremediation by fungi and other microorganisms, hauling away contaminants is not a permanent solution. It just moves the contamination elsewhere. But this practice is not just a matter of greed triumphing over responsibility. Successful mycoremediation, or any bioremediation for that matter (utilizing fungi, plants, or bacteria, or a combination), is difficult. It depends on a detailed understanding of which fungal enzymes can break down what pollutant, the volume of enzymes necessary to do the job, and whether the fungus can even survive the circumstances of the site. It's not just a matter of spreading around microorganisms, a practice that used to be known as "spray and pray." "The main issue is competing microorganisms," said Thom O'Dell, a research biologist who is also vice president of The Remediators. "You can't keep them out."

In order to mycoremediate contaminated land, each site must be independently analyzed for soil pH, for the microbial populations that might be competitive, and for the degree and type of contamination; choices have to be made regarding the species and quantity of fungi needed to address the array of chemicals that may be present. "So far it

---

*Mycelium, with its mat of microscopic, interwoven threads, can capture and disassemble pollutants, both natural and man-made, and has shown promise as a wastewater filter or barrier in a number of studies.

works in 100 cubic yards of diesel-contaminated soil, like an old gas station," said O'Dell. "Some have made it work for more recalcitrant polyaromatic hydrocarbons at a larger scale. It can be more expensive to do, but it's a permanent solution." O'Dell thinks that in time, states will ban the hauling off of less toxic environmental pollutants like diesel-saturated soil and thereby improve the economic competitiveness of on-site mycoremediation.

Bioremediation requires toxicological analysis, too. Many polluted sites are contaminated with heavy metals like lead, mercury, cadmium, and arsenic. Fungi do not molecularly disassemble the majority of heavy metals, though some can be remediated to a degree. Fungi absorb the metals, in a trick called bioaccumulation. "Most fungi," writes the English microbiologist David Moore, "can absorb any particle with which they are challenged."

While fungi may bioremediate the soil of heavy metals, a field of mushrooms containing those metals constitutes a larger plume of contamination. Those same metals that we, and fungi, require in trace amounts can be toxic at concentrations only a few times greater than what's required. So when accumulated in mushrooms, concentrations of metals in potentially unsafe quantities become bioavailable to animals and then travel up the food chain. (The deer eat the fungi, the hunter eats the deer.) As a result, any mycoremediation effort involving metals would require an evaluation of how life is expressed at and around the site.

Indeed, edible mushrooms picked from areas polluted with heavy metals could make you sick. The most notorious example of bioaccumulation is the porcini in the forest outside Sluvuytch, a town about 30 miles from Chernobyl. Big, fat, beautiful porcini grow there and are heartily enjoyed by the local population. But when a BBC news team tested the mushrooms for radiation content, they found the levels to be eight times higher than the safe recommendation. (The locals believe that ample amounts of vodka keep radiation poisoning at bay.) Here in the USA, the amateur mycologist Elinoar Shavit studied morels collected in dying apple orchards that were sprayed years before with lead-arsenate pesticides to combat fruit-tree pests and found a correlation between lead arsenate in the soil and lead and arsenic in morels.

On The Remediators Web site it says, "We clean soil using fungi." Since 2005, the Washington-based company has been treating regional contaminated soils, including petroleum and its derivatives, pesticides, and spent munitions. The Remediators started out working on small-scale petroleum spills, like home heating oil spills and generator fuel spills. "I tell my clients, if [the fungi] don't work, I'll haul the stuff off," said Howard Sprouse. "Mycoremediation is complicated, but it's something that can be done."

✿

I have a hands-off attitude when it comes to guests. I figure Manhattan is entertaining enough, and during the couple of days he stayed with me, Tom Volk made good use of the museums and theaters. He showed me numerous pictures he'd taken of himself, standing in front of various landmarks, but almost always there was a fungal subtext: Tom in front of Andy Warhol's painting of the Campbell's mushroom soup can; Tom in front of the memorial to the Irish victims of the potato blight. The night he spoke to the New York Mycological Society, his lecture was, in part, about how the degrading capabilities of fungi are being used in industry, and how they may be used in the future.

Those cleaning enzymes listed on the label of your contact lens solution, your laundry detergent, and automatic dishwashing detergent bottles? They use fungal (and bacterial) enzymes like lipases and pullulanases to remove greasy stains, and cellulases to soften fabrics. Remember the stonewashed jeans trend? "They are really fungally distressed jeans," said Tom. The jeans are combined in a vat with a cotton-fiber-eating fungus that partially digests the material, leaving that distressed look.

Then Tom showed us a slide of a Bakelite telephone, the old-fashioned kind that must have seemed quaint to some of our younger members. Bakelite, a phenolic resin plastic, is actually one gigantic molecule. His lab determined that certain fungi showed the capability to degrade it.

And indeed, fungi have been found capable of decomposing polymers and plastics by a number of researchers. Polyolefins, which are used in biomedical devices and food packaging, polyethylene (used in the 8 million metric tons of shopping bags produced annually), and polyester resin have all been studied and found to be vulnerable to one or more species of fungi. Fungi have also been found to degrade polyurethane plastic—like foam mattresses—when buried in soil. And the rate of degradation improves when the volume of fungi is increased or nutrients are added to the soil to increase the fungi's activity. Shatterproof polycarbonate plastic—the stuff used to make water bottles, screwdriver handles, and CDs—is a nasty environmental pollutant because it contains bisphenol A (BPA), which may be linked to cancer, metabolic disorders, and endocrine disruption. The problem is, how to dispose of the plastic without releasing the BPA? About 2.7 tons of the stuff is manufactured every year. But scientists found that if the plastic is treated with UV light and heat, which kind of precooks it, before being treated with a trio of fungi, the plastic was substantially degraded and the BPA consumed after 1 year. Sadly, this is not a panacea: The secondary compounds produced by plastics during decomposition can be toxic to the fungi as well.

The potential for fungi to help us deal with wastes of all sorts is clear. The degrading ability of fungi could be utilized to remediate agricultural wastes like untreated fertilizer, sugarcane bagasse (a fibrous residue of sugarcane milling), and cereal straw wastes, of which millions of tons are produced annually; paddy straw, corn straw, horticultural wastes, and coffee pulp, which produces a huge amount of acidic waste. Some studies have suggested it could be used to create pulp for paper, replacing the harsh chemicals like dioxins used to pulp and bleach wood. But the challenges of scaling up the degrading powers of fungal enzymes, and the problems of keeping those organisms alive while they do the job, are complicated and expensive to solve. And then I heard about a company called Ecovative, and I realized fungi could offer an altogether different kind of solution to some of our waste problems.

I drove up to Green Island, New York, one fall morning to visit Ecovative, a business run by 25-year-old Rensselaer Polytechnic Institute graduates. There is a lot of excitement in the mycological and the environmental communities over Ecovative because they have developed a viable alternative to Styrofoam. The prototype facility is producing packaging materials for Steelcase, Dell, and Bloomberg products. Actually, it's more accurate to say they are *growing* packaging. They are making hardy, waterproof, lightweight, and fully biodegradable packaging material from fungal mycelium, grown out on regionally sourced agricultural waste like wheat hulls. I spoke with Gavin McIntyre, the chief scientist, about their technology. We sat in a dusty conference room, among empty wine bottles and a half-eaten container of candy corn. The space felt a little like the living room of a dorm suite. McIntyre is articulate and focused, and was fully decked out in facial piercings. "What we are making," he said, "is a tunable biocomposite," a product that can be as soft or as rigid as you like, in any shape, for a number of packaging purposes, including insulation panels, and other, weirder products.

Here's how it works: Agricultural waste like cereal hulls is pasteurized, inoculated with fungal spawn, and packed into molds made from recycled plastic soda bottles. The mycelium can be grown into any shape (I noticed a test block that had been grown in the shape of a Darth Vader mask). The filled molds are covered and placed in racks, and the fungus is allowed to grow out. In 5 to 10 days, the molds are filled with dense white mycelium. The molded mycelium mass is popped out and baked, which kills the fungus and dehydrates the bricks.

Ecovative packaging material—they call it EcoCradle—costs about the same to produce as petroleum-based Styrofoam, though it takes longer to make. However, mycelium-based packaging produces no by-products and is 100 percent biodegradable. "You just crumble it up and mulch it into your garden," said Sam Harrington, the company's 24-year-old mechanical engineer. Styrofoam doesn't recycle, and as the price of petroleum increases, so will the cost of Styrofoam.

"We see this as a new material for all sorts of things," said Harrington. Like laminates, for one thing. Prior to baking, the mycelium is living. Just as hyphae can fuse together in nature, two independent blocks or forms of the living mycelium can be placed next to each other and they will grow together, fusing in a bond on a microscopic scale. The blocks will also grow into materials like laminated wood, creating a bonded backing for potential use in furniture or paneling.

Ecovative has been experimenting with products like insulation panels called Greensulate (the panels are fire retardant, as the mycelium is grown out on rice hulls, which are mostly silica), impact bolsters like car bumpers, and energy-dissipating foams, which could be inserted into car doors. "We are a material science company," McIntyre told me. "Protective packaging is just our first market, but we want to spread through as many applications as possible." It turns out that the myce-lium can also be grown into flexible membranes of any thickness, even as thin as that scourge of our landfills, the plastic bag.

I was so taken by this product that I asked Gavin McIntyre if I might have a sample to take home. ("Okay," he said. "But not the Darth Vader mask.") Now, when I feel compelled to wax on at dinner parties about the ways fungi can save the planet, I have something to show.

ꙍ

In the process of studying the role fungi might play in mycoreme-diation, I became seriously sidetracked into the realm of biofuels. Any-thing that can improve our energy situation is big news, and fungi have definitely gotten their share of press, and in two categories: as more effi-cient converters of biomass into ethanol and, weirdly, as producers of hydrocarbons that are similar to diesel.

Being a city person, my exposure to cornfields and ethanol plants has been extremely limited. In fact, when Dave Mallery drove me to his morel hunting grounds on the banks of the Illinois River, the weekend that I went to the Illinois State Morel Mushroom Hunting Champion-ship, I'd noticed a huge power plant from the road, steam billowing and quickly evaporating from the smokestacks. I asked Dave if it was a nuclear power plant. He pulled over and opened the window. "Smell that?" he asked. I did: It was sweet and cloying, like corn syrup perfume, an odor created during the purification stage of ethanol production.

Ethanol, or grain alcohol, is produced by the fermentation of sugar. Besides making a martini, ethanol can also be used as fuel for heat, light, and internal combustion engines. (Ethanol, by the way, is not a cleaner fuel source than oil; it's just dirty in a different way. Ethanol made from corn produces more than twice the ozone of gasoline exhaust.) Simply described, corn or other cereals are treated with a fungal enzyme called amylase (the same enzyme used in the malting step of beer production) or dilute sulfuric acid, or a combination, that convert the starch in the plant into sugar. Yeasts ferment the sugar into ethanol.

An ethanol plant will use more than 4,000 bushels of corn an hour, consequently driving up the cost of food for both human and animal consumption. It would be more economical to convert agricultural waste like corncobs and straw into ethanol. However, cellulose from plant debris, while a very common organic compound—it's in all plants—is very tough to break down into sugar. A number of companies are in the business of developing fungal enzymes capable of degrading plant cellulose into fermentable sugar, either by genetically altering the fungi and/or bacteria that does the degrading, or by finding new enzymes in the natural world that can. Even BP is in the game, having financed biofuels research at UC Berkeley in search of fungal enzymes that can both speed up the process of producing ethanol and utilize agricultural waste.

Efficiency is one part of the biofuels picture. But finding an energy source from fungi is the holy grail of mycotechnology, and there are some wild discoveries and ideas out there. Biodiesel is a vegetable- or animal fat–based diesel fuel, usually made from lipids, naturally occurring fats and fatty acids. Biodiesel can be produced from plants like soybeans, palm, and rapeseed, all of which contain burnable oils. However, these products require farmland, fertilizers, and pesticides to grow, and producing a gallon of biofuel realizes a net loss of energy. But mycologists have found a few species of fungi, like *Mucor circinelloides*, that are prolific producers of lipids, comparable to those produced by sunflower, palm, and soy oils, and could theoretically be converted into biodiesel and heating oil.

So how to put this discovery in action? There are some interesting ideas in the works. For example, an Iowa State University research team has been working on a biodiesel product called Mycofuel that is made from treating switchgrass, corn stover, or forestry wastes with ammonia and white rot fungi to degrade the cellulose. The resulting sugars are used to grow another kind of fungus, a mold that's about 60 percent oil. An ultrasonic treatment that causes the fungal cells to explode releases the oil, which is then extracted using an organic solvent system.

Gary Strobel is a bioprospector and longtime professor of microbiology at Montana State University who has licensed more than 20 fungal cultures over his 30-year career to companies like Eli Lilly and Dow Chemical. In a study published in 2008, he reported the discovery of an endophytic fungus from the Patagonian rain forest, *Gliocladium roseum*, which produces volatile hydrocarbons very similar to diesel fuel as a by-product of breaking down cellulose. When I spoke to Strobel about this bizarre phenomenon, he outlined the chain of events that have led him to believe that the fossil fuels we count on today may not only be the result of millions of years of pressure on ancient organic matter but also the busywork of these hydrocarbon-producing fungi.

Strobel is a bit of a Jacques Cousteau personality; an explorer, scientist, and showman who is captured in most photographs wearing a red skull cap (one of which is in the Smithsonian Institution). Strobel discovered an endophytic fungus called *Muscodor albus* (stinky white) that produces volatile chemicals like alcohols, acids, esters, and ketones that are lethal to a wide variety of plant and human pathogenic fungi and bacteria.

"It was 1997," said Strobel. "We were growing endophytes out of surface-sterilized plant tissue we'd brought back from Honduras, and we put all of our petri dishes in a plastic box because we had a problem with microscopic mites that were contaminating the cultures. After 10 or 12 days we opened the box, and there was this strange odor. All the cultures were dead except for a little white fungus. It was a gas bomb. And all its gases, which are composed of simple organic acids, are FDA-approved already." AgraQuest, a corporation specializing in biopesticides, explored "this very interesting fungus," according to Sarah Reiter, the director of global marketing, but they don't plan to commercialize it, as they encountered issues of stability and toxicology. "There is a lot to learn from *Muscodor*," said Reiter, "but *Muscodor* itself may not be that product." Currently, another company, Jeneil Biotech, is working on a *Muscodor*-based product.

Strobel subsequently discovered that some fungi were immune to the gases produced by *Muscodor albus*, like *Gliocladium roseum*, an endophytic fungus that grows inside the ulmo tree of Patagonia, and when grown out in a petri dish, looks like a rose-colored flower, and produces a suite of hydrocarbons that replicate diesel fuel as a by-product of digesting sugars (they produce less quantity if they feed on cellulose). Not all of the hydrocarbons found in diesel fuel are produced by one species, but Strobel claims an array of species produce different hydrocarbons. (His son, Scott Strobel, Yale's chair of the department of molecular biophysics and biochemistry, found one such species in a park near his Connecticut home.)

This has led Gary Strobel to speculate that our crude oil may be the result of a combination of multiple endophytic fungi switching to saprophytic mode once their plant host dies, working together to break down plant materials and, in the process, producing hydrocarbons. "If life created oil," suggested Strobel, "then it should be possible to manipulate these organisms to produce [biofuel]." In 2009, Montana State and Yale Universities joined forces to develop mycodiesel and received a $5 million grant from the Department of Energy to study it and other fungi with similar qualities. But producing ample quantities is going to be the challenge. *Gliocladium* only converts 1 percent of its food into diesel, significantly less than yeasts, which convert 50 percent of their food into ethanol.

These scientists imagine a future where biofuel is not only farmed, but the fungi would produce that fuel as a by-product of degrading agricultural waste.

They're working on it.

ꟿ

Remediation and energy are two of the three most provocative areas of mycotechnological research. The third is pesticides. When I attended Paul Stamets's "Mycelium Running" seminar on Cortes Island, he told a story about how he used the mycelium of *Metarhizium anisopliae*, a mold that kills termites, to destroy a carpenter ant colony that was damaging his home. The ants rejected sporulated mold, but they brought the mycelium back to the nest. "The presporulated mold acts as a Trojan horse," he said. The audience was captivated.

Mycopesticides are in fact already on the market. The most widely used mycoinsecticide is the entomopathogenic fungus *Beauveria bassiana*. It makes products like BotaniGard and Mycotrol effective against whitefly, mealy bug, and weevil infestations of ornamental plants. Their advertising boasts "highest viable spore count," which refers to the problematic stability of live fungal products (and what helped tank AgraQuest's development of *Muscodor*). A new product, Prestop, utilizes the fungus *Gliocladium catenulatum* to tackle fungal diseases of vegetable crops.

Entomopathogenic fungi infect and kill insects, often specializing in particular species. Utilizing these fungi to kill pests is unique in that their target can be species specific, versus the scorched-earth policy of older classes of chemical pesticides, like DDT. Mycoinsecticides are not environmentally hazardous, and the potential market is huge: Killing bugs is an $8 billion a year industry. Fungal spores adhere to the insect's cuticle, germinate, then enter the insect's body through the softer tissues and consume its tissues from within. Most incredible is the sight of those fungi that produce fruiting bodies sprouting tiny mushrooms from the corpses of insects.

There are a range of studies looking into the ability of entomopathogenic fungi to kill different species of insects, from cockroaches

Cordyceps fungi are pathogens of insects. Here, the fungus is fruiting from one corpse of a praying mantis.

to click beetles, malarial mosquitoes to the mites that are decimating honeybees. But there are just as many hurdles to creating commercial mycoinsecticides, the most problematic being the ability of live fungal products to survive distribution. Determining how to extend the shelf life of these fungi is the immediate challenge for many researchers. The problem is some insects have evolved to avoid entomopathogenic spores. Social insects like termites reject infected workers from their nests. The notion of using presporulated mycelium is one possible solution. Additionally, bioinsecticides tend to be inefficient. The bugs don't get killed fast enough. And then, of course, there are the challenges of industrial development. Many of the companies that invest in biopesticide research are small to midsize and lack the kind of long-term funding capabilities often needed to bring a product to market.

But they're working on that, too.

In the end, I wasn't disappointed to discover that mycotechnologies can't save the planet *today*. Instead, I was inspired to learn there are many scientists exploring the possibilities of fungi in remediation, biofuels, and mycopesticides. Good science takes time and money. Nonetheless, there is huge potential in the field for investigation and development. The study of fungi is indeed new territory. And that, in itself, is reason for optimism.

Chapter 12

THE SUPERORGANISM

T he mushroom fruitings in the temperate rain forests of the Pacific Northwest are unparalleled in the United States. There are 20 mycological clubs in Washington and Oregon alone. Most of the wild mushrooms collected for sale are picked there, and it is home to many mycologically inclined research labs and businesses. Since I first got interested in mycology, I had hoped to see those old-growth trees and witness the grand spectacle of countless mushrooms erupting from the forest floor.

When I see a mushroom, I am seeing evidence of what I have learned: trillions of microscopic life-forms living underground, giving rise to titanic trees, green ferns, mosses, and orchids, mushrooms in their myriad incarnations. I wanted to see the forests of the Pacific Northwest the way some people dream of seeing New York City. (New Yorkers are composed of microscopic organisms that support the lives of millions of macro life-forms, too.) Fifty percent of the weight of all life on the planet is microbial. Microorganisms like fungi and bacteria are so endemic to all living things that it is maybe more accurate to describe ourselves not as individuals, but as ecosystems, like forests. Of all the things I've learned about fungi, the one that has struck the deepest chord, that has affected my perspective on life most profoundly, is this: Everything that lives is plural.

So I waited for an opportunity to visit the Pacific Northwest in the fall, when the underworld of fungi reveals itself, when the invisible becomes visible. And then I heard about the Breitenbush Mushroom Conference, held at the end of October.

The Breitenbush Hot Springs are located in Oregon's Cascade Range, part of the Pacific Ring of Fire, a hoop of volcanoes that circles the Pacific Ocean. It's this deep volcanic activity that heats up the natural springs along the fast, shimmering Breitenbush River. Water is everywhere in this part of the world, especially in October, the beginning of the rainy season. I drove east on Route 22, the road silver with moisture, past tall, tall trees in cloaks of green epiphytes, curving beside surprisingly wide rivers, under a thunderhead, then out into gleaming tornados of damp leaves, then under another thunderhead, this one chilly and dumping tiny hail, then through a bank of roiling fog so thick I needed my headlights. It was a theater of moisture: water played out in so many dramatic incarnations.

I pulled into the damp Breitenbush Retreat and Conference Center parking lot, hemmed in by impossibly tall evergreens, which was some

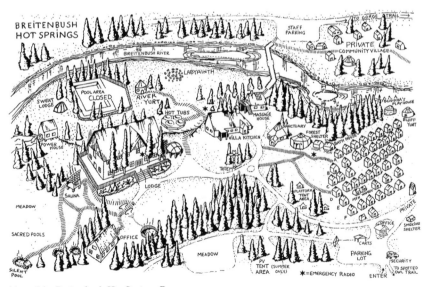

Map of the Breitenbush Hot Springs Retreat

distance from the lodge and cabins—there was no fouling the site with fuel injection engines—and as soon as I stepped out of the car, the dominant smell in the air was mushrooms. Signs directed me to the office, back to the parking lot, and to my cabin, back and forth across the campus along trails that wound through grand conifers and past shabby, mossy buildings. The place had a sort of nurtured run-down aesthetic, like a family beach cottage or mountain cabin. Nothing was in disrepair, but nothing looked new, and the springs themselves were tucked away, down by the river, and in a "sacred meadow." Signs were everywhere: no vehicles, no alcohol, no caffeine (we could bring our own), no nonbiodegradable shampoo (Dr. Bronner's supplied), clothing in the hot springs optional, clothing in the lodge *not* optional, no hair curlers, no hair dryers, and so on. While Breitenbush had the air of being very low-key, my first impression was to be on my best behavior and follow all the rules.

If the New York Mycophilia Association (NAMA) is the science foray, and the Telluride Mushroom Festival is the psychedelic foray, then the Breitenbush Mushroom Conference is the sexy foray. But before you get too excited, let me just throw out this image: nude mycologists.

Gary Lincoff had told me about the antics that had gone on at Breitenbush during its 25-year history: folks cavorting with the likes of Ken Kesey, Andrew Weil, Alexander Shulgin (who discovered and synthesized many psychoactive drugs), and Baba Ram Dass, socializing in the steamy pools, the mushroom-populated old-growth forests, the many private spots ripe for rendezvous.

I'd signed up for the cheapest possible accommodations: a triple without a bathroom, about $300, plus the conference cost, and as before I was the last in our cabin to arrive. It was evening, and my roommates had taken the two beds on the floor, leaving me with an upper bunk. I'd fallen out of bed a few weeks before—just sort of flung myself actually, and still had a scab on my elbow to prove it—so it was not without some trepidation that I set up my sleeping bag, as no linens are provided. Indeed, I backed down the steep ladder like a grandmother. But the cabin was snug and simple, one of 40 or so set up in rows, with a toilet house in the center. Our cabin was very cozy—all the buildings employ ample geothermal heating—and there was a broom in the corner, which struck me as quite nice and practical.

The lodge, where meals were served and lectures presented, was a brisk 10-minute walk away. But forests at night are mighty and intimidating, and since I neglected to bring my headlamp, I had to walk with teeny steps, as if shackled, slowly feeling my way along the dirt trail toward the distant lodge light. At one point a child ran past me, galloping along with his cat eyes and legs like springs, and then a misty rain started up. About a half hour later, I got to the lodge, in time to catch the last of the vegetarian dinner—Breitenbush only serves vegetarian food. Thom O'Dell conducted the first lecture, held after dinner in a room with a grand unlit fireplace and pillows on the floor. O'Dell is the mycologist who helped build the mycoremediation company, The Remediators. He talked some basic biology stuff, which was by now familiar to me, and I started to nod off, lulled by the sound of my stomach digesting quinoa and the increasingly thunderous rain on the lodge roof. The walk home was wet and dark, but at least there were people to follow.

In the middle of the night I woke up. I very carefully climbed out of my bunk bed, quietly, quietly, so as not to disturb my roommates, both lovely women with tousled hair and soft snores under their down quilts, and in my bare feet took a silent, soggy pee outside our front door.

It was dark and chilly when I awoke for the day, and so I went searching for a hot spring to warm up. Fog hung like laundry over the trails, and the first color to be revealed as the sky lightened was green. Virgin forest was all around us, though it seems a misnomer to call those huge trees virgin because they seemed so old and wise and experienced. A deer passed close by me, totally unafraid. The campus felt enchanted as I drifted to the first of three misty pools overlooking a meadow that poured grassily down a low hill to the river. As I shook off my robe and settled into the hot water, I noticed a sign that said, "Please respect your body's limits."

The Breitenbush springs discharge at least 900 gallons of hot water per minute with a maximum temperature of 198 degrees Fahrenheit. The water is several thousand years old, having originated in precipitation in the Cascades and percolated down through the centuries to this one sweet spot. The forests themselves are several hundred years old, and very likely, their fungal partners are, too. The trees were clothed in lichens and moss and tiny ferns that crept down the trunks and onto the ground like robes, from which mushrooms grew in proliferation and squirrels fed, a forestscape of connected life-forms. Life, as the theoretical biologist Lynn Margulis wrote, "is a network of cross-kingdom alliances."

Biologists have reshuffled the taxonomic rank of organisms every 15 years or so since the 1960s. A current classification—and it is not the only proposition out there—suggests that all living things fall under three domains based on their evolutionary path: Bacteria, Archaea, and Eukarya, with kingdoms as subdivisions. Around 2 billion years ago, eukaryotic organisms emerged when a primitive single-celled prokaryote swallowed one of another kind, making for a stable and lasting symbiosis. A eukaryote (from the Greek, *eu* = well or good, *karyon* = nut or kernel) is an organism with a nucleus (their genetic material is contained in membrane). In time, some of these cells combined and formed multicellular organisms—an important development because it allowed for specialized cells to function within a single entity, a kind of biological *e pluribus unum* ("out of many, one"). All higher, complex life, the kingdoms of animals, plants, and fungi, are eukaryotic.

Up until the 1960s, fungi were lumped together with plants because what we could see—mushrooms—resembled plants. They were not mobile, and they seemed to grow from the soil. Indeed, scientists in the 1950s believed that fungi evolved from algae, considered in the past to be the simplest of plants (and some mycologists were teaching the same in the 1970s). The thinking was that photosynthetic plants had to come first because they provided food for other organisms.

Today, it is generally accepted that fungi did not evolve from algae but from a single-celled eukaryote. Eukaryotes followed different evolutionary paths. Some evolved into animals and fungi, and others acquired cyanobacteria, a kind of aquatic photosynthetic bacteria that evolved into chloroplasts that carry out photosynthesis, and became plants.

The timeline for the development of terrestrial fungi is not well understood. The evidence available in the fossil record is scant,* as fungi do not biomineralize. The fossil evidence for the origin of vascular plants is poor as well. So it is not definitive which came on land first. In fact, plants and fungi may have evolved on land together.

Endophytic fungi were found in a fossilized member of the most ancient group of plants, the thalloid liverwort (alive 470 million years ago). There are fossilized hyphae that resemble mycorrhizal fungi and spores from the Ordovician (about 460 million years ago), a time when land plants were nonvascular, and the earliest fossils of vascular land plants, from the Devonian (416 to 359 million years ago), show endophytic fungi living inside the primitive plant structures, even in their rhizoids, the precursors to plant roots. Fossilized lichens have also been found from the Devonian period.† James White, who studies endophytes and evolution and is a professor at Rutgers University, pointed out what seems to be the dominant thinking: "It's possible land plants were able to emerge through the help of fungi."

---

*The molecular estimates suggest the first terrestrial fungi fell into three groups—Basidiomycota, the club fungi, Ascomycota, the cup fungi, and Glomermycota, soil-based mycorrhizal fungi— with particular spore features, and originated about 600 million years ago.

†Since 1859, scientists have tried to figure out a bizarre fossil named prototaxites, a 20-foot-tall tree-trunk-like organism that lived 420 to 350 million years ago and was the largest land organism at the time. The latest findings conclude that the fossil was most likely a giant fungus, although some scientists have suggested it was actually a giant liverwort. Liverwort is technically a plant but is often lumped together with lichen, slime molds, and algae.

White described this hypothetical scenario: Dead aquatic plant remains washed up on ancient shores. Aquatic saprophytic fungi evolved to break down the plant matter on land, in the process building soils. Then, much later, endophytic and parasitic fungi evolved with plants on land, and later still, mycorrhizal relationships evolved, permitting a stable and balanced relationship between fungus and plant. Plants making the transition to land may have taken advantage of fungi's capabilities to mine nutrients from the soil and transfer them to plants. Indeed, there may never have been a time when plants did not have a fungal partner.

At Breitenbush, I noticed a primitive-looking lichen, part fungi, part plant, with leaves that resembled lizard skin. They fell in clusters from their hammocks in the trees with a thwack. It was lungwort, an indicator of undisturbed ecosystems. And indeed, those unfathomable woods and their strange tenants felt trapped in a time before man.

The woods around Breitenbush were all beautiful, though I was never sure where I was. The forays were self-organizing; there was no sign-up list. After breakfast (rice gruel—not as bad as the name implies), a whirlwind of a woman named Patrice informed us about the degree of walkiness (steep, flat, trails, bushwhacking) and we just stood next to the leader we hoped would be leading the walk we wanted to be on. But really, it didn't matter. All the forests were spectacular, and there were mushrooms everywhere, between the cabins, around the bathhouses, along the river. To find mushrooms in that environment, all I had to do was wear my glasses.

The walks had a particular group dynamic I'd seen before. The leader may not cover more than 30 yards of terrain all morning, as they go slow, talking about the mushrooms brought to them. Many of those who cluster around the leaders are new to mycology. Then there are the semiknowledgeable, like me, and some of us are know-it-alls, a vanity that is the curse of not really knowing very much.

I'd spotted a few edible mushrooms and that inspired one or two people to follow me around, though they peeled off when they realized my repertoire was quickly spent. But I was grateful to be left alone, because what I really wanted to do was just look for matsutake, the cinnamon-scented mushroom treasured by the Japanese, without competition. I trucked over and under fallen timber, exhausting myself circling every pine tree. A saucy gal in a conductor's cap and a nose ring who was also a semiknowledgeable type stopped me at one point, a huge matsutake in each hand, and said, "You walked right by these," as if to say I was not who I portrayed myself to be. I looked harder after that, and stewed in a little broth of humiliation, but found none.

But in the afternoon I went to another forest, this one cooler and deeper, with older trees and bear scat on the ground. There I started to find them, peeping under the lumpish groundcover, their white caps mostly submerged. Soon my bag was full of mushrooms, or at least it seemed soon. It wasn't until I got back in the car that I realized I'd been hunting for 4 hours. In the rain.

The Breitenbush conference didn't try to do as many things as other forays I'd been on. The walks were enough. The woods were endless; a field of green columns sprouting ferns like tufts of hair as far as I could see, and within minutes one could hunt alone, footsteps padded by the bouyant moss underfoot, the sunlight falling through the canopy in scant murky puddles. And then there were the springs, where most people hung out as the day waned. I tried them all, like a buffet. The springs by the river were the hottest, and I shared them with a gaggle of teenagers, all self-conscious in bathing suits, despite the fact that their bodies were as beautiful and graceful as the willows that surrounded us. There was a very fine mushroom dyeing seminar, led by a lovely young mycosavant, and an excellent mycophagy seminar, run by a generous and sweet-natured chef who, contrary to typical chefy puffed-upness, allowed everyone to cook whatever mushrooms they wanted their way, and as a result, a variety of well-practiced dishes were produced: aromatic matsutake steamed in soy and rice wine, silky pig's ear sautéed with cream and cognac, crunchy fried slabs of cauliflower mushroom.

In the early evening, I conducted an interview with the mycologist Thom O'Dell in a hot spring, or tried to anyway. I had to hold my large, floppy notebook above the water with one hand while I wrote with the other, and the pages were limp from the condensating steam; afterward my notes looked like runny mascara. And the fact that we were both naked presented its own set of challenges.

Those distractions not withstanding, we talked about how profoundly DNA analyses have affected the study of fungi. Genomics, the study of all the genetic material of an organism, have not only led to a near total reassessment of taxonomy by revealing how different types of fungi relate to each other on a genetic level, but they also reveal how fungi relate to other organisms. For example, a look at the genes of some pathogenic fungi and the plants they parasitize has shown an evolutionary link. For every gene in the plant that is able to mutate to resist the fungal pathogen, there is a gene in the fungus that has mutated to overcome that resistance. Known as the gene-for-gene hypothesis, this pattern of back-and-forth mutation has gone on for a long time, and it may be the mechanism behind mutually beneficial relationships that have evolved between endophytic fungi—fungi that live between the cells of a plant—and their hosts.* Each tree, each flower, each blade of grass is a mini-ecosystem composed of plant and fungal cells (and bacteria cells and viruses). This evolutionary relationship is known as endosymbiosis (from the Greek, *endo* = inside, *sym* = with, and *biosis* = living).

Symbiosis, first conceived by the 19th-century German mycologist

---

*A study conducted in 2011 found that a large cluster of ancient fungal genes jumped from one species to another, a phenomenon called horizontal transfer. It suggests that the tree of life might not be the only model that describes evolution.

Heinrich Anton de Bary, describes close, long-term relationships between organisms. The lifestyles of fungi: mutualism, commensalism, and parasitism, are examples of symbiotic partnerships—evolutionary relationships between two or more organisms. There are countless examples of symbiotic relationships in nature, because all life-forms are symbiotic to some degree, and there are usually more than two partners in a given symbiotic picture. Understanding the symbiotic relationships in an ecosystem is key to retaining the health of that ecosystem. Because we have a history of underestimating the degree to which symbiosis exists, we rarely anticipate the full effect our interventions have on these partnerships.

This point became clear to me when I attended a lecture by Jack States, a retired mycologist from Northern Arizona University, called "Squirrels, Trees, and Truffles." Over the course of many years' study, States proved that the "ancient and highly evolved symbiosis" between tassel-eared squirrels, ponderosa pines, and certain truffles (these truffles are inedible to us: "they stink," said States, "but the squirrels love them") in the American Southwest was key to their well-being, indeed their very survival. Other organisms, the hawk that fed on the squirrels and the beetle that is exclusive to the truffles, were studied as well, and illustrated that the number of symbiotic partners may grow exponentially. His work describing the relationship was so conclusive he was able to change regional logging practices despite numerous challenges by the industry. At the conclusion of his lecture, I jumped up and yelled "Bravo!" It was like attending the symphony. I had never imagined science could be so graceful.

Endosymbiotic relationships are even more mysterious, mainly because they happen on a microscopic scale. Endosymbionts are organisms that have evolved to live among the cells of other organisms, and often the endosymbiont or endosymbionts and the host need each other to thrive. For this reason, they're called obligate endosymbionts, because they are obligated to one another: One cannot live without the other. "When such a mutually agreeable arrangement is in place for a long time," wrote Terrence McKenna, "it will eventually 'institutionalize' itself by progressively blurring the clear genetic distinction between the symbionts. Ultimately, one organism may actually become a part of the other. . . . "

The endosymbiotic theory postulated by the pioneering theoretical biologist Lynn Margulis in the 1960s says that the cells of higher life-forms—animal, fungi, and plants—originated through symbiosis with bacterial cells, and that the ongoing symbiotic relationships between organisms from different kingdoms may even be the driving force of evolution. Today, it is generally agreed that eukaryotic cells, "all of them," said the microbiologist Elio Schaechter, "arose only once by acquisition of a bacterium or something like it, which then whittled down its genome to become mitochondria," the membrane-enclosed packet of organelles, or diminutive organs, found in the cells of higher life-forms.

There are endosymbionts throughout all the kingdoms in nature. Endophytic fungi and endomycorrhizal fungi (fungi that live in—versus on—roots) are endosymbionts of plants. There are fungi that are endosymbionts of other fungi, and bacteria are likely endosymbiotic in all life-forms: Scientists have counted as many as 250,000 live bacteria in a single fungal spore. "If you ask me," said the mycologist Tom Volk, "I think there's probably bacteria living in everything."

When it comes to humans, our microbial partners are ectosymbionts (from the Greek, *ecto* = outside). They live, and do important chores, *on* our skin, and all our internal surfaces, like the lining of our intestines and respiratory tract. (Microbes living in our body are technically living on us.) Certain yeasts are fungal ectosymbionts of animals. "But we don't really know if they are mutualistic or simply in competition with the bacteria," said Volk. "But if you *don't* have yeasts in and on your body, you get more bacterial infections."* Yeasts and bacteria help animals digest food. In some cases, they are obligatory, as in the case of ruminants like cows that cannot digest their food independent of their bacterial flora.

And then there is *our* gut.

"When I went to school, plants were considered competitors, not symbionts," said Gary Lincoff. "That's like calling them communists! After the fall of the Soviets, symbiosis stopped being a dirty word. We think of ourselves as rugged individualists, but where would we be without our *E. coli*? We are conglomerates. It's not a bad thing to be. It means you never have to eat alone." Some scientists are calling the human body a superorganism, that each of us is a colony of organisms, and all our parts—the animal parasites, the fungi and impermanent bacteria in our guts, and the permanently incorporated bacterial descendants in our cells (mitochondria, the membrane-enclosed organelles that give us chemical energy)—have evolved to work in agreement (or maybe it's a kind of deterrence) to compose the organism known as you, and they continue to evolve.

"People assume evolution is done," said Tom Volk. "It's not."

There are 10 trillion or so microbial cells living on us, exceeding human cells by 10 to 1 (but only constituting a pound or two), and they harbor millions of genes (the human genome has 20,000 genes). There are so many bacteria, fungi, and viruses living on us, particularly in our guts, known as gut flora, that this microbial colony functions like a shadow digestive organ, "a collective metabolic activity equal to a virtual organ within an organ," according to Ann M. O'Hara in her article "The Gut

*To wit: There is a fungus, *Pneumocystis*, that lives in human lungs—and cannot survive outside your lungs. Maybe it has a function, maybe it is simply biding its time, because when the host becomes immunocompromised, it becomes pathogenic.

Flora as a Forgotten Organ" (and analogous to the role of endophytic fungi functioning as a virtual immune system for plants, or mycorrhizal fungi functioning as a virtual digestive organ for trees). As a result, massive projects like the Human Microbiome Project are under way in order to actually figure out where the body ends and the microbes begin, and to determine if there is a core microbiome common to all people.* When I refer to my body, I am usually talking about the whole shebang. But the truth is, we have private spaces in our body and public spaces. The microbiologist Terry Hazen likes to say we are "bacteria living on a person."

"I am me, and my symbionts," said Elio Schaechter.

Or, as Tom Volk, who has had a heart transplant, told me, "I am a bunch of organisms, plus one other person."

There are microbes living in all the public spaces in our bodies—our sinuses, mouths, and ears; our throats, esophagus, intestines, colon, vagina, and anus, even our lungs. Scientists at Imperial College in London found there are 6,000 microbes in every square inch of lung tissue. There may be a little or a lot of microbial diversity from person to person and place to place on any individual: Our personal microbial recipe defines us. The community that lives in my gut may be very, very different than the one that lives in yours. The microbes on my tongue and on my hands are different from yours, and not only composed of different species but different quantities of species. There are even different microbial populations on my left hand versus my right. These populations may be different based on all kinds of factors: climatic zone, lifestyle, and genetics. "Although we fall into groups, no two of us are alike," pointed out Elio Schaechter. "*Suum quique*—to each his own—is the way of the microbial world."

*The National Institutes of Health's Human Microbiome Project was launched in 2008 and should be complete by 2013. Previously, the study of the human biota was limited to culturing, or growing out the bacteria in a sample to see what's there, but scientists could only culture about 1 percent of all different bacteria present (lots die when exiled from their habitat—you). The beauty of the Human Microbiome Project is its utilization of genomics: With DNA analysis, scientists can bypass culturing altogether to determine what species are present.

Our fear of microbes is based on misunderstanding. I have a friend who would never dip herself into the Breitenbush Hot Springs, or sit on the rude wood benches to cool off without laying a towel down first, or suck in the steam in the mossy freestanding sauna that resembled a gypsy wagon. But she shouldn't worry. She is filled with microbes that help her stay healthy by keeping invaders out.

Microbes protect their habitats, just as endophytic fungi protect their host plant. You can get sick when the microbial colonies that live in your public spaces become out of whack and certain species overgrow, or when a fungus or bacteria or virus penetrates your private spaces where it doesn't belong (or when you get infected with something neither your immune system nor your microbes can handle). And the makeup of that microbial population could matter. The flora in your lungs may determine whether you are asthmatic or not, or microbe-deficient patients may have under-regulated immune systems, leading to autoimmune disease. From this kind of revelation comes therapy. Someday chronic GI problems may be managed by ingesting a dose of the right microbes. That's what probiotic yogurts are: live microorganisms.

If friendly microbes weren't occupying and defending and modifying the public spaces—their habitats—in our bodies, maybe unfriendly microbes would. Our microbial partners are synonymous with our immune system. They

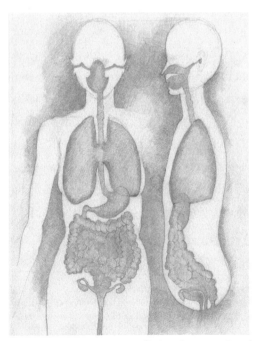

Microbes live in our public spaces (darkened portions of torso).

have other roles, too, like helping us absorb nutrients in our lower intestine, but there is much about the roles played by our microbial colonies that we don't know, and human fungal ectosymbionts—mainly in the form of yeasts—are less studied than bacteria. Our gut flora is composed of far more bacteria, but that doesn't deny fungi's potential importance. The science simply hasn't been done.

The concept of symbiosis has led scientists to utilize the idea of the superorganism in place of the organism. In the past, superorganisms referred to eusocial animals, like ants and bees; colonies composed of multiple individuals acting in concert to produce a collective result. "If humans are thought of as a composite of microbial and human cells," wrote the microbiologist Peter J. Turnbaugh, "the human genetic landscape as an aggregate of the genes in the human genome and the microbiome, and human metabolic features as a blend of human and microbial traits, then the picture that emerges is one of a human 'superorganism.'"

At the end of the weekend, Daniel Winkler, who was one of the speakers at the foray, and Thom O'Dell took off on their own. I tagged along. This was the pros' foray. No identifying mushrooms, just gathering for the table. I was happy to hunt without inhibition. When I search with a group or with people who are new to mushroom hunting, I rein in my impulses. I try to be polite and carry on conversation while walking, but I really prefer to be silent. I try to have eye contact when they talk to me, but it is hard to keep from glancing to the forest floor. I try to stick with the group, but I am restless to move on. Hunting mushrooms seems like a solo sport, but it is not. It is deeply participatory, just not with other people. Instead, the hunter experiences the company of trees and mushrooms and birds. It's a communion with the woods and the grand mosaic of nature.

In the evening, I returned to the spring that overlooked the meadow. Breitenbush is indeed the sexy foray, but I realized it was not because of the company, although one of my roommates did meet a man who had tempted her earlier in the day with a private hunt for matsutake, and she had carefully agreed, and was now tasting the hot waters with him and letting him whisper in her ear. No, for me the Breitenbush foray became sexy when I stepped out of the hot spring and realized the thick green grass under my bare feet was warm, not from the day's sunshine, not from the balmy temperature, but from the primeval hot water that ran through the soil. From the soil, to the grass, to me.

Maybe it is no accident that I became obsessed with mushrooms. I think we all search for a way to connect with something bigger than ourselves, and mycology opened that window for me. I may have started out interested in mushrooms because I liked to eat them, but I ended up with a more profound understanding not only of the natural world but of myself as a symbiotic organism living within it. I came to understand that the traditional idea of an ecosystem, which had been locked in a scale relative to our experience of the world, has both contracted into microecosystems and expanded into macroecosystems. Instead of referring to an area within the natural environment and its interdependent organisms, organisms themselves can be described as ecosystems. Pull back the lens and I could see how organisms are symbionts in an ecosystem, and ecosystems are symbionts in a biome, and biomes are symbionts on the globe. Just as I am a collection of organisms functioning together as a whole, life on the planet—the entire living community—may be considered an organism, one where all life-forms work together to move energy around.

And there's more. The Gaia hypothesis, which was crafted by James Lovelock, a chemist and inventor who turned 90 in 2009, imagines the entire planet as an ecosystem, one that includes the Earth's atmosphere, surface rocks, and water functioning in conjunction with the life cycles of living organisms.* Lovelock proposed that the living and nonliving aspects of Earth, the planet's biologic, climatic, geologic, and chemical aspects, compose an integrated symbiotic system, too.

The degree of complexity that symbiosis suggests is so awesome that creationists consider it evidence of God. "It seems nothing less than a supernatural, super-intelligent Creator can explain all the intricate designs required in advance of launching symbiotic relationships," wrote Hugh Ross, PhD, a Canadian-born former astronomer and current Old Earth creationist. Lynn Margulis suggests that humans—indeed, all higher life-forms—are the work of "thousands of millions of years of interaction among highly responsive microbes." Like the bumper sticker on Paul Stamets's car says: "Evolution *is* God's intelligent design."

"So what are the implications?" the microbiologist Elio Schaechter asked me in his heavy mosh pit of a European accent, his voice musical with intelligence and sass. "It's this. An understanding of what the human being is today is based on an understanding of all our direct and indirect relationships with other creatures."

Indeed, the eternal question is no longer Who am I? but Who are we?

It rained heavier and longer every day I was at Breitenbush. It always rained at night, and all the trails were puddled by the time I packed my bags and dragged my muddy roller bag through the dark, damp pine trees. Somehow I lost a small box containing three Jurassic-size orange chanterelles, two of which I had received in trade for four matsutake. (I think I left it springside after my rather discombobulating nude interview

---

*The name Gaia, pronounced guy-a, comes from the Greek goddess of the Earth. She's a member of the Protogenoi, primeval gods that also include Chaos, Nature, Day, Night, and so on.

with Thom O'Dell.) I was exceedingly bummed about those chanterelles, and as I drove the winding highway out of the mountains, I had to keep talking myself out of turning around and trying to locate them. As I got farther and farther away from Breitenbush and the dark forests receded in my rearview mirror, I began to scan spots beside the road where I could pull over and maybe find a few mushrooms to compensate, and then I did see a spot and parked.

I stepped a few feet into the ferny damp woods, eyes sweeping the terrain for the telltale orange chanterelle color, but it was clear other hunters had been there before. There were mushroom stumps every-where, mixed in with tossed Pampers and beer cans. It was an ugly place, a bit of a dumping ground, and it was stupid to have stopped and I knew it. But as I headed back to the car I noticed, clinging to the side of a fallen log, a *Pseudohydnum gelatinosum,* a strange, clear little fungus that looks like water muscled into the shape of a mushroom. It struck me as basically sex plus water. For all my efforts to understand mushrooms, that simplistic metaphor gave me a sense of completion and an understanding and appreciation of the nature of things that I never

intended or expected to understand or appreciate when I first joined the New York Mycological Society. I pocketed the fungus, because I am a mushroom hunter, got back in the car, and headed home.

Pseudohydnum gelatinosum

ACKNOWLEDGMENTS

Many, many people helped me understand fungi and their role in nature and commerce. They reviewed material for accuracy, patiently explained problematic concepts, and advised me along the way. Three mycologists reviewed the book in its entirety—a very humongous favor for which I will be forever in debt. Many of Mark Miller's pithy insights are incorporated in the text, and his frequent use of the acronym BS was honestifying. I am very grateful to him for his generosity and honored to call him my friend. Elio Schaechter clarified many points in my science reporting, but I am especially grateful to him for providing a kind of moral center for the book. His ear is tuned to ethics, and I thank him especially for steering me away from tacky tendencies. In my opinion, Tom Volk is a national treasure. He's erudite, droll, supportive, and incredibly knowledgeable on a wide array of fungal topics. I learned a great deal from Tom, including some stuff about courage.

My lay reader, Dan Malloy, was an angel for reading the whole manuscript in a matter of weeks. Over the Christmas holidays. In Las Vegas. His careful comments were hugely helpful. Michael McCarthy and Lorraine Cademartori also read the manuscript, and their encouragement was much appreciated, especially coming at a time when I was experiencing more insecurity and self-doubt than usual.

I also benefited from the astute eyes of a few mycologists, both professional and amateur, and other experts, each according to their area of specialty. Rusty Rodriguez reviewed my material on endophytes; David Pilz on fire morels, Rosario Sarafina on the truffle business, Tom Michaels on truffle growing, Peter Grey on exotic mushrooms, Mary Jo

Feeney on mushroom nutrition, Ron Sabourin on nutraceuticals, Denis Benjamin on medicinal and medical mushrooms, Thomas Odell on new technologies, and James White on fungal evolution. Paul Sadowski read very early pages of this book, and his gentle corrections did much to preserve my ego at a critical juncture. Throughout the writing process, Gary Lincoff set me straight on many points of biology and shared hilarious anecdotes about the community of amateur and professional mycologists. Gary is a natural teacher: inspired, generous, and entertaining. It's been a privilege to know him.

I hope I have done their efforts justice, but the truth is, all errors are mine.

I should point out that the mycologists I spoke to almost all have doctorates. I decided not to add their honorifics in the text, but it should be noted that they have dedicated many years to the study of mycology, and their ongoing research is key to the incredible developments in the field that I report on.

I interviewed over a hundred people for this book, many of whom provided general information or clarification on the science and quotes: scientists of all sorts, pickers both amateur and professional, distributors, educators, historians, curators, cultivators, law enforcement, medical doctors, nutritionists, advocates, business people, web masters, myconaughts, archivists, chefs, one aerialist, and one reverend. A few who were especially gracious with their time (and patience) were Ellen Bloch, Britt Bunyard, Bart Byuck, Seth Cagin, David Campbell, George Carroll, Ekaterina Dadachova, Larry Evans, Franklin and Betty Garland, Andrew Geiger, John Getz, Ralph Ghoche, Charles Grob, Sam Harrington, Christopher Hobbs, Charles LeFevre, Gavin McIntyre, Bud Mancinelli, Mark Meisner, Gary Mills, Charlie Novy, Laura Phelps, Jack Ponticelli, David Rose, Elissa Rubin-Mahon, Elinoar Shavit, Suzanne Simard, Denise Smith, Jay Southard, Howard Sprouse, Gary Strobel, John Swayne Jr., Jim Trappe, Amy Tuining, Daniel Winkler, and Michael Wood.

Many thanks to Sophia Lederal and Ana Pulido for their research assistance.

For the illustrations in this book, I am grateful to the uber mushroom photographer Taylor Lockwood, to Ernest Bloch II, Huger Foote, Andrew Geiger, Cathy Kittle of the New York DEP, Gary Mills, Toshiyuki Nakagaki, Cheryl Oakes of the Forest History Society, Jacki Tolley at Science Photo Researchers, Tom Volk, Daniel Winkler, and Gary Lincoff. Thanks to Raye Levine, for her beautiful drawings. Many thanks to Steven Hillyer, director of the Cooper Union's Irwin S. Chanin School of Architecture Archive, for his scans of the artwork.

The production of this book has had many players as well. First, thanks to my literary agent, Angela Miller, cheese-maker, writer, and friend. I feel lucky to have her in my corner. I hold the opinion of my editor Pam Krauss in very high regard, which is important if she is telling you to cut 15,000 words, and I am immensely grateful for her guidance. Her hand is everywhere in this book and it is better because of it. Rodale art director Amy King, a mycophile herself, was inspiring to work with, and kindly held back her annoyance over my technological bumbling. To Aly Mostel, who led the book out of its room and into the world, thank you for your enthusiasm. Managing editor Greg Villepique guided the notes. Never an easy task, but this time more challenging, I think because I was a newbie to writing notes. To Marilyn Hauptly, who navigated the book through production, particularly the copyediting stage. There are many others, of course, who I did not have as much contact with, but are key to the ongoing success of Rodale. Indeed, Rodale is a very decent place to call home. I owe them all my gratitude.

Friends and family played a role in the successful completion of this book as well, mainly by putting up with my inability to talk about anything but fungi for years, and lending support by forgiving the missed birthdays, unreturned calls, date screw-ups, and forgotten hospital procedures, but also for sending me clippings and posts, and offering to help in a myriad of small but important ways. Thanks to Alex Akira, John Bidwell, Art Chandler, the extended Delegato family, Diane Emery, Gia Forakis, Betty Fussell, Charlie and Marilee Gilman, Edward and Elinor Giobbi, Cham Giobbi, Paul Guilfoyle, Bill Haney, Ezra Herman, Sandy Ingber, Arlene Jacobs, Diane and Gerard Koeppel, Lisa Krueger, Dan and Lisa Malloy, Kathryn and Michael McCarthy, Julie Rigby, Wes Rosen, Linda and Steve Rubick, Warren Ser, Tucker Shaw, Susie Siedenburg, Nathalie Smith, Jim and Marie Sullivan, Laine Valentino, Dorian Yates, John Zito, and most of all Lisa Giobbi. I kept her pleasure in mind throughout the writing of this book.

And of course, thanks to my husband Kevin, and kids, Carson and Mo, who, when asked how we were doing, would roll their eyes and report, "It's all mushrooms, all the time."

Sorry guys. Sorry everybody. I'd like to say I'm over it.

NOTES

Introduction

Most of the material in the introduction is first-person narrative; however, I used the following sources where needed. For information on umami, Japanese for "good taste," and its evolution as a food descriptor, the place to go is the Umami Information Center, established in Japan in 1982 (www.umamiinfo.com).

For the overview of mushroom biology and the "explosion of knowledge" of the microbial world, I used *The Fifth Kingdom*, 3rd ed., by Bryce Kendrick (Newburyport, MA: Focus Publishing, 1992); *Mycelium Running: How Mushrooms Can Help Save the World* by Paul Stamets (Berkeley, CA: Ten Speed Press, 2005); and *Introductory Mycology* by C. J. Alexopoulos, C. W. Mims, and M. Blackwell (New York: Wiley, 1996). The quote "scarcely a day . . . " comes from the latter book.

Gary H. Lincoff has written many great books about mushrooms, but his *National Audubon Society Field Guide to North American Mushrooms* is a classic (New York: Knopf, 1981).

Paul Stamets was dubbed "the Steve Jobs of fungus" in the *New York Times* ("Grow your own mushrooms," April 15, 2010, D5). Indeed, he is.

Chapter 1

There are numerous Web sites devoted to morels. Here are a few: www.thegreatmorel .com, www.morels.com, http://morelmania.com, www.morelmushroomhuntingclub .com, http://morelsandmore.com, and www.morel.org. Almost all of these sites have morel sighting maps. The anthropological work I refer to is "Molly mooching on Bradley Mountain: the aesthetic ecology of Appalachian morels" by Mary Hufford, *Gastronomica* (2006) 6(2):49–56.

I learned about the history of the New York Mycological Club from longtime member Ursula Hoffman over a martini in a Chinese restaurant. John Cage's quote comes from "John Cage Interviewed by Jonathan Cott (1963)," www.archive.org/details/Cottinterviews.

I learned much about the evolution of the cultural authority of the sciences from John van Wyhe's essay "Victorian Science, an Introduction" on the Web site www .victorianweb.org. Further information on the evolution of mycological societies in the United States was gleaned from David Rose's article "The poisoning of Count Achilles de Vecchj and the origins of American amateur mycology," *McIlvainea* (2006) 16(1):37–55. Tom Volk of the University of Michigan–La Crosse pointed out the blurring of the lines between amateur and professional mycologists, and Michael Wood's Internet site, www.mykoweb.com, lists all the clubs in the United States.

For the awful details of *Amanita* and other poisonings, I referred to Denis R. Benjamin's excellent *Mushrooms: Poisons and Panaceas: A Handbook for Naturalists, Mycologists, and Physicians* (New York: W.H. Freeman, 1995).

For data about US mushroom poisonings, I referred to the North American Mycological Association (NAMA) Toxicology Committee paper, "Thirty-Plus Years of Mushroom Poisoning: Summary of the Approximately 2,000 Reports in the NAMA Case Registry" by Michael W. Beug, Marilyn Shaw, and Kenneth W. Cochran, *McIlvainea* (2006) 16(2):47–68. Shark attack data came from the International Shark Attack File Statistics of Shark Attacks compiled by the American Elasmobranch Society and the Florida Museum of Natural History (www.flmnh.ufl.edu/fish/sharks/statistics/statistics.htm). Information about specific poisonings were gleaned from Denis Benjamin's *Mushrooms: Poisons and Panaceas*; a lecture by Britt Bunyard on the *Amanita* genus; a lecture by Michael W. Beug, of NAMA's Toxicology Committee, that covered what's new in poisonings; and from the article "Last chance to know? Using literature to explore the biogeography and invasion biology of the death cap mushroom *Amanita phalloides*" by Anne Pringle and Else C. Vellinga, *Biological Invasions* (2006) 8:1131–44. The work on rhabdomyolysis was reported in the article "Wild-mushroom intoxication as a cause of rhabdomyolysis," by Regis Bedry, et al., *New England Journal of Medicine* (2001) 345:798–802. The British papers the *London Telegraph*, *Times*, and *Guardian* have published ongoing accounts of Nicholas Evans's ordeal with orellanine poisoning since September 2008.

Tom Volk told me about most of the mushroom hunter superstitions. For myths about mushroom poisoning, see "Mushrooms" in *Bentley's Miscellany* (London, 1866) 60:412–22.

For information about chitin, the stuff of which fungal cell walls are made, I referred to Kendrick's *Fifth Kingdom*; *Mr. Bloomfield's Orchard: The Mysterious World of Mushrooms, Molds, and Mycologists* by Nicholas P. Money (New York: Oxford University Press, 2002); and "On Eating Raw Mushrooms" by David Campbell, *Mycena News* (2008) 59(8):4–5. For info on the habitat of candy caps, and indeed, for many of the mushrooms mentioned in this book, I used Tom Volk's terrific Fungus of the Month (FOTM) Web site: www.botit.botany.wisc.edu/toms_fungi/fotm/html. Particularly special is the Latin pronunciation feature.

LBM is a well-used acronym, appearing in mushroom-oriented speech and text regularly.

I pulled information from numerous sources in order to describe the classification of fungi. Especially helpful was Tom Volk's lecture series, "The Kingdom Fungi." I also benefited from reading *Mushrooms, Molds, and Miracles: The Strange Realm of Fungi* by Lucy Kavaler (New York: John Day, 1965; Lincoln, NE: iUniverse, Inc., 2007), and Britt Bunyard's article "Morels 101: a primer on the how, when and where of all things morel," *Fungi* (2010) 3(2):49–57, which helped me understand more about Ascomycetes. Lynn Margulis provides an interesting argument against the blanket acceptance of DNA as a classification tool in her magnificent book, *Symbiotic Planet: A New Look at Evolution* (New York: Basic Books, 1998).

The story about *Psilocybe wassonii* is related in *The Sacred Mushroom Seeker: Tributes to R. Gordon Wasson,* Thomas J. Riedlinger, ed. (Rochester, VT: Park Street Press, 1997). It appears in the article "A Twentieth Century Darwin" by Jonathan Ott on pages 183–192.

Women are more adept at mushroom hunting, according to "Sex differences in mushroom gathering: men expend more energy to obtain equivalent benefits" by Luis Pacheco-Cobos, et al., *Evolution and Human Behavior* (2010) 31(4):289–297.

Panic reactions to feared mushroom poisonings are well described in *Mushrooms: Poisons and Panaceas.*

Wild About Mushrooms has a home page, www.wildaboutmushrooms.net. Details about the origins of the company can be found in the WAM brochure, also online.

"Mushroom hunter finds head" is, unfortunately, real. See "Mushroom collector in Japan finds woman's head," *Australian*, November 6, 2009.

In regard to mushroom cookery in the ancient world, I referred to an excellent entry on Apicius in the *Oxford Companion to Food* by Alan Davidson (Oxford: Oxford University Press, 1999); *Cooking and Dining in Imperial Rome,* Joseph Dommers Vehling, ed. and trans. (New York: Dover, 1977); *Roman Cookery: Elegant & Easy Recipes from History's First Gourmet,* rev. ed., by John Edwards (Point Roberts, WA: Hartley & Marks, 1986); *Food in Antiquity: A Survey of the Diet of Early Peoples,* exp. ed., by Don R. Brothwell and Patricia Brothwell (Baltimore: Johns Hopkins University Press, 1997); and a beautiful little book called *Fungi: Folklore, Fiction, & Fact* by W. P. K. Findlay (Richmond, UK: Richmond Publishing, 1982).

A very interesting essay on mycophobia is "A study of cultural bias in field guide determinations of mushroom edibility using the iconic mushroom, *Amanita muscaria,* as an example," by William Rubel and David Arora, *Economic Botany* (2008) 62(3):223–43.

For more information about *Gyromitra*, see Denis Benjamin's *Mushrooms: Poisons and Panaceas* and Tom Volk's FOTM.

There are current, paperback editions of Charles McIlvaine's 1900 book, *One Thousand American Fungi* (New York: Dover, 1973).

Chapter 2

It was Britt Bunyard who first suggested to me that Gary Lincoff had held more mushrooms than anyone alive.

I learned about the tiny size and huge quantity of fungal species from a number of sources, most prominently *In the Company of Mushrooms: A Biologist's Tale* by Elio Schaechter (Cambridge, MA: Harvard University Press, 1997); *From Another Kingdom: The Amazing World of Fungi,* Lynne Boddy and Max Coleman, eds. (Edinburgh: Royal Botanic Garden Edinburgh, 2010); Paul Stamets's *Mycelium Running*; and "Fungi: Eumycota: Mushrooms, Sac Fungi, Yeast, Molds, Rusts, Smuts, etc.," version 10 (April 10, 2009), by Meredith Blackwell, et al., Tree of Life Web Project, http://tolweb.org/Fungi/2377.

About the history of species classification, I looked at "What are we? The social construction of the human biological self" by Lauren H. Seiler, *Journal for the Theory of Social Behavior* (2007) 37(3):243–77; Lucy Kavaler's *Mushrooms, Molds, and Miracles*; and Bryce Kendrick's *The Fifth Kingdom*. Tom Volk's lecture series "The Kingdom Fungi" was enormously helpful.

Regarding the criteria that places fungi closer to animals than plants on the tree of life, I learned much from "Animals and fungi are each other's closest relatives: congruent evidence from multiple proteins" by Sandra L. Baldauf and Jeffrey D. Palmer, *Proceedings of the National Academy of Sciences* (1993) 90(24):11558–62; "The Evolution of Fungi," a terrific paper written in 1997 by New York University students Marianna Melnikova, Bianca Nazzarulo, and Haibin Xie, online at www.nyu.edu/projects/fitch/resources/student_papers/bianca.pdf; *Introductory Mycology*; and the essay "The Origin, Evolution, and Classification of Microbial Life," by Kenneth Todar of the University of Wisconsin–Madison on The Web site the Microbial World: www.textbookofbacteriology .net/themicrobialworld/origins.html.

The notion that spores can ride winds tremendous distances has been suggested by numerous sources, including crop scientists studying the spread of the rust pathogen, Ug99, like Jim Peterson of Oregon State University and researchers like Martin Carson of the USDA Cereal Disease Laboratory. The mycologist Ron Petersen of the University of Tennessee has told interviewers that spores have likely traveled across the Atlantic on hurricane winds. He is just one of many mycologists who have voiced this idea. For details about spore dispersal in general, I was thrilled to encounter University of Hawaii professor George Wong's notes from his botany class "Magical Mushrooms and Mystical Molds." The section on spore dispersal is excellent: www.botany.hawaii.edu/faculty/wong/BOT135/Botany135syllabus.htm.

Other spore dispersal facts were derived from the following sources: the books *Fungi: Delight of Curiosity* by Harold J. Brodie (Toronto: University of Toronto Press, 1978); *Magical Mushrooms, Mischievous Molds* by George Hudler (Princeton, NJ: Princeton University Press, 1998); *Mr. Bloomfield's Orchard*; *In the Company of Mushrooms*; *The Fifth Kingdom*; and the papers "More g's than the space shuttle: ballistospore discharge" by Nicholas P. Money, *Mycologia* (1998) 90(4):547–58; "Dispersal of fungal spores on a cooperatively generated wind" by Marcus Roper, et al., *Proceedings of the National Academy of Sciences* (2010) 107(41):17474–79; the Utah State University Intermountain Herbarium's "Fun Facts About Fungi" by Robert Fogel, http://herbarium.usu .edu/fungi/funfacts/factindx1.htm; "Self-propelled dropwise condensate on superhydrophobic surfaces" by Jonathan B. Boreyko and Chuan-Hua Chen, *Physics Review Letters* (2009) 103(18); and correspondence with Mark Miller on spore sizes, *Pilobolus* shooting contests, and stinkhorns. The source for the Chinese practice of eating stinkhorns at banquets comes from *Mushrooms: Cultivation, Nutritional Value, Medicinal Effect, and Environmental Impact,* 2nd ed., by Shu-Ting Chang and Philip G. Miles (Boca Raton, FL: CRC Press, 2004). I interviewed Dennis Desjardin on bioluminescent fungi—the quote "The bane of mycelium ... " is his. I also read his article (with Anderson G. Oliveria and Cassius V. Stevani) "Fungi bioluminescence revisited" in *Photochemical &*

Photobiological Sciences (2008) 7(2):170–82. Information about wartime use of foxfire comes from multiple sources, like *Steel Boats, Iron Men: History of the U.S. Submarine Force* by Mike H. Rindskopf for the Naval Submarine League (Paducah, KY: Turner Publishing, 1994). I cite spore count figures from *In the Company of Mushrooms*; *Mr. Bloomfield's Orchard*; *Magical Mushrooms, Mischievous Molds*; and the paper "High diversity of fungi in air particulate matter" by Janine Frölich-Nowoisky, et al., *Proceedings of the National Academy of Sciences* (2009) 106(31):12814–19.

The sperm production figures I cite come from *What to Expect When You're Expecting*, 4th ed., by Heidi Murkoff and Sharon Mazel (New York: Workman Publishing, 2008). Tom Volk kept a blog during his heart transplant ordeal, called Tom Volk's Health Update.

I learned how fungi grow from many sources, but most useful were the books *Introductory Mycology*; *Magical Mushrooms, Mischievous Molds*; *In the Company of Mushrooms*; *The Fifth Kingdom*; and *Fungi: Delight of Curiosity*; plus Tom Volk's lecture series "The Kingdom Fungi" and an online class I took at Michigan State University called "The Biology of Fungi." The purpley mycologist I refer to is Harold J. Brodie. Nicholas P. Money's work on turgidity can be found in his paper "Insights on the mechanics of hyphal growth," *Fungal Biology Reviews* (2008) 22(2):71–76.

For mycelium growth volumes, I referred to *Trees, Truffles, and Beasts: How Forests Function* by Chris Maser, Andrew W. Claridge, and James M. Trappe (New Brunswick, NJ: Rutgers University Press, 2008). Paul Stamets refers to fungi as a single-minded organism. I refer to Toshiyuki Nakagaki's work on slime mold, "Smart behavior of true slime mold in a labyrinth," *Research in Microbiology* (2001) 152(9):767–70. For a good overview of the humongous fungus history, see *Inoculum*, a supplement to *Mycologia* (2002) 53(2); and "The Humongous Fungus—Ten Years Later" by Tom Volk, http://botit.botany.wisc.edu/toms_fungi/apr2002.html.

Regarding fungi's remarkable ability to transfer genetic material on contact, I read "Comparative genomics reveals mobile pathogenicity chromosomes in *Fusarium*" by Li-Jun Ma, et al., *Nature* (2010) 464:367–73 (Oregon State University has a good synopsis of the article on its News & Research Communications page, http://oregonstate.edu/ua/ncs/archives/2010/mar/fungi-can-change-quickly-pass-along-infectious-ability); and "Horizontal transfer of a large and highly toxic secondary metabolic gene cluster between fungi" by Jason Slot and Antonis Rokas, *Current Biology* (2010) 21(2):134–39. Regarding the competitive aspects of fungi, I referred to a fascinating 2008 BBC documentary called *Fungi: The Fifth Kingdom*, www.bbc.co.uk/programmes/b008p7vm.

Tom Volk very patiently helped me with the language for describing how mushrooms are made—he told me that the mycologist's favorite plant was the "hedge," which, when it comes to the reproductive cycles of fungi, one must necessarily do. Other helpful sources were *Mr. Bloomfield's Orchard*, *The Fifth Kingdom*, and *Fungi: Delight of Curiosity*. The Japanese study on electricity and mushroom fruiting is ongoing, but a progress report was published on the online site *National Geographic Daily* on April 9, 2010, http://news.nationalgeographic.com/news/2010/04/100409-lightning-mushrooms-japan-harvest.

Regarding polypores, Tom Volk's "Polypore Primer" is an awesome source; see *McIlvainea* (2000) 14(2):74–82. I learned a lot about the noble polypore from Lawrence Millman's article in *Fungi* (2008) 1(4):49–53 as well as Tom Volk's FOTM.

There is a photo of David Hibbet's game on the Hibbet Lab at Clark University Web site, www.clarku.edu/faculty/dhibbett/news.html.

The seminal text on mushroom dyeing is *Let's Try Mushrooms for Color* by Miriam C. Rice (Santa Rosa, CA: Thresh Publications, 1974). For more information about mushroom dyeing, go to www.mushroomsforcolor.com or the International Federation of Fungi and Fibre (http://sonic.net/dbeebee/IFFF.htm). Kremer Pigments in New York City has a terrific Web site (www.kremerpigments.com). The info about lichens comes from *The Fifth Kingdom* and the articles "Lichens survive in space: results from the 2005 LICHENS experiment" by L. G. Sancho, et al., *Astrobiology* (2007) 7(3):443–54; and "A partnership apart" by Susan Milius, *ScienceNews* (2009) 176(10):16–20. The discovery of *Caloplaca obamae* was reported in *Opuscula Philolichenum* (2009) 6:37–40, which publishes short papers on lichenology.

Beyond the books described above in regard to how mushrooms grow (there being a relationship between how they grow and where they grow), a few additional sources I used to describe the variety of environments in which fungi have adapted are "Microbial growth in Arctic tundra soil at –2C" by Shawna K. McMahon, Matthew D. Wallenstein, and Joshua P. Schimel, *Environmental Microbiology Reports* (2009) 1(2):162–66; "Thermophilic fungi: their physiology and enzymes" by Ramesh Maheshwari, et al., *Microbiology and Molecular Biology Reviews* (2000) 64(3):461–88; the statements of Russian cosmonaut Yuri Karash to the press regarding fungi on board the MIR space station, online at http://news.bbc.co.uk/2/hi/world/monitoring/media _reports/1209034.stm, among other sources; "Ionizing radiation changes the electronic properties of melanin and enhances the growth of melanized fungi" by Ekaterina Dadachova, et al., PLoS One (2007) 2(5):e457; "Ionizing radiation: how fungi cope, adapt, and exploit with the help of melanin" by Ekaterina Dadachova, et al., *Current Opinion in Microbiology* (2008) 11(6):525–31; "Aquatic gilled mushrooms: *Psathyrella* fruiting in the Rogue River in southern Oregon" by Jonathan L. Frank, Robert A. Coffan, and Darlene Southworth, *Mycologia* (2010) 102(1):93–107; and "Phylogeny of rock-inhabiting fungi related to *Dothideomycetes*" by C. Ruibal, et al., *Studies in Mycology* (2009) 64(1):123–33. Roland Thaxter's work *Contributions Towards a Monograph of the Laboulbeniaceae* (W. G. Farlow, 1896; Memphis, TN: General Book, 2009) is still in print. The most recent report of fungi attacking the paintings at Lascaux appeared in "Fungus once again threatens French cave paintings" by Marilise Simons, *New York Times*, December 9, 2007. The discovery of fungi on the Bradshaw rock paintings was described in the article "Living pigments in Australian Bradshaw rock art" by J. Pettigrew, et al., *Antiquity* (2010) 84(326).

It is widely held that 90 percent of land plants have mycorrhizal partners, and all plants have endophytic partners. For a good overview, see "The land flora: a phototroph-fungus partnership?" by M-A. Selosse and F. le Tacon, *Trends in Ecology & Evolution* (1998) 13(1):15–20. The odd facts about *Laboulbeniaceous* fungi come from "The characteristics and morphology of a new genus of the Laboulbeniales on an earwig" by Leland Shanor, *American Journal of Botany* (1952) 39(7):498–504.

Chapter 3

For a more detailed history of the North American Mycological Association, see their Web site, www.namyco.org.

For the overview of mycorrhizal fungi, I found *The Fifth Kingdom* and *Mycelium Running* to be most helpful. More specific material came from the following papers: "Biomechanics of spore release in phytopathogens" by Nicholas P. Money and Mark W. F. Fischer, *Mycota* (2009) 5(2):115–33, for the relationship between sugars and spore launching; "Substantial nitrogen acquisition by arbuscular mycorrhizal fungi from organic material has implications for N cycling" by Angela Hodge and Alastair H. Fitter, *Proceedings of the National Academy of Sciences* (2010) 107(31):13754–59, for the important role of fungi in the nitrogen cycle; "Architecture of the wood-wide web: *Rhizopogon* spp. genets link multiple Douglas-fir cohorts" by Kevin J. Beiler, et al., *New Phytologist* (2010) 185(2):543–53; "Net transfer of carbon between ectomycorrhizal tree species in the field" by Suzanne W. Simard, et al., *Nature* (1997) 388:579–82, for insights into mycorrhizal fungi as nutritional pathways between trees; Tom Volk's FOTM on Indian pipes; and "Cryptic bracts facilitate herbivore avoidance in the mycoheterotropic plant *Monotropsis odorata*" by Matthew R. Klooster, David L. Clark, and Teresa M. Culley, *American Journal of Botany* (2009) 96:2197–205, in regard to nonphotosynthesizing mutualistic plants. The notion that tiny fungi actually perform on a landscape scale is the mycologist Amy Tuininga's. The idea that ecosystems with inadequate mycorrhizal fungi suffer a loss in biomass is from "Soil aggregation and carbon sequestration are tightly correlated with the abundance of arbuscular mycorrhizal fungi: results from long-term field experiments," by G. W. Wilson, et al., *Ecology Letters* (2009) 12(5):452–61.

In his book *Magical Mushrooms, Mischievous Molds,* George Hudler describes the role of fungi in the Amazon. In his book *1491: New Revelations of the Americas before Columbus* (New York: Vintage, 2006), Charles C. Mann describes the new archaeology regarding pre-Columbian farmers in the Amazon. I figured mycorrhizal fungi played a role in the successful gardening of the Amazon, but it was Tom Volk who suggested seedlings may have been transplanted to take advantage of mycorrhizal hubs.

My primary sources regarding no-till agriculture were "No-till: the quiet revolution" by David R. Huggins and John P. Reganold, *Scientific American* (2008) 299(1):70–77; "Soil fertility and biodiversity in organic farming" by Paul Maeder, et al., *Science* (2002) 296(5573):1694–97; "Managing soil carbon" by Rattan Lal, et al., *Science* (2004) 304(5669):393; the Natural Resources Conservation Service's "2007 National Resources Inventory on Soil Erosion on Cropland," www.nrcs.usda.gov/technical/NRI/2007/nri07erosion.html; and the article "Glomalin, the Unsung Hero of Carbon Storage" by Don Comis, in "News & Events," USDA Agriculture Research Service, September 6, 2002, www.ars.usda.gov/is/pr/2002/020906.htm.

There is much evidence of mycorrhizal fungi's sensitivity to pollutants. A few of the many good articles are "Mycorrhiza-forming fungi as bioindicators of air pollution" by R. Fellner, *Agriculture, Ecosystems & Environment* (1990) 28(1–4):115–20; "Arbuscular mycorrhizal fungi (AMF) spore abundance is affected by wasterwater pollution in soils of Mezquital Valley in Central Mexico" by M.P. Ortega-Larrocea, in *Sustaining the Global Farm: Selected Papers from the 10th International Soil Conservation Meeting 1999*, D. E. Stott, R. H. Mohtar, and G. C. Steinhardt, eds. (International Soil Conservation Organization, USDA-ARS National Soil Erosion Research Laboratory, and Purdue University, 2001), 676–81; "Effects of industrial pollutants on ectomycorrhizal relationships in temperate forests" by Rostislav Fellner and Vitězslava Pešková, *Canadian Journal of Botany* (1995) 73:1310–1315; and "Fungi and air pollution: is there a general pattern?" by A. L. Ruotsalainen and M. V. Kozlov, in *New Topics in Environmental Research*, Daniel Rhodes, ed. (New York: Nova Science Publications, 2006).

So, about using mycorrhizal fungi in planting and reforestation. The USDA's recommendations can be found in Plant Materials Technical Note No. 3, "Tips for planting trees and shrubs: revegetation and landscaping" by Dale Darris (2001), ftp://ftp-fc.sc .egov.usda.gov/OR/Technical_Notes/Plant%20Materials/PMC03.pdf. New York's guidelines can be found in "Tree Planting Standards" from the City of New York Parks & Recreation (2008); www.nycgovparks.org/sub_permits_and_applications/images _and_pdfs/tree_planting_standards_2009.pdf. Other cities have similar standards. For information about reforestation, see *Mycorrhizae: Benefits and Practical Applications in Forest Tree Nurseries* by Donald H. Marx, et al. (National Forest Service Forest Agriculture Handbook No. 680, 1989), www.rngr.net/authors/donald-h-marx. I also depended on the work of Cathy Cripps at Montana State University. Her publications can be linked through her MSU page http://plantsciences.montana.edu/facultyorstaff/faculty/ cripps/cripps.html. For more information on genetically modified mycorrhizal fungi, see "Segregation in a mycorrhizal fungus alters rice growth symbiosis-specific gene transcription" by Caroline Angelard, et al., *Current Biology* (2010) 20(13):1216–21.

In researching endophytes, I depended on many interviews and research papers, with the following being primary. Regarding the presence of endophytic fungi in marine plants, I used "Bioactive compounds from marine bacteria and fungi" by Abdessamad Debbab, et al., *Microbial Biotechnology* (2010) 3(5):544–63. I benefited hugely from my correspondence with George Carroll, professor emeritus at the University of Oregon, as well as his paper "Fungal endophytes in stems and leaves: from latent pathogen to mutualistic symbiont," *Ecology* (1988) 69(1):2–9, and his book (with Donald T. Wicklow) *The Fungal Community: Its Organization and Role in the Ecosystem* (New York: Marcel Dekker, 1992). Also key was Rusty Rodriguez of the US Geologic Survey and his incredible work on endophytes and stress tolerances, most particularly his papers (in cooperation with other authors) "The role of fungal symbioses in the adaptation of plants to high stress environments," *Mitigation and Adaptation Strategies for Global Change* (2004) 9(3):261–72; "Adaptation and survival of plants in high stress habitats via fungal endophyte conferred stress tolerance," in *Symbioses and Stress: Joint Ventures in Biology*, Joseph Seckbach and Martin Grube, eds. (New York: Springer, 2010); "Habitat-adapted symbiosis as a defense against abiotic and biotic stresses," *Defensive Mutualism in Microbial Symbiosis*, J. White and M. Torres, eds. (Boca Raton, FL: CRC Press, 2009); "Fungal endophytes: diversity and functional roles" in *New Phytologist* (2009) 182(2):314–30; "More than 400 million years of evolution and some plants still can't make it on their own: plant stress tolerance via fungal symbiosis," *Journal of Experimental Botany* (2008) 59(5):1109–14; "Stress tolerance in plants via habitat-adapted symbiosis," *ISME Journal* (2008) 2:404–416; and "A virus in a fungus in a plant: three-way symbiosis required for thermal tolerance," *Science* (2007) 315(5811):513–15. I also found "Fungal endophytes of grasses" by Keith Clay, *Annual Review of Ecology and Systematics* (1990) 21:275–97, to be a great source, as well as "Entomopathogenic fungal endophytes" by Fernando E. Vega, et al., *Biological Control* (2008) 46:72–82.

Mutualistic relationships between fungi and ants and fungi and termites are well documented in most of the books mentioned in these notes: *Magical Mushrooms, Mischievous Molds*; *In the Company of Mushrooms*; and *Fungi: Delight of Curiosity* all tell the story of mushroom-farming insects. For more detail about the role of bacterial symbionts, see "Fungus-growing ants use antibiotic-producing bacteria to control garden parasites" by Cameron R. Currie, et al., *Nature* (1999) 398:701–4. The theory that termite fungus has evolved to be helpful to termites has many sources, but I found the Web page "Termite Mounds as Organs of Extended Physiology" by J. Scott Turner of the State University of New York at Syracuse to be very helpful: www.esf.edu/efb/turner/termite/termhome.htm. His site explains how the mushrooms burst from the flanks of the dirt termite mound, then after a few days sporulate and decompose, leaving a breach in the mound. The termites cover the mound with more dirt, creating another, smaller mound, leading to the distinctive shape of the structures.

For the section on saprophytes, I leaned heavily on the lecture of Tom Volk, "The Kingdom Fungi." Regarding fungi of Antarctica, see "An Antarctic hot spot for fungi at Shackleton's historic hut on Cape Royds" by R. A. Blachette, et al., *Microbial Ecology* (2010) 60(1):29–38. The material on the Chernobyl fungi comes from multiple sources. A terrific BBC television story, "Cooking in the Danger Zone: Chernobyl" with Stefan Gates (series 2, episode 1, 2008), and my interview with Ekaterina Dadachova of Albert Einstein College of Medicine of Yeshiva University were incredibly helpful, as were the papers "Fungi from Chernobyl: mycobiota of the inner regions of the containment structures of the damaged nuclear reactor" by Nelli N. Zhdanova, et al., *Mycological Research* (2000) 104(12):1421–26; "Ionizing radiation changes the electronic properties of melanin and enhances the growth of melanized fungi" by Ekaterina Dadachova, et al., PLoS One (2007) 2(5); "Comparison of the post-Chernobyl 137Cs contamination of mushrooms from eastern Europe, Sweden, and North America" by M. L. Smith, H. W. Taylor and H. D. Sharma, *Applied and Environmental Microbiology* (1993) 59(1):134–39; and "Hot fungi from Chernobyl" by R. T. Moore, *Mycologist* (2001) 15(2):63–64. The business about melanized fungi surviving the Earth's geomagnetic reversal comes from "Ionizing radiation: how fungi cope, adapt, and exploit with the help of melanin" by Ekaterina Dadachova and Artuo Casadevall, *Current Opinion in Microbiology* (2008) 11:525–31.

Regarding the degrading abilities of saprophytic fungi, I found Paul Stamets's *Mycelium Running* to be very helpful. Just about every book on fungi has a chapter on yeasts as they pertain to wine, beer, cheese, and bread, but especially helpful were *Mushrooms, Molds, and Miracles* and *The Fifth Kingdom*. ACH Foods, which owns Fleischmann's Yeast, shared their history of commercial yeast manufacture. Julie Schreiber is the winemaker who tested her wines for uninvited yeasts.

News of dock-eating fungi was reported in the Newsjournalonline.com article "Company attacks dock-eating fungus," January 30, 2010; and reports of fungi decomposing library books was well summarized in "A new approach to treating fungus in small libraries" by William Chamberlain, *Biodeterioration Research 1*, Gerald C. Llewellyn and Charles E. O'Rear, eds. (New York: Plenum Press, 1988): 323–27.

A great deal of the material on *Stachybotrys* and *Aspergillus* and other toxic molds was gleaned from *Carpet Monsters and Killer Spores: A Natural History of Toxic Molds* by Nicholas P. Money (New York: Oxford University Press, 2004). In regard to the history of dry rot in ships, I used W. P. K. Findlay's book *Fungi: Folklore, Fiction & Fact*.

The biology of the lobster mushrooms comes from Tom Volk's FOTM and from the article "Ecology and management of the lobster mushroom in an eastern Canadian jack pine stand" by Caroline Rochon, et al., *Canadian Journal of Forest Research* (2009) 39(11):2080–91.

I learned the background on plant pathology from the University of Florida's Institute of Food and Agricultural Sciences Web site "Basic Plant Pathology," http://mrec .ifas.ufl.edu/lso/SCOUT/Plant%20Pathology.pdf. Information about the bark beetle infestation in the Rocky Mountains can be found at the Colorado Bark Beetle Cooperative page on the Northwest Colorado Council of Government Web site: www.nwc.cog .co.us/index.php/affiliated-programs/colorado-bark-beetle-cooperative. Information about the American chestnut can be found on the American Chestnut Foundation Web site: www.acf.org. Excellent background on Chestnut blight and Dutch elm disease can be found in Nicholas P. Money's fine book, *The Triumph of the Fungi: A Rotten History* (New York: Oxford University Press, 2007).

For more on fusarium, see "A first for *Fusarium*: wheat and barley disease fungus is fully mapped and on the Web" by Don Comis in *Agricultural Research* (2005), http:// findarticles.com/p/articles/mi_m3741/is_2_53/ai_n10300966; "We have no bananas" by Mike Peed, *New Yorker*, January 10, 2011; *Fungi* magazine 1(4) for *Fusarium* in chili seeds; "Killer fungus is no mystery to Afghan poppy growers" by Nushin Arbabzadah, May 17, 2010, www.guardian.co.uk/commentisfree/2010/may/17/poppy-fungus-mystery- afghanistan; as well as "Kill or cure: bio-weapons in the war on drugs" by Tom Fawthrop for *Asia Times*, June 26, 2002, www.atimes.com/se-asia/DF26Ae01.html.

Powdery mildew is well described online at Cornell University's Plant Disease Diagnostic Clinic's page http://plantclinic.cornell.edu/FactSheets/powdery/powdery .htm. The Priscila Chaverri Mycology Lab at the University of Maryland is searching for specialized biocontrol agents to help protect rubber trees from fungal pathogens; visit http://mycology.umd.edu. The Plant Quarantine Act was consolidated, with other statutes, into the Plant Protection Act in 2000; for highlights see www.aphis.usda.gov/lpa/pubs/fsheet_faq_notice/fs_phproact.html.

I leaned on *Introductory Mycology* for the paragraph on smuts and rusts. For the bit about huitlacoche, I turned to Betty Fussell's brilliant book, *The Story of Corn* (New York: Knopf, 1992); Tom Volk's FOTM; "Production of huitlacoche using inoculations techniques developed to screen reactions of sweet corn to common smut," a lecture by Jerald K. Pataky for the World Society for Mushroom Biology and Mushroom Products Fourth International Conference, 2002; "Effect of maize genotype, developmental stage, and cooking process on the nutraceutical potential of huitlacoche" by Maribel Valdez-Morales, et al., *Food Chemistry* (2010) 119:689–97; and "Production and marketing of huitlacoche" by W. F. Tracy, et al., *Issues in New Crops and New Uses,* J. Janick and A. Whipkey, eds. (Alexandria, VA: ASHS Press, 2007). Robigus, the Roman god of the rust pathogen, is described in many places. I used *Famine on the Wind: Man's Battle against Plant Disease* by G. L. Carefoot and E. R. Sprott (Chicago: Rand McNally, 1967), and *Triumph of the Fungi.* Although many sources I read suggested it was so, I tried to find Biblical evidence that rust was the cause of the great Egyptian famine, but despite numerous correspondences with a rabbi in Miami Beach, I couldn't. Current info on Ug99 came from an excellent *Wired* article by Brendan I. Koerner, "Red Menace: Stop the Ug99 fungus before its spores bring starvation," March 2010. For more info on Norman Borlaug, see his obituary, "Norman Borlaug, plant scientist who fought famine, dies at 95" by Justin Gillis, *New York Times,* September 13, 2009.

Good information about aflatoxin and the other mycotoxins mentioned in this section can be found on the Cornell University Department of Animal Science's "Plants Poisonous to Livestock" page under "Toxic Agents in Plants," www.ansci.cornell.edu/plants/toxicagents/index.html. Regarding the handling of toxic molds, I referred to the USDA Safe Food Handling Fact Sheet "Molds on Food: Are They Dangerous?" www.fsis.usda.gov/factsheets/molds_on_food/index.asp.

I used three sources for the paragraph on the Irish potato blight: *Triumph of the Fungi;* "Monoculture and the Irish potato famine: cases of missing genetic variation" on the Web page "Understanding Evolution" from the University of California Museum of Paleontology, http://evolution.berkeley.edu/evolibrary/article//agriculture_02; and Tom Volk's FOTM.

For more information on noble rot, see *Great Wine Made Simple: Straight Talk from a Master Sommelier* by Andrea Immer Robinson (New York: Broadway Books, 2005).

I learned that fungi predate and keep eelworm populations at bay from *Fungi: Delight of Curiosity.* But that's not the only case of fungi predating animals. Larry Evans told me a story about a group of Swedish scientists—I've been unable to track them down—who sprinkled springtail mites on a collection of fungal cultures, including *Laccaria laccata,* to see which fungi the mites were using as food. When they checked back, they found the fungi had consumed the mites. According to Larry, the biologist involved said it was like leaving a football player in a room with a pizza overnight, and when you came back the football player was gone.

For the material on fungal parasites of animals, I benefited from many papers, including *"Fusarium oxysporum* is responsible for mass mortalities in nests of logger-head sea turtle, *Caretta caretta,* in Boavista, Cape Verde" by Julie M. Samiento-Ramirez, et al., *FEMS Microbiology Letters* (2010) 312:192–200: "Iridovirus and microsporidian linked to honey bee colony decline" by Jerry J. Bromenshenk, et al., *PLoS One* (2010) 5(10); "Emerging infectious disease and the loss of biodiversity in a neotropical amphibian community" by Karen R. Lips, et al., *Proceedings of the National Academy of Sciences* (2006) 103(9):3165–70; "Spread of chytridiomycosis has caused the rapid global decline and extinction of frogs" by Lee Francis Skerratt, et al., *EcoHealth* (2007) 4(2):125–34; *"Geomyces destructans* sp. nov. associated with bat white-nose syndrome" by A. Gargas, et al., *Mycotaxon* (2009) 108:147–53; "White-nose syndrome: Something is killing our bats," from the US Fish and Wildlife Service, www.fws.gov/whitenosesyndrome; and "Closing caves, sparing bats" by Leslie Newell Peacock, *Arkansas Times,* March 25, 2010, 8–9.

The most visceral way to understand *Cordyceps* fungi is by watching an amazing video clip from the 2006 BBC series *Planet Earth,* narrated by Richard Attenborough. Called "Cordyceps Fungus," this clip is found on YouTube and similar sites; otherwise, read *Mr. Bloomfield's Orchard* and the papers "The life of a dead ant: the expression of an adaptive extended phenotype" by Sandra B. Andersen, et al., *American Naturalist* (2009) 174(3):424–33; "Respect for the Fungus Overlords" by Carl Zimmer on his great blog, the Loom, at http://blogs.discovermagazine.com/loom/2009/07/28/respect-for-the-fungus-overlords; "Yartsa gunbu (*Cordyceps senensis*) and the fungal commodifica-tion of Tibet's rural economy" by Daniel Winkler, *Economic Botany* (2008) 62(3):291–305; and "Present and historic relevance of yartsa gunbu" by Daniel Winkler, *Fungi* (2008) 1(4).

Chapter 4

Much of the information about morel harvesting in forest fire burns comes from the following sources: "Ecology and management of morels harvested from the forests of western North American" by David Pilz, et al., General Technical Report PNW-GTR-710 (Portland, OR: USDA Forest Service, Pacific Northwest Research Station, 2007); "Commercial harvests of edible mushrooms from the forests of the Pacific Northwest United States: issues, management, and monitoring for sustainability" by David Pilz and Randy Molina, *Forest and Ecology Management* (2001) 5593:1–14; "Com-mercial morel harvesters and buyers in Western Montana: an exploratory study of the 2001 harvesting season" by Rebecca J. McLain, et al., General Technical Report PNW-GTR-643 (Portland, OR: USDA Forest Service, Pacific Northwest Research Station, 2005); "Constructing a wild mushroom panopticon" by Rebecca J. McLain, *Economic Botany* (2008) 62(3):343–55; *Selected Laws Affecting Forest Service Activities* by Amie M. Brown (Washington, DC: USDA Forest Service, 2004), www.fs.fed.us/publications/laws/selected-laws.pdf; the morel issue of *Fungi* magazine (2010) 3(2); "High-elevation gray morels and other *Morchella* species harvested as non-timber forest products in Idaho and Montana" by Erika M. McFarlane, et al., *Mycologist* (2005) 19:62–68; "Surviving and thriving in urban-edge agriculture" by Deb Stenberg, *Sustaining the Pacific Northwest* (2005) 3(3):1–3, http://csanr.wsu.edu/publications/SPNW/SPNW-v3-n3.pdf; and Tom Volk's FOTM.

I also used the following articles: "Bears and Menstruating Women" by Kerry A. Gunther of the Bear Management Office in Yellowstone National Park, found online at Bearman's Yellowstone Outdoor Adventures Web site: www.yellowstone-bearman.com/menstruation_data.html; the Grizzly Bear Recovery home page on the US Fish and Wildlife Service Web site, www.fws.gov/mountain-prairie/species/mammals/grizzly; and "Migrant mushroomers" by David Arora, *Whole Earth* (Spring 2000):60–69 as well as Arora's book *Mushrooms Demystified: A Comprehensive Guide to the Fleshy Fungi* (Berkeley, CA: Ten Speed Press, 1986). I used *The Cooks and Confectioners Dictionary; Or, the Accomplish'd Housewife's Companion* by John Nott (London: C. Rivington, 1723) for the archaic morel recipes; and *Last Dinner on the Titanic* by Rick Archbold and Dana McCauley (New York: Hyperion, 1997).

The overview of the wild mushroom market here and abroad and the observation that wild mushroom harvesting figures have stabilized are David Pilz's.

Regarding the Flathead Fire, I benefited greatly from the coverage of the morel picking scene over the years by the *Daily Inter Lake* newspaper out of Kalispell, Montana (including a story on the Kalispell mushroom wars).

Marijuana plantations in national forests are a growing problem. See "Cartels turn U.S. forests into marijuana plantations, creating toxic mess" by Phil Taylor, *New York Times,* July 30, 2009.

The paper by Paul S. Taylor, "Migratory Farm Labor in the United States," can be found on the Web site New Deal Network at http://newdeal.feri.org/misc/taylor.htm. It was originally presented before a joint meeting of the American Farm Economic Association and Rural Sociology Section of the American Sociological Society in 1936. The percentage of different ethnic groups that pick wild mushrooms commercially varies, but 1994 permit data from national forests in eastern Oregon indicated that 51.3 percent of the pickers obtaining permits had Southeast Asian surnames, 44.2 percent had Euro-American surnames, and 4.5 percent had Latino surnames (*Commercial Morel Harvesters and Buyers in Western Montana: An Exploratory Study of the 2001 Harvesting Season,* General Technical Report PNW-GTR-643, by Rebecca J. McLain, Erika Mark McFarlane, and Susan J. Alexander [USDA Forest Service Pacific Northwest Research Station, 2005]). The same data indicated that 73 percent of the pickers who had obtained permits came from other locations, and only 27 percent lived near the harvesting location. Circuit pickers typically participate in both the spring and fall mushroom seasons and are likely to spend from 6 to 10 months of the year harvesting mushrooms. They may fill in the gaps between seasons with other activities, such as gathering other non-timber forest products, panning gold, or doing construction work. Others, however, rely primarily upon income from picking.

Information about distribution was gleaned from interviews with David Pilz, Jay Southard, Charles Novy, Connie Green, John Getz, among other experts in the field. The buyers establish the "grade" of the mushroom based on criteria that have to do with how the mushroom is going to be used, whether it is sold as a fresh product or one to be dried or canned. Freshness, cleanliness, and age are always considered, and pickers will gravitate toward buyers who they think are more generous in their grading standards.

Guidelines about wild mushroom picking vary from state to state, as does enforcement. But in Europe, there are definitely tighter regulations. For example, the Web site www.angloinfo.com sports a page called "Mushroom Picking in France," as well as another page for Italy, that describes the relevant regulations. The paper "Patois and paradox in a Boy Scout treasure hunt" by Jay Mechling, *Journal of American Folklore* (1984) 97(383):24–42 was useful in understanding attitudes toward wild harvesters.

Much of the information I learned about matsutake harvesting comes from these articles and sources: "Effects of mushroom harvest technique on subsequent American matsutake production" by Daniel L. Luoma, et al., *Forest Ecology and Management* (2006) 236:65–75; "Ectomycorrhizal fungi with edible fruiting bodies 1. *Tricholoma matsutake* and related fungi" by Wang Yun, et al., *Economic Botany* (1997) 51(3):311–27; "Matsutake madness seizes the Japanese every autumn" by James Sterngold, *New York Times*, November 11, 1992; "Kim thanks Roh with million-dollar mushrooms," *Reuters*, October 5, 2007; an excellent video produced by John Getz titled *North American Matsutake: Harvest Technique for the Oregon Dunes*; the Web site www.matsiman.com (including the page dedicated to *Allotropa virgata*); and Tom Volk's FOTM.

The story about North Korean farmers selling matsutake mushrooms was reported in the *Daily NK*, October 23, 2007, www.dailynk.com/english/read.php?cataId =nk00100&num=2817. For information on pine wilt disease, see "History of pine wilt disease in Japan" by Y. Mamiya, *Journal of Nematology* (1998) 20(2):219–26.

The English mushroom picking code is called *The Conservation of Wild Mushrooms* (Peterborough, UK: English Nature, 1998), www.britmycolsoc.org.uk/index .php/download_file/225.

Larry Evans conducted a panel discussion called "The Ethics of Harvesting." A transcript can be found on the Web site www.fungaljungal.org. A good article on ethics is "What the natives know: wild mushrooms and forest health" by Rebecca Templin Richards, *Journal of Forestry* (1997) 95(9):5–10. French criminal gangs were reported in "Organized crime mushrooms as French fungi trade becomes lucrative" by Adam Sage, *Times*, November 21, 2009.

Chapter 5

For a fine, detailed, and often hilarious look at the evolution of the American food scene, see *The United States of Arugula: How We Became a Gourmet Nation* by David Kamp (New York: Broadway Books, 2006).

The statistics I report on concerning commercial mushroom crops come from numerous sources, primarily *Factors Affecting US Mushroom Consumption* by Gary Lucier, Jane Allshouse, and Biing-Hwan Lin (USDA Economic Research Service, 2003), www.ers.usda.gov/publications/VGS/mar03/vgs29501/vgs29501.pdf; *Mushroom Industry Report (94003)* (USDA National Agricultural Statistics Service, 2009), http://usda .mannlib.cornell.edu/MannUsda/viewDocumentInfo.do?documentID=1395; and *Pennsylvania Agricultural Statistics 2008–2009* (USDA National Agricultural Statistics Service, 2009), www.nass.usda.gov/Statistics_by_State/Pennsylvania/Publications/ Annual_Statistical_Bulletin/2008_2009/Section%204.pdf.

Information on the early years of shiitake cultivation in this country came from a seminal report by Gary F. Leatham, "Cultivation of shiitake, the Japanese forest mushrooms, on logs: a potential industry for the United States," *Forest Products Journal* (1981) 32(8):29–35. Regarding the quarantine of shiitake mushrooms, see "Getting a Year-Round Harvest from Japanese Forest Mushrooms" by Albert Bates, www.shroomery .org/8531/Getting-a-Year-round-Harvest-from-Japanese-Forest-Mushrooms.

The oyster-mushroom-growing monks live in Mepkin Abbey in South Carolina. Their Web site is www.mepkinabbey.org. The *BTTR* in BTTR Ventures stands for Back to the Roots, and they sell mushroom home-growing kits online at www.bttrventures.com.

Kristopher Setchfield's review of Masaru Emoto's *The Hidden Messages in Water* can be found at www.is-masaru-emoto-for-real.com.

About growing morels: Tom Volk's morel Web page is extremely useful, and his papers on morels are referenced at the conclusion of the first article at http://botit .botany.wisc.edu/toms_fungi/morel.html. Ronald T. Ower's article on morel cultivation appeared in *Mycologia* (1982) 74:142–44. My interviews with Gary Mills, Ower's business partner, were extremely useful. The patents they held, along with James Malachowski, are US Patent No. 4,594,809 (Cultivation of Morchella, 1986) and US Patent No. 4,757,640 (Cultivation of Morchella, 1988). Other useful sources were *Cropping the French Black Morel: A Preliminary Investigation* by S. Barnes and A. Wilson (Australia: Rural Industries Research and Development Corporation Publication no. 98/44, 1998); www.answers.com/topic/neogen-corporation; "Resources for mushroom growers morel mushroom cultivation," *Mushroom Grower's Newsletter,* updated October 29, 2010, www.mushroomcompany.com/resources/morels/index .shtml; "Morel-growing rights are sold," *New York Times,* April 13, 1994; and an unpublished presentation the CEO of Neogen, James Herbert, gave in 2001 that was forwarded to me by his office. Stewart Miller's morel cultivation technique is described on his Web site www.morel-farms.com.

Chapter 6

For truffle and truffle product statistics, I referred to the USDA National Agricultural Statistics Service's 2009 *Mushroom Industry Report*, particularly tables 40, 41, 50, 51, 54. You can see the auction for the biggest and most expensive truffle, won by Stanley Ho, on YouTube: "Auction of the biggest truffle of the year.flv."

For more on the fascinating biology and lore of truffles, see *Secondary Metabolites in Soil Ecology* (*Soil Biology,* vol. 14), Petr Karlovsky, ed. (Berlin: Springer, 2008); *Trees, Truffles, and Beasts: Taming the Truffle* by Ian Hall, Gordon Brown, and Alessandra Zambonelli (Portland, OR: Timber Press, 2008); *Truffles* by Elisabeth Luard (London: Berry & Co., 2006); *Fungi* magazine's special truffle issue (2008) 1(3); "Truffles and climate change" by Ulf Buntgen, et al., *Frontiers in Ecology and Environment* (2011) 9:150–51; "Desert truffles of the African Kalahari: ecology, ethnomycology, and taxonomy" by James M. Trappe, et al., *Economic Botany* (2008) 62(3):521–29; "Ascomycota truffles: cup fungi go underground" by Karen Hansen, *Newsletter of the Friends of the Farlow* (2006) 47:1–4; "The secret of truffles: a steroidal pheromone?" by R. Claus, H. O. Hoppen, and H. Karg, *Cellular and Molecular Life Sciences* (1981) 37(11):1178–79; "The hidden life of truffles" by James M. Trappe and Andrew W. Claridge, *Scientific American* (2010) 302:78–84; France's National Institute for Agricultural Research Web site, www.international.inra.fr (the institute is part of INRA, the leading agricultural research institute in Europe); and Tom Volk's FOTM. There is a link on Volk's January 2007 page "*Terfezia* and *Tirmania,* Desert Truffles (terflez, kama, p/faqa): Delicacies in the Sand or Manna from Heaven?" (written with Elinoar Shavit) to the page "Manna: White Truffles in the Sand," which provides a good overview of the desert-truffle-as-manna argument.

Theophrastes' description of truffles was reported in *The Deipnosophists or Banquet of the Learned of Athenaeus,* vol. 1, C. D. Yonge, trans. (London: Henry G. Bohn, 1754), www.onread.com/book/The-Deipnosophists-or-Banquet-of-the-learned-of-Athenaeus-Literally-translated-by-C-D-Yonge-B-A-With-an-appendix-of-poetical-fragments-rendered-into-English-verse-by-various-authors-and-a-general-index-1-1371835/. The cooking methods described for desert truffles with rice was found on RecipeZaar.com; for truffles with stewed meat, see "Desert truffles *Tirmania nivea* in the Emirates" by Phil Iddison on the Emirates Natural History Group Web site at www.enhg.org/trib/trib10.htm; and for grilled truffles, see *Saha: A Chef's Journey Through Lebanon and Syria* by Greg and Lucy Malouf (Prahran, Victoria: Hardie Grant Books, 2005; Singapore: Peripius Editions, 2007).

The Italian chemist Sandro Silveri now works for Rosario Safina, whose company, daRosario, sells organic products made with truffles. The story about the Roman official who broke a tooth on a truffle was reported in *The Natural History of Pliny,* vol. 4, John Bostock and H. T. Riley, trans. (London: Henry G. Bohn, 1756), www.archive.org/stream/naturalhistoryof06plin/naturalhistoryof06plin_djvu.txt.

I found information on truffle growing and history on the North American Truffling Society Web site (www.natruffling.com); "Selection of fungi for ecotmycorrhizal inoculation in nursuries" by James M. Trappe, *Annual Review of Phytopathology* (1977) 15:203–22; "Oregon culinary truffles: an emergent industry for forestry, agriculture & culinary tourism" by David Pilz, et al., www.oregontruffles.org/truffles_feasibility_final.pdf 2009; "Truffles" by W. Collett-Sandars in *The Gentleman's Magazine,* vol. 261 (London: Chatto & Windus, 1877); "Oak truffles" by M. de Gasparin, *The Technologist,* vol. 2 (London: Kent & Co., 1862): 17–19; the INRA Web site (they are doing the DNA truffle tracking work); "The socioeconomic impact of truffle cultivation in rural Spain" by Nicklas Samils, et al., *Economic Botany* (2008) 62(3):331–40; "Black Truffles of Sweden" by Christina Wedén (see Comprehensive Summaries of Uppsala Dissertations from the Faculty of Science and Technology, 2004 uu.diva-portal.org/smash/get/diva2:165461 /FULLTEXT01); and the Web site for New World Truffieres, Inc. (www.truffletrees. com). The world's largest truffle plantation is owned by Arotz (www.arotz.com). There is a terrific *New York Times* article on Chinese truffles, "The invasion of the Chinese truffle" by Florence Fabricant, February 15, 1995; and another, from the *Telegraph* of London: "Chinese import threat to gourmet truffles" by Malcolm Moore, May 16, 2008.

Regarding the American truffle scene, see "Coveted, French, and now in Tennessee" by Molly O'Neill, *New York Times,* February 28, 2007; "For hire: truffle hunter" by Robin T. Reid, November 12, 2007, www.smithsonianmag.com/arts-culture/truffle .html; "Black Diamonds" by Alastair Bland, December 3, 2008, www.bohemian.com /bohemian/06.23.10/eats-1025.html; "Californians claim to unearth secret of raising truffles" by Joan Rigdon, *Wall Street Journal,* March 25, 1994; and "Useful fungi of the world: morels and truffles" by D. N. Pegler, *Mycologist* (2003) 17:174–75. For more information on eastern filbert blight (and other plant diseases), see http://plantclinic .cornell.edu. For the North Carolina Tobacco Trust Fund, see www.tobaccotrustfund. org and the Rural Advancement Foundation International, located in Pittsboro, North Carolina (www.rafiusa.org). For a picture of the lagotto breed, see enci.it/razze/lagotto /lagin. Regarding the you-pick scam in the Hamptons, see "Psst! you pick it, but they grow it someplace else" by Julia C. Mead, *New York Times,* October 8, 2005.

Chapter 7

Most of this chapter was built from interviews with Mark Miller, Steve Register, Pete Gray, and J. B. Swayne. Additionally, the Mushroom Council (www.mushroomcouncil .org) and the American Mushroom Institute (www.americanmushroom.org) were invaluable resources. Otherwise, the sources below were particularly useful.

For the history of spawn making, I checked a Russian mushroom-growing technology Web site (http://agaricus.ru/en/doc/show/296/), The Mushroom People: Ireland's Mushroom Community online (www.themushroompeople.com), and the Kennett Township history (www.kennett.pa.us/geninfothstory.html). I read "Origin of spawn" by Richard Kerrigan in *Mushroom News* (July 2004) 52(7); *Celebrating the Wild Mushroom* by Sara Ann Friedman (New York: Dodd, Mead, 1986); *Fungi: Folklore, Fiction & Fact*; "Origin and improvement of spawn of the cultivated mushroom *Agaricus brunnescens* Peck" by James P. San Antonio, *Horticultural Reviews* (1984) (6):85–118; and "Nutrition and the development of mushroom flavor in *Agaricus campestris* mycelium" by Ahmad M. Moustafa, *Applied Microbiology* (1960) 8(1):63–67.

More about Kennett Square and its symphony and wines can be found on the Web site www.historickennettsquare.com and on the Kennett Square Borough Historical Commission site at www.kennettsquarehistory.org. "American Fancy" antiques are described on the antique flag dealer Jeff Bridgman's Web site, www.jeffbridgman.com.

The white button mushroom production statistics came from the following sources: USDA Economic Research Service "Mushrooms Industry and Trade Summary," Office of Industries Publication ITS-07 (United States International Trade Commission, June 2010), www.usitc.gov/publications/332/ITS_7.pdf; "Mushroom sales volume up, value down from last year," *Wisconsin Ag News,* August 26, 2009, www.wisconsinagconnection .com/story-state.php?Id=1026&yr=2009; "Mushrooms leads Chesco's powerful mark in farming" by Gretchen Metz, *Daily Times,* April 7, 2009; "Economic impact of the mushroom industry in Chester County, PA" by Spiro E. Stefanou (Community Awareness Committee of the American Mushroom Institute, May 2008), www.mushroomfarmcommunity .org/truimg/EconomicImpactReport.pdf); USDA National Agricultural Statistics Service "Mushroom Industry Report 2009," http://usda.mannlib.cornell.edu/MannUsda/ viewDocumentInfo.do?documentID=1395; and the "Pennsylvania Statistical Bulletin 2008–2009," www.nass.usda.gov/Statistics_by_State/Pennsylvania/Publications/Annual _Statistical_Bulletin/2008_2009/Section%204.pdf.

For the Swayne family history and the roots of mushroom cultivation, I depended on the Web site www.kennett.pa.us for much of the Kennett Township history; "Swaynes descended from Francis Swayne of East Marlborough Township, Chester County, Pennsylvania, Compiled by Norman Walton Swayne, Great-great-great-great-great-grandson, eldest in line of succession from Francis in 1955," http://swayne.0catch .com/swayne1.html; and "Tracing the roots of mushroom cultivation" by Kelly Ivors, *New York Mycological Society Newsletter* (fall 2003).

About compost, I referred to "Managing Microbial Activity During Phase II Composting" by David M. Beyer, Department of Plant Pathology, College of Agricultural Sciences, Pennsylvania State University, www.mushroomspawn.cas.psu.edu; and "The case of the exploding haystacks: spontaneous combustion of natural products in New Zealand" by Max Kennedy, *Australasian Biotechnology* (1997) 7(2). Almost all of the information about *Agaricus* mushroom pathology was provided to me by Mark Miller in a series of encyclopedic e-mails.

Regarding the labor issues surrounding the mushroom industry and the industry's later history, I found especially useful "The Evolution of the Mushroom Industry in Kennett Square" by Samuel E. Flammini, June 17, 1999, http://courses.wcupa.edu/jones/ his480/reports/mushroom.htm; and consumption data from "Factors affecting mushroom consumption" by Gary Lucier, Jane Allshouse, and Biing-Hwan Lin, ERS USDA, March 2003, www.ers.usda.gov/publications/VGS/mar03/vgs29501/vgs29501.pdf.

Chapter 8

The quote from Galenus comes from *Fungi: Folklore, Fiction & Fact.* Otto Carqué's *Vital Facts About Food: A Guide to Health and Longevity* was first published in 1933 and reprinted in 1974 (Pomeroy, WA: Health Research Books, 1974). The 2008 study about dieticians was reported in "The value of research: achieving super food status," *Mushroom News* (2008) 56(12).

General mushroom nutritional information was gleaned from many sources, but most helpful were *Mushrooms: Poisons and Panaceas*; The Mushroom Council's Web pages on nutrition (www.mushroomcouncil.org/Nutrition); *Dietary Reference Intakes: Essential Guide Nutrient Requirements*, Jennifer J. Otten, Jennifer Pitzi Hellwig, Linda D. Meyers, eds. (Washington, DC: National Academies Press, 2006); "Edible mushrooms as a source of valuable nutritive constituents" by Emilia Bernas, Grazyna Jaworska, and Zofia Lisiewska, *ACTA Scientiarum Polonorum—Technologia Alimentaria* (2006) 5(1):5–20; "A study of the nutritive value of mushrooms" by F. W. Quackenbush, W. H. Peterson, and H. Steenbock, *Journal of Nutrition* (1935) 10(6):625–43; *The New Good Housekeeping Family Health and Medical Guide* (New York: Hearst, 1989); "Mushrooms—intake, composition, and research: a mini-review" by Mary Jo Feeney, *Nutrition Today* (2006) 41(5):219–26; the USDA National Nutrient Database for Standard Reference, Release 22, "Mushrooms, white, raw," 2009, www.ars.usda.gov/SP2UserFiles/Place/12354500/Data/SR22/nutrlist/sr22a430.pdf; and "Nutrient Data on Mushrooms Updated" by Rosalie Marion Bliss, USDA Agricultural Research Service News & Events 2006, www.ars.usda.gov/is/pr/2006/060818.htm. I used the Dietary Reference Intake Tables on the USDA Food and Nutrition Information Center's Dietary Guidance Web site for human intake of elements, macronutrients, and vitamins: http://fnic.nal.usda.gov/nal_display/index.php?info_center=4&tax_level=2&tax_subject=256&topic_id=1342.

Since it isn't particularly nutritious, I don't mention the dominant sugar alcohol in mushroom carbs. It's mannitol, which is also a sweetener in Dentyne gum.

Dr. Cheskin's preliminary findings about mushrooms as a food substitution for beef were published in "Lack of energy compensation over 4 days when white button mushrooms are substituted for beef" by L. J. Cheskin, et al., *Appetite* (2008) 51(1):50–57. You can find chitosan products on the Web. For a response to the producers' claims, see "Chitosan: A Critical Look" by S. Barrett, online at www.quackwatch.org/04ConsumerEducation/QA/chitosan.html. While the essay focuses on crustacean-derived chitosan, the criticism is valid in regard to fungal chitosan as well. See the chapter "Chitin and Chitosan in Fungi" by Martin G. Peter, in *Biopolymers Online* (John Wiley, 2005), for a more detailed description of fungal chitin.

For more detail on the concept of prebiotics, see "Dietary modulation of the human colonic microbiota: introducing the concept of prebiotics" by G. R. Gibson and M. B. Roberfroid, *Journal of Nutrition* (1995) 125(6):1401–12; and "Mushrooms as a potential source of prebiotics: a review" by F.M.N.A. Aida, et al., *Trends in Food Science & Technology* (2009) 20(11–12):567–75.

Information about minerals and vitamins is widely available. I bounced around, using the National Institutes of Health Office of Dietary Supplements fact sheets at http://ods.od.nih.gov; state university cooperative extension services (for example, I used the Colorado State University extension for information on potassium, as well as "Potassium and Health" by J. Anderson, L. Young, and E. Long, et al., Fact sheet no. 9.355 [August 2008], online at www.ext.colostate.edu/pubs/foodnut/09355.html); the Institute of Medicine's Web site (www.iom.edu); and the Agency for Toxic Substances and Disease Registry (www.atsdr.cdc.gov), which was helpful in describing what might go wrong if you had too little or too much of a given mineral, as in the case of the paragraph on selenium. Material about selenium and chemotherapy treatment can be found in the article "Selenium and vitamin E: cell type and intervention-specific tissue effects in prostate cancer" by Dimitra Tsavachidou, et al., *Journal of the National Cancer Institute* (2009) 101(5):306–20. Other sites or papers I used were "Copper & Human Health," www.copperinfo.co.uk/health/downloads/pub-34-copper-and-human-health.pdf; "Potential use of copper surfaces to reduce survival of epidemic meticillin-resistant *Staphylococcus aureus* in the healthcare environment" by J. O. Noyce, H. Michels, and C. W. Keevil, *Journal of Hospital Infection* (2006) 63(3):289–97; "Human zinc deficiency" by Michael Hambidge, *Journal of Nutrition* (2000) 130:1344S–49S; "Dietary Sources of Iron," McKinley Health Center Health Information Handouts, www.mckinley.illinois.edu/handouts/dietary_sources_iron.html; "Iron deficiency anemia" by Shersten Killip, et al., *American Family Physician* (2007) 75(5):671–78; "Lack energy? Maybe it's your magnesium level" by Rosalie Marion Bliss, *Agricultural Research* (May 2004), www.ushrl.saa.ars.usda.gov/is/ar/archive/may04/energy0504.htm?pf=1; "Contents of vitamins, mineral elements, and some phenolic compounds in cultivated mushrooms" by P. Mattila, et al., *Journal of Agricultural and Food Chemistry* (2001) 49(5):2343–48; and "Vitamin B_{12} synthesis by human small intestinal bacteria" by M. J. Albert, V. I. Mathan, and S. J. Baker, *Nature* (1980) 283:781–82.

For information about mushrooms and vitamin D, I looked at the Institute of Medicine's 2010 report *Dietary Reference Intakes for Calcium and Vitamin D* (access at www.iom.edu/Reports/2010/Dietary-Reference-Intakes-for-Calcium-and-Vitamin-D.aspx) and the Mushroom Council's press release "Mushrooms may offer natural solution for vitamin D deficiency" (at www.mushroomcouncil.com/wp-content/uploads/MushroomCouncilFINALRelease21208.pdf); "Vitamin D deficiency is associated with low mood and worse cognitive performance in older adults" by Consuelo Wilkins, et al., *American Journal of Geriatric Psychiatry* (2006) 14(12):1032–40; "Vitamin D deficiency treated by consuming UVB-irradiated mushrooms" by Andrew Ozzard, et al., *British Journal of General Practice* (2008) 58(554):644–45; "Sterol and vitamin D_2 contents in some wild and cultivated mushrooms" by Pirjo Mattila, et al., *Food Chemistry* (2002) 76(3):293–98; "Ultraviolet irradiation increased vitamin D_2 content in edible mushrooms" by Jeng-Leun Mau, Pei-Ru Chen, and Joan-Hwa Yang, *Journal of Agricultural and Food Chemistry* (1998) 46(12): 5269–72; "Vitamin D: more is not necessarily better, long-awaited diet guidelines show" by Lauran Neergaard, *Huffington Post,* November 30, 2010; "Vitamin D" fact sheet from the National Institutes of Health Office of Dietary Supplements (http://ods.od.nih.gov/factsheets/VitaminD-HealthProfessional/); "Vitamin D_2 formation from post-harvest UV-B treatment of mushrooms (*Agaricus bisporus*) and retention during storage" by John S. Roberts, A. Teichert, and T. H. McHugh, *Journal of Agricultural and Food Chemistry* (2008) 56(12): 4541–44; "Vitamin D_2 enrichment in fresh mushrooms using pulsed UV light" by Michael D. Kalaras and Robert B. Beelman (Department of Food Science,

Pennsylvania State University 2008), www.xenoncorp.com/Images/VitaminDEnrichment
.pdf; *The UV Advantage* by Michael Holick (Ibooks, Inc., 2004); and *The Vitamin D Solution: A 3-Step Strategy to Cure Our Most Common Health Problems* by Michael Holick
(New York: Hudson Street Press, 2010).

For the paragraphs on nutraceuticals, I benefited from the article "Wild and commercial mushrooms as a source of nutrients and nutraceuticals" by Lillian Barros, et al.,
Food and Chemical Toxicology (2008) 46(8):2742–47; and "Mushroom nutriceuticals" by
S. T. Chang and J. A. Buswell, *World Journal of Microbiology and Biotechnology* (1996)
12(5):473–476. The analogy of homeopathy and eating the heart of a lion is Stephen Barrett's (www.homeowatch.org/basic/similars.html). George Hudler's quote comes from
his marvelous book *Magical Mushrooms, Mischievous Molds*. For more on red yeast rice,
see "An analysis of nine proprietary Chinese red yeast rice dietary supplements: implications of variability in chemical profiles and contents" by David Heber, et al., *Journal of
Alternative and Complementary Medicine* (2004) 7(2):133–39; "Tolerability of red yeast
rice (2400 mg twice daily) versus pravastatin (20 mg twice daily) in patients with previous statin intolerance" by S. C. Halbert, et al., *American Journal of Cardiology* (2010)
105(2):198–204; and "Red yeast rice for dyslipidemia in statin-intolerant patients; a randomized trial" by D. J. Becker, et al., *Annals of Internal Medicine* (2009) 150(12):830–39.

The evolution of dietary guidelines reads like a history of eating habits in the
United States. I used "The Report of the Dietary Guidelines Advisory Committee on
Dietary Guidelines for Americans, 2005, Appendix G-5: History of the Dietary Guidelines for Americans," www.health.gov/dietaryguidelines/dga2005/report/HTML/G5
_History.htm. The Harvard School of Public Health produces an excellent Web site
called the Nutrition Source: www.hsph.harvard.edu/nutritionsource. Their response to
the 2010 Dietary Guidelines for Americans is on the site.

Chapter 9

There are a variety of books covering the subject of medicinal mushrooms on the
market, but I found the following to be the most helpful: *MycoMedicinals: An Informa-
tional Treatise on Mushrooms* by Paul Stamets (Olympia, WA: MycoMedia, 2002);
Mushrooms: Poisons and Panaceas by Denis Benjamin; *Medicinal Mushrooms: An
Exploration of Tradition, Healing & Culture* by Christopher Hobbs (Summertown, TN:
Botanica Press, 1986); as well as *Mushrooms: Cultivation, Nutritional Value, Medicinal
Effect, and Environmental Impact,* 2nd ed., by Philip G. Miles and Shu-Ting Chang;
Magical Mushrooms, Mischievous Molds by George Hudler; and *Fungi: Folklore, Fiction
& Fact* by W. P. K. Findlay. It was Stamets who describes the mushroom mycelium's
ultimate potency to be at the point where the fungus is "most hungry," although in
TCM the mycelium is often regarded as the more potent aspect of the fungus. Many of
Stamets's descriptions of the therapeutic actions of mushrooms are described on his
Web site http://fungi.com and in the Fungi Perfecti catalog. Other extremely useful
overviews were "Mycology and medicine" by Chester W. Emmons, *Mycologia* (1961)
53(1):1–10; "Medicinal mushroom science: history, current status, future trends, and

unsolved problems" by Solomon P. Wasser, *International Journal of Medicinal Mushrooms* (2010) 12(1):1–16; and "Novel antimicrobials from mushrooms" by Paul Stamets, *HerbalGram* (2002) 54:29–33. There are many places where the penicillin story has been told, but I like Lucy Kavaler's telling in *Mushrooms, Molds, and Miracles* best.

On more specific topics, I found the following to be especially illuminating: "Natural products from endophytic microorganisms" by Gary Strobel, et al., *Journal of Natural Products* (2004) 67(2):257–68; "Discovery of a small molecule insulin mimetic with antidiabetic activity in mice" by Bei Zhang, et al., *Science* (1999) 284(5416):974–77; "Medicinal mushrooms as a source of antitumor and immunomodulating polysaccharides" by S. P. Wasser, *Applied Microbial Biotechnology* (2002) 60:258–74; "Medicinal mushrooms: a rapidly developing area of biotechnology for cancer therapy and other bioactivities" by John E. Smith, Neil J. Rowan, and Richard Sullivan, *Biotechnology Letters* (2002) 24(2):1839–45; "Novel medicinal mushrooms blend suppresses growth and invasiveness of human breast cancer cells" by Jiahua Jiang and Daniel Sliva, *International Journal of Oncology* (2010) 37:1529–36; "Mushroom antivirals" by Curtis R. Brandt and Frank Piraino, *Recent Research Developments in Antimicrobial Agents & Chemotherapy* (2000) 4:11–26; and "A selective inhibitor of myxoviruses from shiitake (*Lentinus edodes*)" by R. Yamamura and K. W. Cochran, *Mushroom Science* (1976) 9(1):495–507. The theory of antigen evolution was kindly explained to me by Christopher Hobbs.

The philology of agarikon is interesting. In brief, Greek physician and botanist Dioscorides described the mushroom as growing in Agaria, a Sarmatian country. Multiple sources from the ancient world describe the Agari as a Scythian people from southwest Russia. The Greek historian Diodorus Siculus wrote of Agarus, a Scythian king. The Agari were also known as the Sarmatians (5th century BC to AD 4th century), and the Greek historian Herodotus reported a story that claimed the Sarmatians originated from a band of Scythian men and a group of Amazons. In the 4th century AD, the Sarmatians were overrun by the Goths, who were in turn conquered by the Romans, who captured Ariaricus, the son of the Goth king. Christopher Hobbs pointed out that the name *agaric* was applied to a range of shelf fungi during the Middle Ages and Renaissance, until Linnaeus (1707–1778) reapplied it to fleshy gilled fungi, where it is used today in the genus name *Agaricus* (as in *Agaricus bisporus*, the white button mushroom). For more on agarikon, see *The Romance of the Fungus World* by R. T. Rolie and F. W. Rolie (London: Chapman & Hall, 1925). For Warburg's tincture, see *American Journal of the Medical Sciences* (1876) 71(141):256–57 and *American Medical Digest* (1884) 3:134–35 (the squeamish may wish to avoid the front matter). Agaracin is recommended in *Journal of the American Medical Association* (1901) 36. The attributions to Pliny were found in *The Natural History of Pliny*, vol. 5, John Bostock and H. T. Riley, trans. (London: Henry G. Bohn, 1856).

Descriptions of Western versus Eastern medical practices are described in many books and articles, but I found Denis Benjamin's *Mushrooms: Poisons and Panaceas* to be the most helpful.

New medicines are found in part by bioprospecting. For information on bio-prospecting for fungi living in stressed habitats, see "Bioactive compounds from marine bacteria and fungi" by Abdessamad Debbab, et al., *Microbial Biotechnology* (2010) 3(5):544–63.

There is a lot of good information on shiitake and reishi mushrooms in *Medicinal Mushrooms* and in *Mushrooms: Poisons and Panaceas*. Additionally, other very helpful sources were the papers "Medicinal and therapeutic value of the shiitake mushroom" by S. C. Jong and J. M. Birmingham, *Advances in Applied Microbiology* (1993) 39:153–84; "*Pleurotus ostreatus* inhibits proliferation of human breast and colon cancer cells through p53-dependent as well as p53-independent pathway" by A. Jedinak and D. Sliva, *International Journal of Oncology* (2008) 33:1307–13; "Present and historic rele-vance of yartsa gunbu" by Daniel Winkler, *Fungi* (2008) 1(4); "Rush for cure-all fungus puts plateau ecology at risk" by Zhou Yan and Wu Guangyu, *Xinhua News*, April 29, 2011, http://English.news.cn; the Memorial Sloan-Kettering Cancer Center's Cancer Information Web site (www.mskcc.org/mskcc/html/457.cfm); and the Cancer Research UK "News and Resources" page (http://info.cancerresearchuk.org). Also, "White but-ton mushroom phytochemicals inhibit aromatase activity and breast cancer cell prolif-eration" by Baiba J. Grube, et al., *Journal of Nutrition* (2001) 131:3288–93.

What's happening in psilocybin research is very interesting. The books I leaned upon most were *Psilocybin Mushrooms of the World: An Identification Guide* by Paul Sta-mets (Berkeley, CA: Ten Speed Press, 1996); *Shroom: A Cultural History of the Magic Mushroom* by Andy Letcher (London: Faber and Faber, 2006); and *Toxic and Hallucino-genic Mushroom Poisoning: A Handbook for Physicians and Mushroom Hunters* by Gary Lincoff and D. H. Mitchel, MD (New York: Van Nostrand Reinhold, 1977) and the articles "Safety, tolerability, and efficacy of psilocybin in 9 patients with obsessive-compulsive disorder" by F. A. Moreno, et al., *Journal of Clinical Psychiatry* (2006) 67(11):1735–40; "Response of cluster headaches to psilocybin and LSD" by R. Andrew Sewell, et al., *Neu-rology* (2006) 66(12):1920–22; "Pilot study of psilocybin treatment for anxiety in patients with advanced-stage cancer" by Charles S. Grob, et al., *Archives of General Psychiatry* (2011) 68(1):71–78; "Human hallucinogen research: guidelines for safety" by M. W. John-son, et al., *Journal of Psychopharmacology* (2008) 22(6):603–20; and "Commentaries and editorial on article by Griffths et al.," *Psychopharmacology* (2006) 187(3):283–91. The Web site Erowid (www.erowid.org), which covers all aspects of psychedelia in as serious a man-ner as possible considering the subject matter, was very useful.

I owe a great deal to Tom Volk for helping me understand the mycoses, the types, where they occur on and in the body, the diseases they cause, and the fungi that cause them (he teaches medical mycology at the University of Wisconsin–La Crosse, among other mycology subjects).

Among other sources I used were the Web sites www.doctorfungus.com, www .physorg.com, www.microbiologybytes.com, and www.merckmanuals.com; the online textbook *Microbiology and Immunology On-Line* from the University of South Carolina School of Medicine (http://pathmicro.med.sc.edu/book/mycol-sta.htm); the papers

"Skin, hair and nail fungal infections" by Raza Aly, *Current Opinion in Infectious Diseases* (1998) 11(2):113–18; "Mammalian endothermy optimally restricts fungi and metabolic costs" by Aviv Bergman and Arturo Casadevall, *mBio* (2010) 1(5); and "New discovery: lethal fungus reproduces sexually," *CORDIS News,* December 2, 2008, http://cordis.europa.eu/fetch?CALLER=NEWSLINK_=EN_C&RCN=30197&ACTION =D.

Regarding the deep mycoses, the stunning valley fever statistics come from www .valleyfeversurvivor.com, a patients' advocacy group. The information about histoplasmosis comes from eMedicine (http://emedicine.medscape.com); the American Lung Association (www.lungusa.org); and *Mushrooms, Molds, and Miracles.* The Bob Dylan quote was circulated by his record producer, Sony Music, in a press release.

Besides the sources mentioned above, the following sources were very helpful in understanding the "toxic mold" issue: "Infants' lung bleeding traced to toxic mold" by Robyn Meredith, *New York Times,* January 24, 1997; the American Society of Home Inspectors (www.ashi.org); Washington State Department of Health's Division of Environmental Health Web pages "Got Mold?" www.doh.wa.gov/ehp/ts/iaq/got_mold.html; "High diversity of fungi in air particulate matter" by Janine Fröhlich-Nowoisky, et al., *Proceedings of the National Academy of Sciences* (2009) 106(31):12814–19; *The Fifth Kingdom*; the American College of Occupational and Environmental Medicine; "Indoor fungal composition is geographically patterned and more diverse in temperate zones than in the tropics" by Anthony Amend, et al., *Proceedings of the National Academy of Sciences* (2010) 107(31):13748–53; and the Centers for Disease Control and Prevention's "Facts about Mold and Dampness," www.cdc.gov. The mold litigation stories included "Beware: toxic mold" by Anita Hamilton, *Time,* July 2, 2001; "Mold getting a costly hold on homes" by Rochelle Sharpe, *USA Today,* June 19, 2002; "Ed McMahon settles suit over mold for $7.2 million" by Jean Guccione, *Los Angeles Times,* May 9, 2003; and "Spore war" by Alex Williams, *New York* magazine, March 8, 2004. Information about sick building syndrome was found on the Environmental Protection Agency's Web site page "Indoor Air Facts No. 4 (revised) Sick Building Syndrome," www.epa.gov/iaq/ pubs/sbs.html; the Institute of Medicine report *Damp Indoor Spaces and Health* (Washington, DC: National Academies Press, 2004) online at www.nap.edu/openbook .php?isbn=0309091934; the American Academy of Allergy and Immunology "Table 1: National Allergy Bureau Outdoor Mold Counts" and "Table 2: Indoor Mold Classifications: Residential Buildings," www.nrdc.org/health/effects/katrinadata/mold.asp; "Airborne mold and endotoxin concentrations in New Orleans, Louisiana, after flooding, October through November 2005" by Gina M. Solomon, et al., *Environmental Health Perspectives* (2006) 114(9):1381–86; the Natural Resources Defense Council Web report "New Orleans Environmental Quality Test Results," www.nrdc.org/health/effects/ katrinadata/contents.asp; and *Molds, Toxic Molds, and Indoor Air Quality* by Pamela J. Davis (Sacramento: California Research Bureau, 2001). Davis's paper is not only an excellent report, but she introduces the idea of black mold being associated with leprosy in the Old Testament.

To find out about the Melina Bill, the only mold-related legislation ever submitted, see the Web site of Representative John Conyers Jr. (D-MI): http://conyers.house.gov.

Regarding mycotoxins, I used many sources, including Tom Volk's lecture on "Mycotoxins" (modified from a presentation by Nik Zitomer, 2004); *Carpet Monsters and Killer Spores* by Nicholas P. Money; and *Immunotoxicology and Immunopharmacology*, 3rd ed., Robert Luebke, Robert V. House, Ian Kimber, eds. (Boca Raton, FL: CRC Press, 2006); among other books. Of the papers, the following were all very helpful: "Public health significance of molds and mycotoxins in fermented dairy products (*Penicillium roqueforti*)" by L. B. Bullerman, *Journal of Dairy Science* (1981) 64(12):2439–52; "The concentration of no toxicologic concern (CoNTC) and airborne mycotoxins" by Bryan D. Hardin, et al., *Journal of Toxicology and Environmental Health, Part A* (2009) 72(9):585–98; "Mycotoxins: the cost of achieving food security and food quality" by K. F. Cardwell, et al. (American Phytopathological Society, 2001), www.apsnet.org; "Fumonisin exposure through maize in complementary foods is inversely associated with linear growth of infants in Tanzania" by Martin E. Kimanya, et al., *Molecular Nutrition and Food Research* (2010) 54(11):1659–667; and "Trichothecenes: from yellow rain to green wheat" by Anne Desjardins, *ASM News* (2003) 69(4):182–85.

John G. Fuller wrote a fantastic report on ergot poisoning in *The Day of St. Anthony's Fire* (New York: Macmillan, 1968). Tom Volk's FOTM also provided an excellent description of ergot's biology. Also of great use: "Convulsive ergotism: epidemics of the serotonin syndrome?" by Mervyn J. Eadie, *Lancet Neurology* (2003) 2(7):429–34; "Skeleton of St. Anthony goes on display to public more than 750 years after his death," *Daily Mail Reporter*, February 15, 2010; "Ergotism: the satan loosed in Salem?" by Linda Caporael, *Science* (1976) 192(4234):21–26; and "Ergotism and its effects on society and religion" by Larry R. Sherman, and Michael R. Zimmerman, *Journal of Nutritional Immunology* (1994) (2)3:127–36.

Chapter 10

There are lots of books on the subject of hallucinogenics. On the subject of psilocybin biology, I used *Psilocybin Mushrooms of the World* by Paul Stamets and *Toxic and Hallucinogenic Mushroom Poisoning* by Gary Lincoff and D. H. Mitchel, both of which are important resources in their field; *Psilocybin Mushroom Handbook: Easy Indoor & Outdoor Cultivation* by L. G. Nicholas and Kerry Ogamé (San Francisco: Quick American, 2006), which focuses on growing; *Mushrooms: Poisons and Panaceas* by Denis Benjamin; and *Alkaloids: Biochemistry, Ecology, and Medicinal Applications*, Margaret F. Roberts and Michael Wink, eds. (New York: Plenum Press, 1998)—which has a great chapter on the history of alkaloids.

The subjects of entheogenic substances and ethnomycology often overlap, and as a result, the library is quite large and very eccentric. Of the sources pertaining to prehistoric use, I leaned most upon *Tassili n'Ajjer: Art Rupestre du Sahara Prehistorique* by Jean-Dominique Lajoux (Paris: Chene, 1977); the *Florentine Codex: Book 10; The People*

(*General History of the Things of New Spain*) by Bernardino de Sahagun, Charles E. Dibble, and Arthur J. O. Anderson, trans. (Salt Lake City: University of Utah, 1961); *The Ancient Maya*, 6th ed., by Robert J. Sharer (Palo Alto, CA: Stanford University Press, 2006); and the papers "The sacred mushroom in Scandinavia" by Reid W. Kaplan, *Man* (1975) 10(1):72–79; "Stonehenge and sacred mushrooms: the inspiration behind the circle of stones" by Mathew Calloway, *Shaman's Drum* (2001) 58:26; "New records of mushroom stones from Guatemala" by B. Lowy, *Mycologia* (1971) 63(5):983–93; and various Web sites, particularly the Metropolitan Museum of Art's Heilbrunn Timeline of Art History online article "African Rock Art: Tassili-n-Ajjer (?8000 B.C.–?)," www.metmuseum.org/toah/hd/tass/hd_tass.htm; and www.erowid.org

Other texts on entheogenics and ethnomycology are *Persephone's Quest: Entheogens and the Origins of Religion* by R. Gordon Wasson, Stella Kramrisch, Jonathan Ott, and Carl Ruck (New Haven: Yale University Press, 1992); *The Sacred Mushroom and the Cross*, by John M. Allegro (Garden City, NY: Doubleday, 1970); *Food of the Gods: The Search for the Original Tree of Knowledge* by Terence McKenna (New York: Bantam, 1992); and the article "Seeking the Magic Mushroom" by R. Gordon Wasson and Valentina P. Wasson, *Life*, June 10, 1957. The point that Wasson had deceived the Mixtec shaman into administering mushrooms was well made by Andy Letcher in *Shroom*. Indeed, Letcher's argument that Wasson was motivated as much by ambition as altruism is persuasive.

The materials I found most useful in learning about the culture of hallucinogenics were *Shroom*, an erudite, beautifully written cultural history; the classic *Doors of Perception* by Aldous Huxley (New York: Harper, 1954); and *Acid Dreams: The Complete Social History of LSD: The CIA, the Sixties, and Beyond*, an excellent history by Martin A. Lee and Bruce Shlain (New York: Grove Weidenfeld, 1985). I also read *The Politics of Psychopharmacology* by Timothy Leary (Berkeley, CA: Ronin Publishing, 1988) and referred to *The Harvard Psychedelic Club: How Timothy Leary, Ram Dass, Huston Smith, and Andrew Weil Killed the Fifties and Ushered in a New Age for America* by Don Lattin (New York: HarperOne, 2010), *Sacred Mushrooms and the Law* by Richard Glen Boire (Berkeley, CA: Ronin, 2002), and *Castaneda's Journey: The Power and the Allegory* by Richard de Mille (son of Cecil) (Santa Barbara, CA: Capra Press, 1970). For an interesting discussion on Carlos Castaneda's books, see "Vistas beyond the Horizon of This Life" by Peter T. Furst in *The Sacred Mushroom Seeker: Tributes to R. Gordon Wasson*, Thomas J. Riedlinger, ed. (Rochester, VT: Park Street Press, 1997).

The *Amanita muscaria* stories were found in *Fungi: Folklore, Fiction & Fact* by W. P. K. Findlay; *The General Gazetteer: or, Compendious Geographical Dictionary* compiled by Richard Brookes (London: A. Piquot, 1827); *The Botany and Chemistry of Hallucinogens* by Richard Evans Schultes and Albert Hofmann (Springfield, IL: Thomas, 1980); *Soma: Divine Mushroom of Immortality* by R. Gordon Wasson (New York: Harcourt Brace Jovanovich, 1972); *Travelers' Tales, a Book of Marvels* by Henry Cadwallader Adams (London: George Routledge and Sons, 1883); *The Road to Eleusis: Unveiling the Secret of the Mysteries* by Carl A. Ruck, et al. (Los Angeles: William Dailey Antiquarian Books, 2004); and *Mushrooms and Mankind* by James Arthur (Escondido, CA: Book Tree, 2000).

I also benefited from the papers "Mushroom hunting in Oregon" by Andrew Weil, *Journal of Psychedelic Drugs* (1975) 7(1); "Human hallucinogen research: guidelines for safety" by M. W. Johnson, et al., *Journal of Psychopharmacology* (2008) 22(6):603–20; and the article "A final turn-on lifts Timothy Leary off" by Marlise Simons, *New York Times*, April 22, 1997. I referred many times throughout the chapter to the excellent Cornell Mushroom Blog (http://blog.mycology.cornell.edu) and Tom Volk's FOTM.

Besides those sources mentioned above, specific books about the use of psychedelic mushrooms that I found useful were *The Psychedelic Experience: A Manual Based on the Tibetan Book of the Dead* by Timothy Leary (Secaucus, NJ: Citadel, 1964); and *Hallucinogenic Plants of North America* by Jonathan Ott (Berkeley, CA: Wingbow Press, 1976); as well as the article "The strange case of the Harvard drug scandal" by Andrew Weil, *Look*, November 5, 1963.

The *Psilocybe* usage statistics come from the University of Maryland's Center for Substance Abuse Research, www.cesar.umd.edu/cesar/drugs/psilocybin.asp; the US Department of Health and Human Services, Substance Abuse and Mental Health Services Administration's "Results from the 2009 National Survey on Drug Use and Health: Volume 1. Summary of National Findings," www.oas.samhsa.gov/ NSDUH/2k9NSDUH/2k9ResultsP.pdf; and the National Institute on Drug Abuse research report series "Hallucinogens and Dissociative Drugs," www.nida.nih.gov/ PDF/RRHalluc.pdf.

About the current research in psilocybin and religious experience, I found the following papers most useful: "Psilocybin can occasion mystical-type experiences having substantial and sustained personal meaning and spiritual significance" by R. R. Griffiths, et al., *Psychopharmacology* (2006) 187(3):268–83; "Mystical-type experiences occasioned by psilocybin mediate the attribution of personal meaning and spiritual significance 14 months later" by R. R. Griffiths, et al., *Journal of Psychopharmacology* (2008) 22(6):621–32; plus the commentaries by Charles R. Schuster, Herbert D. Kleber, Solomon H. Snyder, David E. Nichols and the editorial "Toward a science of spiritual experience" by Harriet De Wit, collectively titled "Commentary on: Psilocybin can occasion mystical-type experiences having substantial and sustained personal meaning and spiritual significance," *Psychopharmacology* (2006) 187(3):284–92.

Chapter 11

I used two newspaper sources for the material on the BP oil spill: the *New York Times* and the *Guardian* (UK). For an excellent report and analysis of the use of dispersants on the spill, see "The Gulf War" by Raffi Khatchadourian, *New Yorker*, March 14, 2011. News about Wisconsin's state microbe was reported in "And now, a state microbe" by Monica Davey, *New York Times*, April 15, 2010.

Paul Stamets's mycoremediation project is described in his wonderful book *Mycelium Running* as well as on his Web site, Fungi Perfecti (www.fungi.com). There are very few secondary sources when it comes to mycoremediation—a few books, or chapters in books—but almost all the literature is composed of research papers and reviews or roundups of research papers.

Nonetheless, the books and chapters within books that I found most helpful to my understanding of the current state of mycoremediation include: "Fungal Remediation of Contaminated Sites" by Fotis Rigas and Vicky Dritsa in *Environmental Research at the Leading Edge,* Robert W. Gore, ed. (New York: Nova Science Publishers, 2007); "Aerobic degradations of cloroaromatics by Pseudomona(d)s" by D. H. Pieper, et al., in *The Pseudomonads, vol. 3: Biosynthesis of Macromolecules and Molecular Metabolism,* J. L. Ramos, ed. (New York: Kluwer Academic/Plenum Publishers, 2004); "Recent Advances in the Use of Fungi in Environmental Remediation and Biotechnology" by Andrzej Paszczynski and Ronald L. Crawford in *Soil Biochemistry, vol. 10,* Jean-Marc Bollag and Guenther Stotzky, eds. (New York: Marcel Dekker, 2000); "The Valdez Oil Spill: Environmental, Economic and Social Impacts" by E. Willard Miller in *Natural and Technological Disasters: Causes, Effects and Preventive Measures,* Shyamal K. Majumdar, et al., eds. (Pennsylvania Academy of Science, 1992); "The Cavalry Is Coming. Fungi to the Rescue" in *Slayers, Saviors, Servants, and Sex: An Expose of Kingdom Fungi* by David Moore (New York: Springer-Verlag, 2001); and *Fungi in Bioremediation,* Geoffrey M. Gadd, ed. (Cambridge, UK: Cambridge University Press, 2001).

The papers that I leaned on most heavily were "The fungus among us: use of white rot fungi to biodegrade environmental polutants" by S. D. Aust and J. T. Benson, *Environmental Health Perspectives* (1993) 101(3):232–33; "Pollutants biodegradation by fungi" by C. Pinedo-Rivilla, J. Aleu, and I. G. Collado, *Current Organic Chemistry* (2009) 13(12):1194–214; "Toxic Avengers" by Dawn Stover, *Popular Science* special issue on Environment & Technology (1992) 241(1):70,73; "Diverse fungal and bacterial communities promote Mn(II)-oxidation and remediation of coal mine drainage in passive treatment systems" by Cara M. Santelli, et al., *Applied and Environmental Microbiology* (2010) 76(14):4871–75, doi:10.1128/AEM.03029-09; "Heavy metals in edible mushrooms in Italy" by Luigi Cocchi, et al., *Food Chemistry* (2006) 98(2): 277–84; "Lead and arsenic in *Morchella esculenta* fruitbodies collected in lead arsenate contaminated apple orchards in the northeastern United States: a preliminary study" by Elinoar Shavit and Efrat Shavit, *Fungi* (2010) 3(2):11–18; "Assessing bioaccumulation of heavy metals in sporocarp of *Pleurotus ostreatus*" by Arshid Pervez, et al., *World Applied Sciences Journal* (2009) 7(12):1498–503; and "Geomycology: biogeochemical transformations of rocks, minerals, metals and radionuclides by fungi, bioweathering and bioremediation" by Geoffrey M. Gadd, *Mycological Research* (2007) 111(Pt 1): 3–49.

I also referred to the Web sites www.globalsecurity.org and www.matteroftrust.org and to the BBC series episode "Cooking in the Danger Zone: Chernobyl."

Regarding other uses to which the remediating or biodegrading capability of fungi can be put, I found useful the following papers: "Decolourization of bagasse-based paper mill effluent by the white-rot fungus *Trametes versicolor*" by Dinesh R. Modi, Satyandra K. Garg, and Harish Chandra, *Bioresource Technology* (1998) 66(1):79–81; "Bioremediation of paper and pulp mill effluents" by K. Murugesan, *Indian Journal of Experimental Biology* (2003) 41(11):1239–48; "Enzymes used in detergents," an enzymology paper written by Mayank Jain, a student at the Amity Institute of Biotechnology in 2008; "Effect of biostimulation and bioaugmentation on degradation of polyurethane buried in soil" by Lee Cosgrove, et al., *Applied and Environmental Microbiology* (2010) 76(3):810–19; "Fungal communities associated with degradation of polyester polyurethane in soil" by Lee Cosgrove, et al., *Applied and Environmental Microbiology* (2007) 73(18):5817–24; "Degradation of bisphenol A by white rot fungi, *Stereum hirsutum* and *Heterobasidium insulare*, and reduction of its estrogenic activity" by Soo-Min Lee, et al., *Biological and Pharmaceutical Bulletin* (2005) 28(2):201–7; "Biodegradation of bisphenol A by fungi" by W. Chai, et al., *Applied Biochemistry and Biotechnology* (2005) 120(3):175–82; Tom Volk's FOTM February 2007, "*Phanerochaete chrysosporium*"; "Use of filamentous fungi for wastewater treatment and production of high value fungal byproducts: a review" by Sindhuja Sankaran, et al., *Critical Reviews in Environmental Science and Technology* (2010) 40(5):400–49; "Removal of biocide pentachlorophenol in water system by the spent mushroom compost of *Pleurotus pulmonarius*" by M. W. Law, et al., *Chemosphere* (2003) 52(9):1531–37; "Silica-alginate-fungi biocomposites for remediation of polluted water" by Mercedes Perullini, et al., *Journal of Materials Chemistry* (2010) 20:6479–83; "Fungi decolorization of dye wastewaters: a review" by Yuzhu Fu and T. Viraraghavan, *Bioresource Technology* (2001) 79(3):251–62; and "Utilization of fungi for biotreatment of raw wastewaters" by Lacina Coulibaly, et al., *African Journal of Biotechnology* (2003) 2(12):620–30.

For the section on fungi and biofuels, I depended on a variety of papers, including "Megascience" by J. Thomas Ratchford and Umberto Colombo, UNESCO World Science Report, 1996; "The production of myco-diesel hydrocarbons and their derivatives by the endophytic fungus *Gliocladium* roseum" by Gary Strobel, et al., *Microbiology* (2008) 154(Pt 11):3319–28; "Perspectives of microbial oils for biodiesel production" by Qiang Li, Wei Du, and Dehua Liu, *Applied Microbiology and Biotechnology* (2008) 80(5):749–56; "Driving on Mushroom Fumes" by Christopher Helman, *Forbes*, May 25, 2009; "Volatile antimicrobials from *Muscodor albus*, a novel endophytic fungus" by Gary Strobel, et al., *Microbiology* (2001) 147(pt 11):2943–50; and "Scientist looks to find ways to turn fungus into biofuel" by Stephen Dunn, *Hartford Courant*, October 20, 2009.

I also used the Web sites www.checkbiotech.org; the US Department of Energy Joint Genome Institute's Fungal Genomics Program (www.jgi.doe.gov); http://mycoinnovations .com; and Iowa State Daily.com's "Professor wins innovation awards," www.iowastatedaily .com/news/article_a8639315-2b5e-55fc-b209-a7ec33556a3b.html?mode=story.

The material on mycopesticides was primarily based on online articles. A selection: "Pesticide Industry Sales and Usage," www.epa.gov/opp00001/pestsales); "Green Alternative to Traditional Pesticides," www4.agr.gc.ca/AAFC-AAC/display-afficher.do?id =1261420797857&lang=eng; "Biotec company aims to bridge the green gap" by Helen Twose, October 15, 2010, www.nzherald.co.nz/business/news/article.cfm?c_id=3&objectid= 10680587; "Breakthrough technology harnesses microorganism for use as green bio-pesticide," www.lifesciencesworld.com/news/view/116188; "Fungus foot baths could save bees," July 28, 2008, www.sciencedaily.com/releases/2008/07/080728081621.htm; "Fungus enhances susceptibility of resistant malaria mosquito to pesticides," September 24, 2009, www.sciencedaily.com/releases/2009/09/090923110320.htm; "Fighter fungus" by Mary MacKay, June 15, 2009, www.theguardian.pe.ca/Business/Agriculture/2009-06-15/article-1374015/Fighter-fungus/1; "Penn State entomologists seek fungus to blunt mosquitoes' sense of smell," May 7, 2009, www.eurekalert.org/pub_releases/2009-05/ps-pse050709.php; "Mode of action: insecticides" by Scott W. Ludwig, www.golfcourseindustry.com/Article.aspx?article_id=108091; and the articles "Mushrooms assist in generating human vaccines, researchers say" by Tiffany Peden, December 6, 2007, www.collegian.psu.edu/archive/2007/12/06/mushrooms_assist_in_generating.aspx; and "Mushrooms may aid rapid vaccine response," *Mushroom News,* January 1, 2008.

Other weird new products produced by mushrooms can be found in the papers "Self-repairing oxetane-substituted chitosan polyurethane networks" by Biswajit Ghosh and Marek W. Urban, *Science* (2009) 323(5920):1458–60, about a scratch-repairing car paint; "Antioxidative activity and antidiscoloration efficacy of ergothioneine in mushroom (*Flammulina velutipes*) extract added to beef and fish meats" by Huynh Bao, Hideki Ushio, and Toshiaki Ohshima, *Journal of Agricultural and Food Chemistry* (2008) 56(21):10032–40, about using fungi to color foods; and "Fungi-infected violins best Stradivarius" by Eric Bland, September 30, 2009 (http://news.discovery.com/tech/fungi-violin-better-stradivarius.html), which reports that a violin made from fungi-infested wood sounds better than a Stradivarius. Check out www.curbmedia.com to learn about a company making signs with bioluminescent fungi.

Chapter 12

For a wonderful description of the geology of the Cascade mountains, of which the Breitenbush Hot Springs are a part, see "The search for hot rocks—geothermal exploration, northwest" by J. Eric Schuster, *Pacific Search* (State of Washington, Department of Natural Resources, Division of Mines and Geology, 1973), www.dnr.wa.gov/Publications/ger_reprint11_geotherm_explor_nw.pdf; and "Using springs to study groundwater flow and active geologic processes" by Michael Manga, *Annual Review of Earth Planetary Sciences* (2001) 29:201–28. Lynn Margulis's quote is from her excellent book (with Dorion Sagan) *What is Life?* (Berkeley, CA: University of California Press, 2000). "What Lies Beneath" in *Mr. Bloomfield's Orchard* by Nicholas P. Money has a terrific explanation of fungal evolution. Even though it doesn't spend much time on fungi, I think *Life: A Natural History of the First Four Billion Years of Life on Earth* by Richard Fortey (New York: Vintage, 1999) is a pretty cool place to start any investigation of biology.

Ah, fungal evolution. I read a lot of material before getting some serious help from James White, chair of the department of plant pathology at Rutgers. It's a mishmash, but here are the more significant papers I read: "Towards a natural system of organisms: proposal for the domains Archaea, Bacteria, and Eucarya" by Carl R. Woese, Otto K. Kandler, and Mark L. Wheelis, *Proceedings of the National Academy of Sciences* (1990) 87:4576–79; "Five-kingdom classification and the origin and evolution of cells" by Lynn Margulis, *Evolutionary Biology* (1974) 7:45–78; "Evolutionary biology: a kingdom revised" by Thomas D. Bruns, *Nature* (2006) 443(7113):758–61; "Are fungi plants?" by G. W. Martin, *Mycologia* (1955) 47(6):779–91; "Reconstructing the early evolution of fungi using a sex-gene phylogeny" by Timothy Y. James, et al., *Nature* (2006) 443(7113):818–22; "Glomalean fungi from the Ordovician" by Dirk Redecker, R. Kodner, and L. E. Graham, *Science* (2000) 289(5486):1920–21; "Animals and fungi are each other's closest relatives: congruent evidence from multiple proteins" by Sandra L. Baldauf and Jeffrey D. Palmer, *Proceedings of the National Academy of Sciences* (1993) 90:11558–62; "Mutualistic mycorrhizae-like symbiosis in the most ancient group of land plants" by Claire P. Humphreys, et al., *Nature Communications* (2010), doi:10.1038/ncomms1105; "Evolutionary studies of ectomycorrhizal fungi: recent advances and future directions" by Thomas D. Bruns and Richard P. Shefferson, *Canadian Journal of Botany* (2004) 82(8):1122–132; "The energetics of genome complexity" by Nick Lane and William Martin, *Nature* (2010) 467(7318):929–35; "Chemical constitution of a Permian-Triassic disaster species" by Mark A. Sephton, et al., *Geology* (2009) 37(10):875–78; "Molecular evidence for the early colonization of land by fungi" by Daniel S. Heckman, et al., *Science* (2001) 293(5532):1129–33; "The terminal Paleozoic fungal event: evidence of terrestrial ecosystem destabilization and collapse" by Henk Visscher, et al., *Proceedings of the National Academy of Sciences* (1996) 93:2155–58; "Plant-driven fungal weathering: early stages of mineral alteration at the nanometer scale" by Steeve Bonneville, et al., *Geology* (2009) 37(7):615–18; "The land flora: a phototroph-fungus partnership?" by M-A. Selosse and F. Le Tacon, *Trends in Ecology and Evolution* (1998) 13(1):15–20; "Four-hundred-million-year-old vesicular arbuscular mycorrhizae" by Winfried Remy, et al., *Proceedings of the National Academy of Sciences* (1994) 91:11841–43; and "The most ancient terrestrial lichen *Winfrenatia reticulata*: a new find and new interpretation" by I. V. Karatygin, N. S. Snigirevskaya, and S. V. Vilkulin, *Paleontological Journal* (2009) 43(1):107–14.

The prototaxites story can be found in numerous places. I used "Prototaxites: a 400 million year old giant fossil, a saprophytic holobasidiomycete, or a lichen?" by Marc-André Selosse, *Mycological Research* (2002) 106:641–44; "Comparative geochemistry suggests Prototaxites was a gigantic fungus" by Charles Kevin Boyce, *Abstracts with Programs* (2003) 35(6); "Structural, physiological, and stable carbon isotopic evidence that the enigmatic Paleozoic fossil Prototaxites formed from rolled liverwort mats" by L. E. Graham, et al., *Journal of Botany* (2010) 97:268–75. For a good summation, see "The enigmatic *Prototaxites*: curiouser still" by Britt Bunyard, *Fungi* (2010) 3(4):8–9. There are two renderings of the Prototaxites online: one of *Prototaxites* the fungus by Mary Parrish at the National Museum of Natural History, and another of *Prototaxites* the liverwort by Linda E. Graham of the University of Wisconsin. Both images are found at http://coo.fieldofscience.com/2010/02/prototaxites-giant-that-never-was.html.

On symbiosis, I'd have to put *Symbiotic Planet* by Lynn Margulis at the top of my list, followed by *Plant-Animals: A Study in Symbiosis* by Frederick Keeble (Cambridge, UK: Cambridge University Press, 1910), and Bryce Kendrick's *The Fifth Kingdom*. The International Symbiosis Society Web site is a marvelous resource: http://iss-symbiosis.org.

Terence McKenna's quote comes from his book *Food of the Gods*. I also benefited from reading "Current status of the gene-for-gene concept" by H. H. Flor, *Annual Review of Phytopathology* (1971) 9:275–96; "Horizontal transfer of a large and highly toxic secondary metabolic gene cluster between fungi" by Jason C. Slot and Antonis Rokas, *Current Biology* (2010) 21(2):134–39; and the chapter "Arbuscular mycorrhizal fungi and their endobacteria" by P. Bonfante, et al., in *Symbiosis: Mechanisms and Model Systems*, Joseph Seckbach, ed. (Dordrecht, Netherlands: Kluwer Academic Press, 2002).

The gut flora story is very interesting. A good place to start is "The human microbiome project" by Peter J. Turnbaugh, et al., *Nature* (2007) 449(7164):804–10; "Microbiology: the inside story" by Asher Mullard, *Nature* (2008) 454(7205):690–91; "Microbiology: Straight from the gut" by Apoorva Mandavilli, *Nature* (2008) 453(7195):581–82; "A human gut microbial gene catalogue established by metagenomic sequencing" by Junje Qin, et al., *Nature* (2010) 464(7285):59–65; "Who are we?" *Nature* (2008) 453(7195):563; "A microbial symbiosis factor prevents intestinal inflammatory disease" by Sarkis K. Mazmanian, June L. Round, and Dennis L. Kasper, *Nature* (2008) 453(7195):620–25; "The gut flora as a forgotten organ" by Ann M. O'Hara and Fergus Shanahan, *EMBO Reports* (2006) 7:688–93; "How microbes defend and define us" by Carl Zimmer, *New York Times*, July 12, 2010; and an NPR interview with Jeffrey Gorden, "Bacterial bonanza: microbes keep us alive" on *Fresh Air*, September 15, 2010, www.scpr.org/news/2010/09/15/bacterial-bonanza-microbes-keep-us-alive.

Other books I recommend in relation to this chapter are: James Lovelock's *Gaia: A New Look at Life on Earth* (New York: Oxford University Press, 1979); Lovelock's *The Revenge of Gaia: Earth's Climate in Crisis and the Fate of Humanity* (New York: Basic Books, 2006); and *Spinoza: His Life and Philosophy* by Frederick Pollock (London: Duckworth and Co.; New York: Macmillan, 1899). I got into Spinoza because he questions what determines the individual.

More or less, don't we all?

PHOTOGRAPHY AND ARTWORK CREDITS

(Frontspiece) Andrew Geiger

(Page xiii) Dan Malloy

(Page 6) Dan Malloy

(Page 9) Taylor Lockwood

(Page 13) Taylor Lockwood

(Page 20) John Serrao/Photo Reserachers, Inc.

(Page 44) Eugenia Bone

(Page 46) Taylor Lockwood

(Page 50) Taylor Lockwood

(Page 51) Toshiyuki Nakagaki, Future University Hakodate, Japan

(Page 52) US Forest Service

(Page 54) Eugenia Bone

(Page 72) Taylor Lockwood

(Page 79) Taylor Lockwood

(Page 83) Tom Volk

(Page 86) The Forest History Society

(Page 88) Inga Spence/Photo Researchers, Inc.

(Page 90) New York State Department of Environmental Conservation, All Rights Reserved

(Page 91) Daniel Winkler

(Page 102) Andrew Geiger

(Page 120) Gary Lincoff

(Page 133) Eugenia Bone

(Page 138) Gary Mills

(Page 143) Daniel Winkler

(Page 168) Mark Miller

(Page 179) George Weigel

(Page 197) Biophoto Associates/ Photo Researchers, Inc.

(Page 199) http://GetKombucha.com

(Page 206) Eugenia Bone

(Page 208) Eugenia Bone

(Page 217) Eugenia Bone

(Page 219) Eugenia Bone

(Page 223) Eugenia Bone

(Page 232) Tanya Solomon/ ShutterPoint Photography

(Page 233) Tom Volk

(Page 237) Eugenia Bone

(Page 244) Raye Levine

(Page 250) Gary Lincoff

(Page 256) Permission granted by the Ernst Bloch Legacy Foundation

(Page 264) Eugenia Bone

(Page 282) Taylor Lockwood

(Page 284) Permission granted by the Breitenbush Hot Springs Retreat and Conference Center

(Page 296) Raye Levine

(Page 300) Taylor Lockwood

INDEX

Boldface page references indicate photographs or illustrations. <u>Underscored</u> references indicate footnote material.